Ancestors of Raymond Donald Burton:

From the Mayflower and Salem to California, 2nd Edition.

Scott R Mackay

ISBN: 9781708971670

Table of Contents

Introduction

This genealogy has been many years in the making, and I tried to make it as accurate as possible. However, I can not guarantee that there are no mistakes despite my best efforts to make it accurate, at the expense of leaving people out if I wasn't certain they belonged in the tree.

This book is a combination of other people's research with my own. Whenever possible, I tried to use multiple sources and primary documents (or at least images of primary documents) to verify information. Information that could not be verified or traced to a reputable source was not used. For recent generations I am grateful for the use of documents that my mother saved, but further back I looked for images of documents at sites like *FamilySearch* and *Ancestry.com.* However, I did not use internet trees as evidence, including those at *FamilySearch* and *Ancestry.com* because of uneven quality. I did use works by Savage, Cutter, and others for the American side of the genealogy, when their work in the US was generally in line with primary sources that I could find. However, they were too often unreliable in genealogy that was in England. For English ancestry, articles from *The New England Historical and Genealogical Register* and *The American Genealogist* were helpful and often well sourced.

Sometimes transcriptions are in error due to transcribers not understanding the difference between the Julian calendar of the 1600's as used by the English, and the modern Gregorian calendar in use today. The English Julian calendar ended the year in late March, rather than December. So dates between January 1 and March 24 were recorded as being in the prior year. For example, January 1, 1650 by the Gregorian calendar was usually recorded in England and the colonies as being in 1649. One way to reconcile the overlap is to write the date and January 1, 1649/50.

I had to end the book around the twelfth generation back. Some lines that went a little further back were noted, but several lines that continued well beyond the twelfth generation will have to be covered elsewhere. I believe the families that can be continued further back to ancient and medieval aristocrats and royals are the Palgrave, Southworth, Carleton, Newton, Appleton, and Bulkeley families.

While reviewing the original book to meet standards in possibly getting a credential, I found a mistake due to there being two ladies named Abigail Carleton living in Haverhill, Massachusetts at the same time. I once thought Abigail Carleton [B7-5f in Burton book 1rst ed] was born in 1789 to Israel Carleton and Abigail Whittier in Haverhill. That Abigail Carleton apparently died under her maiden name in 1851 according to the Massachusetts Town Clerk database at FamilySearch. The Abigail who married Moses Johnson was having children as late as 1844 and in the 1850 Census gave her age as 47, which would make 1803 the correct birth year. Additionally, her death record under the name (Carleton) Johnson gives Michael and Ruth Carleton as her parents. Even though they were cousins and shared some ancestors, this unfortunately led to a major revision in the Carleton portion of the genealogy.

The numbering system is based on the Ahnentafel system of numbering, which is the genealogical standard for credentialed genealogists. The first number is the generation number, and the number followed by the dash is the Ahnentafel number. That starts with the number 1 for the starting individual, 2 for the father, 3 for the mother, 4 for the paternal grandfather, etc.

[01-01] Raymond Donald Burton and Betty Lou Webb

Raymond Donald Burton was born on July 13, 1929 to Raymond Dwight Burton [02-02] and Ruth Elma Johnson [02-03] in San Jose, Santa Clara Co, California.[1] He grew up in the San Jose area and served in the Naval Reserves from 1948 to 1956.[2] From 1960 to the 1970's he worked in Maintenance and Air Conditioning at Lockheed in Sunnyvale, Santa Clara Co, California.[3] There he was also active in the Lockheed Employer Recreation Association. Outside of work, he was social and involved in the Freemasons, Cub Scouts, PTA, and Little Leagues.[4] In April 1982, Raymond received the Hiram Award for Distinguished and Dedicated Service, which is the highest award in California freemasonry.[5]

On August 19, 1949, by a Methodist minister, he married Betty Lou Webb[6], who was born in San Jose, California on July 9, 1931 to Dorothy Mae (Prueske) Webb.[7] They had four children and lived at 2400 Quantico Ct in San Jose after 1965.[8]

Raymond Donald Burton died of lung cancer on September 12, 1986 at the Kaiser Santa Clara Hospital in Santa Clara, Santa Clara Co, California.[9] His wife Betty followed him on February 25, 1997 at their home at Quantico Ct of ovarian cancer. They are buried together at Oak Hill Cemetery in San Jose,

---

1 California, Department of Health Services, *Certified Copy of Birth Record* (California: Office of the State Registrar of Vital Statistics, 13 July 1929) certificate number RE: Z-442, Raymond Donald Burton; privately held by Scott Mackay, Irondale, MO.

2 Burton, Raymond Donald (Department of Defense Personnel Security Questionnaire, DD-49, 13 Jan 1976) p. 4; privately held by Scott Mackay, Irondale, MO.

3 Ibid., p. 1

4Ibid., p. 6.

5 N.A., "Raymond Donald Burton" (eulogy, San Jose, California, 16 September 1986); privately held by Scott Mackay, Irondale, MO.

6 California, Santa Clara County, County Clerk, *Marriage Certificate* (Santa Clara County: County Clerk, 1949) Raymond D Burton and Betty Lou Webb; privately held by Scott Mackay, Irondale, MO.

7 California, Department of Health Services, *Certified Copy of Birth Record* (California: Office of the State Registrar of Vital Statistics, 13 April 1981) certificate number RE: 7-522, Betty Lou Webb; privately held by Scott Mackay, Irondale, MO.

8 Burton, Raymond Donald (Department of Defense Personnel Security Questionnaire, DD-49, 13 Jan 1976) p. 4; privately held by Scott Mackay, Irondale, MO.

9 California, Santa Clara County, Health Department, *Certificate of Death* (Santa Clara County: Vital Records Section, Department of Public Health, 19 September 1986) death certificate no. 4300-05813, Raymond D Burton Jr; privately held by Scott Mackay, Irondale, MO.

California.[10]

[02-02] Raymond Dwight Burton and [02-03] Ruth Elma Johnson

Raymond Dwight Burton was born on October 22, 1907 in Gilroy, Santa Clara County, California to Harold Elmer Burton [03-04] and Bertha Viola Fine [03-05].[11] By the 1920 Census the family had moved a little north to 773 San Carlos in San Jose, Santa Clara County, California.[12]

Raymond Dwight Burton married Ruth Elma Johnson, the daughter of Fred Henry Johnson [03-06] and Caroline Susan Newsom [03-07]. Ruth's birth was in Fowler, Meade Co, Kansas on April 1, 1910.[13] Raymond's brother Harold Heber Burton had already married into the Johnson family in 1924, since he had married Ruth's sister Ellen "Ella" C Johnson. The 1930 census shows Raymond and Ruth living with Raymond's parents on 860 Polhemus St in San Jose, California.[14] Raymond was a railroad mechanic in 1930. The 1940 census shows that Raymond was a cannery mechanic and Ruth was a canner in a cannery, and they lived at 409 San Carlos in San Jose, California.[15] In 1930 Raymond was registered as a Republican, but by 1934 he had changed his voter registration to the Democrats. Ruth was active in Butcher's Union, Local 506, being a member of the executive board of the Egg Worker's Division and a delegate to the Central Labor Council.[16]

Together Raymond and Ruth had 3 children, one of whom (Nancy) died as an infant. Then on June 16, 1951 Ruth took ant poison and was found dead by

---

10 California, Santa Clara County, Health Department, *Certificate of Death* (Santa Clara County: Vital Records Section, Department of Public Health, 3 March 1997), certificate number H 933225, Betty Lou Burton; privately held by Scott Mackay, Irondale, MO.

11. Darling-Fischer Garden Chapel, *In Remembrance* (funeral leaflet, San Jose, California, 18 June 1970) Funeral Leaflet for Raymond Dwight Burton; privately held by Scott Mackay, Irondale, MO.

12. 1920 U.S. Census, Santa Clara County, California, population schedule, San Jose Township, Crandalville Precinct #2, ED 147, sheet 13A, dwelling 303, family 321, Elmer Burton Jr and Bertha Burton family; database with digital images, *FamilySearch*, accessed 2 June 2016.

13. "Family Record," digital image of undated pages from a family Bible or genealogy book for the Fred H Johnson family; privately held by Scott Mackay, Irondale, MO.

14. 1930 U.S. Census, Santa Clara County, California, population schedule, San Jose Township, ED 43-73, sheet 3B, dwelling 74; family 77, Raymond and Ruth Burton family; database with digital images, *FamilySearch*, accessed before June 2016.

15. 1940 U.S. Census, Santa Clara County, California, population schedule, San Jose Township, ED 43-87, 2B, household 59, Raymond and Ruth Burton; database with digital images, *FamilySearch*, accessed before June 2016.

16. Ruth Burton obituaries, digital images of June 1951 obituaries for Ruth Burton from unidentified newspapers; privately held by Scott Mackay, Irondale, MO.

Raymond after he got home from work. She was buried at Oak Hill Cemetery in San Jose, California.[17] Raymond then married Ruby, and lived until June 16, 1970 when he died of cancer in San Jose, California and was buried at Oak Hill Cemetery.[18]

The children of Raymond Dwight Burton and Ruth Johnson are below:

1. Raymond Donald Burton [01-01], who was born July 13, 1929 in San Jose, CA and died on September 12, 1986 at Kaiser Hospital in Santa Clara, California. He married Betty Lou Webb on August 19, 1949 in San Jose, California. He was buried at Oak Hill Cemetery in San Jose, California.
2. Elaine Ruth Burton, who was born on September 23, 1931 in San Jose, California, married Robert George Farry on October 22, 1950 in San Jose, CA, and died on May 8, 1973 in Mountain View, Santa Clara County, California. She was buried at Oak Hill Cemetery in San Jose, California.
3. Nancy Jean Burton, who was born and died in 1937 in San Jose, California.

[03-04] Harold Elmer Burton and [03-05] Bertha Viola Fine

Harold "Harry" Elmer Burton was born on June 18th, 1881 to Henry Heber Burton [04-08] and Mary Frances Robb [04-09] in Yamhill, Yamhill County, Oregon.[19] [20] Some sources say he was born on June 10, 1881, but Harold had reported June 18, 1881 in his registration for the draft. In the 1900 census he was living with his parents and working as a messenger.[21]

By 1903, Harry had moved to California, and he married Bertha Viola Fine in Hollister, San Benito County, California on December 10th, 1903.[22] Bertha was the daughter of Spencer Pettis Fine [04-10] and Margeline McCutchen

17. Ruth Burton obituaries, digital images of June 1951 obituaries for Ruth Burton from unidentified newspapers; privately held by Scott Mackay, Irondale, MO.
18. Raymond Dwight Burton obituaries, digital images of June 1951 obituaries for Raymond Dwight Burton from *San Jose Mercury News*; privately held by Scott Mackay, Irondale, MO.
19. Eugene T Sawyer, *History of Santa Clara County California: with Biographical Sketches* (Los Angeles: Historic Record Company, 1922), p. 1034, PDF e-book, https://archive.org , (accessed February 2016).
20. "United States World War I Draft Registration Cards, 1917-1918," s.v. "Harry Elmer Burton", database with digital images, *FamilySearch*, accessed before June 2016.
21. 1900 U.S. Census, Multnomah County, Oregon, population schedule, ED Portland, 22nd Precinct, Ward 5, sheet 6A, dwelling 81 or 77, family 132 or 128, Henry and Mary Burton family; database with digital images, *FamilySearch*, accessed 2 March 2017.
22. "California, County Marriages, 1850-1952," s.v. "H E Burton and Bertha Fine" (married 1903), database with digital images, *FamilySearch*, accessed 2 March 2017.

[04-11],[23] [24] and was born in Gilroy, Santa Clara County, California on August 26th, 1880.[25] Together they had four children for whom I found mention.

In California, Harry was working as a bookkeeper in Gilroy, California by the 1910 census[26], but by the time of his World War I draft registration he worked as a railway inspector in San Jose, California.[27] He was described in the draft registration as being of medium height and build with black hair, and lived at 773 West San Carlos in San Jose. By the 1920 census he still lived at the same address on West San Carlos in San Jose, but had become an Electric Railway adjuster.[28] He continued moving up by the 1930 census, becoming an Assistant Superintendent in the railroad industry. He had moved by 1930 to 860 Polhemus St in San Jose.[29] Harry died in San Jose on June 9, 1940[30] and was buried at Oak Hill Cemetery in San Jose, California.[31] Bertha lived until November 13, 1944, when she died in San Jose.[32]

1. Harold Heber Burton, who was born on January 8, 1905 in Portland, Multnomah County, Oregon and died on January 17, 1924 in San Joaquin County, California. His first wife was Ella Christina Johnson, who he married on January 17, 1924 in San Joaquin County, California. His second wife was Edna Fritz Saunders.

2. Raymond Dwight Burton [02-02] who was born on October 22, 1907 in Gilroy, Santa Clara County, California and died on June 16, 1970 in

---

23. Dorothy Wilson Fine, *A Fine Branch of the Family Tree*, (San Jose, CA: El Camino Real Chapter, DAR, 1991), p. 53.

24. J. P. Munro-Fraser, *History of Santa Clara County, California: including its Geography, Geology, Topography, Climatography and Description*, (San Francisco: Alley, Bowen & Co, 1881) p. 609; PDF e-book, https://archive.org , (accessed 16 March 2017).

25. "California Death Index, 1940-1997," s.v. "Bertha Viola Burton" (death 1944), database, *FamilySearch,* accessed 2 March 2017.

26. 1910 U.S. Census, Santa Clara County, California, population schedule, Gilroy Township, ED 72, sheet 6A, dwelling 80; family 80, Harry E Burton family; database with digital images, *FamilySearch*, accessed 2 June 2016.

27. "United States World War I Draft Registration Cards, 1917-1918," s.v. "Harry Elmer Burton", database with digital images, *FamilySearch*, accessed before June 2016.

28. 1920 US Census, Santa Clara County, California, population schedule, San Jose Township, Crandalville Precinct #2, ED 147, sheet 13A, dwelling 303, family 321, Elmer Burton Jr and Bertha Burton family; database with digital images, *FamilySearch*, accessed 2 June 2016.

29. 1930 US Census, Santa Clara County, California, population schedule, San Jose Township, ED 43-73, sheet 3B, dwelling 74, family 76, Harry and Bertha Burton family; database with digital images, *FamilySearch*, accessed before June 2016.

30. Dorothy Wilson Fine, *A Fine Branch of the Family Tree*, (San Jose, CA: El Camino Real Chapter, DAR, 1991), p. 50.

31. Harry E Burton, grave marker, Oak Hill Memorial Park, San Jose, Santa Clara County, California, digital image s.v. "Harry E Burton" (death 1940, memorial 151551984) , database with digital images, *FindAGrave,* accessed 7 July 2018.

32. "California Death Index, 1940-1997," s.v. "Bertha Viola Burton" (death 1944), database, *FamilySearch,* accessed 2 March 2017.

San Jose, California. His first wife was Ruth Elma Johnson [02-03] who he married on March 20, 1928. His second wife was Ruby Hanson.

3. Elmer DeForest (aka Harry Elmer) Burton, who was born on August 5, 1912 in Gilroy, California and died on June 14, 2004 in Sparks, Washcoe County, Nevada. He married Elsie Irene Swagerty on June 6, 1936 in San Jose, California.

4. Ada Frances Burton, who was born on November 12, 1914 in San Jose, California and died on June 7, 1986 in Campbell, Santa Clara County, California. She married John Earl Nevis on August 12, 1937 in Campbell, California.

[03-06] Fred Henry Johnson and [03-07] Caroline Susan Newsom

Fred Henry Johnson was born on May 24, 1860 in La Crosse County, Wisconsin[33] to William Henry Carleton Johnson [04-12] and Mary Eliza Cowdrey [04-13], as indicated in the 1860, 1870, and 1880 Census records which will be described next. Fred's father was a farmer by 1860 and moved around. So in the 1860 census, Fred was in Harmony, Bad Ax County (now Vernon County), Wisconsin,[34] then in Jefferson, Vernon County, Wisconsin for the 1870 census.[35] Then he was in Center Township, Russell County, Kansas in the 1880 census, in which he was recorded as working on the farm.[36]

Fred married Caroline Susan Newsom on May 3, 1883 in Carrollton, Carroll County, Missouri.[37] Caroline was the daughter of William Newsom [04-14] and Sarah Jane Ryan [04-15] and was born on April 1, 1867 in Missouri.[38] (The marriage record for Fred Henry Johnson and Caroline Newsom listed William Newsom as the father,[39] and William Newsom's wife was Sarah J

---

33. Fred Henry Johnson Obituary, digital image of undated clipping from unidentified newspaper in Rocky Ford, Colorado, 1932; privately held by Scott Mackay, Irondale, MO.

34. 1860 U.S. Census, Bad Ax County, Wisconsin, population schedule, Harmony, p 237, dwelling 1954, family 1867, Henry C and Mary Johnson family; database with digital images, *FamilySearch*, accessed before June 2016.

35. 1870 U.S. Census, Vernon County, Wisconsin, population schedule, Jefferson, p 19, dwelling 137, family 137, Henry and Mary Johnson family; database with digital images, *FamilySearch*, accessed 3 March 2017.

36. 1880 U.S. Census, Russell County, Kansas, population schedule, Center Township, ED 290, page 11, dwelling 104, family 105, William and Mary Johnson family; database with digital images, *FamilySearch*, accessed 3 March 2017.

37. "Missouri Marriages, 1750-1920," s.v. "Fred H Johnson and Caroline S Newsom" (marriage in 1883), database, *FamilySearch*, accessed 7 Feb 2016.

38. "Family Record," digital image of undated pages from a family Bible or genealogy book for the Fred H Johnson family; privately held by Scott Mackay, Irondale, MO.

39. "Missouri, County Marriage, Naturalization, and Court Records, 1800-1991," film

Ryan).[40] Fred and Caroline had eleven children together in Kansas, but Fred continued to move the family around. He was a farmer in West Naron, Pratt County, Kansas for the 1900 census,[41] a farm employee in Fowler, Meade County, Kansas for the 1910 census,[42] a grocer in Rocky Ford, Otero County, Colorado for the 1920 census,[43] and finally a Pentecostal church pastor in Tuolumne, Tuolumne County, California for the 1930 census.[44] By the time of his death on April 18, 1932 Fred was back in Rocky Ford, Otero County, Colorado again, according to a clipping of an obituary from a Rocky Ford area newspaper for which I could not find the name.[45] Caroline died in 1946.[46]

The children of Fred Henry Johnson and Caroline Susan Newsom are listed below:

1. Louisa Johnson, who was born on February 10, 1884 in Carrollton, Missouri, and died on February 12, 1884.
2. Bertha May Johnson, who was born on February 22, 1885 in Dubuque, Russell County, Kansas and died in November 1966. She married John Swafford on February 25, 1903.
3. Cora Jane Johnson, who was born on February 29, 1888 in Dubuque, Kansas and died on August 17, 1904.
4. William Henry Johnson, who was born on April 6, 1891 in Dubuque, Kansas and died on February 14, 1970 in Santa Cruz County, California.
5. Charles M Johnson, who was born on May 16, 1893 in Dubuque, Kansas.
6. Carrie Mabel Johnson, who was born on April 27, 1895 in Dubuque, Kansas and died on December 26, 1895.

#007424511, image 151; digital images (not indexed), *FamilySearch*, accessed 2 May 2019.

40. "Missouri, County Marriage, Naturalization, and Court Records, 1800-1991," Carroll County, Marriage Records 1848-1887, Vol B, image 189; digital images (not indexed), *FamilySearch*, accessed 2 May 2019.

41. 1900 US Census, Pratt County, Kansas, population schedule, West Naron Township, ED 183, Sheet 1B, dwelling 11, family 11, Fred and Susan Johnson family; database with digital images, *FamilySearch*, accessed before June 2016.

42. 1910 US Census, Meade County, Kansas, population schedule, Fowler Township, ED 109, Sheet 7A, dwelling 108, family 114, Fred and Susan Johnson family; database with digital images, *FamilySearch*, accessed before June 2016.

43. 1920 US Census, Otero County, Colorado, population schedule, Rocky Ford, Sheet 5A, dwelling 106, family 118, Fred Johnson; database with digital images, *FamilySearch*, accessed before June 2016.

44. 1930 US Census, Tuolumne County, California, population schedule, Township 5 of Tuolumne, 55-14; 11B, dwelling 294, family 296, Fred and Caroline Johnson; database with digital images, *FamilySearch,* accessed before June 2016.

45. Fred Henry Johnson Obituary, digital image of undated clipping from unidentified newspaper in Rocky Ford, Colorado, 1932; privately held by Scott Mackay, Irondale, MO.

46. "Family Record," digital image of undated pages from a family Bible or genealogy book for the Fred H Johnson family; privately held by Scott Mackay, Irondale, MO.

7. Mabel Almeda Johnson, who was born on February 24, 1897 in Dubuque, Kansas and married Dorsey Kreible Staples on June 22, 1916. She died in 1980.
8. Lester Earl Johnson, who was born on March 6, 1899 in West Naron, Pratt County, Kansas.
9. Earnest Thesyl Johnson, who was born on July 18, 1901 in West Naron, Kansas and died on April 1, 1965 in Santa Clara County, California.
10. Esther Ivora Johnson, who was born on November 1, 1903 in West Naron, Kansas.
11. Reuben Larango Johnson, who was born on September 13, 1905 in Pratt County, Kansas.
12. Ella Christina Johnson, who was born on July 28, 1907 in Fowler, Meade County, Kansas and died on May 4, 1941 in Santa Clara County, California. She married Harold Heber Burton on January 17, 1924 in San Joaquin County, California.
13. Ruth Elma Johnson [02-03], who was born on April 1, 1910 in Fowler, Kansas and died on June 16, 1951 in San Jose, California. She married Raymond Dwight Burton [02-02] on March 29, 1928.[47]

[04-08] Henry Heber Burton and [04-09] Mary Frances Robb

Henry Heber Burton was born on November 2, 1843 on the ship *Heber* in the Pacific Ocean as it crossed the equator. Henry was named for the ship captain and his middle name was for the ship. His parents were John James Burton [05-16] and Margaret W Watson [05-17], who were traveling from Australia to Oregon.[48] The family had a farm in the North Fork Precinct of Yamhill County, Oregon, where Henry worked as a farm laborer[49] [50] until enlisting into B Company of the 1rst Oregon Infantry in 1864.[51] During the war Henry's unit stayed in the Northwest and fought Indians.[52] After the Civil War

---

47. "Family Record," digital image of undated pages from a family Bible or genealogy book for the Fred H Johnson family; privately held by Scott Mackay, Irondale, MO.
48. Eugene T Sawyer, *History of Santa Clara County California: with Biographical Sketches* (Los Angeles: Historic Record Company, 1922), p. 1033, PDF e-book, https://archive.org , (accessed February 2016).
49. 1850 U.S. Census, Yamhill County, Oregon Territory, population schedule, p 33, dwelling 135, family 135, John and Martha Burton family; database with digital images, *FamilySearch*, accessed 2015.
50. 1860 U.S. Census, Yamhill County, Oregon, population schedule, North Fork Precinct, p 454, dwelling 4199, family 3588, John and Margaret Burton; database with digital images, *FamilySearch*, accessed 2015.
51. "U.S., Union Soldiers Compiled Service Records, 1861-1865," s.v. "Henry H Burton" (Oregon), database, *Ancestry.com*, accessed 7 July 2018.
52. Eugene T Sawyer, *History of Santa Clara County California: with Biographical Sketches* (Los Angeles: Historic Record Company, 1922), p. 1033, PDF e-book,

Henry farmed and drove livestock throughout the west and mid-west. Sometime after his first marriage in August of 1873 to Lizzie Scott in Missouri, Henry settled down in the Fort Worth area of Texas running a wagon yard and livery stable. Lizzie died in 1877, at which point Henry joined the police force for two years before returning home to Oregon to farm. Henry married Mary Frances Robb in Fort Worth, Texas sometime between Lizzie's death and his return to Oregon.[53]

Mary Frances Robb was born in 1852 in Pike County, Missouri to Benjamin Franklin Robb [05-18] and Nancy A Nickelson [05-19].[54][55] Henry and Mary stayed in Oregon until 1918 when they moved to San Jose, California. Mary suffered a paralytic stroke in 1918 and died on February 14, 1920 in San Jose,[56] where she is buried at Oak Hill Cemetery. Henry had a third marriage before dying on August 15th, 1922 in San Jose, and is also buried at Oak Hill Cemetery.[57]

The son of Henry Heber Burton and Mary Frances Robb was Harold Elmer Burton [03-04], who was born on June 18, 1881 in Yamhill, Oregon and died on June 9, 1940 in San Jose, Santa Clara County, California. His wife was Bertha Viola Fine [03-05], who he married on December 10, 1903 in Hollister, San Benito County, California.[58]

[04-10] Spencer Pettis Fine and [04-11] Margeline McCutchen

Spencer Pettis Fine was born on May 13, 1836 in Lafayette County, Missouri[59] to Lidgard Fine, Jr [05-20] and Martha Ann Cox [05-21].[60] Spencer

---

https://archive.org , (accessed February 2016).

53. Ibid., p 1034.

54. Ibid., p 1034.

55. "Kentucky, County Marriages, 1797-1954," s. v. "Benjamin F Robb and Nancy Nicholson" (marriage 1833), database with digital images, *FamilySearch*, accessed 27 March 2017.

56. Eugene T Sawyer, *History of Santa Clara County California: with Biographical Sketches* (Los Angeles: Historic Record Company, 1922), p. 1034, PDF e-book, https://archive.org , (accessed February 2016).

57. Henry H Burton, grave marker, Oak Hill Memorial Park, San Jose, Santa Clara County, California, digital image s.v. "Corp H H Burton" (death 1922, memorial 73357500) , database with digital images, *FindAGrave*, accessed 7 July 2018.

58. Dorothy Wilson Fine, *A Fine Branch of the Family Tree*, (San Jose, CA: El Camino Real Chapter, DAR, 1991), p. 53.

59. J. P. Munro-Fraser, *History of Santa Clara County, California: including its Geography, Geology, Topography, Climatography and Description*, (San Francisco: Alley, Bowen & Co, 1881) p. 609; PDF e-book, https://archive.org , (accessed 16 March 2017).

60. Dorothy Wilson Fine, *A Fine Branch of the Family Tree*, (San Jose, CA: El Camino Real Chapter, DAR, 1991), p. 53.

Fine was also listed in Lidgard Fine's household in the 1860 Census.[61] He stayed in Missouri until 1854 when he went with his family in a wagon train to California. Spencer was a cattle rancher in the mountains of California from 1857 to 1864, except for part of 1859 and 1860 when he was at Jones Commercial School in Chicago, Illinois.

On May 13, 1868, Spencer married Margeline McCutchen in Gilroy, Santa Clara County, California.[62] In many records, it is spelled McCutcheon. Margeline was born in Gilroy to John McCutchen [05-22] and Keziah Anson [05-23].[63] Margeline's gravestone gives March 30, 1847 as her date of birth.[64] Spencer and Margeline had seven children, all born in Gilroy, California where they had a farm. Margeline died on November 25, 1903 and was buried at Gavilan Hills Memorial Park and Catholic Cemetery in Gilroy, California.[65] Spencer continued farming in Gilroy until he died on Jan 10, 1912.[66] He also was buried at the Gavilan Hills Cemetery.[67]

The children of Spencer Fine and Margeline McCutchen are listed below:
1. Spencer Fine, Jr was born on February 26, 1870 in Gilroy, California and married Juana Catalina Mead on April 12, 1895. He died on April 20, 1928 in San Jose, California.
2. Lidgard Fine was born on May 22, 1872 in Gilroy, California and died on May 25, 1946 in Gilroy.
3. Milbra Fine was born on July 16, 1874 in Gilroy, California and died on November 17, 1880 in Gilroy.
4. Ada Louise Fine was born on January 20, 1878 in Gilroy, California and married Jasper F Martin on February 10, 1912 in Gilroy. She died on March 31, 1949 in San Jose, California and was buried in Gilroy.
5. Bertha Viola Fine [03-05] was born on August 26, 1880 in Gilroy, California and married Harold Elmer Burton [03-04] on December 10,

---

61. 1860 U.S. Census, Santa Clara County, California, population schedule, Gilroy Township, p. 19, dwelling 150, family 129, Lidgard Fine family; database with digital images, *Ancestry.com,* accessed 2015.
62. "California Marriages, 1850-1877," s.v. "Margeline Mc Cutcheon and S P Fine" (married 1868), database, *Ancestry.com,* accessed 5 August 2012.
63. Dorothy Wilson Fine, *A Fine Branch of the Family Tree*, (San Jose, CA: El Camino Real Chapter, DAR, 1991), p. 31.
64. Margeline McCutchen Fine, grave marker, Gavilan Hills Memorial Park, Gilroy, Santa Clara County, California, digital image s.v. "Margeline McCutchen Fine" (death 1903, memorial 19318389), database with digital images, *FindAGrave,* accessed 7 July 2018.
65. Margeline McCutchen Fine, grave marker, Gavilan Hills Memorial Park, Gilroy, Santa Clara County, California, digital image s.v. "Margeline McCutchen Fine" (death 1903, memorial 19318389), database with digital images, *FindAGrave,* accessed 7 July 2018.
66. "California Death Index, 1905-1939," s.v. "Spencer Fine" (death 1912), database, *FamilySearch,* accessed 17 March 2017.
67. Spencer Fine, grave marker, Gavilan Hills Memorial Park, Gilroy, Santa Clara County, California, digital image s.v. "Spencer Pettis Fine" (died 1912, memorial 17714304), database with digital images, *FindAGrave,* accessed 7 July 2018.

1903 in Hollister, California. She died on November 13, 1944 in San Jose, California and was buried in San Jose.

6. Leonidas Bernard Fine was born on January 29, 1884 in Gilroy, California and married Cecil Rose on November 16, 1914 in Gilroy. He died on April 7, 1938 in Gilroy and was buried there.

7. Raymond Fine was born on April 8, 1887 in Gilroy, California and married Emily Lemke Barclay on August 11, 1928 in San Jose, California. He died on November 25, 1954 in San Jose, California and was buried in Gilroy.[68] [69]

[04-12] William Henry Carlton Johnson and [04-13] Mary Eliza Cowdrey

William Henry Carleton Johnson was born in 1827 in Vermont[70] to Moses Johnson [05-24][71] and Abigail Carleton [05-25].[72] By 1849, William had moved to Bradford, Essex County, Massachusetts where he married Mary Eliza Cowdrey on April 10, 1849. He was a shoemaker according to his marriage record.[73] Some genealogies give Providence, Rhode Island as the marriage location, but the record image actually says Providence Road, which is in Bradford, Massachusetts.

Mary Eliza Cowdrey was born on February 12, 1830 in Billerica, Middlesex County, Massachusetts to Joseph Cowdrey [05-26] and Ann Eliza Foster [05-27].[74] [75] William and Mary Johnson had seven children that I could find records

68. Dorothy Wilson Fine, *A Fine Branch of the Family Tree*, (San Jose, CA: El Camino Real Chapter, DAR, 1991), p. 31.

69. J. P. Munro-Fraser, *History of Santa Clara County, California: including its Geography, Geology, Topography, Climatography and Description*, (San Francisco: Alley, Bowen & Co, 1881) p. 609; PDF e-book, https://archive.org , (accessed 16 March 2017).

70. "California Death Index, 1905-1939," s.v. "William H Johnson" (died 1910), database, *FamilySearch,* accessed 17 March 2017.

71. "Massachusetts, Town Clerk, Vital and Town Records, 1626-2001" s.v. "Henry C Johnson" (spouse "Mary Eliza Cowdry", marriage 1849), database with images, *FamilySearch,* accessed 2 May 2019.

72. "Vermont Vital Records, 1760-1954" s.v. "Moses Johnson" (spouse "Abigail Carleton", marriage 1818), database with images, *FamilySearch*, accessed 19 April 2016.

73. "Massachusetts Marriages, 1841-1915," s.v. "Henry C Johnson and Mary E Cowdrey" (marriage 1849), database with images, *FamilySearch*, accessed 17 March 2017.

74. "Massachusetts Births and Christenings, 1639-1915," s.v. "Mary Eliza Cowdrey" (born 1830), database, *FamilySearch,* accessed 17 March 2017.

75. "Massachusetts, Town Clerk, Vital and Town Records, 1626-2001," s.v. "Joseph Cowdry" (spouse "Ann E Foster," marriage 1829), database with images, *FamilySearch*, accessed 20 April 2017.

for. Three were born in Massachusetts and four in Wisconsin, where they had moved by the 1860 census.[76] When the Civil War came, William served in Union Army. (His gravestone has 12 Wis.L.A. which is probably the 12th Wisconsin Light Artillery.)[77] Then between the 1870 census and the 1880 census William and Mary moved to Center Township in Russell County, Kansas.[78]

It appears that Mary died before the 1900 census was taken, because at that point William lived with a friend at 165 West 37th St in Los Angeles, California.[79] William died on August 19th, 1910 in Orange County, California[80] and was buried in Santa Ana Cemetery, Santa Ana, Orange County, California.[81]

The children of William Henry Carleton Johnson and Mary Eliza Cowdrey are listed below:

1. Henrietta Johnson, who was born about 1850 in Massachusetts.
2. Marietta F Johnson, who was born about 1850 in Massachusetts[82] and married Isaac Laylan on July 23, 1868 in Genoa, Vernon County, Wisconsin.[83]
3. Ann Eliza Johnson, who was born on August 23, 1851 in Groveland, Essex County, Massachusetts[84] and married Thomas R Riley on June 12, 1870 in Genoa, Vernon County, Wisconsin.[85]
4. Fred Henry Johnson [03-06], who was born on May 24, 1860 in La Crosse County, Wisconsin and married Caroline Susan Newsom [03-

---

76. 1850 US Census, Essex County, Massachusetts, population schedule, Bradford, p 26, dwelling 154, family 193, Henry C and Mary Johnson family; database with digital images, *FamilySearch*, accessed 17 March 2017.
77. William Johnson, grave marker, Santa Ana Cemetery, Santa Ana, Orange County, California, digital image s.v. "William H C Johnson" (death 1910, memorial 8722020), database with digital images, *FindAGrave*, accessed 7 July 2018.
78. 1880 US Census, Russell County, Kansas, population schedule, Center Township, ED 290, page 11, dwelling 104, family 105, William and Mary Johnson family; database with digital images, *FamilySearch*, accessed 3 March 2017.
79. 1900 US Census, Los Angeles County, California, population schedule, Los Angeles Precinct 39, ED 48, sheet 16B, dwelling 358, family 370, William HC Johnson; database with digital images, *FamilySearch*, accessed 17 March 2017.
80. "California Death Index, 1905-1939," s.v. "William H Johnson" (died 1910), database, *FamilySearch,* accessed 17 March 2017.
81. William Johnson, grave marker, Santa Ana Cemetery, Santa Ana, Orange County, California, digital image s.v. "William H C Johnson" (death 1910, memorial 8722020), database with digital images, *FindAGrave,* accessed 7 July 2018.
82. 1860 US Census, Bad Ax County, Wisconsin, population schedule, Harmony, p. 237, dwelling 1,954, family 1,827, Henry C and Mary Johnson family; database with digital images, *FamilySearch*, accessed 2016.
83. "Wisconsin, County Marriages, 1836-1911," s.v. "Isaac Laylan" (marriage 1868, spouse "Marietta F Johnson"), database, *FamilySearch*, accessed 30 June 2017.
84. "Massachusetts Births, 1841-1915," s.v. "Annie Eliza Johnson" (birth 1851), database, *FamilySearch,* accessed 30 June 2017.
85. "Wisconsin, County Marriages, 1836-1911," s.v. "Thomas R Riley" (marriage 1870, spouse "Anne Eliza Johnson"), database, *FamilySearch*, accessed 30 June 2017.

07] on May 3, 1883. He died on April 18, 1932 in Rocky Ford, Otero County, Colorado.
5.   Clarence C Johnson, who was born about 1862 in Wisconsin.[86]
6.   Eddie M Johnson, who was born about 1864 in Wisconsin.
7.   Charles Johnson, who was born about 1869 in Wisconsin.[87]

[04-14] William Newsom and [04-15] Sarah Jane Ryan

William Newsom was born in North Carolina in 1841,[88] but by the time he registered for the Civil War draft in July 1863 he lived in Hurricane, Carroll County, Missouri.[89] I do not know if he served in the military during the war or not, but after the war he married Sarah Jane Ryan in Carroll County, Missouri on April 10, 1866.[90] Due to a combination of sources which will be mentioned below, I believe that Sarah Jane Ryan was the daughter of Morgan Ryan [05-30] and Susan Jane Patton [05-31] and was born in 1850 in Missouri. The 1880 census for Sarah Jane (Ryan) Newsom indicates that Sarah was born in Missouri in 1850 and that her parents were born in Tennessee.[91] The marriage record shows that Sarah's maiden name was Ryan,[92] and the 1860 census shows a Sarah J Ryan who is born in Missouri in 1850, living with parents who were born in Tennessee.[93] I believe this is strong enough evidence to establish a family connection.

William and Sarah Newsom continued in Carroll County, Missouri according to records. There are records of them having seven children in Missouri. William was a farmer in the 1870 census at Grand River Township,

86. 1870 US Census, Vernon County, Wisconsin, population schedule, Jefferson, p. 19, dwelling 137, family 137, Henry and Mary Johnson family; database with digital images, *FamilySearch,* accessed 3 March 2017.
87. 1880 US Census, Russell County, Kansas, population schedule, Center Township, ED 290, p. 11, dwelling 104, family 105, William and Mary Johnson family; database with digital images, *FamilySearch*, accessed 3 March 2017.
88. 1880 U.S. Census, Carroll County, Missouri, population schedule, Rea Township, ED 156, 3, dwelling 27, family 27, William and Sarah Newsim family; database with digital images, *FamilySearch*, accessed 4 March 2016.
89. "U.S., Civil War Draft Registrations Records, 1863-1865," s.v. "William Newsom" (residence 1863 Missouri), database with digital images, *Ancestry.com*, accessed 7 July 2018.
90. "Missouri Marriages, 1750-1920," s.v. "William Newsome and Sarah J Ryan" (marriage 1866), database, *FamilySearch*, accessed 17 March 2017.
91. 1880 U.S. Census, Carroll County, Missouri, population schedule, Rea Township, ED 156, 3, dwelling 27, family 27, William and Sarah Newsim family; database with digital images, *FamilySearch*, accessed 4 March 2016.
92. "Missouri Marriages, 1750-1920," s.v.. "William Newsome and Sarah J Ryan" (marriage 1866), database, *FamilySearch*, accessed 17 March 2017.
93. 1860 US Census, Texas County, Missouri, population schedule, Burdine, p 14, dwelling 93, family 83, Morgan and Susan Ryan family; database with digital images, *FamilySearch*, accessed 20 April 2017.

Carroll County, Missouri,[94] again a farmer at Rea Township, Carroll County, Missouri in the 1880 census,[95] and still a farmer at Combs Township, Carroll County, Missouri at the birth of their last child Emma Newsom on March 15, 1884.[96] I found no records of William and Sarah after 1884. Below are their children for whom I could find records:

1. Caroline Susan Newsom [03-07] who was born April 1, 1867 in Carrollton, Carroll County, Missouri[97] and married Fred Henry Johnson [03-06] on May 3, 1883 in Carrollton.[98] She died in 1946.[99]
2. Ollie J Newsom, born 1869.
3. Henry Newsom, born 1872.
4. Zana Newsom, born 1874.
5. Samuel J Newsom, born 1876.
6. Larcena Newsom, born 1878.[100]
7. Emma Newsom, born May 15, 1884 in Combs Township, Carroll County, Missouri.[101]

[05-16] John James Burton and [05-17] Margaret W. Watson

John James Burton was born in Shaldon in Devon, England on February 19, 1815 (according to his gravestone)[102] to James Burton [06-32] and Jemima Champion [06-33]. John was christened on March 5, 1815 in the Anglican parish of St Nicholas in Shaldon.[103] By 1832, John had become an architect and

---

94. 1870 US Census, Carroll County, Missouri, population schedule, Grand River Township, p 41, dwelling 323, family 325, William and Sarah Newsom family; database with digital images, *FamilySearch*, accessed 20 April 2017.
95. 1880 U.S. Census, Carroll County, Missouri, population schedule, Rea Township, ED 156, 3, dwelling 27, family 27, William and Sarah Newsim family; database with digital images, *FamilySearch*, accessed 4 March 2016.
96. "Missouri Birth & Death Records Database," s.v. "Emma Newsom" (born in Carroll County), database, *Missouri Digital Heritage*, accessed 3 March 2017.
97. "Missouri Marriages, 1750-1920," s.v. "Fred H Johnson and Caroline S Newsom" (marriage in 1883), database, *FamilySearch*, accessed 7 Feb 2016.
98. "Family Record," digital image of undated pages from a family Bible or genealogy book for the Fred H Johnson family; privately held by Scott Mackay, Irondale, MO.
99. "Missouri Marriages, 1750-1920," s.v. "Fred H Johnson and Caroline S Newsom" (marriage in 1883), database, *FamilySearch*, accessed 7 Feb 2016.
100   1880 U.S. Census, Carroll County, Missouri, population schedule, Rea Township, ED 156, 3, dwelling 27, family 27, William and Sarah Newsim family; database with digital images, *FamilySearch*, accessed 4 March 2016.
101   "Missouri Birth & Death Records Database," vs. "Emma Newsom" (born in Carroll County), database, *Missouri Digital Heritage*, accessed 3 March 2017.
102   John James Burton, grave marker, Yamhill Carlton Pioneer Memorial Cemetery, Yamhill, Yamhill County, Oregon, s.v. "John James Burton" (death 1879, memorial 41229693), database with digital images, *FindAGrave*, accessed 7 July 2018.
103   'Devon Baptisms Transcriptions," s.v. "John James Burton" (birth 1815), database with digital images, *FindMyPast*, accessed 25 March 2017.

moved to Australia,[104] where he met his wife Margaret "Martha" Watson and married her on May 12, 1839 in a Roman Catholic marriage at Hobart on the island of Tasmania in Australia.[105]

Margaret W. Watson was born on June 21, 1822 in Lancashire, England[106] to Charles Watson [06-34] and Bridget Linnoir [06-35], although Bridget apparently also went by Mary.[107] Margaret grew up in England, but at a young age her father was sent to Australia under the harsh laws of the time in England[108], and her mother eventually brought the rest of the family to Australia to be with him.

In 1843, John and Margaret emigrated to Oregon, where he became a stock raiser and farmer. During the gold rush in California, John did some gold mining between 1848 and 1850.[109] They were in Yamhill, Oregon for the 1850 census[110] and had the rest of their fifteen children (that I know of) at Yamhill. By 1879 John and Margaret had moved to Portland in Multnomah County, Oregon, where John died on September 15, 1879. He is buried at Yamhill Carlton Pioneer Memorial Cemetery in Yamhill in Yamhill Co, Oregon.[111] Margaret left for California before 1892 and died of Meningitis in Oakland, Alameda County, California on October 18, 1900.[112] She was also buried at Yamhill Carlton Pioneer Memorial Cemetery.[113] The children of John James

---

104   The Lewis Publishing Company, *The Bay of San Francisco: The Metropolis of the Pacific Coast and its Suburban Cities*, (Chicago: The Lewis Publishing Company, 1892), p. 625; PDF e-book, https://archive.org , accessed November 2017.

105   "Tasmania Marriages 1803-1899," *s.v.* "John James Burton and Margaret Watson" (marriage 1839) *FindMyPast*, accessed 2015.

106   Margaret Watson Burton, grave marker, Yamhill Carlton Pioneer Memorial Cemetery, Yamhill, Yamhill County, Oregon, s.v. "Margaret Watson Burton" (death 1900, memorial 41229727), database with digital images, *FindAGrave*, accessed 25 March 2017.

107   The Lewis Publishing Company, *The Bay of San Francisco: The Metropolis of the Pacific Coast and its Suburban Cities*, (Chicago: The Lewis Publishing Company, 1892), p. 625; PDF e-book, https://archive.org , accessed November 2017.

108   "Convict Records," s.v. "Charles Watson" (sentenced 1827), database, *Convict Records of Australia,* accessed 3 July 2017.

109   The Lewis Publishing Company, *The Bay of San Francisco: The Metropolis of the Pacific Coast and its Suburban Cities*, (Chicago: The Lewis Publishing Company, 1892), p. 626; PDF e-book, https://archive.org , accessed November 2017.

110   1850 US Census, Yamhill County, Oregon Territory, population schedule, p 33, dwelling 135, family 135, John and Martha Burton family; database with digital images, *FamilySearch*, accessed 2015.

111   John James Burton, grave marker, Yamhill Carlton Pioneer Memorial Cemetery, Yamhill, Yamhill County, Oregon, s.v. "John James Burton" (death 1879, memorial 41229693), database with digital images, *FindAGrave*, accessed 7 July 2018.

112   "Return of a Death—Physician's Certificate", Margaret Watson Burton; privately held by Scott Mackay, Irondale, MO.

113   Margaret Watson Burton, grave marker, Yamhill Carlton Pioneer Memorial Cemetery, Yamhill, Yamhill County, Oregon, s.v. "Margaret Watson Burton" (death 1900, memorial 41229727), database with digital images, *FindAGrave*, accessed 7 July 2018.

Burton and Margaret Watson are listed below:

1. Mary Ann Burton, born March 2, 1840 in New Zealand and died September 7, 1856 in Oregon.
2. Jemima B. Burton, born November 11, 1841 in New Zealand and died September 13, 1850 in Oregon.
3. Henry Heber Burton [04-08] who was born November 2, 1843 on ship in the Pacific Ocean. He married Lizzie Scott in August 1873 in Missouri, his second marriage was to Mary Frances Robb [04-09] after 1877 in Texas,[114] and his third marriage was to Mary Elizabeth Matthis about 1921. He died on August 15, 1922.[115]
4. Sarah Kate Burton who was born on October 19, 1846 in Yamhill, Yamhill County, Oregon and married John R Lake.
5. Charles Watson Burton, who was born about 1849 in Yamhill and married Annie Squires.
6. Eliza B. Burton, who was born in 1852 in Yamhill, married Major P. Moore, and died on April 25, 1888 in Yamhill.
7. Kisiah Burton, who was born about 1852 in Yamhill and married Dwight Rogers.
8. John James Burton, who was born about 1854 in Yamhill and married Mary Brady.
9. Edward Ransom Burton, who was born about August 1856 in Yamhill and married Mary Withycomb.
10. Benjamin Turner Burton, born about 1858 in Yamhill.
11. Linnoir Lord Burton, who was born on December 23, 1859 and died on July 4, 1908.
12. Lincoln Creswell Burton, who was born about 1862 in Yamhill and married Nellie Graham.
13. Clara Eloise Elizabeth Burton, who was born on December 27, 1865 in Yamhill and married E. H. Anthony.
14. George Launcelot William Burton, who was born on July 27, 1866 in Yamhill and married Nellie Gregor.
15. Margaret Edith Alma Burton, who was born on May 14, 1868 in Yamhill.[116]

---

114   The Lewis Publishing Company, *The Bay of San Francisco: The Metropolis of the Pacific Coast and its Suburban Cities*, (Chicago: The Lewis Publishing Company, 1892), p. 626; PDF e-book, https://archive.org , accessed November 2017.

115   Henry H Burton, grave marker, Oak Hill Memorial Park, San Jose, Santa Clara County, California, digital image s.v. "Corp H H Burton" (death 1922, memorial 73357500) , database with digital images, *FindAGrave,* accessed 7 July 2018.

116   The Lewis Publishing Company, *The Bay of San Francisco: The Metropolis of the Pacific Coast and its Suburban Cities*, (Chicago: The Lewis Publishing Company, 1892), p. 626; PDF e-book, https://archive.org , accessed November 2017.

[05-18] Benjamin Franklin Robb and [05-19] Nancy A Nickelson

Benjamin Franklin Robb was born about 1814 near Frankfort, Kentucky to Hugh W Robb [06-36] and Elizabeth Waller[117] [06-37]. He married Nancy A Nickelson in Union County, Kentucky on December 19, 1833.[118] Nancy had to get permission to marry from her father, who signed the permission as M D Nickelson [06-38]. That is all I could find on her parents, although they were described as Scottish in ancestry and lived in Illinois.[119] However in the 1880 census Nancy was said to have been born in Kentucky, and so was her mother although her father was born in Pennsylvania.[120]

In 1834, the Robb family moved to Marion County, Missouri.[121] They moved around and farmed in different states, being in Adams County, Illinois for the 1860 census,[122] back in Marion County, Missouri for the 1870 census,[123] and in Fannin County, Texas for the 1880 census.[124] Benjamin was back in Adams County, Illinois when he died in 1900.[125] He is buried at New Town Cemetery in Adams County, Illinois along with his wife who died in 1881.[126]

---

117   Chapman Bros., *Portrait and Biographical Album of Johnson and Pawnee Counties, Nebraska*, (Chicago: Chapman Bros., 1889), pp. 599-601; PDF e-book, https://books.google.com accessed 27 March 2017.
118   "Kentucky, County Marriages, 1797-1954," s.v. "Benjamin F Robb and Nancy Nicholson" (marriage 1833), database with digital images, *FamilySearch*, accessed 27 March 2017.
119   Chapman Bros., *Portrait and Biographical Album of Johnson and Pawnee Counties, Nebraska*, (Chicago: Chapman Bros., 1889), pp. 599-601; PDF e-book, https://books.google.com accessed 27 March 2017.
120   1880 US Census, Fannin Co, Texas, population schedule, Precinct 7, ED 30, p 6B, dwelling 58, family 58, Benjamin and Nancy Robb family; database with digital images, *FamilySearch*, accessed before June 2016.
121   Chapman Bros., *Portrait and Biographical Album of Johnson and Pawnee Counties, Nebraska*, (Chicago: Chapman Bros., 1889), pp. 599-601; PDF e-book, https://books.google.com accessed 27 March 2017.
122   1860 US Census, Adams County, Illinois, population schedule, Liberty Post Office, p 533, dwelling 55, family 55, Benjamin F and Nancy Robb; database with digital images, *FamilySearch*, accessed 16 March 2016.
123   1870 US Census, Marion County, Missouri, population schedule, Fabius Township, p 8, dwelling 48; family 49, Benjamin F and Nancy Robb family; database with digital images, *FamilySearch*, accessed before June 2016.
124   1880 US Census, Fannin Co, Texas, population schedule, Precinct 7, ED 30, p 6B, dwelling 58, family 58, Benjamin and Nancy Robb family; database with digital images, *FamilySearch*, accessed before June 2016.
125   Benjamin Robb, grave marker, New Town Cemetery, Burton Township, Adams County, Illinois, s.v. "Benjamin Franklin Robb" (death 1900, memorial 92514846), database with digital images, *FindAGrave*, accessed 2 April 2017).
126   Nancy Nickelson Robb, grave marker, New Town Cemetery, Burton Township, Adams County, Illinois, s.v. "Nancy A. Nichols Robb" (death 1881, memorial 92514878), database with digital images, *FindAGrave*, accessed 1 July 2017.

Benjamin was described as an abolitionist who had been a Whig but became a Republican at the formation of the Republican party. He was a Justice of the Peace and a Sheriff in Missouri. His religion was Baptist.[127] The children of Benjamin Franklin Robb and Nancy A. Nickelson are listed below:

1. Julia A Robb.
2. Hugh W. Robb, born on January 17, 1836 in West Ely, Marion County, Missouri.
3. Nancy J. Robb.
4. Franklin M. Robb.[128]
5. Thomas J. Robb, born about 1841 in Missouri.
6. James M. Robb, born about 1842 in Missouri.
7. Newton J. Robb, born about 1844 in Missouri.
8. George W. Robb, born about 1846 in Missouri.
9. Zachary T. Robb, born about 1849 in Missouri.[129]
10. Mary Frances Robb, [04-09] born about 1852 in Pike County, Missouri. She married first to James H. Davis on October 8, 1867 in Pike County, and then her second marriage was to Henry Heber Burton [04-08] after 1877 in Barnum, Polk County, Texas. She died on February 14, 1920 in San Jose, Santa Clara County, California.[130]
11. John H. Robb, born about 1854 in Illinois.
12. Benjamin F. Robb, born about 1856 in Illinois.
13. Emma E. Robb, born about 1858 in Illinois.[131]
14. Martha J. Robb.[132]

---

127   Chapman Bros., *Portrait and Biographical Album of Johnson and Pawnee Counties, Nebraska*, (Chicago: Chapman Bros., 1889), pp. 599-601; PDF e-book, https://books.google.com accessed 27 March 2017.
128   Chapman Bros., *Portrait and Biographical Album of Johnson and Pawnee Counties, Nebraska*, (Chicago: Chapman Bros., 1889), pp. 599-601; PDF e-book, https://books.google.com accessed 27 March 2017.
129   1860 US Census, Adams County, Illinois, population schedule, Liberty Post Office, p 533, dwelling 55, family 55, Benjamin F and Nancy Robb; database with digital images, *FamilySearch*, accessed 16 March 2016.
130   Eugene T Sawyer, *History of Santa Clara County California: with Biographical Sketches* (Los Angeles: Historic Record Company, 1922), p. 1034, PDF e-book, https://archive.org , (accessed February 2016).
131   1860 US Census, Adams County, Illinois, population schedule, Liberty Post Office, p 533, dwelling 55, family 55, Benjamin F and Nancy Robb; database with digital images, *FamilySearch*, accessed 16 March 2016.
132   Chapman Bros., *Portrait and Biographical Album of Johnson and Pawnee Counties, Nebraska*, (Chicago: Chapman Bros., 1889), pp. 599-601; PDF e-book, https://books.google.com accessed 27 March 2017.

[05-20] Lidgard Fine, Jr and [05-21] Martha Ann "Patsey" Cox

Lidgard Fine, Jr was born on March 22, 1808 in Cocke County, Tennessee to Lidgard Fine, Sr [06-40] and Elizabeth Netherton [06-41].[133] By 1833 he was in Missouri, and on August 6th, 1833 he married Martha Ann "Patsey" Cox.[134] Martha was born on January 13th, 1813 to Solomon Cox [06-42] and Deborah Collins [06-43].[135]

In 1849, Lidgard went on his first of three trips between Missouri and California. This first trip was by wagon train, possibly with his brothers but without his wife and children. Then he came back to Missouri and in 1854 took his wife, two children, and a herd of cattle to California by wagon train. For his final trip, Lidgard went by sea and got the rest of his children while selling his land in Missouri about 1855.[136] Lidgard farmed in Gilroy, Santa Clara County, California until his wife Martha died on August 9, 1873 in Gilroy. She is buried at Gavilan Hills Memorial Park in Gilroy.[137]

After his wife died, Lidgard moved to Paraiso Springs, near Soledad in Monterrey County, California. He became a hotel keeper and purchased 1/3 interest in the resort, where people believed the hot springs could cure many kinds of ailments. Paraiso Springs is where Lidgard died on 21 March 1891,[138] and he is buried at Gavilan Hills Memorial Park in Gilroy.[139] The children of Lidgard Fine and Martha Cox are listed below:

1. Leonidas Fine, born September 19, 1834 in Dover, Lafayette County, Missouri and died November 13, 1834 in Dover.
2. Spencer Pettis Fine [04-10], born May 13, 1836 in Lafayette County, Missouri and died January 10, 1912 in Santa Clara County, California. He married Margeline McCutchen [04-11] on May 13, 1868 in Gilroy, Santa Clara County, California.
3. Missouri Ann Fine, born January 4, 1839 in Dover, Lafayette County,

---

133   Dorothy Wilson Fine, *A Fine Branch of the Family Tree*, (San Jose, CA: El Camino Real Chapter, DAR, 1991), p. 3.
134   "Missouri, Marriage Records, 1805-2002," s.v. "Lidgard Fine Jr and Patsa Cors" (marriage 1833), database with digital images, *Ancestry.com*, accessed 1 July 2017.
135   Dorothy Wilson Fine, *A Fine Branch of the Family Tree*, (San Jose, CA: El Camino Real Chapter, DAR, 1991), p. 25.
136   Dorothy Wilson Fine, *A Fine Branch of the Family Tree*, (San Jose, CA: El Camino Real Chapter, DAR, 1991), p. 23.
137   Martha Fine, grave marker, Gavilan Hills Memorial Park, Gilroy, Santa Clara County, California, s.v. "Martha Fine" (death 1873, memorial 17714143), database with digital images, *FindAGrave*, accessed 13 April 2017.
138   Dorothy Wilson Fine, *A Fine Branch of the Family Tree*, (San Jose, CA: El Camino Real Chapter, DAR, 1991), p. 25.
139   Lidgard Fine, Jr, Gavilan Hills Memorial Park, Gilroy, Santa Clara County, California, s.v. "Lidgard Fine, Jr" (death 1891, memorial 17714257), database with digital images, *FindAGrave*, accessed 2 April 2017.

Missouri and died December 13, 1870 in California. She married William C Miller on March 22, 1860 in Gilroy, Santa Clara County, California.

4. Mary Jane Fine, born July 4, 1841 in Dover, Lafayette County, Missouri and died November 23, 1927 in Gilroy, Santa Clara County, California. She married Oscar Reeve about 1865.

5. Priscilla Y Fine, born January 17, 1843 in Dover, Lafayette County, Missouri and died June 10, 1874 in Gilroy, Santa Clara County, California. She married Samuel Eldridge on April 2, 1868 in Gilroy.

6. Deborah Cox Fine, born April 4, 1847 in Dover, Lafayette County, Missouri and died on July 31, 1927 in Gilroy, Santa Clara County, California. She married Henry F Reeve, Jr on May 14, 1868 in Gilroy.

7. Eliza R Fine, born July 24, 1855 in Mayfield, Santa Clara County, California and died on January 10, 1941 in Gilroy, Santa Clara County, California.[140]

[05-22] John McCutchen and [05-23] Keziah Anson

Not much is known for sure about John McCutchen, or McCutcheon. His daughter Margeline said he was born in Virginia.[141] He married Keziah Anson in Lewis County, Missouri on October 6, 1836,[142] and later took the family to California by wagon train about 1848. Then family history says he went to Oregon and no one heard from him again.[143] It is possible that John went back to Virginia, because in the 1850 census there is a John J McCutchen born about 1812 living as a farmer on James McCutchen's property in Augusta, Virginia. This John J McCutchen could be the same John that married Keziah, but the evidence is not strong. There is also another John McCutchen born in 1799 in Virginia, but he is less likely to be the right John McCutchen.

Keziah (also spelled Kisiah) Anson was born on December 20, 1805 in Logan County, Kentucky to Henry Anson [06-46] and Elizabeth Bierley [06-47]. A year after John J McCutchen disappeared, Keziah McCutchen married William Campbell, who founded Campbell, California, on July 5th, 1849 at Mission Santa Clara in Santa Clara County, California. She divorced William Campbell in 1855.[144] Keziah died in Gilroy, Santa Clara County, California on

---

140   Dorothy Wilson Fine, *A Fine Branch of the Family Tree*, (San Jose, CA: El Camino Real Chapter, DAR, 1991), p. 25.

141   1880 US Census, Santa Clara County, California, population schedule, Gilroy Township, ED 258, page 24D, dwelling 151, family 151, S P and Margeline Fine family; database with digital images, *FamilySearch*, accessed 17 March 2017.

142   Dorothy Wilson Fine, *A Fine Branch of the Family Tree*, (San Jose, CA: El Camino Real Chapter, DAR, 1991), p. 34.

143   Dorothy Wilson Fine, *A Fine Branch of the Family Tree*, (San Jose, CA: El Camino Real Chapter, DAR, 1991), p. 39.

144   Dorothy Wilson Fine, *A Fine Branch of the Family Tree*, (San Jose, CA: El Camino Real Chapter, DAR, 1991), p. 34.

January 10, 1884 and is buried at Gavilan Hills Memorial Park in Gilroy.[145]
The children of John McCutchen and Keziah Anson are listed below:
1.   Maxie McCutchen, born April 1840.
2.   Newton McCutchen, born June 19, 1842.
3.   Margeline McCutchen [04-11], born March 30, 1847 in Santa Clara, Santa Clara County, California and died November 25, 1903 in California. She married Spencer Pettis Fine [04-10] on May 13, 1868 in Gilroy, Santa Clara County, California.[146]

[05-24] Moses Johnson and [05-25] Abigail Carleton

Moses Johnson was born on November 6, 1794 in Newbury, Orange County, Vermont to Joab Johnson [06-48] and Jemima Ball [06-49].[147] He married Abigail Carleton in Newbury on December 24, 1818.[148]

Abigail was the daughter of Michael Carleton [06-50] and Ruth Ayer [06-51], and was born on July 17, 1802 in Haverhill, Essex County, Massachusetts.[149] [150] There were two Abigail Carleton's born in Haverhill 13 years apart, so they are easy to confuse for each other. However the death record for Abigail Carleton Johnson makes it clear that the Abigail Carleton who married Moses Johnson was born about 1802 and was the daughter of Michael and Ruth Carleton.

By 1850, Moses was a farmer in Bradford, Essex County, Massachusetts.[151] Abigail died on December 14, 1873 in Haverhill with paralysis listed as cause of death. Even though she was listed as a widow,[152] Moses didn't die until June 28, 1880 in Vermont.[153] There are possible reasons for this inconsistency,

---

145   Keziah Anson Campbell, grave marker, Gavilan Hills Memorial Park, Gilroy, Santa Clara County, California, s.v. "Kasih Cambell" (death 1884, memorial 17800925), database with digital images, *FindAGrave*, accessed 20 April 2017.
146   Dorothy Wilson Fine, *A Fine Branch of the Family Tree*, (San Jose, CA: El Camino Real Chapter, DAR, 1991), p. 31.
147   "Vermont Vital Records, 1760-1954," s.v. "Moses Johnson" (born 1794 in Dover), database with digital images, *FamilySearch*, accessed 19 April 2016.
148   "Vermont Vital Records, 1760-1954," s.v. "Moses Johnson and Abigail Carleton" (marriage 1818), database with digital images, *FamilySearch*, accessed 19 April 2016.
149   "Massachusetts Deaths, 1841-1915," s.v."Abigail Carleton Johnson" (death 1873), database with digital images, *FamilySearch*, accessed 15 June 2019.
150   "Massachusetts Births and Christenings, 1639-1915," s.v. "Abigail Carleton" (birth 1802), database, *FamilySearch*, accessed 16 June 2019.
151   1850 US Census, Essex County, Massachusetts, population schedule, Bradford, p 445, dwelling 169, family 217, Moses and Abigail Johnson family; database with digital images, *FamilySearch*, accessed before June 2016.
152   "Massachusetts Deaths, 1841-1915," s.v."Abigail Carleton Johnson" (death 1873), database with digital images, *FamilySearch*, accessed 15 June 2019.
153   "Vermont Vital Records, 1760-1954," s.v. "Moses Johnson" (death 1880),

including clerical error, or that they separated and she might or might not have known that he went back to Vermont. The children of Moses Johnson and Abigail Carleton are listed below:
1. William Henry Carleton Johnson [04-12], born 1827 in Vermont, died August 19, 1910 in Orange County, California.[154] He married Mary Eliza Cowdrey [04-13] on April 10, 1849 in Bradford, Essex County, Massachusetts.[155]
2. Abby G Johnson, born about 1840 in New Hampshire.
3. Ellen F Johnson, born about 1842 in New Hampshire.
4. Emily A Johnson, born about 1844 in New Hampshire.[156]

[05-26] Joseph Cowdrey and [05-27] Ann Eliza Foster

Joseph Cowdrey was born on January 18, 1807 in Billerica, Middlesex County, Massachusetts to Joseph Cowdry [05-52] and Lucy Brown [05-53].[157] [158] He married Ann Eliza Foster on March 22nd, 1829 in Danvers, Essex County, Massachusetts.[159] It is not clear where or to whom Ann was born, except that she was 44 when she died on November 26th, 1847 in Billerica, Middlesex County, Massachusetts.[160] Sometime before the 1850 census, Joseph had married again to a Louisa A, but her last name is unknown. He was a shoemaker in Haverhill for the 1850 census.[161] The children of Joseph Cowdrey and Ann Eliza Foster are listed below:
1. Mary Eliza Cowdrey [04-13] born February 12, 1830 in Billerica,

---

database with digital images, *FamilySearch*, accessed 19 April 2016.
154   "California Death Index, 1905-1939," s.v. "William H Johnson" (died 1910), database, *FamilySearch*, accessed 17 March 2017.
155   "Massachusetts Marriages, 1841-1915," s.v. "Henry C Johnson and Mary E Cowdrey" (marriage 1849), database with images, *FamilySearch*, accessed 17 March 2017.
156   1850 US Census, Essex County, Massachusetts, population schedule, Bradford, p 445, dwelling 169; family 217, Moses and Abigail Johnson family; database with digital images, *FamilySearch*, accessed before June 2016.
157   "Massachusetts Births and Christenings, 1639-1915," s.v. "Joseph Cowdrey" (born 1807), database, *FamilySearch*, accessed 20 April 2017.
158   Henry A Hazen, *History of Billerica, Massachusetts: With a Genealogical Register,* (Boston: A Williams and Co, 1883) p. 26 of Genealogical Register; PDF e-book, https://archive.org/details/historyofbilleri00hazenhe , accessed 9 July 2018.
159   "Massachusetts, Town Clerk, Vital and Town Records, 1626-2001," s.v. "Joseph Cowdrey and Ann Foster" (marriage 1829), database with digital images, *FamilySearch,* accessed 20 April 2017.
160   "Massachusetts, Town Death Records, 1620-1850," s.v. "Ann E Cowdrey" (death 1847), database, *Ancestry.com,* accessed 1 July 2017.
161   1850 US Census, Essex County, Massachusetts, population schedule, Haverhill, 187, dwelling 194, family 288, Joseph and Louisa Cowdrey family; database with digital images, *FamilySearch,* accessed 20 April 2017.

Middlesex County, Massachusetts.[162] She married William Henry Carleton Johnson [04-12] on April 10, 1849.[163]

2. Warren Cowdrey, born May 12, 1833 in Billerica,[164] married first to Deborah W Langmaid on November 18, 1855 in Lowell, Middlesex County, Massachusetts[165] and second to Hattie T Morse on June 19, 1890 in Groveland, Essex County, Massachusetts.[166]

3. Lucy Ann Cowdrey, born July 5, 1835 in Billerica[167] and married Amos P Austin on April 28, 1855 in Haverhill.[168]

4. Sargent F Cowdrey, born December 23, 1837 in Billerica.[169]

5. Joseph Sargent Cowdrey, born March 26, 1838 in Billerica,[170] and died July 10, 1854.

6. Emma Frances Cowdrey, born January 31, 1846 in Haverhill.[171]

[05-30] Morgan Ryan and [05-31] Susan Jane Patton

Morgan Ryan was born on September 1, 1817[172] in Tennessee to Henry Fuller Ryan [06-60] and Nancy Brakebill [06-61]. Morgan was a farmer, a soldier in the Seminole War, a Methodist, and his father is described as being of

---

162	Henry A Hazen, *History of Billerica, Massachusetts: With a Genealogical Register,* (Boston: A Williams and Co, 1883) p. 26 of Genealogical Register; PDF e-book, https://archive.org/details/historyofbilleri00hazenhe , accessed 9 July 2018.

163	"Massachusetts, Town Clerk, Vital and Town Records, 1626-2001," s.v. "Henry C Johnson" (spouse "Mary Eliza Cowdry", marriage "1849"), database with digital images, *FamilySearch,* accessed 2 May 2019.

164"Massachusetts Births and Christenings, 1639-1915," s.v. "Warren Cowdrey" (birth "1833"), database, *FamilySearch*, accessed 20 April 2017.

165"Massachusetts Marriages, 1841-1915," s.v. "Warren Cowdrey" (spouse "Deborah Langmaid" year "1855"), database, *FamilySearch*, accessed 20 April 2017.

166"Massachusetts Marriages, 1841-1915," s.v. "Warren Cowdry" (spouse "Hattie Morse" year "1890"), database, *FamilySearch*, accessed 20 April 2017.

167"Massachusetts Births and Christenings, 1639-1915," s.v. "Lucy Ann Cowdrey" (birth "1835"), database, *FamilySearch*, accessed 20 April 2017.

168	"Massachusetts Marriages, 1841-1915," s.v. "Lucy Cowdrey" (spouse "Amos Austin" year "1855"), database, *FamilySearch*, accessed 20 April 2017.

169	Henry A Hazen, *History of Billerica, Massachusetts: With a Genealogical Register,* (Boston: A Williams and Co, 1883) p. 26 of Genealogical Register; PDF e-book, https://archive.org/details/historyofbilleri00hazenhe , accessed 9 July 2018.

170	"Massachusetts Births and Christenings, 1639-1915," s.v. "Joseph Sargent Cowdrey (year "1838"), database, *FamilySearch*, accessed 20 April 2017.

171	Henry A Hazen, *History of Billerica, Massachusetts: With a Genealogical Register,* (Boston: A Williams and Co, 1883) p. 26 of Genealogical Register; PDF e-book, https://archive.org/details/historyofbilleri00hazenhe , accessed 9 July 2018.

172	Morgan Ryan, grave marker, Clintonville Cemetery, El Dorado Springs, Cedar County, Missouri, s.v. "Morgan Ryan" (death 1895, memorial 30187046), database with digital images, *FindAGrave*, accessed 20 April 2017.

Irish descent. Morgan married Susan Jane Patton about 1837.[173] Some family trees give Henry as a first name for Morgan, but I have not seen the evidence to support this.

Susan Jane Patton was born on November 3rd, 1821 in Jefferson County, Tennessee to John M Patton [06-62] and Grizzy Moyers [06-63].[174] She was christened at Westminster and St. Paul's Presbyterian Church in Jefferson County, Tennessee on March 24, 1822.[175] By 1848, Morgan and Susan moved to Missouri, but they did not stay at one place in Missouri.[176] Susan died on July 21rst, 1883 in El Dorado Springs, Cedar County, Missouri and is buried at Clintonville Cemetery in El Dorado Springs.[177] Morgan died on June 4, 1895 in Mooney, Polk County, Missouri but is also buried at Clintonville Cemetery.[178] The children of Morgan Ryan and Susan Jane Patton are listed below:

1. Nancy Ryan, born about 1846 in Tennessee.
2. John Ryan, born about 1847 in Arkansas.
3. Sarah Jane Ryan [04-15], born about 1850 in Missouri[179] and married William Newsom [04-14] on April 10, 1866 in Carrollton, Carroll County, Missouri.[180]
4. Jerry Ryan, born about 1852 in Missouri.
5. Alfred Ryan, born about 1858 in Missouri.[181]
6. [illegible male on Census] Ryan, born about 1860 in Missouri.
7. Caroline Ryan, born about 1862 in Missouri
8. George Ryan, born about 1863 in Iowa.[182]

---

173   The Goodspeed Publishing Co., *History of Hickory, Polk, Cedar, Dade, and Barton Counties, Missouri*, (Chicago: The Goodspeed Publishing Co, 1889), Vol II: pp 772-3; PDF e-book, https://books.google.com , accessed 20 April 2017.
174   The Goodspeed Publishing Co., *History of Hickory, Polk, Cedar, Dade, and Barton Counties, Missouri*, (Chicago: The Goodspeed Publishing Co, 1889), Vol II: pp 772-3; PDF e-book, https://books.google.com , accessed 20 April 2017.
175   "Tennessee Births and Christenings, 1828-1939," s.v. "Susan Jane Patton" (born 1822), database, *FamilySearch*, accessed 5 May 2017.
176   The Goodspeed Publishing Co., *History of Hickory, Polk, Cedar, Dade, and Barton Counties, Missouri*, (Chicago: The Goodspeed Publishing Co, 1889), Vol II: pp 772-3; PDF e-book, https://books.google.com , accessed 20 April 2017.
177   Susan Ryan, grave marker, Clintonville Cemetery, El Dorado Springs, Cedar County, Missouri, s.v. "Susan Jane Ryan" (death 1883, memorial 28019815), database, *FindAGrave*, accessed 20 April 2017.
178   Morgan Ryan, grave marker, Clintonville Cemetery, El Dorado Springs, Cedar County, Missouri, s.v. "Morgan Ryan" (death 1895, memorial 30187046), database with digital images, *FindAGrave*, accessed 20 April 2017.
179   1860 US Census, Texas Co, Missouri, population schedule, Burdine, p. 14, dwelling 93, family 83, Morgan and Susan Ryan family, database with digital images, *FamilySearch*, accessed 20 April 2017.
180   "Missouri Marriages, 1750-1920," s.v.. "William Newsome" (spouse "Sarah J Ryan" marriage "1866"), database, *FamilySearch*, accessed 17 March 2017.
181   1860 US Census, Texas Co, Missouri, population schedule, Burdine, p. 14, dwelling 93, family 83, Morgan and Susan Ryan family, database with digital images, *FamilySearch*, accessed 20 April 2017.
182   1870 US Census, Polk Co, Missouri, population schedule, Mooney, p. 27,

[06-32] James Burton and [06-33] Jemima Champion

James Burton [06-32] was born at Teignmouth House in Shaldon, Devon, England about 1783. His father was Reverend John Burton [07-64][183] and it is not clear at this time where the Reverend John Burton came from. James Burton [06-32] had a marriage banns with Jemima Champion [06-33] on January 21, 1800 at St Nicholas Parish in Shaldon, Devon, England.[184] Jemima was christened at an Anglican church in Shaldon on May 4th, 1782.[185] Her parents were John Champion [07-66] and Catherine Periman [07-67].[186] [187]

James Burton became a sea captain. During the Napoleonic War James was captured and held prisoner for seven years.[188] He was released by 1815, when his son John James was christened. The baptism record for John James shows that James was still a Mariner.[189] James Burton died of yellow fever in Cuba in 1821.[190] Then Jemima moved to Oregon and married a Mr Cooper. She died in Oregon on December 17th, 1862 and is buried at Lafayette Pioneer Cemetery in Lafayette, Yamhill County, Oregon.[191] The children of James Burton [06-32] and Jemima Champion [06-33] are listed below:

1. Jemima Burton, born about 1802 and died in 1802 in Shaldon.[192]

---

dwelling 186, family 186, Morgan and Susan Ryan family, database with digital images, *FamilySearch*, accessed 20 April 2017.

183   The Lewis Publishing Company, *The Bay of San Francisco: The Metropolis of the Pacific Coast and its Suburban Cities*, (Chicago: The Lewis Publishing Company, 1892), p. 625; PDF e-book, https://archive.org , accessed November 2017.

184   "Devon Marriages," s.v. "James Burton and Jemima Champion" (marriage 1800), database with digital images, *FindMyPast*, accessed 2015.

185   "Devon Baptisms Transcriptions," s.v. "Jemima Champion" (birth 1782), database with digital images, *FindMyPast*, accessed 2015.

186   The Lewis Publishing Company, *The Bay of San Francisco: The Metropolis of the Pacific Coast and its Suburban Cities*, (Chicago: The Lewis Publishing Company, 1892), p. 626; PDF e-book, https://archive.org , accessed November 2017.

187   "Devon Marriages," s.v. "John Champion and Catherine Periman" (marriage 1778), database with digital images, *FindMyPast*, accessed 2015.

188   The Lewis Publishing Company, *The Bay of San Francisco: The Metropolis of the Pacific Coast and its Suburban Cities*, (Chicago: The Lewis Publishing Company, 1892), pp. 625-6; PDF e-book, https://archive.org , accessed November 2017.

189   "Devon Baptisms Transcriptions," s.v. "John James Burton" (baptism 1815), database with digital images, *FindMyPast*, accessed 25 March 2017.

190   The Lewis Publishing Company, *The Bay of San Francisco: The Metropolis of the Pacific Coast and its Suburban Cities*, (Chicago: The Lewis Publishing Company, 1892), p. 626; PDF e-book, https://archive.org , accessed November 2017.

191   Jemima Champion Cooper, grave marker, Lafayette Pioneer Cemetery, Lafayette, Yamhill County, Oregon, s.v. "Jemima Champion Cooper" (death 1862, memorial 36922950), database with digital images, *FindAGrave*, accessed 2 July 2017.

192   "Devon Burials," s.v. "Jemima Burton" (burial "1802"), database with digital images, *FindMyPast*, accessed 2015.

2. John James Burton [05-16], born February 19, 1815 in Shaldon. He married Margaret W Watson [05-17] on May 12, 1839 in Hobart, Tasmania,[193] and died on September 15, 1879 in Portland, Multnomah County, Oregon.[194]
3. Sarah Burton, christened on November 4, 1817 in Shaldon.[195]
4. Amy Jemima Burton, christened on December 7, 1819 at Exeter, Devon, England.[196]

[06-34] Charles Watson and [06-35] Bridget Linnoir

Charles Watson was born in England in 1797 to Joseph Watson [07-68] and Phoebe Whitman [07-69].[197] [198] He married the widow Bridget (Linnoir) Barker on February 18th, 1817 in Burnley, Lancashire, England at St Peter's Church.[199] Bridget was the daughter of William Linnoir [07-70] and also went by Mary, but not much else is known by me about her birth.[200]

In 1827, Charles Watson was convicted in the Gloucester Assizes in Gloucester, Gloucestershire, England of receiving stolen goods. He received a sentence of fourteen years and was transported aboard the *Asia*, arriving in Van Dieman's Island (Tasmania), Australia on November 30th, 1827. His occupation was a draftsman, and he built lighthouses in Australia. Bridget eventually was able to bring the family to Australia to be with him. Charles died in Tasmania on November 11th, 1849.[201] Charles Watson and Bridget Linnoir had at least one child, Margaret W Watson [05-17], who was born on

---

193   "Tasmania Marriages 1803-1899," s.v. "John James Burton" (spouse "Margaret Watson" year "1839"), database with digital images, *FindMyPast*, accessed 2015.

194   John James Burton, grave marker, Yamhill Carlton Pioneer Memorial Cemetery, Yamhill, Yamhill County, Oregon, s.v. "John James Burton" (death 1879, memorial 41229693), database with digital images, *FindAGrave*, accessed 7 July 2018.

195 "England, Devon Bishop's Transcripts, 1558-1887," s.v. "Sarah Burton" (year "1817"), database, *FamilySearch*, accessed 21 April 2017.

196 "England Births and Christenings, 1538-1975," s.v. "Amy Jemima Burton" (year "1819"), database, *FamilySearch*, accessed 21 April 2017.

197   The Lewis Publishing Company, *The Bay of San Francisco: The Metropolis of the Pacific Coast and its Suburban Cities*, (Chicago: The Lewis Publishing Company, 1892), p. 625; PDF e-book, https://archive.org , accessed November 2017.

198   "Convict Records," s.v. "Charles Watson" (sentenced 1827), database, *Convict Records of Australia*, accessed 3 July 2017.

199   "England, Lancashire, Parish Registers 1538-1910," s.v. "Charles Watson" (spouse "Bridget Barker" marriage "1817"), database, *FamilySearch*, accessed 3 July 2017.

200   The Lewis Publishing Company, *The Bay of San Francisco: The Metropolis of the Pacific Coast and its Suburban Cities,* (Chicago: The Lewis Publishing Company, 1892), p. 625; PDF e-book, https://archive.org , accessed November 2017.

201   "Convict Records," s.v. "Charles Watson" (sentenced 1827), database, *Convict Records of Australia,* accessed 3 July 2017.

June 21, 1822 in Lancashire, England and died on October 18, 1900.[202] Margaret married John James Burton [05-16] on May 12, 1839 in Hobart, Tasmania.[203]

[06-36] Hugh W Robb and [06-37] Elizabeth Waller

Hugh W Robb may have been born in Pennsylvania or Virginia, depending on the source. His parents were James Robb [07-72] and Margaret Barr [07-73], and they were from Ireland.[204] [205] Hugh's brother was Col David Robb at the Battle of Tippecanoe, and Hugh was a Presbyterian missionary in Kentucky at the age of 35. Hugh continued in the service of the Presbyterian church until he died at the age of 87.[206] He married Elizabeth Waller on June 2, 1803 in Washington County, Kentucky.[207] The children of Hugh W Robb and Elizabeth Waller are listed below:

1. Benjamin Franklin Robb [05-18] born about 1814 in Kentucky and died in 1900 in Illinois.[208] He married Nancy A Nickelson on December 19, 1833 in Union County, Kentucky.[209]
2. Massey Ann Robb, who married Nathan Waller in August 1832 in Union County, Kentucky.[210]

---

202   Margaret Watson Burton, grave marker, Yamhill Carlton Pioneer Memorial Cemetery, Yamhill, Yamhill County, Oregon, s.v. "Margaret Watson Burton" (death 1900, memorial 41229727), database with digital images, *FindAGrave*, accessed 7 July 2018.
203   "Tasmania Marriages 1803-1899," s.v. "John James Burton" (spouse "Margaret Watson" year "1839"), database with digital images, *FindMyPast*, accessed 2015.
204   Chapman Bros., *Portrait and Biographical Album of Johnson and Pawnee Counties, Nebraska*, (Chicago: Chapman Bros., 1889), pp. 599-601; PDF e-book, https://books.google.com accessed 27 March 2017.
205   Jas. A Tartt & Co, *History of Gibson County, Indiana*, (Edwardsville, Ill: Jas. A Tartt & Co, 1884), pp 49-50; PDF e-book, https://books.google.com accessed 3 July 2017.
206   Chapman Bros., *Portrait and Biographical Album of Johnson and Pawnee Counties, Nebraska*, (Chicago: Chapman Bros., 1889), pp. 599-601; PDF e-book, https://books.google.com accessed 27 March 2017.
207   "Kentucky, County Marriages, 1797-1954," s.v. "Hugh Robb" (spouse "Elizabeth Waller" marriage "1803"), database with digital images, *FamilySearch*, accessed 31 March 2017.
208   Benjamin Robb, grave marker, New Town Cemetery, Burton Township, Adams County, Illinois, s.v. "Benjamin Franklin Robb" (death 1900, memorial 92514846), database with digital images, *FindAGrave*, accessed 2 April 2017).
209   "Kentucky, County Marriages, 1797-1954," s.v. "Benjamin F Robb" (spouse "Nancy Nicholson" marriage "1833"), database with digital images, *FamilySearch*, accessed 27 March 2017.
210   "Kentucky, County Marriages, 1797-1954," s.v. "Nathan Waller" (spouse "Massey Ann" year "1832"), database with digital images, *FamilySearch*, accessed 31

3.   John Robb, who married Polly Girtin in January 1828 in Union County, Kentucky.[211]

[06-40] Lidgard Fine, Sr and [06-41] Elizabeth Netherton

Lidgard Fine was born on September 1rst, 1775 in a part of the former Dunmore County which is now Shenandoah County, Virginia to Peter Fine [07-80] and Rebecca Stats [07-81].[212]   He married Elizabeth Netherton on May 1, 1797 in Jefferson County, Tennessee.[213]   Elizabeth was born on February 12, 1773 in Shenandoah County, Virginia to Henry Netherton [07-82] and Elizabeth [07-83].[214]   Lidgard was a Lieutenant in the Tennessee militia, specifically a cavalry regiment in the Hamilton District of Cocke County, Tennessee.[215]   He was also a Lieutenant in the War of 1812 in the 2 Regiment of East Tennessee Volunteers.[216]   About 1816, Lidgard and Elizabeth moved to Missouri, settling in Lafayette County of Missouri in 1819.[217]   Lidgard died before March 11, 1834.[218]   The children of Lidgard Fine, Sr and Elizabeth Netherton are listed below:

1.   John Fine, born on September 2, 1798 in Newport, Cocke County, Tennessee and died on August 14, 1878 in Linden, San Joaquin County, California. He married Agnes Mitchell on September 30, 1826 in Dover, Lafayette County, Missouri.

2.   Morgan Fine, born on December 31, 1800 in Newport, Cocke County, Tennessee and died on July 17, 1879 in Santa Clara, Santa Clara County, California. He married Louisa (Belt) Porter on January 30, 1834 in Dover, Lafayette County, Missouri.

3.   Cornelius Fine, born on July 14, 1803 in Newport, Cocke County, Tennessee and died before September 6, 1841 in Dover, Lafayette

---

March 2017.

211   "Kentucky, County Marriages, 1797-1954," s.v. "John Robb" (spouse "Polly Girtin" year "1828"), database with digital images, *FamilySearch*, accessed 31 March 2017.

212   Dorothy Wilson Fine, *A Fine Branch of the Family Tree*, (San Jose, CA: El Camino Real Chapter, DAR, 1991), p. 16.

213   "Tennessee, Marriage Records, 1780-2002" s.v. "L Fine and E Netherson" (marriage 1797), database with digital images, *Ancestry.com*, accessed 8 July 2018.

214   Dorothy Wilson Fine, *A Fine Branch of the Family Tree*, (San Jose, CA: El Camino Real Chapter, DAR, 1991), p. 16.

215   "Record of Commissions of Officers in the Tennessee Militia," s.v. "Ledgard Fine," database with digital images, *Ancestry.com*, accessed 19 August 2017.

216   "United States War of 1812 Index to Service Records, 1812-1815," s.v. "Lidgard Fine," database with digital images, *FamilySearch*, accessed 21 April 2017.

217   Dorothy Wilson Fine, *A Fine Branch of the Family Tree*, (San Jose, CA: El Camino Real Chapter, DAR, 1991), p. 13.

218   Dorothy Wilson Fine, *A Fine Branch of the Family Tree*, (San Jose, CA: El Camino Real Chapter, DAR, 1991), p. 15.

County, Missouri. He married Harriette Hill on January 30, 1834 in Dover.

4. William Fine, born on May 10, 1805 in Newport, Cocke County, Tennessee and died on July 4, 1874 in Lafayette County, Missouri. He married Mary Sheets on April 1, 1841.

5. Lidgard Fine, Jr [05-20], born on March 22, 1808 in Cocke County, Tennessee and died on March 21, 1891 at Paraiso Springs, Soledad, Monterrey County, California. He married Martha Ann Cox [05-21] on August 6, 1833 in Dover, Lafayette County, Missouri.

6. Rebecca Ann Fine, born on August 19, 1810 at Newport, Cocke County, Tennessee and died on March 15, 1883 in Santa Clara County, California. She married James W Easton on April 13, 1843 in Dover, Lafayette County, Missouri.

7. Eliza Fine, born on October 22, 1812 in Newport, Cocke County, Tennessee and died on April 23, 1887. She married James Findla.

8. Abigail Fine, born on January 5, 1815 in Newport, Cocke County, Tennessee.[219]

[06-42] Solomon Cox and [06-43] Deborah Collins

Solomon Cox was born May 17, 1788 in Grayson Co, Virginia to Enoch Cox [07-84] and Mary Mackey [07-85].[220] On June 12, Solomon Cox married Deborah Collins.[221] I have not found much on Deborah except that she died on October 20, 1872 in Dover, Lafayette County, Missouri at the age of about 83 years old according to her gravestone. She is buried at Dover Cemetery, in Dover, Missouri.[222]

Solomon and Deborah lived in White County, Tennessee in 1818, but after 1818 they moved to Lafayette County in Missouri. Solomon engaged in farming and milling, but in 1849 he was a part of the gold rush in California. Solomon died near Gilroy, California on November 25, 1849.[223] The children of Solomon Cox and Deborah Collins are listed below:

1. Ellis Cox, married ___ Dustin.

219   Dorothy Wilson Fine, *A Fine Branch of the Family Tree*, (San Jose, CA: El Camino Real Chapter, DAR, 1991), p. 16.

220   National Historical Society, *History of Caldwell and Livingston Counties, Missouri*, (St Louis: National Historical Society, 1886), p. 273; PDF e-book, https://books.google.com , accessed 19 April 2017.

221   Elizabeth Berry Buffa, "Cox Family Outline," (report, 1977), A IX b 3; p 11; PDF e-book, https://archive.org/details/coxfamilyoutline00buff accessed 8 July 2018.

222   Deborah Cox, grave marker, Dover Cemetery, Dover, Lafayette County, Missouri, s.v. "Deborah Collins Cox" (death 1872, memorial 91175358), database with digital images, *FindAGrave*, accessed 21 April 2017.

223   National Historical Society, *History of Caldwell and Livingston Counties, Missouri*, (St Louis: National Historical Society, 1886), p. 273; PDF e-book, https://books.google.com , accessed 19 April 2017.

2. Martha Ann Cox [05-21] aka "Patsy",[224] born January 13, 1813 in Tennessee and died on August 9, 1873 in Gilroy, Santa Clara County, California. She married Lidgard Fine, Jr [05-20] on August 6, 1833 in Dover, Lafayette County, Missouri.[225]
3. James Cox, born on March 12, 1817 in Virginia and died September 4, 1859. He married Sarah Brown on December 28, 1851.
4. Ruth Cox, born on July 4, 1818, and married Jesse Cole on March 27, 1836.
5. Elizabeth Cox, born in 1822 and died February 11, 1864. She married J J Hampton on July 24, 1839.
6. Malvina Cox, born on June 10, 1823 and died in 1898. She married Daniel Ray.
7. John Dennis Cox, born on September 29, 1824 in Lafayette County, Missouri and died in August 1893. He married Mary C Robinson, who died in 1860, and second married Amanda Bufort in July 1867.
8. Lewis William Cox, born March 15, 1834 and died January 12, 1908. He married Eliza Preston Fletcher on November 17, 1858.
9. William B Cox.
10. Robert Watson Cox, who married Lucy Fleming.
11. Mary Cox, who married John Johnson.[226]

[06-46] Henry Anson and [06-47] Elizabeth Bierley

Henry Anson [06-46] (or Ansell) was born about 1773[227] in Baltimore, Maryland to Philaris Ansell [07-92].[228] Some people say Henry [06-46] was born later, which would make the 1778 marriage date of Philaris Ansell [07-92] and Catherine Fresh before the birth of Henry [06-46]. However there is no evidence from the time he lived that I have found to support a birth date later than 1778 so that Catherine Fresh would be his birth mother. He married Elizabeth Bierley (spelled Buerly in marriage record transcriptions) on August 26, 1803 in Baltimore. Many online trees and my Fine source give the

---

224   Elizabeth Berry Buffa, "Cox Family Outline," (report, 1977), A IX b 3; p 12; PDF e-book, https://archive.org/details/coxfamilyoutline00buff accessed 8 July 2018.
225   Dorothy Wilson Fine, *A Fine Branch of the Family Tree*, (San Jose, CA: El Camino Real Chapter, DAR, 1991), p. 25.
226   Elizabeth Berry Buffa, "Cox Family Outline," (report, 1977), A IX b 3; pp. 11-12; PDF e-book, https://archive.org/details/coxfamilyoutline00buff accessed 8 July 2018.
227   "Iowa Mortality Schedules, 1850-1880," s.v. "Henry Anson" (death "1850"), database with digital images, FamilySearch, accessed 12 November 2019.
228   Dorothy Wilson Fine, *A Fine Branch of the Family Tree*, (San Jose, CA: El Camino Real Chapter, DAR, 1991), p. 35.

marriage date as the 20th, but the marriage record transcriptions give the 26th.[229] [230] Elizabeth was born about 1784 to Peter Bierley [07-94], possibly in Maryland.[231]

Shortly after marrying, Henry and Elizabeth moved to Kentucky and bought 200 acres in Logan County, Kentucky on Dec 6, 1803. In 1826 they were in Pike County, Missouri, and about 1836 they were in Van Buren County, Iowa.[232] Elizabeth died on April 10, 1847 in Van Buren County[233] but is said to be buried at Anson Cemetery in Anson, Clark County, Missouri.[234] Henry may have died on April 5, 1850 and is also said to be buried at Anson Cemetery,[235] however the 1850 Census mortality schedule said he died in March 1850.[236] The children of Henry Anson and Elizabeth Bierley are listed below:

1. Peter Ansell, born about 1804[237] and died in Lafayette County, Missouri.[238]
2. Keziah Anson [05-23], born on December 20, 1805 in Logan County, Kentucky[239] and died January 10, 1884.[240] She married first to John McCutchen [05-22] on October 6, 1836 in Lewis County, Missouri, and second to William Campbell on July 5, 1849 at Mission Santa Clara, Santa Clara County, California, whom she divorced in 1855.
3. Francis Ansell, born on January 10, 1808.[241]
4. Catherine Anson, born in 1811 and died in 1890.[242] She married Isaac

---

229   "Maryland Marriages, 1666-1970," s.v. "Henry Anson and Elizabeth Buerly" (marriage 1803), database, *FamilySearch*, accessed 21 April 2017.
230   Dorothy Wilson Fine, *A Fine Branch of the Family Tree*, (San Jose, CA: El Camino Real Chapter, DAR, 1991), p. 35.
231   Ibid., p 35.
232   Ibid., p 35.
233   Ibid., p 35.
234   Elizabeth Anson, memorial, s.v. "Elizabeth Anson" (death 1847, memorial 131435800), database, *FindAGrave*, accessed 21 April 2017.
235   Henry Anson, memorial, s.v. "Henry Anson" (death 1850, memorial 45616743), database, *FindAGrave*, accessed 21 April 2017.
236   "Iowa Mortality Schedules, 1850-1880," s.v. "Henry Anson" (death "1850"), database with digital images, FamilySearch, accessed 12 November 2019.
237   Dorothy Wilson Fine, *A Fine Branch of the Family Tree*, (San Jose, CA: El Camino Real Chapter, DAR, 1991), p. 35.
238   Lake City Publishing, *Portrait and Biographical Album of Jefferson and Van Buren Counties, Iowa*, (Chicago: Lake City Publishing, 1890), p. 596; PDF e-book, https://archive.org/details/portraitbiograph02lake/page/596 accessed 5 May 2019.
239   Dorothy Wilson Fine, *A Fine Branch of the Family Tree*, (San Jose, CA: El Camino Real Chapter, DAR, 1991), p. 34.
240   Keziah Anson Campbell, grave marker, Gavilan Hills Memorial Park, Gilroy, Santa Clara County, California, s.v. "Kasih Cambell" (death 1884, memorial 17800925), database with digital images, *FindAGrave*, accessed 20 April 2017.
241   Dorothy Wilson Fine, *A Fine Branch of the Family Tree*, (San Jose, CA: El Camino Real Chapter, DAR, 1991), p. 34-35.
242   Catherine Anson Rigsby, grave marker, Center Chapel Cemetery, Vernon, Van Buren County, Iowa, s.v. "Catherine Anson Rigsby" (death "1890" memorial "140774235"), database with digital images, *FindAGrave*, accessed 27 April 2017.

Rigsby.[243]

5. Henry Ansell, Jr, born about 1815[244] and died in 1882 in Lick Creek Township, Davis County, Iowa.[245]
6. George Anson, born on January 18, 1815 and died on January 31, 1904.[246]
7. Flarious Ansell, born about 1817[247] and died in 1889 in California.[248]
8. Eliza Anson, born on October 20, 1819[249] and died on June 3, 1903.[250]
9. John Ansell, born on December 30, 1821.
10. Christiana Ansell, born on May 3, 1824[251] and died in 1883 in Van Buren County, Iowa.
11. Thomas Anson, born on July 24, 1826 in Pike County, Missouri.[252]
12. William Anson, born on December 10, 1827 in Pike County, Missouri, and married Charlotta Martin in 1862.[253]

[06-48] Joab Johnson and [06-49] Jemima Ball

Joab Johnson was born on March 9, 1765 in Hardwick, Worcester County,

---

243   Lake City Publishing, *Portrait and Biographical Album of Jefferson and Van Buren Counties, Iowa,* (Chicago: Lake City Publishing, 1890), p. 596; PDF e-book, https://archive.org/details/portraitbiograph02lake/page/596 accessed 5 May 2019.
244   Dorothy Wilson Fine, *A Fine Branch of the Family Tree,* (San Jose, CA: El Camino Real Chapter, DAR, 1991), p. 34-35.
245   Lake City Publishing, *Portrait and Biographical Album of Jefferson and Van Buren Counties, Iowa,* (Chicago: Lake City Publishing, 1890), p. 596; PDF e-book, https://archive.org/details/portraitbiograph02lake/page/596 accessed 5 May 2019.
246   George Anson, grave marker, Center Chapel Cemetery, Vernon, Van Buren County, Iowa, s.v. "George Anson" (death "1904" memorial "150259866"), database with digital images, *FindAGrave,* accessed 27 April 2017.
247   Dorothy Wilson Fine, *A Fine Branch of the Family Tree,* (San Jose, CA: El Camino Real Chapter, DAR, 1991), p. 34-35.
248   Lake City Publishing, *Portrait and Biographical Album of Jefferson and Van Buren Counties, Iowa,* (Chicago: Lake City Publishing, 1890), p. 596; PDF e-book, https://archive.org/details/portraitbiograph02lake/page/596 accessed 5 May 2019.
249   Dorothy Wilson Fine, *A Fine Branch of the Family Tree,* (San Jose, CA: El Camino Real Chapter, DAR, 1991), p. 34-35.
250   Eliza Anson, grave marker, Center Chapel Cemetery, Vernon, Van Buren County, Iowa, s.v. "Eliza Anson" (death "1903" memorial "150259853"), database with digital images, *FindAGrave,* accessed 27 April 2017.
251   Dorothy Wilson Fine, *A Fine Branch of the Family Tree,* (San Jose, CA: El Camino Real Chapter, DAR, 1991), p. 34-35.
252   Lake City Publishing, *Portrait and Biographical Album of Jefferson and Van Buren Counties, Iowa,* (Chicago: Lake City Publishing, 1890), p. 596; PDF e-book, https://archive.org/details/portraitbiograph02lake/page/596 accessed 5 May 2019.
253   Lake City Publishing, *Portrait and Biographical Album of Jefferson and Van Buren Counties, Iowa,* (Chicago: Lake City Publishing, 1890), p. 408; PDF e-book, https://archive.org/details/portraitbiograph02lake/page/596 accessed 5 May 2019.

Massachusetts to Zebadiah Johnson [07-96] and Alice "Ales" Mirrick [07-97].[254] [255] Joab's wife was Jemima Ball and their first child, Virtue Johnson, was born April 13, 1793 so they were probably married in 1792 or earlier.[256] I could not find evidence linking Jemima Ball to any parents. Jemima died on March 25, 1816 and was buried at Hathaway Cemetery in Dover, Windham County, Vermont.[257] Joab died on May 6, 1840 in Dover, Vermont[258] and was also buried at Hathaway Cemetery in Dover.[259] The children of Joab Johnson and Jemima Ball are listed below:

1. Virtue Johnson, born April 13, 1793 in Vermont.
2. Moses Johnson [05-24], born on November 6, 1794 in Vermont,[260] and died on June 28, 1880 in Vermont.[261] He married Abigail Carleton [05-25] on December 24, 1818 in Newbury, Orange County, Vermont.[262]
3. Jemima Johnson, born on October 27, 1796 in Vermont.
4. Joab Johnson, Jr, born on August 6, 1798 in Vermont.
5. Tryphena Johnson, born on February 26, 1800 in Vermont, and died on March 7, 1801.
6. Tryphena Johnson, born on August 31, 1802 in Vermont.
7. Hope Johnson, born on September 27, 1803 in Vermont.
8. Gary Johnson, born on December 8, 1806 in Vermont.
9. Almira Johnson, born on February 4, 1809 in Vermont.
10. Otis Johnson, born on March 2, 1813 in Vermont.[263]

---

254   "Massachusetts Births and Christenings, 1639-1915," s.v. "Joab Johnson" (birth 1765), database, *FamilySearch*, accessed 20 April 2016.
255   Joab Johnson, grave marker, Hathaway Cemetery, Dover, Windham County, Vermont, s.v. "Joab Johnson" (death 1840, memorial 137191568), database, *FindAGrave*, accessed 20 April 2016.
256   "Vermont, Town Clerk, Vital and Town Records, 1732-2005" digital image not indexed, *FamilySearch*, https://www.familysearch.org/ark:/61903/3:1:3QS7-L999-Q7HP?i=139&cc=1987653 , accessed 26 April 2016.
257   Jemima Johnson, grave marker, Hathaway Cemetery, Dover, Windham County, Vermont, s.v. "Jemima Johnson" (death 1816, memorial 137191601), database with digital images, accessed 26 April 2016.
258   "Vermont Vital Records, 1760-1954," s.v. "Joab Johnson" (death 1840), database with digital images, *FamilySearch*, accessed 20 April 2016.
259   Joab Johnson, grave marker, Hathaway Cemetery, Dover, Windham County, Vermont, s.v. "Joab Johnson" (death 1840, memorial 137191568), database, *FindAGrave*, accessed 20 April 2016.
260   "Vermont, Town Clerk, Vital and Town Records, 1732-2005" digital image not indexed, *FamilySearch*, https://www.familysearch.org/ark:/61903/3:1:3QS7-L999-Q7HP?i=139&cc=1987653 , accessed 26 April 2016.
261   "Vermont Vital Records, 1760-1954," s.v. "Moses Johnson" (death "1880"), database with digital images, *FamilySearch*, accessed 19 April 2016.
262   "Vermont Vital Records, 1760-1954," s.v. "Moses Johnson" (spouse "Abigail Carleton" year "1818"), database with digital images, *FamilySearch*, accessed 19 April 2016.
263   "Vermont, Town Clerk, Vital and Town Records, 1732-2005" digital image not indexed, *FamilySearch*, https://www.familysearch.org/ark:/61903/3:1:3QS7-L999-Q7HP?i=139&cc=1987653 , accessed 26 April 2016.

[06-50] Michael Carleton and [06-51] Ruth Ayer

Michael Carleton was born on May 23, 1757 in Bradford, Essex County, Massachusetts to Dudley Carleton [07-100] and Abigail Willson [07-101]. Bradford was later annexed by Haverhill, Essex County, Massachusetts so some records say he was in Bradford and others say he was in Haverhill. Michael served as a soldier in the American Revolution from 1778 to 1779, and possibly more. However, there was another Michael Carleton of similar age in Massachusetts, who lived in Andover. Since both Michael Carleton's fought in the Revolution, it is a little confusing to sort out which one did what in the Revolution. But the Michael Carleton [06-50] of Bradford and Haverhill in this genealogy did draw a pension in Haverhill for being in the Revolution, so it is certain that he was in the Revolution too.[264]

After being in the Revolution, Michael Carleton married Ruth Ayer on November 20, 1795 in Haverhill.[265] Ruth Ayer was born on August 12, 1776 in Haverhill to Nathaniel Ayer [07-102] and Lydia White [07-103],[266] although Cutter mistakenly gave 1778. Michael Carleton lived the rest of his life in Haverhill/Bradford, and he died there on June 20, 1836. Ruth died on September 13, 1847and they are buried next to each other at Pentucket Cemetery in Haverhill.[267] The children of Michael Carleton and Ruth Ayer are listed below:

1. Michael Carleton, born on April 8, 1796 in Haverhill and died on April 13, 1796.
2. William Carleton, born on May 20, 1797 in Haverhill. His first marriage was to Lydia Hunting and his second was to Susan Willis on March 11, 1875. He died on December 5, 1876.
3. David Carleton, born on April 17, 1799 in Haverhill.
4. Nathaniel Carleton, born on November 29, 1800 in Haverhill and died on December 8, 1801.[268]
5. Abigail Carleton [05-25], born on July 17, 1802 in Haverhill[269] and died

---

264   William Richard Cutter, ed., *New England Families: Genealogical and Memorial,* (New York: Lewis Historical Publishing Co, 1913), Vol I: p. 8; PDF e-book, https://archive.org/details/newenglandfamili01cutt_1 accessed 10 July 2018.
265   Ibid., Vol I: p. 8.
266   "Massachusetts, Town Clerk, Vital and Town Records, 1626-2001," family group s.v. "Nathaniel Ayer" (spouse "Lydia White" marriage "1757"), database with digital images, *FamilySearch*, accessed 23 June 2019.
267   Michael Carleton, Pentucket Cemetery, Haverhill, Essex County, Massachusetts, s.v. "Michael Carleton" (death "1836", memorial "52198349"), database with digital images, *FindAGrave*, accessed 15 June 2019.
268   William Richard Cutter, ed., *New England Families: Genealogical and Memorial,* (New York: Lewis Historical Publishing Co, 1913), Vol I: p. 8; PDF e-book, https://archive.org/details/newenglandfamili01cutt_1 accessed 10 July 2018.
269   "Massachusetts Births and Christenings, 1639-1915," s.v. "Abigail Carleton"

on December 14, 1873 in Haverhill.[270] Abigail married Moses Johnson [05-24] on December 24, 1818 in Newbury, Orange County, Vermont.[271]

6. Nathaniel Carleton, born 1807 and died in April 1833.[272]

[06-52] Joseph Cowdry and [06-55] Lucy Brown

Joseph Cowdrey was born on March 19, 1781 to Nathaniel Cowdry [07-104] and Rebecca Parker [07-105] in Westford, Middlesex County, Massachusetts.[273] I did not find a marriage record for Joseph Cowdry, but his first child with Lucy Brown was born about 1798 so he would have been married around that time.[274] Lucy Brown was born on September 6, 1778 in Billerica, Middlesex County, Massachusetts to Thomas Brown [07-106] and Lucy Kemp [07-107].[275] Lucy died on December 25, 1856 and is buried at North Cemetery in Billerica.[276] Joseph died a few years later, on January 15, 1859 of "lung fever" in Billerica[277] and is also buried at North Cemetery.[278] The children of Joseph Cowdry and Lucy Brown are listed below:

1. Ebenezer Cowdrey, born about 1798 in Billerica, and died on

---

(birth "1802"), database, *FamilySearch*, accessed 16 June 2019.

270   "Massachusetts Deaths, 1841-1915," s.v. "Abigail Carleton Johnson" (death "1873"), database with digital images, *FamilySearch*, accessed 15 June 2019.

271   "Vermont Vital Records, 1760-1954," s.v. "Moses Johnson" (spouse "Abigail Carleton" year "1818"), database with digital images, *FamilySearch*, accessed 19 April 2016.

272   William Richard Cutter, ed., *New England Families: Genealogical and Memorial,* (New York: Lewis Historical Publishing Co, 1913), Vol I: p. 8; PDF e-book, https://archive.org/details/newenglandfamili01cutt_1 accessed 10 July 2018.

273   "Massachusetts, Town Clerk, Vital and Town Records, 1626-2001," s.v. "Joseph Cowdry" (birth "1781"), database with digital images, *FamilySearch*, accessed 30 April 2017.

274   "Massachusetts Deaths, 1841-1915," s.v. "Ebenezer Cowdry" (death "1860"), database, *FamilySearch*, accessed 30 April 2017.

275   "Massachusetts, Town Clerk, Vital and Town Records, 1626-2001," s.v. "Lucy Brown" (birth "1778"), database with digital images, *FamilySearch*, accessed 18 May 2017.

276   Lucy Cowdry, North Cemetery, Billerica, Middlesex County, Massachusetts, s.v. "Lucy Cowdry" (death "1856", memorial "107626476"), database with digital images, *FindAGrave*, accessed 30 April 2017.

277   "Massachusetts Deaths, 1841-1915," s.v. "Joseph Cowdry" (death "1859"), database with digital images, *FamilySearch*, accessed 30 April 2017.

278   Joseph Cowdry, grave marker, North Cemetery, Billerica, Middlesex County, Massachusetts, s.v. "Joseph Cowdry" (death "1859", memorial "107626419"), database with digital images, *FindAGrave*, accessed April 2017.

September 2, 1860 in Billerica.[279] He married Betsey Gibson.[280]

2. Maria Cowdrey, born on February 16, 1805 in Billerica[281] and married a Wyers.[282]
3. Joseph Cowdrey [05-26], born on January 18, 1807 in Billerica,[283] and married first to Ann Eliza Foster on March 22, 1829 in Danvers, Essex County, Massachusetts,[284] and second to Louisa A before 1850,[285]
4. Silas H Parker Cowdrey, born on February 16, 1810 in Billerica,[286] and died on August 24, 1881 in Billerica.[287]
5. Elias Cowdrey, born on February 5, 1812 in Billerica.[288]
6. Isaac Brown Cowdrey, born on May 10, 1814 in Carlisle, Middlesex County, Massachusetts.[289]
7. Lucy Cowdrey.[290]

[06-60] Henry Fuller Ryan and [06-61] Nancy Brakebill

Henry Fuller Ryan was born about 1795 in Virginia[291] to T Houston Ryan

---

279   "Massachusetts Deaths, 1841-1915," s.v. "Ebenezer Cowdry" (death "1860"), database, *FamilySearch*, accessed 30 April 2017.
280   Henry A Hazen, *History of Billerica, Massachusetts: With a Genealogical Register,* (Boston: A Williams and Co, 1883) p. 26 of Genealogical Register; PDF e-book, https://archive.org/details/historyofbilleri00hazenhe , accessed 9 July 2018.
281   "Massachusetts Births and Christenings, 1639-1915," s.v. "Maria Coudre" (birth "1805"), database, *FamilySearch*, accessed 30 April 2017.
282   Henry A Hazen, *History of Billerica, Massachusetts: With a Genealogical Register,* (Boston: A Williams and Co, 1883) p. 26 of Genealogical Register; PDF e-book, https://archive.org/details/historyofbilleri00hazenhe , accessed 9 July 2018.
283   "Massachusetts Births and Christenings, 1639-1915," s.v. "Joseph Cowdrey" (birth "1807"), database, *FamilySearch*, accessed 30 April 2017.
284   "Massachusetts, Town Clerk, Vital and Town Records, 1626-2001," s.v. "Joseph Cowdry" (spouse "Ann Foster" marriage "1829"), database with digital images, *FamilySearch*, accessed 20 April 2017.
285   1850 US Census, Essex County, Massachusetts, population schedule, Haverhill, 187, dwelling 194, family 288, Joseph and Louisa Cowdrey family; database with digital images, *FamilySearch*, accessed 20 April 2017.
286   "Massachusetts Births and Christenings, 1639-1915," s.v. "Silas Parker Coudre" (birth "1810"), database, *FamilySearch*, accessed 30 April 2017.
287   "Massachusetts Deaths, 1841-1915," s.v. "Silas Cowdrey" (death "1881"), database, *FamilySearch*, accessed 30 April 2017.
288   "Massachusetts Births and Christenings, 1639-1915," s.v. "Elias Coudre" (birth "1812"), database, *FamilySearch*, accessed 30 April 2017.
289   "Massachusetts Births and Christenings, 1639-1915," s.v. "Isaac Brown Cowdery" (birth "1814"), database, *FamilySearch*, accessed 30 April 2017.
290   Henry A Hazen, *History of Billerica, Massachusetts: With a Genealogical Register,* (Boston: A Williams and Co, 1883) p. 26 of Genealogical Register; PDF e-book, https://archive.org/details/historyofbilleri00hazenhe , accessed 9 July 2018.
291   1850 US Census, Knox County, Tennessee, population schedule, Knoxville,

[07-120].[292] Henry was a carpenter and had Irish ancestry.[293] By 1816 he was in Blount County, Tennessee, where he married Nancy Brakebill on September 25, 1816.[294] Many internet sites give the parents of Nancy as Peter Brakebill and Katherine Rorex, which I believe is probably correct but I have seen no conclusive evidence so I will not continue her genealogy. She reported being 40 years old in the 1850 census which would make her birth year as 1810, but I am very skeptical of that because she would have been six years old when married and seven years old when she had her son Morgan Ryan. So the little I know for sure about her is that she believed she was born in Tennessee. The 1850 census is the last record I could find of Henry and Nancy, when they lived in Knoxville, Knox County, Tennessee.[295] Henry died in Knoxville at some point after 1850.[296] The known children of Henry Fuller Ryan and Nancy Brakebill are listed below:

1. Morgan Ryan [05-30], born September 1, 1817, and died on June 4, 1895.[297] He married Susan Jane Patton about 1837.[298]
2. Elizabeth Ryan, born about 1830 in Tennessee.
3. Henry Ryan, born about 1832 in Tennessee.
4. Sally Ryan, born about 1834 in Tennessee.
5. William Ryan, born about 1836 in Tennessee.
6. Susan Ryan, born about 1838 in Tennessee.[299]

---

dwelling 45, family 48, Fuller and Nancy Ryan family; database with images, *FamilySearch*, accessed 4 May 2017.

292   "Tennessee State Marriage Index, 1780-2002," s.v. "Fuller Ryan and Nancy Brakebill" (married 1816), database with images, *FamilySearch*, accessed 4 May 2017.

293   The Goodspeed Publishing Co., *History of Hickory, Polk, Cedar, Dade, and Barton Counties, Missouri*, (Chicago: The Goodspeed Publishing Co, 1889), Vol II: pp 772-3; PDF e-book, https://play.google.com/store/books/details? id=WdMyAQAAMAAJ&rdid=book-WdMyAQAAMAAJ&rdot=1 , accessed 20 April 2017.

294   "Tennessee State Marriage Index, 1780-2002," s.v. "Fuller Ryan and Nancy Brakebill" (married 1816), database with images, *FamilySearch*, accessed 4 May 2017.

295   1850 US Census, Knox County, Tennessee, population schedule, Knoxville, dwelling 45, family 48, Fuller and Nancy Ryan family; database with images, *FamilySearch*, accessed 4 May 2017.

296   The Goodspeed Publishing Co., *History of Hickory, Polk, Cedar, Dade, and Barton Counties, Missouri*, (Chicago: The Goodspeed Publishing Co, 1889), Vol II: pp 772-3; PDF e-book, https://play.google.com/store/books/details? id=WdMyAQAAMAAJ&rdid=book-WdMyAQAAMAAJ&rdot=1 , accessed 20 April 2017.

297   Morgan Ryan, grave marker, Clintonville Cemetery, El Dorado Springs, Cedar County, Missouri, s.v. "Morgan Ryan" (death "1895" memorial "30187046"), database with digital images, *FindAGrave*, accessed 20 April 2017.

298   The Goodspeed Publishing Co., *History of Hickory, Polk, Cedar, Dade, and Barton Counties, Missouri*, (Chicago: The Goodspeed Publishing Co, 1889), Vol II: pp 772-3; PDF e-book, https://play.google.com/store/books/details? id=WdMyAQAAMAAJ&rdid=book-WdMyAQAAMAAJ&rdot=1 , accessed 20 April 2017.

299   1850 US Census, Knox County, Tennessee, population schedule, Knoxville,

[06-62] John M Patton and [06-63] Grizzy Moyers

John M Patton was born about 1793 in Tennessee.[300] There appears to be more information available on his ancestry in copyrighted books to which I have no access so I have to stop here due to lack of accessible evidence. On April 14, 1813, John married Grizzy Moyers in Jefferson County, Tennessee.[301] Once again, there is a further genealogy for Grizzy but all I could find was excerpts on the internet and I have no access to the copyrighted information, so I have to stop due to lack of obtainable evidence. Grizzy apparently died before 1831 when the Tennessee State Marriage Index shows John marrying Elizabeth Lyle in Jefferson County, Tennessee on November 6, 1831.[302] Then John married again on November 2 1834 to Eddy Lions in Jefferson County, Tennessee.[303]

In 1830 and 1840 John Patton shows up in Census records in Jefferson County, Tennessee.[304] [305] Unfortunately, the Census in those years do not give family member names. The 1850 Census shows him being a farmer in Grainger County, Tennessee,[306] but in the 1860 Census he is back in Jefferson County, Tennessee as a farmer.[307] I could find no further records of John Patton after 1860. The children of John M Patton and Grizzy Moyers are listed below:

1. Mary Blackburn Patton, christened on July 15, 1821 in Jefferson County, Tennessee.[308]

---

dwelling 45, family 48, Fuller and Nancy Ryan family; database with images, *FamilySearch*, accessed 4 May 2017.

300   1850 US Census, Grainger County, Tennessee, population schedule, District 21, p 26, dwelling 183, family 195, John M and Eda Patton family; database with digital images, *FamilySearch*, accessed 5 May 2017.

301   "Tennessee State Marriage Index, 1780-2002," s.v. "John Patton and Grizzy Moyers" (marriage 1813), database, *FamilySearch*, accessed 5 May 2017.

302   Tennessee State Marriage Index, 1780-2002," s.v. "John Patton and Elizabeth Lyle" (marriage 1831), database, *FamilySearch*, accessed 5 May 2017.

303   Tennessee State Marriage Index, 1780-2002," s.v. "John Patton and Eddy Lions" (marriage 1834), database, *FamilySearch*, accessed 5 May 2017.

304   1830 US Census, Jefferson County, Tennessee, population schedule, p 284, family 172, John Patton; database with digital images, *FamilySearch*, accessed 5 May 2017.

305   1840 US Census, Jefferson County, Tennessee, population schedule, p 291, John M Patton; database with digital images, *FamilySearch*, accessed 5 May 2017.

306   1850 US Census, Grainger County, Tennessee, population schedule, District 21, p 26, dwelling 183, family 195, John M and Eda Patton family; database with digital images, *FamilySearch*, accessed 5 May 2017.

307   1860 US Census, Jefferson County, Tennessee, population schedule, , p 191, dwelling 1349; family 1376, J M and E Patton; database with digital images, *FamilySearch*, accessed 5 May 2017.

308   "Tennessee Births and Christenings, 1828-1939," s.v. "Mary Blackburn Patton" (year "1821"), database, *FamilySearch*, accessed 5 May 2017.

2. James Mayers Patton, christened on July 15, 1821 in Jefferson County, Tennessee.[309]
3. Elizabeth Wood Patton, christened July 15, 1821 at Jefferson County, Tennessee.[310]
4. John Jefferson Patton, christened July 15, 1821 in Jefferson County, Tennessee.[311]
5. Susan Jane Patton [05-31], born November 3, 1821 and died July 21, 1883.[312] She married Morgan Ryan [05-30] about 1837 in Tennessee.[313]
6. Samuel Alexander Patton, born on January 30, 1824 in Jefferson County, Tennessee.[314]
7. William Mathes Patton, born on January 22, 1827 in Jefferson County, Tennessee.[315]

[07-64] Rev John Burton

The Reverend John Burton had two children for whom I have a record, Captain James Burton [06-32] and another Reverend John Burton born about 1798. The second John Burton was recorded as being alive in 1890 at the age of ninety-two, and their father also lived to be ninety.[316] As for the specific years that John Burton was born and died or whom he married, I have not found sufficient evidence to include that information. I have seen evidence of a Reverend John Burton in Devon, England at this time but I have not seen proof that they were the same people.

---

309   "Tennessee Births and Christenings, 1828-1939," s.v. "James Mayers Patton" (year "1821"), database, *FamilySearch*, accessed 5 May 2017.
310   "Tennessee Births and Christenings, 1828-1939," s.v. "Elizabeth Wood Patton" (year "1821"), database, *FamilySearch*, accessed 5 May 2017.
311   "Tennessee Births and Christenings, 1828-1939," s.v. "John Jefferson Patton" (year "1821"), database, *FamilySearch*, accessed 5 May 2017.
312   Susan Jane Ryan, Clintonville Cemetery, El Dorado Springs, Cedar County, Missouri, s.v. "Susan Jane Ryan" (year "1883" memorial "28019815"), database with digital images, *FindAGrave*, accessed 20 April 2017.
313   The Goodspeed Publishing Co., *History of Hickory, Polk, Cedar, Dade, and Barton Counties, Missouri*, (Chicago: The Goodspeed Publishing Co, 1889), Vol II: pp 772-3; PDF e-book, https://play.google.com/store/books/details?id=WdMyAQAAMAAJ&rdid=book-WdMyAQAAMAAJ&rdot=1 , accessed 20 April 2017.
314   "Tennessee Births and Christenings, 1828-1939," s.v. "Samuel Alexander Patton" (year "1824"), database, *FamilySearch*, accessed 5 May 2017.
315   "Tennessee Births and Christenings, 1828-1939," s.v. "John Mathes Patton" (year "1827"), database, *FamilySearch*, accessed 5 May 2017.
316   The Lewis Publishing Company, *The Bay of San Francisco: The Metropolis of the Pacific Coast and its Suburban Cities*, (Chicago: The Lewis Publishing Company, 1892), Vol I: p. 626; PDF book, https://archive.org/details/bayofsanfrancisc00lewi , accessed November 2017.

[07-66] John Champion and [07-67] Catherine Periman

Captain John Champion was christened on December 30, 1748 as an Anglican in Shaldon, Devon, England to Jonas Champion [08-132] and Margaret [08-133].[317] At some point, John Champion is recorded as being a sea captain,[318] but as of February 12, 1778 when he married Catherine Periman as Anglicans in Shaldon, John Champion was recorded as being a mariner.[319] Catherine Periman was christened on November 5, 1753 as an Anglican in Shaldon to Jonas Periman [08-134] and Catherine[320] Squarry [08-135].[321] The only child I found for John Champion and Catherine Periman was Jemima Champion [06-33], who was christened May 4, 1782 in Shaldon[322] and died on December 17, 1862 in Oregon.[323] Jemima married first to James Burton [06-32] in Shaldon on January 21, 1800,[324] and second to Mr. Cooper.[325]

[07-68] Joseph Watson and [07-69] Phoebe Whitman

Joseph Watson was said to have been born in Scotland about 1747 and brought to England at the age of 6 weeks due to religious persecution. Since a later generation married in a Roman Catholic ceremony and since the 1745 Rebellion dominated by Roman Catholics and allied Clans in Scotland was very recent, I believe it is likely that the Watson's were Roman Catholics

---

317   "Devon Baptisms," s.v. "John Champion" (birth 1748), database with digital images, *FindMyPast*, accessed 2015.

318   The Lewis Publishing Company, *The Bay of San Francisco: The Metropolis of the Pacific Coast and its Suburban Cities*, (Chicago: The Lewis Publishing Company, 1892), Vol I: p. 626; PDF e-book, https://archive.org/details/bayofsanfrancisc00lewi , accessed November 2017.

319   "Devon Marriages," s.v. "John Champion and Catherine Periman" (marriage 1788) database with digital images, *FindMyPast*, accessed 2015.

320   "Devon Baptisms Transcriptions," s.v. "Catherine Periman" (birth 1753), database with digital images, *FindMyPast*, accessed 2015.

321   "Devon Marriages," s.v. "Jonas Perryman" (spouse "Catherine Squarry" marriage "1749"), database with digital images, *FindMyPast*, accessed 2015.

322   "Devon Baptisms Transcriptions," s.v. "Jemima Champion" (birth "1782"), database with digital images, *FindMyPast*, accessed 2015.

323   Jemima Champion Cooper, Lafayette Pioneer Cemetery, Lafayette, Yamhill County, Oregon, s.v. "Jemima Champion Cooper" (death "1862" memorial "36922950"), database with digital images, *FindAGrave*, accessed 2 July 2017.

324   "Devon Marriages," s.v. "James Burton" (spouse "Jemima Champion" marriage "1800"), database with digital images, *FindMyPast*, accessed 2015.

325   Jemima Champion Cooper, Lafayette Pioneer Cemetery, Lafayette, Yamhill County, Oregon, s.v. "Jemima Champion Cooper" (death "1862" memorial "36922950"), database with digital images, *FindAGrave*, accessed 2 July 2017.

fleeing the backlash against the failed rebellion.[326]

I found no record of a Joseph Watson born in Scotland around 1747. However there is a record of a Joseph Watson born on June 27, 1748 in the "Castle Garth" (which was used as a prison) at Newcastle upon Tyne, England as the son of another Joseph Watson,[327] That Joseph had married Ann Goodale on the other side of the Scottish border in 1747.[328] Since Newcastle is near the border with Scotland, this fits with the account of him being brought to England at a young age and so he would have been christened in England. I consider this match of Joseph being the son of Joseph as possible but needing more evidence to include in this genealogy. Another database match was the Joseph Watson christened in 1746 in Northumbria, England as the son of Robert Watson. However, Robert Watson can be traced as being born in Northumbria so that is not a likely match. Other Joseph Watson birth records between 1746 and 1750 were further from the border so I do not consider them likely either.

Joseph Watson married Phoebe Whitman but I have not found the marriage record. She was born in 1749, probably in England but not verified since I could not find her birth record. Both Joseph Watson and Phoebe Whitman Watson died in a cholera epidemic in 1831. The son of Joseph Watson and Phoebe Whitman was Charles Watson [06-34],[329] who was born in 1797 in England and died on November 11, 1849 in Australia.[330] Charles Watson married Bridget Linnoir, a widow, on February 18, 1817 in Burnley, Lancashire, England.[331]

[07-70] William Linnoir

William Linnoir was in Great Britain sometime before 1774 when he was drafted into the British Army and sent to the American colonies. He deserted the British Army in North America and fought for the colonists for the next

---

326   The Lewis Publishing Company, *The Bay of San Francisco: The Metropolis of the Pacific Coast and its Suburban Cities*, (Chicago: The Lewis Publishing Company, 1892), Vol I: p. 625; PDF e-book, https://archive.org/details/bayofsanfrancisc00lewi , accessed November 2017.
327   "England Births and Christenings, 1538-1975" s.v. "Joseph Watson" (birth 1748), database, *American Ancestors*, accessed 3 July 2018.
328   "Scotland: Marriages, 1561-1910" s.v. "Joseph Watson" (spouse "Ann Goodale" marriage "1747"), database, *American Ancestors*, accessed 3 July 2018.
329   The Lewis Publishing Company, *The Bay of San Francisco: The Metropolis of the Pacific Coast and its Suburban Cities*, (Chicago: The Lewis Publishing Company, 1892), Vol I: p. 625; PDF e-book, https://archive.org/details/bayofsanfrancisc00lewi , accessed November 2017.
330   "Convict Records," s.v. "Charles Watson" (sentenced "1827"), database, *Convict Records of Australia*, accessed 3 July 2017.
331   "England, Lancashire, Parish Registers 1538-1910," s.v. "Charles Watson" (spouse "Bridget Barker" marriage "1817"), database, *FamilySearch*, accessed 3 July 2017.

seven years instead. Sometime after the American Revolution was over, he was back in Ireland where he died fighting for the Irish rebellion in the Battle of Vinegar Hill on June 21, 1798.[332] However, another source reported that he stayed in the US and also fought in the War of 1812 for the US, but did not return to his wife and family in Lancashire, England until right before he died in 1816.[333] As I could not find a death record for William Linnoir around 1798 nor around 1816 at *FamilySearch*, I do not know which death story is more accurate. William's daughter was Bridget Linnoir, aka Mary, [06-35], who first married Mr. Barker[334] and second married Charles Watson on February 18, 1817 in Burnley, Lancashire, England.[335]

[07-72] James Robb and [07-73] Margaret Barr

James Robb and Margaret Barr were both born in Ireland as were at least three of their children, and most of the family emigrated to Philadelphia in 1773. They probably came from Northern Ireland, considering the time period they emigrated in and that their son Hugh W Robb (B08-03m) was a Presbyterian missionary. By 1786 James and Margaret migrated to Kentucky. However in 1807 they were in Indiana where Margaret died. James Robb apparently moved back to Jefferson County in Kentucky sometime after the death of his wife, where he died in 1825.[336] The children of James Robb and Margaret Barr are listed below:

1. Thomas Robb, born before 1773 in Ireland.
2. James Robb, born before 1773 in Ireland.
3. David Robb, born before 1773 in Ireland and died on April 15, 1844. He married Nancy Eckley on March 20, 1800 in Jefferson County,

---

332 The Lewis Publishing Company, *The Bay of San Francisco: The Metropolis of the Pacific Coast and its Suburban Cities*, (Chicago: The Lewis Publishing Company, 1892), Vol I: p. 625; PDF e-book, https://archive.org/details/bayofsanfrancisc00lewi , accessed November 2017.

333 Eugene T Sawyer, *History of Santa Clara County California: with Biographical Sketches*, (Los Angeles: Historic Record Company, 1922) p. 1033; PDF e-book, https://archive.org/details/historyofsantacl00sawy/page/n1129 accessed 19 February 2016.

334 The Lewis Publishing Company, *The Bay of San Francisco: The Metropolis of the Pacific Coast and its Suburban Cities*, (Chicago: The Lewis Publishing Company, 1892), Vol I: p. 625; PDF e-book, https://archive.org/details/bayofsanfrancisc00lewi , accessed November 2017.

335 "England, Lancashire, Parish Registers 1538-1910," s.v. "Charles Watson" (spouse "Bridget Barker" marriage "1817"), database, *FamilySearch*, accessed 3 July 2017.

336 Jas. A Tartt & Co, *History of Gibson County, Indiana*, (Edwardsville, Ill: Jas. A Tartt & Co, 1884), pp 49-50; PDF e-book, https://play.google.com/store/books/details/Jas_T_Tartt_Co_History_of_Gibson_Count y_Indiana?id=XTtEAQAAMAAJ accessed 3 July 2017.

Kentucky.

4. Hugh W Robb [06-36], who was born in Virginia[337] and married Elizabeth Waller on June 2, 1803 in Washington County, Kentucky.[338]

[07-80] Peter Fine and [07-81] Rebecca Stats

Peter Fine was born on May 5, 1753 to Thomas Fine (B10-17m) and Agnes Merchant (B10-17f). Peter married Rebecca Stats on October 6, 1773. She was born on May 8, 1756,[339] but I could not find any record of a birth for Rebecca Stats around 1756 except in England. So her parents are unclear at this time. Around 1776 Peter Fine joined the colonists in the American Revolution in North Carolina and rose to the rank of Major, according to his gravestone.[340]

Rebecca died on September 7, 1802 in Newport, Cocke County, Tennessee, and Peter remarried twice after she died. On September 6, 1803 Peter married Anne Mitchell Murrel, and on November 26, 1816 he had his third marriage, this time with Elizabeth Alexandra.[341] Peter Fine died on August 11, 1826 and was buried at Roadman Cemetery in Newport, Cocke County, Tennessee.[342] The children of Peter Fine and Rebecca Stats are listed below:

1. Lidgard Fine, Sr [06-40], born September 1, 1775 in Shenandoah County (formerly Dunmore County), Virginia and died before March 10, 1834 in Dover, Lafayette County, Missouri. He married Elizabeth Netherton [06-41] on May 1, 1797 in Jefferson County, Tennessee.

2. Aron Fine, born on July 5, 1777 in Shenandoah County.

3. Jonathan Fine, born on May 11, 1779 in Shenandoah County and died on May 11, 1862 in Santa Rosa, Sonoma County, California. He married Hannah Rector on September 7, 1791 in Jefferson County, Tennessee, and then Rachel Houx.

---

337   Chapman Bros., *Portrait and Biographical Album of Johnson and Pawnee Counties, Nebraska*, (Chicago: Chapman Bros., 1889), pp. 599-601; PDF e-book, https://play.google.com/store/books/details/Portrait_and_Biographical_Album_of_John son_and_Paw?id=ev40AQAAMAAJ accessed 27 March 2017.

338   "Kentucky, County Marriages, 1797-1954," s.v. "Hugh Robb" (spouse "Elizabeth Waller" marriage "1803"), database with digital images, *FamilySearch*, accessed 31 March 2017.

339   Dorothy Wilson Fine, *A Fine Branch of the Family Tree*, (San Jose, CA: El Camino Real Chapter, DAR, 1991), p. 11.

340   Peter Fine, grave marker, Roadman Cemetery, Newport, Cocke County, Tennessee, s.v. "Maj Peter Fine" (death 1826, memorial 51911118), database with digital images, *FindAGrave*, accessed 2015.

341   Dorothy Wilson Fine, *A Fine Branch of the Family Tree*, (San Jose, CA: El Camino Real Chapter, DAR, 1991), p. 11.

342   Peter Fine, grave marker, Roadman Cemetery, Newport, Cocke County, Tennessee, s.v. "Maj Peter Fine" (death 1826, memorial 51911118), database with digital images, *FindAGrave*, accessed 2015.

4. John Fine, born on January 1, 1781 in Shenandoah County and died on January 26, 1857 in Sweetwater, Monroe County, Tennessee. He married Nancy Lee in 1800 in Cocke County, Tennessee.
5. David Fine, born on August 12, 1783 in Greene County, North Carolina and died on October 15, 1843. He married Agnes Mitchell in 1813.
6. Peter Fine, born on September 18, 1786 in Greene County, North Carolina.
7. Elizabeth Fine, born on January 21, 1788 in Greene County, North Carolina and died in 1845. She married Edom Kendrick.
8. Abraham Fine, born on March 24, 1789 in Greene County, North Carolina and died on September 26, 1861 in Cocke County, Tennessee. He married Elizabeth Smith.
9. Aron Fine, born June 7, 1792 in Jefferson County, Tennessee.
10. Mariann Fine, born May 5, 1794 in Jefferson County, Tennessee and died on October 15, 1812 in Cocke County, Tennessee.
11. Rebecca Fine, born on August 25, 1796 in Jefferson County, Tennessee.
12. Patsey Tirevelan Fine, born on September 10, 1799 in Cocke County, Tennessee.[343]

[07-82] Henry Netherton and [07-83] Elizabeth

Henry Netherton was born about 1740 to Henry Netherton [08-164] and Sarah Rhodes [08-165], probably in Virginia. About 1763 Henry married Elizabeth, probably in Frederick County, Virginia. Elizabeth's birth date and parents are not established with certainty at this time. On April 30, 1778, Henry became a Lieutenant in the Shenandoah County Militia during the American Revolution. After the Revolution, Henry and Elizabeth were living in Greene County, North Carolina as of October 15, 1788, where they were members of the Big Pigeon Baptist Church. Elizabeth probably died in North Carolina about 1789, and about 1796 Henry had moved to Kentucky. He died about 1808.[344] The children of Henry Netherton and Elizabeth are listed below:
1. Abigail Netherton, born February 7, 1765 in Frederick County, Virginia and married Evan Morgan on October 15, 1788 in Greene County, North Carolina
2. Henry Netherton, born about 1766/7 in Frederick County, Virginia.
3. Sarah Netherton, born about 1768/9 in Frederick County, Virginia.
4. Elizabeth Netherton [06-41], born on February 12, 1773 in Shenandoah County, Virginia and married Lidgard Fine, Sr [06-40] on May 1, 1797

---

343   Dorothy Wilson Fine, *A Fine Branch of the Family Tree*, (San Jose, CA: El Camino Real Chapter, DAR, 1991), p. 11.

344   Dorothy Wilson Fine, *A Fine Branch of the Family Tree*, (San Jose, CA: El Camino Real Chapter, DAR, 1991), pp 19-20.

in Jefferson County, Tennessee.
5. John Netherton, born on October 12, 1774 in Shenandoah County, Virginia.
6. Esther Netherton, born in 1775/6 in Shenandoah County, Virginia.
7. Moses Netherton, born on October 16, 1780 in Shenandoah County, Virginia.
8. James Netherton, born on January 18, 1782 in Shenandoah County, Virginia.
9. Enoch Netherton, born in 1789 in Greene County, North Carolina.

[07-84] Enoch Cox and [07-85] Mary Mackey

Enoch Cox was born about 1755 to Solomon Cox [08-168] and Ruth Cox [08-169]. Enoch was a Quaker, and married Mary Mackey about 1785.[345] Mary's birth date and parents are not established. She died in 1829 and is buried at the Old Quaker Cemetery in Pipers Gap, Carroll County, Virginia.[346] By 1832 Enoch married again, to Sally Stoneman.[347] Enoch died in Grayson, Virginia on March 28, 1840 and was also buried at the Old Quaker Cemetery in Pipers Gap.[348] The children of Enoch Cox and Mary Mackey are listed below:
1. Ruth Cox, born January 29, 1784 and died on May 6, 1845. She married William Rodney Cole.
2. Nathan Cox, born November 25, 1785 and died on August 28, 1840 in Wyoming, Stark County, Illinois. He married Anne Dixon on November 10, 1806 in Ross County, Ohio.
3. Solomon Cox [06-42], born May 17, 1788 in Grayson County, Virginia and died on November 25, 1849 near Gilroy, Santa Clara County, California. He married Deborah Collins [06-43] on June 12, 1806.
4. Enoch Cox, Jr, born on August 19, 1793 and married Nancy Davis.
5. Mary Cox, born on December 17, 1794 and died on April 17, 1892 in Dover, Lafayette County, Missouri. She married John Weir Lovelady on October 18, 1817 in Lafayette County, Missouri.
6. William Cox, born on January 4, 1796.
7. Jesse Cox, born on June 12, 1800 and married Sally Cox.
8. Jeremiah Cox, born on March 12, 1804 and died on October 22, 1883.

---

345   Elizabeth Berry Buffa, "Cox Family Outline," (report, 1977), A IX b; p 10; PDF e-book, https://archive.org/details/coxfamilyoutline00buff accessed 8 July 2018.
346   Mary Cox, grave marker, Old Quaker Cemetery, Pipers Gap, Carroll County, Virginia, s.v. "Mary Mackey Cox" (death 1829, memorial 53211001), database with digital images, *FindAGrave,* accessed 23 April 2017.
347   Elizabeth Berry Buffa, "Cox Family Outline," (report, 1977), A IX b; p 14; PDF e-book, https://archive.org/details/coxfamilyoutline00buff accessed 8 July 2018.
348   Enoch Cox, grave marker, Old Quaker Cemetery, Pipers Gap, Carroll County, Virginia, s.v. "Enoch Cox, Sr" (death 1840, memorial 53210721), database with digital images, *FindAGrave,* accessed 23 April 2017.

He married Edith Davis.[349]

[07-92] Philaris Ansell

Philaris (or Valerius) Ansell was the son of Henry Ansell [08-184] and Catherine [08-185]. Philaris married Catherine Fresh on March 14, 1778 in St Paul's Parish, Baltimore, Maryland,[350] but Henry Ansell [06-46] was born about 1773.[351] So Philaris possibly had a prior marriage to marrying Catherine Fresh. Philaris died before December 20, 1786, as that is the date that his estate account was filed in Baltimore, Maryland.[352] The known children of Philaris Ansell are listed below:

1. Henry Ansell [06-46], born about 1773[353] in Baltimore, Maryland[354] and died on April 5, 1850 in Van Buren County, Iowa.[355] He married Elizabeth Bierley [06-47] on August 26, 1803 in Baltimore, Maryland.[356]
2. Elizabeth Ansell, born 1780/1.
3. Francis Ansell, born 1784.[357]

[07-96] Zebadiah Johnson and [07-97] Ales Mirrick

Zebadiah Johnson was born on July 25, 1732 in Shrewsbury, Worcester County, Massachusetts to Zebadiah Johnson [08-192] and Esther Richardson

---

349   Elizabeth Berry Buffa, "Cox Family Outline," (report, 1977), A IX b; pp. 10-14; PDF e-book, https://archive.org/details/coxfamilyoutline00buff accessed 8 July 2018.
350   Dorothy Wilson Fine, *A Fine Branch of the Family Tree*, (San Jose, CA: El Camino Real Chapter, DAR, 1991), p. 35.
351   "Iowa Mortality Schedules, 1850-1880," s.v. "Henry Anson" (death "1850"), database with digital images, *FamilySearch*, accessed 12 November 2019.
352   Dorothy Wilson Fine, *A Fine Branch of the Family Tree*, (San Jose, CA: El Camino Real Chapter, DAR, 1991), p. 35.
353   "Iowa Mortality Schedules, 1850-1880," s.v. "Henry Anson" (death "1850"), database with digital images, *FamilySearch*, accessed 12 November 2019.
354   Dorothy Wilson Fine, A Fine Branch of the Family Tree, (San Jose, CA: El Camino Real Chapter, DAR, 1991), p. 35.
355   Henry Anson, Anson Cemetery, Anson, Clark County, Missouri, s.v. "Henry Anson" (death "1850" memorial "45616743"), database with digital images, *FindAGrave*, accessed 21 April 2017.
356   "Maryland Marriages, 1666-1970," s.v. "Henry Anson" (spouse "Elizabeth Buerly" marriage "1803"), database, *FamilySearch,* accessed 21 April 2017.
357   Dorothy Wilson Fine, *A Fine Branch of the Family Tree*, (San Jose, CA: El Camino Real Chapter, DAR, 1991), p. 35.

[08-193].[358] [359]   They baptized Zebadiah as a child on April 1, 1733 in Shrewsbury.   By 1753 Zebadiah lived in Hardwick, Worcester County, Massachusetts[360] and in Hardwick married Ales (Alice) Mirrick on November 25, 1756.[361] Ales Mirrick was born August 29, 1737 in Hardwick to Constant Merrick [08-194] and Sarah Freeman [08-195].[362] Together Zebadiah and Ales had at least six children between 1758 and 1769. Some online genealogies as of 2016 gave the death of Zebadiah Johnson and Ales Mirrick as 1752, which is obviously false since they weren't married until 1756 and are not on record as having children until 1769.[363] The children of Zebadiah Johnson and Ales Mirrick are listed below:

1. Samuel Johnson, born on May 23, 1758.
2. Mary Johnson, born on March 10, 1760 and died on October 5, 1837.
3. Constant Johnson, born on January 9, 1762.[364]
4. Joab Johnson [06-48], born on March 9, 1765 in Hardwick[365] and died on May 6, 1840 in Dover, Windham County, Vermont.[366] He married Jemima Ball [06-49] before 1793.[367]
5. Zebadiah Johnson, born on June 16, 1767.
6. John Johnson, born on June 4, 1769.[368]

---

358   Lucius R. Paige, *History of Hardwick, Massachusetts. with a Genealogical Register*, (Boston, MA: Houghton, Mifflin and Company, 1883), p. 404; PDF e-book, https://play.google.com/store/books/details?id=cxipJ2yyiygC&rdid=book-cxipJ2yyiygC&rdot=1 accessed 9 July 2018.
359   Mrs. Ellwood Kimball, "The Solomon Johnson Family," *The New England Historical and Genealogical Register*, Vol 66, p 238; database, *American Ancestors*, accessed 9 July 2018.
360   Lucius R. Paige, *History of Hardwick, Massachusetts. with a Genealogical Register*, (Boston, MA: Houghton, Mifflin and Company, 1883), p. 404; PDF e-book, https://play.google.com/store/books/details?id=cxipJ2yyiygC&rdid=book-cxipJ2yyiygC&rdot=1 accessed 9 July 2018.
361   "Massachusetts Marriages, 1695-1910," s.v. "Zebadiah Johnson and Allis Mirick" (marriage 1756), database, *FamilySearch*, accessed 9 July 2018.
362   "Massachusetts Births and Christenings, 1639-1915." s.v. "Ales Mirrick" (birth 1737), database, *FamilySearch,* accessed 3 May 2016.
363   Lucius R. Paige, *History of Hardwick, Massachusetts. with a Genealogical Register*, (Boston, MA: Houghton, Mifflin and Company, 1883), p. 405; PDF e-book, https://play.google.com/store/books/details?id=cxipJ2yyiygC&rdid=book-cxipJ2yyiygC&rdot=1 , accessed 9 July 2018.
364   Ibid., p. 405.
365   "Massachusetts Births and Christenings, 1639-1915," s.v. "Joab Johnson" (birth "1765"), database, *FamilySearch*, accessed 20 April 2016.
366   "Vermont Vital Records, 1760-1954," s.v. "Joab Johnson" (death "1840"), database with digital images, *FamilySearch*, accessed 20 April 2016.
367   "Vermont, Town Clerk, Vital and Town Records, 1732-2005," s.v. "Joab Johnson" (spouse "Jemima"), database with digital images, *FamilySearch,* accessed 2 May 2019.
368   Lucius R. Paige, *History of Hardwick, Massachusetts. with a Genealogical Register*, (Boston, MA: Houghton, Mifflin and Company, 1883), p. 405; PDF e-book, https://play.google.com/store/books/details?id=cxipJ2yyiygC&rdid=book-

[07-100] Dudley Carleton and [07-101] Abigail Wilson

Dudley Carleton was born on January 5, 1721/2 in Bradford, Essex County, Massachusetts to Benjamin Carleton [08-200] and Abigail [08-201],[369] [370] whose last name was likely Dalton[371] as will be explained in more detail in her own section. As he was too old to fight in the Revolution when it happened, he got involved by getting on a committee to raise recruits for campaigns in New York and Canada.[372]

Dudley Carleton married Abigail Wilson on February 25, 1745 in Bradford. Abigail was the daughter of Joseph Wilson [08-202] and Rebecca Kimball [08-203], and was born on November 25, 1725 in Bradford.[373] Abigail Wilson died on October 23, 1799 and was buried at the Ancient Burial Ground in Bradford.[374] Dudley died on September 15, 1807 and was also buried at the Ancient Burial Ground in Bradford.[375] The children of Dudley Carleton and Abigail Wilson are listed below:

1. Rebecca Carleton, born on May 26, 1746 in Bradford.
2. Dudley Carleton, born on May 16, 1748 in Bradford.
3. Abigail Carleton, born on March 30, 1750 in Bradford.
4. David Carleton, born on December 7, 1751 in Bradford.
5. Hannah Carleton, born on January 7, 1753 in Bradford.
6. Michael Carleton [06-50], born on May 23, 1757 in Bradford and died on June 20, 1836 in Bradford. He married Ruth Ayer [06-51] in

---

cxipJ2yyiygC&rdot=1 , accessed 9 July 2018.

369   William Richard Cutter, ed., *New England Families: Genealogical and Memorial,* (New York: Lewis Historical Publishing Co, 1913), Vol I: p. 8; PDF e-book, https://archive.org/details/newenglandfamili01cutt_1 accessed 9 July 2018.

370   "Massachusetts, Town Clerk, Vital and Town Records, 1626-2001," digital images not indexed, Massachusetts, Essex County, Bradford 1670-1796, *FamilySearch,* accessed 21 June 2019.

371   William Henry Gove, *The Gove Book: History and Genealogy of the American Family of Gove and Notes of European Goves,* (Salem, MA: Sydney Perley, 1922), p. 50; PDF e-book, https://archive.org/details/govebookhistoryg00gove/page/50 , accessed 22 June 2019.

372   William Richard Cutter, ed., *New England Families: Genealogical and Memorial,* (New York: Lewis Historical Publishing Co, 1913), Vol I: p. 8; PDF e-book, https://archive.org/details/newenglandfamili01cutt_1 accessed 9 July 2018.

373   "Massachusetts, Town Clerk, Vital and Town Records, 1626-2001," digital images not indexed, Massachusetts, Essex County, Bradford 1670-1796, *FamilySearch,* accessed 21 June 2019.

374   Abigail Wilson Carleton, Ancient Burial Ground, Bradford, Essex County, Massachusetts, s.v. "Abigail Wilson Carleton" (death "1799" memorial "38056602"), database with digital images, *FindAGrave,* (accessed 21 June 2019).

375   Dudley Carleton, Ancient Burial Ground, Bradford, Essex County, Massachusetts, s.v. "Dudley Carleton" (death "1807" memorial "38056642"), database with digital images, *FindAGrave,* (accessed 21 June 2019).

Haverhill, Essex County, Massachusetts on November 20, 1795.
7. Moses Carleton, born on January 17, 1759 in Bradford.
8. Mercy Carleton, born on September 17, 1760 in Bradford.
9. Edward Carleton, born on July 2, 1762 in Bradford.
10. William Carleton, born on June 1, 1764 in Bradford.
11. Ebenezer Carleton, born on April 4, 1766 in Bradford.
12. Phoebe Carleton, born on March 4, 1769 in Bradford.

[07-102] Nathaniel Ayer and [07-103] Lydia White

Nathaniel Ayer was born on February 24, 1734/5 in Haverhill, Essex County, Massachusetts[376] to David Ayer [08-204] and Hannah Shepard [08-205].[377] Nathaniel married Lydia White on November 17, 1757 in Haverhill,[378] although one source mistakenly gave the marriage date as November 7, 1759.[379] Lydia White was the daughter of John White [08-206] and Martha Appleton [08-207], and she was born on January 24, 1736/7 in Haverhill.[380] Nathaniel died on January 18, 1784 and is buried at the Pentucket Cemetery in Haverhill.[381] Lydia lived until February 9, 1817 and is also buried at the Pentucket Cemetery in Haverhill.[382] The children of Nathaniel Ayer and Lydia White are listed below:

1. John Ayer, born on October 15, 1758.
2. Hannah Ayer, born on June 11, 1760.
3. David Ayer, born on November 19, 1762 and died on March 24, 1789.
4. Lydia Ayer, born on April 15, 1765, and who married Samuel White.

---

376   "Massachusetts, Town Clerk, Vital and Town Records, 1626-2001," family group s.v. "David Ayer" (spouse "Hannah Shepard" marriage "1733"), database with digital images, *FamilySearch*, accessed 23 June 2019.

377   William Richard Cutter, ed., *New England Families: Genealogical and Memorial,* (New York: Lewis Historical Publishing Co, 1913), Vol I: p. 8; PDF e-book, https://archive.org/details/newenglandfamili01cutt_1 accessed 9 July 2018.

378   "Massachusetts, Town Clerk, Vital and Town Records, 1626-2001," family group s.v. "Nathaniel Ayer" (spouse "Lydia White" marriage "1757"), database with digital images, *FamilySearch*, accessed 23 June 2019.

379   Daniel Appleton White and Annie Frances Richards, *The Descendants of William White, of Haverhill, Mass.,* (Boston: American Printing and Engraving Company, 1889), p. 57; PDF e-book, https://archive.org/details/descendantswill00richgoog/page/n10 accessed 23 June 2019.

380   "Massachusetts, Town Clerk, Vital and Town Records, 1626-2001," family group s.v. "John White" (spouse "Martha Appleton" marriage "1737"), database with digital images, *FamilySearch*, accessed 23 June 2019.

381   Nathaniel Ayer, Pentucket Cemetery, Haverhill, Essex County, Massachusetts, s.v. "Nathaniel Ayer" (death "1784" memorial "166801201"), database with digital images, *FindAGrave*, accessed 23 June 2019.

382   Lydia Ayer, Pentucket Cemetery, Haverhill, Essex County, Massachusetts, s.v. "Lydia White Ayer" (death "1817" memorial "143121807"), database with digital images, *FindAGrave*, accessed 23 June 2019.

5. Ann Ayer, born on November 27, 1768.
6. Timothy Ayer, born on April 23, 1773.[383]
7. Ruth Ayer [06-51], who was born on August 12, 1776 in Haverhill,[384] and died on September 13, 1847. She married Michael Carleton [06-50].
8. Nathaniel Ayer, who was born on September 20, 1780 and died on February 18, 1817.[385]

[07-104] Nathaniel Cowdry and [07-105] Rebecca Parker

Nathaniel Cowdry was born about 1745 in Westford, Middlesex County, Massachusetts to John Cowdry [08-208] and Hannah Davis [08-209].[386] Unfortunately his birth date is not marked clearly in the town clerk record[387] so some sites claim 1741. However 1745 is more likely since his parents married in 1744. Nathaniel married Rebecca Parker on March 11, 1773 in Chelmsford, Middlesex County, Massachusetts.[388] Rebecca Parker was the daughter of Samuel Parker [08-110] and Anne Tarbell [08-111], and was born on May 16, 1752 in Billerica, Middlesex County, Massachusetts.[389] Rebecca Parker's first child was Samuel Lovejoy, born December 6, 1771, whose father is not known.[390] Nathaniel was recorded on the Revolutionary War Rolls as a

---

383   Daniel Appleton White and Annie Frances Richards, *The Descendants of William White, of Haverhill, Mass.,* (Boston: American Printing and Engraving Company, 1889), p. 57; PDF e-book,
https://archive.org/details/descendantswill00richgoog/page/n10 accessed 23 June 2019.
384   "Massachusetts, Town Clerk, Vital and Town Records, 1626-2001," family group s.v. "Nathaniel Ayer" (spouse "Lydia White" marriage "1757"), database with digital images, *FamilySearch,* accessed 23 June 2019.
385   Daniel Appleton White and Annie Frances Richards, *The Descendants of William White, of Haverhill, Mass.,* (Boston: American Printing and Engraving Company, 1889), p. 57; PDF e-book,
https://archive.org/details/descendantswill00richgoog/page/n10 accessed 23 June 2019.
386   William Richard Cutter, ed., *Genealogical and Family History of Western New York,* (New York: Lewis Historical Publishing Company, 1912), Vol III: p 1428; PDF e-book, https://archive.org/details/genealogicalfami03incutt accessed 9 July 2018.
387   "Massachusetts, Town Clerk, Vital and Town Records, 1626-2001," s.v. "Nathaniel Cowdry" (birth "1741"), database with digital images, *FamilySearch,* accessed 30 April 2017.
388   "Massachusetts Marriages, 1695-1910," s.v. "Nathaniel Cowdry" (spouse "Rebecca Parker" marriage "1773"), database, *FamilySearch,* accessed 30 April 2017..
389   Henry A Hazen, *History of Billerica, Massachusetts: With a Genealogical Register,* (Boston: A Williams and Co, 1883) p. 105; PDF e-book, Internet Archive, https://archive.org/details/historyofbilleri00hazenhe , accessed 9 July 2018.
390   "Massachusetts, Town Clerk, Vital and Town Records, 1626-2001," family group s.v. "Nathaniel Cowdry" (spouse "Rebeckah Parker"), database with digital images, *FamilySearch,* accessed 23 June 2019.

Private,[391] but survived the war and had at least seven children with Rebecca between 1774 and 1790, who are listed below:

1. Lucy Cowdry, born on July 16, 1774 in Westford, Middlesex County, Massachusetts.
2. Nathaniel Cowdry, born on July 27, 1776 in Westford.
3. Rebeckah Cowdry, born on March 27, 1778 in Westford.
4. Joseph Cowdry [06-52], born on March 19, 1781 in Westford[392] and died on January 15, 1859 in Billerica.[393] He married Lucy Brown [06-53].[394]
5. Mighill (Michael?) Cowdry, born on October 27, 1784 in Westford.
6. Naomi Cowdry, born on September 20, 1787 in Westford.
7. Betty Cowdry, born on February 13, 1790 in Westford.[395]

[07-106] Thomas Brown and [07-107] Lucy Kemp

Thomas Brown was born February 20, 1723/4 in Billerica, Middlesex County, Massachusetts to John Brown [08-212] and Susanna Dutton [08-213]. His first marriage was with Ester before 1752.[396] Then on January 4, 1775, he married Lucy Kemp in Billerica.[397] [398] Lucy Kemp was the daughter of Jason Kemp [08-214] and Hannah Meers [08-215], and was born February 22, 1752 in Billerica.[399] This would have made Thomas Brown about 51 and Lucy Kemp

---

391   "United States Revolutionary War Rolls, 1775-1783," s.v. "Nathl Cowdry," database with digital images, *FamilySearch*, accessed 30 April 2017.
392   "Massachusetts, Town Clerk, Vital and Town Records, 1626-2001," family group s.v. "Nathaniel Cowdry" (spouse "Rebeckah Parker"), database with digital images, *FamilySearch*, accessed 23 June 2019.
393   "Massachusetts Deaths, 1841-1915," s.v. "Joseph Cowdry" (death "1859"), database, *FamilySearch*, accessed 30 April 2017.
394   Henry A Hazen, *History of Billerica, Massachusetts: With a Genealogical Register*, (Boston: A Williams and Co, 1883) p. 26; PDF e-book, Internet Archive, https://archive.org/details/historyofbilleri00hazenhe , accessed 9 July 2018.
395   "Massachusetts, Town Clerk, Vital and Town Records, 1626-2001," family group s.v. "Nathaniel Cowdry" (spouse "Rebeckah Parker"), database with digital images, *FamilySearch*, accessed 23 June 2019.
396   Henry A Hazen, *History of Billerica, Massachusetts: With a Genealogical Register*, (Boston: A Williams and Co, 1883) p. 19 of Genealogical Register; PDF e-book, Internet Archive, https://archive.org/details/historyofbilleri00hazenhe , accessed 9 July 2018.
397   "Massachusetts, Town Clerk, Vital and Town Records, 1626-2001," s.v. "Thomas Brown" (spouse "Lucy Kemp" marriage "1775"), database with digital images, *FamilySearch*, accessed 9 July 2018.
398   Henry A Hazen, *History of Billerica, Massachusetts: With a Genealogical Register*, (Boston: A Williams and Co, 1883) p. 19 of Genealogical Register; PDF e-book, Internet Archive, https://archive.org/details/historyofbilleri00hazenhe , accessed 9 July 2018.
399   "Massachusetts, Town Clerk, Vital and Town Records, 1626-2001," s.v. "Lucy

23 when they got married, which has confused some people. So some online genealogies put Lucy Kemp as marrying the son of this Thomas Brown [07-106] and his first wife Ester. That son was also named Thomas Brown and just a few years younger than Lucy Kemp. Also, Thomas Brown and Lucy Kemp had nine recorded children between 1775 and 1794. However, the town records clearly record the elder Thomas Brown [07-106] marrying Lucy Kemp, and Hazen also wrote that the elder Thomas Brown [07-106] married Lucy Kemp. Plus, the son Thomas Kemp was married to Rachel Procter in 1785,[400] so he was not the one who married Lucy Kemp. So in this genealogy I followed what the sources indicate and have the elder Thomas Brown [07-106] as having a marriage with the much younger Lucy Kemp. The children of the elder Thomas Brown and Lucy Kemp are listed below:

1. Sarah Brown, who was born on October 15, 1775 in Billerica.
2. Rebecca Brown, who was born on March 25, 1777 in Billerica.
3. Lucy Brown [06-53], who was born on September 6, 1778 in Billerica[401] and died on December 25, 1856.[402] She married Joseph Cowdry [06-52].[403]
4. Joab Brown, who was born on March 10, 1780 in Billerica.
5. Elisha Brown, who was born on July 13, 1782 in Billerica.
6. Jonas Brown, who was born on January 25, 1785 in Billerica.
7. Isaac Brown, who was born on November 9, 1788 in Billerica.
8. Jacob Brown, who was born on May 10, 1792 in Billerica.
9. Rebecca Brown, who was born on December 3, 1794 in Billerica[404] and married Benoni Spaulding.[405]

Kemp" (birth "1752"), database with digital images, *FamilySearch,* accessed 18 May 2017.

400   Henry A Hazen, *History of Billerica, Massachusetts: With a Genealogical Register,* (Boston: A Williams and Co, 1883) p. 20 of Genealogical Register; PDF e-book, Internet Archive, https://archive.org/details/historyofbilleri00hazenhe , accessed 9 July 2018.

401   "Massachusetts, Town Clerk, Vital and Town Records, 1626-2001," family group s.v. "Thomas Brown" (spouse "Lucy Kemp"), database with digital images, *FamilySearch,* accessed 18 May 2017.

402   Lucy Kemp Cowdry, North Cemetery, Billerica, Middlesex County, Massachusetts, s.v. "Lucy Cowdry" (death "1856" memorial "107626476"), database with digital images, *FindAGrave,* accessed 30 April 2017.

403   Henry A Hazen, *History of Billerica, Massachusetts: With a Genealogical Register,* (Boston: A Williams and Co, 1883) p. 26 of Genealogical Register; PDF e-book, Internet Archive, https://archive.org/details/historyofbilleri00hazenhe , accessed 9 July 2018.

404   "Massachusetts, Town Clerk, Vital and Town Records, 1626-2001," family group s.v. "Thomas Brown" (spouse "Lucy Kemp"), database with digital images, *FamilySearch,* accessed 18 May 2017.

405   Henry A Hazen, *History of Billerica, Massachusetts: With a Genealogical Register,* (Boston: A Williams and Co, 1883) p. 20 of Genealogical Register; PDF e-book, Internet Archive, https://archive.org/details/historyofbilleri00hazenhe , accessed 9 July 2018.

[08-134] Jonas Periman and [08-135] Catherine Squarry

Jonas Periman was christened into the Anglican church on October 12, 1721 in Shaldon, Devon, England, and was the son of Jonas Periman [09-268] and Eliza [09-269].[406] Jonas married Catherine Squarry on December 26, 1749 at St Mary (Anglican) in Wolborough, Devon, England.[407] Catherine was the daughter of Will Squarry [09-270] and Grace [09-271], and was christened into the Anglican church on December 16, 1721 in Shaldon.[408] Jonas Periman and Catherine Squarry had at least one child, Catherine Periman [07-67], who was christened at an Anglican church on November 5, 1753 in Shaldon.[409] She married John Champion [07-66] on February 12, 1778 in Shaldon.[410]

[08-164] Henry Netherton and [08-165] Sarah Rhodes

Henry Netherton was born about 1710 to Henry Netherton [09-328] and Sarah Tucker [09-329]. He married Sarah Rhodes about 1737 and they had at least four children between 1739 and about 1755. Henry died after 1786. Sarah Rhodes was born in 1715 in Virginia to John Rhodes [09-330] and Ann [09-331].[411] Some genealogies connect Sarah Rhodes to the Rhodes family in Christchurch, Middlesex County, Virginia but this Sarah Rhodes reportedly came from Stafford County. I have not been able to reliably trace the Rhodes family in Stafford County as of 2017. Known children of Henry Netherton and Sarah Rhodes are listed below:

1. Sarah Netherton, who was born on April 25, 1739 in Virginia.
2. Henry Netherton [07-82], who was born about 1740 and died about 1808. He married Elizabeth [07-83] probably about 1763 in Frederick County, Virginia.
3. John Netherton, who was born about 1747.
4. Rebecca Netherton, who was born about 1755.[412]

---

406   "Devon Baptisms Transcriptions," s.v. "Jonas Perriman" (baptism "1721"), database with digital images, *FindMyPast*, accessed 2015.

407   "Devon Marriages," s.v. "Jonas Perryman" (spouse "Catherine Squarry" marriage "1749"), database with digital images, *FindMyPast*, accessed 2015.

408   "Devon Baptisms," s.v. "Catherine Squarry" (baptism "1721"), database with digital images, *FindMyPast*, accessed 2015.

409   "Devon Baptisms," s.v. "Catherine Periman" (birth "1753"), database with digital images, *FindMyPast*, accessed 2015.

410   "Devon Marriages," s.v. "John Champion" (spouse "Catherine Periman" marriage "1778"), database with digital images, *FindMyPast*, accessed 2015.

411   Dorothy Wilson Fine, *A Fine Branch of the Family Tree*, (San Jose, CA: El Camino Real Chapter, DAR, 1991), p. 19.

412   Ibid., pp. 19-20.

[08-168] Solomon Cox and [08-169] Ruth Cox

Solomon Cox was born about 1730 in New Castle County, Delaware to William Cox [09-336] and Catherine Kinkey [09-337].[413] He married Ruth Cox about 1755, and she was the daughter of John Cox [09-338] and Mary [09-339].[414] Some genealogies put Ruth Cox in another family but I have not seen good evidence to support this. Solomon and Ruth Cox were Quakers, and apparently finished their lives in Ohio. Ruth was buried after 1805 in Peecher Cemetery in Londonderry, Ross County, Ohio,[415] and Solomon died in 1812 and was also buried at Peecher Cemetery in Londonderry.[416] The children of Solomon Cox and Ruth Cox are listed below:

1. Enoch Cox [07-84] who was born about 1755 and died on March 28, 1840 in Grayson County, Virginia. He married Mary Mackey [07-85] about 1784.
2. Solomon Cox, who was born about 1755 and died in 1840 in Ohio. He married Rebecca Cox.
3. Catherine Cox, born about 1759 and died before 1828. She married John Cox about 1792.
4. Ruth Cox, born about 1761 or 1767 and died on August 22, 1825. She married William Cox before December 1789.
5. Samuel Cox, born in Orange County, North Carolina and died in 1808 in Ross County, Ohio. He married Lydia Hadley on September 1, 1783.
6. Mary Cox, born about 1766 and died after 1828. She married John Dixon.
7. Joseph Cox, born about 1768 and died on August 5, 1828 in Ohio. He married Lydia Dixon about 1807.
8. William Cox, born about 1764 and died before 1810 in Ohio. He married Phebe Cox about 1793.
9. Jesse Cox, born about 1770 and died on August 5, 1822. He married Margery Cox on September 25, 1789 in Tennessee.[417]

---

413   Elizabeth Berry Buffa, "Cox Family Outline," (report, 1977), E IV, p 24; PDF e-book, https://archive.org/details/coxfamilyoutline00buff accessed 8 July 2018.

414   Elizabeth Berry Buffa, "Cox Family Outline," (report, 1977), A IX; p 10; PDF e-book, https://archive.org/details/coxfamilyoutline00buff accessed 8 July 2018.

415   Ruth Cox, Peecher Cemetery, Londonderry, Liberty Township, Ross County, Ohio, s.v. "Ruth Cox Cox" (death "1805" memorial "131720554"), database with digital images, *FindAGrave,* accessed 9 July 2018.

416   Solomon Cox, grave marker, Peecher Cemetery, Londonderry, Liberty Township, Ross County, Ohio, s.v. "Solomon Cox" (death "1812" memorial "5688796"), database with digital images, *FindAGrave,* accessed 9 July 2018.

417   Elizabeth Berry Buffa, "Cox Family Outline," (report, 1977), A IX; pp. 10 and 26; PDF e-book, https://archive.org/details/coxfamilyoutline00buff accessed 8 July 2018.

[08-184] Henry Ansell and [08-185] Catherine

Henry Ansell showed up in colony records when he bought 142 acres of "Murray's Plains" in Maryland. Then about 1774 his wife Catherine administered Henry's estate after his death. I have not been able to verify much else with this family. The known son of Henry Ansell and Catherine was Philaris Ansell [07-92], who married Catherine Fresh [07-93] on March 14, 1778 in Baltimore, Maryland and died before December 20, 1786.[418]

[08-192] Zebadiah Johnson and [08-193] Esther Richardson

Zebadiah Johnson was born on April 28, 1704 in Marlborough, Middlesex County, Massachusetts to Daniel Johnson [09-384] and Dorothy Lambe [09-385].[419] Zebadiah married Esther Richardson on October 17, 1731 in Leicester, Worcester County, Massachusetts[420] and they had at least fifteen children between 1732 and 1756 in Shrewsbury, Worcester County, Massachusetts. Esther Richardson was born October 8, 1713 in Malden, Middlesex County, Massachusetts to Thomas Richardson [09-386] and Elizabeth Green [09-387].[421] Esther died on May 5, 1796 and was buried at the West Main Street Cemetery in Shrewsbury.[422] Zebadiah followed on September 7, 1796 and was also buried at the West Main Street Cemetery in Shrewsbury.[423] The children of Zebadiah Johnson and Esther Richardson are listed below:

1. Zebadiah Johnson [07-96], born on July 25, 1732 in Shrewsbury[424] and married Ales Mirrick [07-97] on November 25, 1756 in Hardwick,

---

418   Dorothy Wilson Fine, *A Fine Branch of the Family Tree*, (San Jose, CA: El Camino Real Chapter, DAR, 1991), p. 35.

419 Mrs. Ellwood Kimball, "The Solomon Johnson Family," *The New England Historical and Genealogical Register*, Vol 66,   p 238; database, *American Ancestors*, accessed 9 July 2018.

420   "Massachusetts Marriages, 1695-1910," s.v. "Zebadiah Johnson and Esther Richardson" (marriage "1731"), database, *FamilySearch*, accessed 24 April 2016.

421   "Massachusetts Births and Christenings, 1639-1915," s.v. "Esther Richardson" (birth "1713"), database, *FamilySearch*, accessed 26 April 2016.

422   Esther Johnson, grave marker, West Main Street Cemetery, Shrewsbury, Worcester County, Massachusetts, s.v. "Esther Richardson Johnson" (death "1796", memorial "26087298"), database with digital images, *FindAGrave*, accessed 9 July 2018.

423   Zebadiah Johnson, grave marker, West Main Street Cemetery, Shrewsbury, Worcester County, Massachusetts, s.v. "Zebadiah Johnson" (death "1796", memorial "26087320"), accessed 9 July 2018.

424 Mrs. Ellwood Kimball, "The Solomon Johnson Family," *The New England Historical and Genealogical Register*, Vol 66,   p 238; database, *American Ancestors*, accessed 9 July 2018.

Worcester County, Massachusetts.[425]

2. Esther Johnson, born on June 23, 1734 in Shrewsbury.
3. Seth Johnson, born on February 15, 1736 in Shrewsbury.
4. Israel Johnson, born on September 11, 1737 in Shrewsbury.
5. Solomon Johnson, born on October 13, 1739 in Shrewsbury.
6. Esther Johnson, born on July 20, 1741 in Shrewsbury.
7. Elizabeth Johnson, born on April 11, 1743 in Shrewsbury.
8. Phebe Johnson, born on October 2, 1744 in Shrewsbury.
9. Thomas Johnson, born on July 2, 1746 in Shrewsbury.
10. John Johnson, born on March 19, 1747 in Shrewsbury.
11. Philip Johnson, born on October 19, 1749 in Shrewsbury.
12. Issacher Johnson, born on January 7, 1751 in Shrewsbury.
13. Lemuel Johnson, born on April 7, 1752 in Shrewsbury.
14. Jonah Johnson, born on December 22, 1754 in Shrewsbury.
15. David Johnson, born on February 16, 1756 in Shrewsbury.[426]

[08-194] Constant Merrick and [08-195] Sarah Freeman

Constant Merrick was born about 1701 in Hardwick, Worcester County, Massachusetts to Nathaniel Merrick [09-388] and Alice Freeman [09-389]. He was active in the community, being an assessor for nine years, a deacon in the church, a Captain in the militia, and a Selectman for eleven years. He married a Merrick cousin, Sarah Freeman, and they had at least seven children between around 1728 to around 1740. Sarah Freeman was born on January 26, 1704 in Massachusetts to John Freeman (B11-68m) and Mercy Watson (B11-68f). I don't have the death date for Sarah, but Constant died on March 17, 1792.[427] The children of Constant Merrick and Sarah Freeman are listed below:

1. William Merrick, born on April 22, 1728.
2. Nathaniel Merrick, born on May 22, 1730.
3. Sarah Merrick, born on September 30, 1732 and married Timothy Newton on July 5, 1751.
4. Constant Merrick, born on February 21, 1734 and died before 1740.[428]
5. Ales Mirrick [07-97] (or Merrick), born on August 29, 1737 in Hardwick[429] and married Zebadiah Johnson [07-96] on November 25,

---

425   "Massachusetts Marriages, 1695-1910," s.v. "Zebadiah Johnson" (spouse "Allis Mirick" marriage "1756"), database, *FamilySearch*, accessed 20 April 2016.

426   Mrs. Ellwood Kimball, "The Solomon Johnson Family," *The New England Historical and Genealogical Register*, Vol 66,   p 238; database, *American Ancestors*, accessed 9 July 2018.

427   George Byron Merrick, *Genealogy of the Merrick-Mirick-Myrick Family of Massachusetts: 1636-1902*, (Madison, WI: Tracy, Gibbs & Co, 1902), p 25; PDF e-book, *Internet Archive*, https://archive.org/details/genealogymerric00merrgoog , accessed 9 July 2018.

428   Ibid.

429   "Massachusetts Births and Christenings, 1639-1915," s.v. "Ales Mirrick"

1756 in Hardwick.[430]
6.   Constant Merrick, born on September 13, 1740.
7.   Elizabeth Merrick.[431]

[08-200] Benjamin Carleton and [08-201] Abigail Dalton

Benjamin Carleton [08-200] was born on April 23, 1693 in Bradford, Essex County, Massachusetts to Edward Carleton [09-400] and Elizabeth Kimball [09-401]. Benjamin first married Abigail Dalton [08-201] on February 23, 1721.[432] She was the daughter of Philemon Dalton [09-402] and Abigail Gove [09-403],[433] since she is mentioned as Abigail Carleton in Philemon Dalton's will,[434] and was born on September 2, 1699.[435] Abigail died young on June 29, 1726, and is buried at the Ancient Burial Ground in Bradford.[436] Abigail apparently only had one child with Benjamin Carleton before she died, and the child's name was Dudley Carleton [07-100]. Dudley was born on January 5, 1721/2 and married Abigail Wilson [07-101]. After Abigail Dalton [08-201] died, Benjamin Carleton [08-200] married Elizabeth and had more children with her. Benjamin lived until May 3, 1772.[437]

(birth "1737"), database, *FamilySearch,* accessed 3 May 2016.
430   "Massachusetts Marriages, 1695-1910," s.v. "Zebadiah Johnson" (spouse "Allis Mirick" marriage "1756"), database, *FamilySearch,* accessed 20 April 2016.
431   George Byron Merrick, *Genealogy of the Merrick-Mirick-Myrick Family of Massachusetts: 1636-1902*, (Madison, WI: Tracy, Gibbs & Co, 1902), p 25; PDF e-book, *Internet Archive*, https://archive.org/details/genealogymerric00merrgoog , accessed 9 July 2018.
432   William Richard Cutter, *New England Families: Genealogical and Memorial,* (New York: Lewis Historical Publishing Co, 1913), Vol II: p. 510; PDF e-book, https://archive.org/details/newenglandfamili02cutt accessed 2017.
433   William Henry Gove, *The Gove Book: History and Genealogy of the American Family of Gove and Notes of European Goves*, (Salem, MA: Sydney Perley, 1922), p. 50; PDF e-book, https://archive.org/details/govebookhistoryg00gove/page/50 accessed 22 June 2019.
434   Henry Harrison Metcalf, ed., *Probate Records of the Province of New Hampshire*, (Bristol, NH: R W Musgrove, Printer, 1914), Vol 32: p. 131; PDF e-book, https://archive.org/details/probaterecordsof1914newh/page/n4 accessed 22 June 2019.
435   William Henry Gove, *The Gove Book: History and Genealogy of the American Family of Gove and Notes of European Goves*, (Salem, MA: Sydney Perley, 1922), p. 50; PDF e-book, https://archive.org/details/govebookhistoryg00gove/page/50 accessed 22 June 2019.
436   Abigail Carleton, Ancient Burial Ground, Bradford, Essex County, Massachusetts, s.v. "Abigail Dalton Carleton" (death "1726" memorial "38056585"), database with digital images, *FindAGrave*, accessed 21 June 2019.
437   William Richard Cutter, *New England Families: Genealogical and Memorial,* (New York: Lewis Historical Publishing Co, 1913), Vol I: p. 8; PDF e-book, https://archive.org/details/newenglandfamili01cutt_1 accessed 2017.

[08-202] Joseph Wilson and [08-203] Rebecca Kimball

Joseph Wilson [08-202] was the son of Joseph Wilson [09-404] and Mary Lovejoy [09-405], and was born on June 6, 1677 in Andover, Essex County, Massachusetts. Joseph Wilson [08-202] married first to Mary Richardson on January 25, 1699/1700, and had five children with her.[438] Then Joseph married a younger woman named Rebecca Kimball [08-203] on December 18, 1724 in Bradford, Essex County, Massachusetts.[439] Rebecca Kimball was the daughter of David Kimball [09-406] and Elizabeth Gage [09-407], and was born on August 16, 1703 in Bradford.[440] The children of Joseph Wilson and Rebecca Kimball are listed below:

1. Abigail Wilson [07-101], born on November 25, 1725 in Bradford, and married Dudley Carleton [07-100].
2. Elizabeth Wilson, born on March 20, 1726 in Haverhill, Essex County, Massachusetts.
3. David Wilson, born on April 12, 1729 in Bradford.
4. Phebe Wilson, born on March 12, 1730/1.
5. Rebecca Wilson, born on February 26, 1732/3.[441]

[08-204] David Ayer and [08-205] Hannah Shepard

David Ayer [08-204] was born on May 2, 1714 in Haverhill, Essex County, Massachusetts to Nathaniel Ayer [09-408] and Esther [09-409].[442] [443]   He

---

438   William Richard Cutter, *New England Families: Genealogical and Memorial,* (New York: Lewis Historical Publishing Co, 1914), Vol II: p. 576; PDF e-book, https://archive.org/details/newenglandfamili02cutt_1 accessed 10 July 2018.

439   "Massachusetts, Town Clerk, Vital and Town Records, 1626-2001," "Joseph Wilson and Rebeca Kimball marriage in 1724," Massachusetts, Essex County, Bradford 1670-1796, digital image not indexed, *FamilySearch,* accessed June 2019.

440   Leonard Allison Morrison and Stephen Paschall Sharples, *History of the Kimball Family in America: From 1634 to 1897, and of its Ancestors the Kemballs or Kemboldes of England,* (Boston: Damrell & Upham, 1897), p. 60; PDF e-book, https://archive.org/details/historyofkimball00morr , accessed 14 July 2018.

441   William Richard Cutter, *New England Families: Genealogical and Memorial,* (New York: Lewis Historical Publishing Co, 1914), Vol II: p. 576; PDF e-book, https://archive.org/details/newenglandfamili02cutt_1 accessed 10 July 2018.

442   William Richard Cutter, ed., *New England Families: Genealogical and Memorial,* (New York: Lewis Historical Publishing Co, 1913), Vol I: p. 8; PDF e-book, https://archive.org/details/newenglandfamili01cutt_1 accessed 9 July 2018.

443   Topsfield Historical Society, *Vital Records of Haverhill Massachusetts: to the End of the Year 1849,* (Topsfield, MA: Topsfield Historical Society, 1911), Vol I: p. 16; PDF e-book, https://archive.org/details/vitalrecordsofha00byuhave/page/1 (accessed 25 June 2019).

married Hannah Shepard [08-205] on September 13, 1733 in Haverhill.[444] Hannah was the daughter of John Shepard [09-410] and Hannah Ayer [09-411], and was born on April 9, 1714 in Haverhill.[445] David Ayer died on March 27, 1767 in Haverhill and was buried at the Pentucket Cemetery.[446] The children of David Ayer and Hannah Shepard are listed below:

1. Nathaniel Ayer [07-102], born on February 24, 1734/5 in Haverhill.
2. Hannah Ayer, born on August 16, 1739 in Haverhill and died on September 17, 1754 in Haverhill.
3. Ruth Ayer, born on June 23, 1742 in Haverhill.
4. Abigail Ayer, born on November 24, 1746 in Haverhill.[447]

[08-206] John White and [08-207] Martha Appleton

John White [08-206] was born on September 8, 1707 in Haverhill, Essex County, Massachusetts to John White [09-412] and Lydia Gilman [09-413].[448] The younger John [08-206] married Martha Appleton [08-207] before 1732 in Haverhill.[449] Martha was the daughter of Isaac Appleton [09-414] and Priscilla[450] Baker[451] [09-415]. John White [08-206] died on May 10, 1745 in

---

444   "Massachusetts, Town Clerk, Vital and Town Records, 1626-2001," family group s.v. "David Ayer" (spouse "Hannah Shepard" marriage "1733"), database with digital images, *FamilySearch,* accessed 23 June 2019.

445   Topsfield Historical Society, *Vital Records of Haverhill Massachusetts: to the End of the Year 1849,* (Topsfield, MA: Topsfield Historical Society, 1911), Vol I: p. 272; PDF e-book, https://archive.org/details/vitalrecordsofha00byuhave/page/1 (accessed 25 June 2019).

446   David Ayer, Pentucket Cemetery, Haverhill, Essex County, Massachusetts, s.v. "David Ayer" (death "1767" memorial "51711778"), database with digital images, *FindAGrave,* accessed 25 June 2019.

447   "Massachusetts, Town Clerk, Vital and Town Records, 1626-2001," family group s.v. "David Ayer" (spouse "Hannah Shepard" marriage "1733"), database with digital images, *FamilySearch,* accessed 23 June 2019.

448   Topsfield Historical Society, *Vital Records of Haverhill Massachusetts: to the End of the Year 1849,* (Topsfield, MA: Topsfield Historical Society, 1911), Vol I: p. 311; PDF e-book, https://archive.org/details/vitalrecordsofha00byuhave/page/1 (accessed 25 June 2019).

449   Topsfield Historical Society, *Vital Records of Haverhill Massachusetts: to the End of the Year 1849,* (Topsfield, MA: Topsfield Historical Society, 1911), Vol I: p. 329; PDF e-book, https://archive.org/details/vitalrecordsofha00byuhave/page/1 (accessed 25 June 2019).

450   "Massachusetts Births and Christenings, 1639-1915" s.v. "Martha Appleton" (birth "1708"), database, *FamilySearch,* accessed 25 June 2019.

451   James Savage, *A Genealogical Dictionary of the First Settlers of New England: Showing Three Generations of Those Who Came Before May 1692,* (Boston: Little, Brown and Company, 1860), Vol I: p. 60; PDF e-book, http://archive.org/details/ genealogicaldic01savarich accessed 17 July 2018.

Haverhill, and was said to be in his 38th year at time of death.[452] The children of
John White and Martha Appleton are listed below:
1. John Appleton White, born on September 26, 1732 in Haverhill.
2. Martha White, born on September 11, 1734 in Haverhill.
3. Lydia White [07-103], born on January 24, 1736/7 in Haverhill.
4. Joanna White, born on March 6 1738/9 in Haverhill and died there on
    October 25, 1741.
5. John White, born on December 31, 1740 in Haverhill.
6. Priscilla White, born on August 21, 1743 in Haverhill, and died there
    on September 10, 1807.[453]

[08-208] John Cowdry and [08-209] Hannah Davis

John Cowdry was born after 1710 in Massachusetts to Matthias Cowdrey
[08-416] and Sarah [08-417]. His first marriage was to Abigail, before maybe
1731.[454] Then on May 30, 1744 John married Hannah Davis [08-209] in
Westford, Middlesex County, Massachusetts.[455] Cutter wrote that she was "of
Groton"[456] but there were multiple girls named Hannah or Anna Davis born in
the area around 1710 to 1730, so I could not establish her parents with certainty
through vital records. Davis might not have even been her maiden name. John
Cowdry and Hannah Davis had at least five children between 1745 and 1756,
then John died about 1760 and Hannah died on May 15, 1761.[457] The children
of John Cowdry and Hannah Davis are listed below:
1. Nathaniel Cowdry [07-104], born about 1745 in Westford.
2. Mary Cowdry, born February 2, 1747 in Westford.
3. John Cowdry, born April 11, 1750 in Westford.

---

452   Topsfield Historical Society, *Vital Records of Haverhill Massachusetts: to the
End of the Year 1849*, (Topsfield, MA: Topsfield Historical Society, 1911), Vol II: p.
490; PDF e-book, https://archive.org/details/cu31924099427654/page/n8 accessed 25
June 2019.
453   "Massachusetts, Town Clerk, Vital and Town Records, 1626-2001," family
group s.v. "John White" (spouse "Martha Appleton" marriage "1737"), database with
digital images, *FamilySearch*, accessed 23 June 2019.
454   William Richard Cutter, ed., *Genealogical and Family History of Western
New York*, (New York: Lewis Historical Publishing Company, 1912), Vol III: p 1428;
PDF e-book, https://archive.org/details/genealogicalfami03incutt   accessed
.....9 July 2018.
455   "Massachusetts, Town Clerk, Vital and Town Records, 1626-2001," family
group s.v. "John Cowdry" (spouse "Hannah Davis" (marriage "1744)", database,
FamilySearch, accessed 30 April 2017.
456   William Richard Cutter, *Genealogical and Family History of Western New
York*, (New York: Lewis Historical Publishing Company, 1912), Vol III: p 1428; PDF
e-book, https://archive.org/details/genealogicalfami03incutt   accessed   9 July
2018.
457   Ibid.

4. Jonathan Cowdry, born January 30, 1752 in Westford.
5. David Cowdry, born on February 18, 1756 in Westford.[458]

[08-210] Samuel Parker and [08-211] Anna Tarbell

Samuel Parker was born December 10, 1722 in Billerica, Middlesex County, Massachusetts to John Parker [09-420] and Sarah [09-421]. Samuel married Anna Tarbell probably before 1743, and they had at least six children between 1743/4 and 1752. Anna (or Anne in some sources) was born on April 20, 1716 in Salem, Essex County, Massachusetts to John Tarbell [09-422] and Hannah Flint [09-423].[459] [460] Some, like the Hazen source, give a 17 July 1717 birth date for her,[461] but are probably confused by her christening being on 7 July 1717 in Salem.[462] After Samuel died on November 21, 1752, Anna got married to Nathan Crosby.[463]
1. Samuel Parker, born on February 9, 1743/4 in Billerica.
2. Anne Parker, born on February 7, 1745 in Billerica.
3. Ruth Parker, born on February 27, 1747/8 in Billerica.
4. John Parker, born on August 15, 1750 in Billerica.
5. Jonathan Parker, born on August 15, 1750 in Billerica.
6. Rebecca Parker [07-105], born on May 16, 1752 in Billerica.[464]

[08-212] John Brown and [08-213] Susanna Dutton

John Brown was born on January 22, 1684/5 in Woburn, Middlesex County, Massachusetts to John Browne [09-424] and Elizabeth Polly [09-425].[465] He

---

458   "Massachusetts, Town Clerk, Vital and Town Records, 1626-2001," family group s.v. "John Cowdry" (spouse "Hannah Davis" (marriage "1744)", database, *FamilySearch*, accessed 30 April 2017.
459   Henry A Hazen, *History of Billerica, Massachusetts: With a Genealogical Register,* (Boston: A Williams and Co, 1883) p. 105; PDF e-book, https://archive.org/details/historyofbilleri00hazenhe , accessed 9 July 2018.
460   "Massachusetts Births and Christenings, 1639-1915," s.v. "Anna Tarbell" (christened 1717), database, *FamilySearch,* accessed 21 Dec 2017.
461   Henry A Hazen, *History of Billerica, Massachusetts: With a Genealogical Register,* (Boston: A Williams and Co, 1883) p. 105; PDF e-book, https://archive.org/details/historyofbilleri00hazenhe , accessed 9 July 2018.
462   "Massachusetts Births and Christenings, 1639-1915," s.v. "Anna Tarbell" (christened 1717), database, *FamilySearch,* accessed 21 Dec 2017.
463   Henry A Hazen, *History of Billerica, Massachusetts: With a Genealogical Register,* (Boston: A Williams and Co, 1883) p. 105; PDF e-book, https://archive.org/details/historyofbilleri00hazenhe , accessed 9 July 2018.
464   Ibid.
465   "Massachusetts, Town Clerk, Vital and Town Records, 1626-2001," s.v. "John Browne" (birth 1683, parents Jno Browne and Elizabeth Poll Browne), database with

married Susanna Dutton in 1709 in Haverhill, Essex County, Massachusetts[466] and they had at least seven children between 1716/7 and 1733 in Billerica, Middlesex County, Massachusetts.[467] Susanna Dutton was born on November 4, 1689 in Billerica to Thomas Dutton [09-426] and Rebeckah Brabrooks [09-427].[468] I do not have records for when John Brown and Susanna Dutton died, but it would have been after 1733 when their last known child was born.

1. Thomas Brown, born on February 21, 1716/7 in Billerica and died there on October 14, 1718.
2. Sarah Brown, born on June 26, 1719 in Billerica and married Isaac Foster.
3. Rebecca Brown, born on June 17, 1721 in Billerica.
4. Thomas Brown [07-106], born on February 20, 1723/4 in Billerica.
5. Mary Brown, born on May 1, 1726 in Billerica.
6. Mehitable Brown, born on February 13, 1729/30 in Billerica.
7. David Brown, born on October 10, 1733 in Billerica.[469]

[08-214] Jason Kemp and [08-215] Hannah Meers

Jason Kemp was born November 11, 1725 in Billerica, Middlesex County, Massachusetts to Joseph Kemp [09-428] and Elizabeth Chamberlain [09-429].[470] He married Hannah Meers and had at least eight children between 1748 and 1767 in Billerica.[471] Hannah Meers was born April 21, 1728 in Billerica to Robert Meers [09-430] and Hannah Frost [09-431][472] I do not have death dates for Jason Kemp and Hannah Meers but it would have been after

images, *FamilySearch,* accessed 21 May 2017.

466   "Massachusetts Marriages, 1695-1910," s.v. "John Browne and Susannah Dutton" (marriage 1709), database, *FamilySearch,* accessed 21 May 2017.

467   Henry A Hazen, *History of Billerica, Massachusetts: With a Genealogical Register,* (Boston: A Williams and Co, 1883) p. 19 of Genealogical Register; PDF e-book, https://archive.org/details/historyofbilleri00hazenhe , accessed 9 July 2018.
468   "Massachusetts, Town Clerk, Vital and Town Records, 1626-2001," s.v. "Susannah Dutton" (birth 1689), database with images, *FamilySearch,* accessed 10 July 2018.
469   Henry A Hazen, *History of Billerica, Massachusetts: With a Genealogical Register,* (Boston: A Williams and Co, 1883) p. 19 of Genealogical Register; PDF e-book, https://archive.org/details/historyofbilleri00hazenhe , accessed 9 July 2018.
470   Henry A Hazen, *History of Billerica, Massachusetts: With a Genealogical Register,* (Boston: A Williams and Co, 1883) p. 80 of Genealogical Register; PDF e-book, https://archive.org/details/historyofbilleri00hazenhe , accessed 9 July 2018.
471   "Massachusetts, Town Clerk, Vital and Town Records, 1626-2001," family group s.v. "Lucy Kemp" (birth "1752"), database with images, *FamilySearch,* accessed 18 May 2017.
472   "Massachusetts, Town Clerk, Vital and Town Records, 1626-2001," s.v. "Hannah Meers" (birth "1728"), database with images, *FamilySearch,* accessed 21 June 2017.

1767 when their last child was born.
1. Hannah Kemp, born on April 12, 1748 in Billerica.
2. William Kemp, born on January 10, 1752 in Billerica.
3. Lucy Kemp [07-107], born on February 22, 1752 in Billerica.
4. Thaddeus Kemp, born on January 22, 1757 in Billerica.
5. Levi Kemp, born on June 20, 1760 in Billerica.
6. Elijah Kemp, born on February 4, 1762 in Billerica.
7. Keziah Kemp, born on March 17, 1764 in Billerica.
8. Rhoda Kemp, born on October 3, 1767 in Billerica.[473]

[09-328] Henry Netherton and [09-329] Sarah Tucker

Henry Netherton was born about 1680.[474] Some say that Richard Netherton, who immigrated to Maryland around 1670, was the father of Henry Netherton, but I have not found strong evidence to support that line. Richard was not the only Netherton in the area at the time, because there was also a William Netherton who arrived in Virginia around 1670 and a John Netherton who arrived in Maryland about 1650. There was also a family of Nethertons in the records of Bishopsgate in London at this time period, but I have not found strong evidence to support a connection to them either.

Henry Netherton [09-328] married Sarah Tucker [09-329] about 1706 in Westmoreland County, Virginia. She was the daughter of John Tucker [10-658]. The Fine book gives Sarah's mother as Rebecca, but John Tucker's will says his wife was Mary.[475] Henry Netherton died before November 8, 1716 and Sarah died before 1735.[476]
1. Elizabeth Netherton, born about 1708.
2. Henry Netherton [08-164], born about 1710.
3. Hester Netherton, born about 1712.[477]

[09-330] John Rhodes and [09-331] Ann

There is some disagreement about the lineage of John Rhodes [09-330] and

---

473   "Massachusetts, Town Clerk, Vital and Town Records, 1626-2001," family group s.v. "Lucy Kemp" (birth "1752"), database with images, *FamilySearch,* accessed 18 May 2017.
474   Dorothy Wilson Fine, *A Fine Branch of the Family Tree,* (San Jose, CA: El Camino Real Chapter, DAR, 1991), p. 18.
475   "Virginia, Wills and Probate Records, 1652-1983," s.v. "John Tucker" (will "1718"), database with digital images, *Ancestry.com,* accessed 14 January 2018.
476   Dorothy Wilson Fine, *A Fine Branch of the Family Tree,* (San Jose, CA: El Camino Real Chapter, DAR, 1991), pp. 18-19.
477   Ibid.

Ann [09-331], who were the parents of Sarah Rhodes [08-165].[478]   Some connect them to the Rhodes family that was in Christchurch, Middlesex County, Virginia in the 1600's, but John Rhodes [09-330] was in Stafford County, Virginia. I have not found evidence to support the connection between the Christchurch Rhodes family and the Stafford County Rhodes family, but it is certainly possible. Due to lack of evidence I will stop the Rhodes line here.

[09-336] William Cox and [09-337] Catherine Kinkey

William Cox [09-336] was born about 1692.   In Chester County, Pennsylvania about 1716, he married Catherine Kinkey [09-337].   Catherine was born about 1698 in Cecil County, Maryland to Harmon Kinkey [10-674] and Margery [10-675]. She died between 1760 and 1767, and William died January 20, 1767 in Orange County, North Carolina. They had at least ten children together.[479] William and Catherine were both Quakers and said to be buried at Mill Creek Friends Cemetery in Asheboro, Randolph County, North Carolina, but FindAGrave shows no gravestone for either of them so it is not certain.[480] [481]

1. Harmon Cox, born about 1723 in New Castle County, Delaware and died in 1812 in North Carolina. He married Jane John on October 25, 1745 in Virginia.
2. William Cox, born about 1726 in New Castle County, Delaware and married Juliantha Carr on September 6, 1755.
3. John Cox, born on April 25, 1728 in New Castle County, Delaware and died in 1803.   He married Mary Scarlett on May 25, 1755 in "Londongrove", Pennsylvania.
4. Solomon Cox [08-168], born about 1730 in New Castle County, Delaware and died in 1812 in Ohio. He married Ruth Cox [08-169] in 1755.
5. Thomas Cox, born about 1736 in New Castle County, Delaware and died in 1809 in Ross County, Ohio. He married Sarah Davis on January 24, 1760 in North Carolina.
6. Rebecca Cox, born about 1717 in New Castle County, Delaware and married John Dixon on March 26, 1742 in Delaware.
7. Mary Cox, born about 1719 in New Castle County, Delaware and married James Lindley on may 5, 1753 in Delaware.

---

478   Dorothy Wilson Fine, *A Fine Branch of the Family Tree*, (San Jose, CA: El Camino Real Chapter, DAR, 1991), p. 19.
479   Elizabeth Berry Buffa, "Cox Family Outline," (report, 1977), E, p 18; PDF e-book, https://archive.org/details/coxfamilyoutline00buff accessed 8 July 2018.
480   "FindAGrave," s.v. "William Cox" (death 1767, memorial 115077675), database, *FindAGrave*, accessed 23 April 2017.
481   "FindAGrave," s.v. "Catherine Kinkey Cox" (death 1744, memorial 131766789), database, *FindAGrave*, accessed 23 April 2017.

8. Martha Cox, born about 1721 in New Castle County, Delaware, and married William Ferrell on July 26, 1744 in Chester County, Pennsylvania.
9. Margery Cox, born about 1724 in New Castle County, Delaware and married Isaac Nichols on March 26, 1742 in Delaware.
10. Catherine Cox, born about 1732 in New Castle County, Delaware and married Eleazor Hunt.[482]

[09-338] John Cox and [09-339] Mary

John Cox was born in England about 1688-90 and married Mary in 1713. They moved around occasionally. Between 1722 and 1735 they were in "London Grove" in Chester County, Pennsylvania (possibly Linden Grove?). From 1736 to 1754 they were in Huntingdon, York County, Pennsylvania, and after 1755 they were in Randolph County, North Carolina. They had at least 11 children[483] who are listed below:

1. John Cox, born about 1714 and married Mary Harlan on August 9, 1735.
2. Sarah Cox, born about 1721 and married Nicholas Wierman on August 24, 1745.
3. Ann Cox, who married William Ruddock on August 23, 1746.
4. Samuel Cox, born about 1727 and married Hannah Wierman on August 22, 1747.
5. William Cox, who married Naomi Garretson about 1748.
6. Benjamin Cox, who married Martha Garretson about 1751 and died in 1817.
7. Hannah Cox, who married Daniel Winter about 1752.
8. Amy Cox, born on September 27, 1729 and married William Wierman on June 28, 1753.
9. Ruth Cox [08-169], who married Solomon Cox [08-168] about 1755.
10. Thomas Cox, who married Martha Jenkins about 1757 and died in 1771.
11. Solomon Cox, born between about 1735 and 1738, and married Naomi Hussey about 1759 or 1760. He died in 1844.[484]

---

482   Elizabeth Berry Buffa, "Cox Family Outline," (report, 1977), E, p 18; PDF e-book, https://archive.org/details/coxfamilyoutline00buff accessed 8 July 2018.
483   Elizabeth Berry Buffa, "Cox Family Outline," (report, 1977), A; p 1; PDF e-book, https://archive.org/details/coxfamilyoutline00buff accessed 8 July 2018.
484   Ibid.

[09-384] Daniel Johnson and [09-385] Dorothy Lambe

Daniel Johnson [09-384] was born on April 5, 1675 in Marlborough, Middlesex County, Massachusetts to John Johnson [10-768] and Deborah Ward [10-769].[485] [486] He married Dorothy Lambe [09-385] on December 23, 1697 in Framingham, Middlesex County, Massachusetts[487] and they had at least five children together between 1698 and 1709. Dorothy was the daughter of Joshua Lambe [10-770] and Mary Alcock [10-771] and was born on June 8, 1679 in Roxbury, Suffolk County, Massachusetts.[488] Daniel Johnson made a will dated December 11, 1721 and died in 1722.[489]

1. Solomon Johnson, born on October 13, 1698.
2. Deborah Johnson, born on March 8, 1701.
3. Martha Johnson, born on October 6, 1702.
4. Zebadiah Johnson [08-192], born on April 28, 1704 in Marlborough.
5. Daniel Johnson, born on August 23, 1709.[490]

[09-386] Thomas Richardson and [09-387] Elizabeth Green

Thomas Richardson [09-386] was born on April 15, 1687 in Woburn, Middlesex County, Massachusetts to Nathaniel Richardson [10-772] and Mary [10-773].[491] He married Elizabeth Green [09-387] in Malden, Middlesex County, Massachusetts in 1712 and they had at least eight children together. Elizabeth was the daughter of Samuel Green [10-774] and Elizabeth Upham [10-775] and was born on April 4, 1693 in Malden.[492] [493] Around 1717,

---

485 Mrs. Ellwood Kimball, "The Solomon Johnson Family," *The New England Historical and Genealogical Register*, Vol 66, p 236; database, *American Ancestors*, accessed 9 July 2018.

486 "Massachusetts Births and Christenings, 1639-1915," s.v. "Daniel Johnson" ("birth 1675"), database, *FamilySearch,* accessed 26 April 2016.

487 "Massachusetts, Town Clerk, Vital and Town Records, 1626-2001," s.v. "Daniel Johnson" (spouse "Dorothia Lamb" marriage "1697"), database with images, *FamilySearch,* accessed 3 May 2016.

488 "Massachusetts Births and Christenings, 1639-1915," s.v. "Dorothy Lambe" (birth 1679), database, *FamilySearch,* accessed 5 May 2016.

489 Mrs. Ellwood Kimball, "The Solomon Johnson Family," *The New England Historical and Genealogical Register*, Vol 66, p 236; database, *American Ancestors*, accessed 9 July 2018.

490 Ibid., Vol 66: pp. 236-38.

491 Massachusetts, Town Clerk, Vital and Town Records, 1626-2001," s.v. "Thomas Richardson" (born 1687), database with images, *FamilySearch,* accessed 8 July 2017.

492 John Adams Vinton, *The Richardson Memorial: Comprising a Full History and Genealogy of the Posterity of the Three Brothers,* (Portland, Maine: Brown Thurston and Co, 1876), p. 521; PDF e-book, https://archive.org/details/richardsonmemori00vint , accessed 10 July 2018.

493 Samuel S. Greene, *A Genealogical Sketch of the Descendants of Thomas*

Thomas and Elizabeth moved to Leicester, Worcester County, Massachusetts where in 1729 Thomas was assessed for 300 acres of land. Elizabeth died after 1736 and Thomas remarried to a lady named Jane.[494]   The children of Thomas Richardson and Elizabeth Green are listed below:

1. Esther Richardson [08-193], who was born October 8, 1713 in Malden, and died on May 5, 1796. She married Zebadiah Johnson [08-192].
2. Thomas Richardson, born on July 22, 1716 in Malden, and married Hannah Smith.
3. Elizabeth Richardson, born in 1718 in Leicester, and died on June 21, 1780. She married first to Jonathan Lamb, and then to Ms. Nichols.
4. Samuel Richardson, born in 1722 in Leicester.
5. James Richardson, born in 1723 in Leicester, and married Levinah Johnson.
6. Phillip Richardson, born in 1725 in Leicester. He first married Catherine Briggs, and then Esther Webster.
7. Mary Richardson, born in 1729 in Leicester.
8. Rebecca Richardson, born in 1731 in Leicester, and married James Smith.[495]

[09-388] Nathaniel Merrick and [09-389] Alice Freeman

Nathaniel Merrick [09-388] was born in 1675 in Eastham, Barnstable County, Massachusetts to William Merrick [10-776] and Abigail Hopkins [10-777]. Nathaniel married Alice Freeman [09-389] and they had at least ten children together. Alice Freeman was the daughter of Samuel Freeman [10-778] and Mercy Southworth [10-779]. Nathaniel Merrick was a Captain in the Colonial militia and died November 13, 1743 in Hardwick, Worcester County, Massachusetts.[496] The children of Nathaniel Merrick and Alice Freeman are listed below:

1. William Merrick.
2. Gideon Merrick.
3. Constant Merrick [08-194], born about 1701, and married Sarah Freeman [08-195].
4. Benjamin Merrick, born on March 20, 1717/8 and married Elizabeth

Green of Malden, Mass., (Boston: Henry W. Dutton & Son, 1858), pp. 12-13; PDF e-book, https://archive.org/details/genealogicalsket00gree , accessed 10 July 2018.
494   John Adams Vinton, *The Richardson Memorial: Comprising a Full History and Genealogy of the Posterity of the Three Brothers,* (Portland, Maine: Brown Thurston and Co, 1876), p. 521; PDF e-book, https://archive.org/details/richardsonmemori00vint , accessed 10 July 2018.
495   Ibid., p. 522.
496   George Byron Merrick, *Genealogy of the Merrick-Mirick-Myrick Family of Massachusetts: 1636-1902,* (Madison, WI: Tracy, Gibbs & Co, 1902), p 19; PDF e-book, *Internet Archive,* https://archive.org/details/genealogymerric00merrgoog , accessed 9 July 2018.

Davis in 1738.
5. Hannah Merrick, who married John Snow.
6. Mercy Merrick, who married Ebenezer King.
7. Ruth Merrick, who married Thomas Hinckley.
8. Priscilla Merrick, who married Elisha Cobb.
9. Alice Merrick, who married Capt Benjamin Ruggles on October 19, 1736.
10. Sarah Merrick, born on July 5, 1720 and married Abner Lee of New Rutland in October 1744.[497]

[09-390] John Freeman and [09-391] Mercy Watson

John Freeman [09-390] was born in July 1678 in Eastham, Barnstable County, Massachusetts to John Freeman [10-780] and Sarah Merrick [10-781]. John was in Harwich, Barnstable County, Massachusetts on October 17, 1700 and was one of the original members of the church in Harwich. About 1701 he married Mercy Watson [09-391] and they had at least eleven children.[498] Mercy Watson was born in October 1683 in Plymouth, Plymouth County, Massachusetts to Elkanah Watson [10-782] and Marcy Hedge [10-783].[499] [500] After her marriage to John Freeman, Mercy [09-391] was admitted to the Harwich church on September 14, 1701. In 1728 the Harwich church dismissed John and Mercy to the Rochester church and that is the last I could find of them.[501] The children of John Freeman and Mercy Watson are listed below:
1. Elkanah Freeman, born on October 28, 1702 in Harwich and died on January 21, 1713/4.
2. Sarah Freeman [09-195], born on January 26, 1704.
3. Mercy Freeman, born on April 24, 1707 in Harwich.
4. John Freeman, born on August 3, 1709 in Harwich and died on January 24, 1804. He married Joanna Rickett on January 29, 1730/1.
5. Phebe Freeman, born on November 28, 1711.

---

497   Ibid., p. 20.
498   William Richard Cutter, ed., *New England Families: Genealogical and Memorial*, (New York: Lewis Historical Publishing Company, 1914), Vol II: p. 854; PDF e-book, https://archive.org/details/newenglandfamili02cutt_1 accessed 10 July 2018.
499   "Massachusetts Births and Christenings, 1639-1915," s.v. "Mercy Watson" (birth 1683) database, *FamilySearch*, accessed, 17 Dec 2017.
500   Henry Cole Quinby, ed., "The Watsons," *New England Family History*, Vol III: p 469; PDF e-book, https://archive.org/details/newenglandfamily03quin accessed 10 July 2018.
501   William Richard Cutter, ed., *New England Families: Genealogical and Memorial*, (New York: Lewis Historical Publishing Company, 1914), Vol II: p. 854; PDF e-book, https://archive.org/details/newenglandfamili02cutt_1 accessed 10 July 2018.

6. Thankful Freeman, born on October 6, 1714.
7. Elkanah Freeman, born on February 6, 1716/7.
8. Mary Freeman, born on October 13, 1719.
9. Eli Freeman, born on April 27, 1722.
10. Elisha Freeman, born on May 21, 1724.
11. Hannah Freeman, christened on January 17, 1728 in Harwich.[502]

[09-400] Edward Carleton and [09-401] Elizabeth Kimball

Edward Carleton [09-400] was born on March 22, 1665 in Bradford, Essex County, Massachusetts (which is now Haverhill, Massachusetts) to John Carleton [10-800] and Hannah Jewett [10-801].[503] Edward married Elizabeth Kimball [09-401] before 1699 in what is now Haverhill,[504] and they had at least six children between 1691 and 1707. Elizabeth was born July 24, 1669 in Bradford to Benjamin Kimball [10-802] and Mercy Hazeltine [10-803]. Edward Carleton died on August 29, 1708 in Bradford and Elizabeth died on August 24, 1727, also in Bradford.[505] They are both buried at the Ancient Burial Ground in Bradford.[506] [507] The children of Edward Carleton and Elizabeth Kimball are listed below:

1. Edward Carleton, born on February 20, 1691 in Bradford. He married first Hannah Kimball on June 13, 1734 and second Abiah Clement on July 2, 1734.
2. Benjamin Carleton [08-200], born on April 23, 1693 in Bradford.[508] He

---

502   Ibid.
503   William Richard Cutter, ed., *New England Families: Genealogical and Memorial,* (New York: Lewis Historical Publishing Co, 1913), Vol II: p 509; PDF e-book, https://play.google.com/store/books/details?id=ofcsAAAAYAAJ&rdid=book-ofcsAAAAYAAJ&rdot=1 accessed 9 July 2018.
504   Topsfield Historical Society, *Vital Records of Haverhill, Massachusetts: to the End of the Year 1849,* (Topsfield, MA: Topsfield Historical Society, 1911); PDF e-book, https://archive.org/details/cu31924099427654/page/n8 accessed 25 June 2019.
505   William Richard Cutter, ed., *New England Families: Genealogical and Memorial,* (New York: Lewis Historical Publishing Co, 1913), Vol II: p 510; PDF e-book, https://play.google.com/store/books/details?id=ofcsAAAAYAAJ&rdid=book-ofcsAAAAYAAJ&rdot=1 accessed 9 July 2018.
506   Edward Carleton, gravestone, Ancient Burial Ground, Bradford, Essex County, Massachusetts, s.v. "Edward Carleton" (death "1708" memorial "18149370"), database with digital images, *FindAGrave,* accessed 27 June 2019.
507   Elisabeth Carlton, gravestone, Ancient Burial Ground, Bradford, Essex County, Massachusetts, s.v. "Elisabeth Kimball Carlton" (death "1727" memorial "18149371"), database with digital images, *FindAGrave,* accessed 27 June 2019.
508   William Richard Cutter, ed., *New England Families: Genealogical and Memorial,* (New York: Lewis Historical Publishing Co, 1913), Vol II: p 510; PDF e-book, https://play.google.com/store/books/details?id=ofcsAAAAYAAJ&rdid=book-ofcsAAAAYAAJ&rdot=1 accessed 9 July 2018.

married first to Abigail Dalton on February 23, 1721,[509] and second to Elizabeth.[510]

3. Nehemiah Carleton, born April 15, 1695 in Bradford.
4. Nathaniel Carleton, born on June 20, 1697 in Bradford.
5. Ebenezer Carleton, born on December 22, 1704 in Bradford.
6. Mehitable Carleton, born on March 28, 1707 in Bradford.[511]

[09-402] Philemon Dalton and [09-403] Abigail Gove

Philemon Dalton [09-402] was born on December 15, 1664 in Hampton, Rockingham County, New Hampshire to Samuel Dalton [10-804] and Mehitable[512] [513] [10-805]. He married Abigail Gove [09-403] on September 25, 1690 in Hampton.[514] Although the cursive of the image of the transcription of the marriage record is not clear on whether the "v" in Gove is really a "r" or a "v", a search of the *FamilySearch* database does not show an Abigail Gore being born in New Hampshire in the 1600's and it seems well established that Abigail was a Gove. So Abigail Gove [09-403] was born on April 17, 1670 in Hampton to Edward Gove [10-806] and and Hannah[515] Partridge[516] [10-807].

Philemon was a Deacon and died on April 5, 1721. He was buried at the

---

509   William Henry Gove, *The Gove Book: History and Genealogy of the American Family of Gove and Notes of European Goves*, (Salem, MA: Sydney Perley, 1922) p. 50; PDF e-book, https://archive.org/details/govebookhistoryg00gove/page/50 accessed 22 June 2019.

510   William Richard Cutter, ed., *New England Families: Genealogical and Memorial*, (New York: Lewis Historical Publishing Co, 1913), Vol I: p. 8; PDF e-book, https://archive.org/details/newenglandfamili01cutt_1 accessed 2017.

511   William Richard Cutter, ed., *New England Families: Genealogical and Memorial*, (New York: Lewis Historical Publishing Co, 1913), Vol II: p 510; PDF e-book, https://play.google.com/store/books/details?id=ofcsAAAAYAAJ&rdid=book-ofcsAAAAYAAJ&rdot=1 accessed 9 July 2018.

512   "New Hampshire Birth Records, Early to 1900," s.v. "Philemon Dalton" (birth "1664"), database with digital images, *FamilySearch*, accessed 28 June 2019.

513   William Henry Gove, *The Gove Book: History and Genealogy of the American Family of Gove and Notes of European Goves*, (Salem, MA: Sydney Perley, 1922) p. 50; PDF e-book, https://archive.org/details/govebookhistoryg00gove/page/50 accessed 22 June 2019.

514   "New Hampshire Marriage Records, 1637-1947," s.v. "Philemon Dalton" (spouse "Abigail Gore" marriage "1690"), database with digital images, *FamilySearch*, accessed 28 June 2019.

515   "New Hampshire Birth Records, Early to 1900," s.v. "Abigail Gove" (birth "1670"), database with digital images, *FamilySearch*, accessed 28 June 2019.

516   William Henry Gove, *The Gove Book: History and Genealogy of the American Family of Gove and Notes of European Goves*, (Salem, MA: Sydney Perley, 1922) p. 50; PDF e-book, https://archive.org/details/govebookhistoryg00gove/page/50 accessed 22 June 2019.

Pine Grove Cemetery in Hampton.[517]   Abigail married again to Deacon Benjamin Sanborn on November 1724, and a third time to James Prescott on June 17, 1746. She died on May 8, 1751 and is also buried at the Pine Grove Cemetery in Hampton.[518]   The children of Philemon Dalton [09-402] and Abigail Gove [09-403] are listed below:

1. Hannah Dalton, who was baptized on June 27, 1697 and married John Sargent.
2. Timothy Dalton, who was baptized on June 27, 1697 and married Sarah Mason on February 2, 1721.
3. Samuel Dalton, who was born on July 22, 1694 and died on December 26, 1755. He married Mary Leavitt on April 28, 1720.
4. Philemon Dalton, who was born on August 16, 1697 and married Bethiah Bridges of Andover on July 15, 1720.
5. Abigail Dalton [08-201], who was born on September 2, 1699 in Hampton and married Benjamin Carleton [08-200] on February 23, 1721.
6. John Dalton, born on February 10, 1702 and died on December 10, 1717.
7. Sarah Dalton, born on April 19, 1704 and died in July 1770. She married Joseph Towle.
8. Jeremiah Dalton, born on May 25, 1707 and died on December 17, 1707.
9. Michael Dalton, born on February 22, 1709.
10. Mehitable Dalton, born on September 25, 1713 and married Benjamin Prescott of Hampton on October 16, 1728.[519]

[09-404] Joseph Wilson and [09-405] Mary Lovejoy

Joseph Wilson [09-404] was born on November 10, 1643 in Boston, Suffolk County, Massachusetts to William Wilson [10-808] and Patience[520] Grindall [10-809]. (The maiden name of Patience will be explained in her own section.) As a child, he was apprenticed to Thomas Faxon in Braintree, Norfolk County,

---

517   Philemon Dalton gravestone, Pine Grove Cemetery, Hampton, Rockingham County, New Hampshire, s.v."Deacon Philemon Dalton" (death "1721" memorial "7376033"), database with digital images, *FindAGrave*, accessed 28 June 2019.
518   Abigail Prescott gravestone, Pine Grove Cemetery, Hampton, Rockingham County, New Hampshire, s.v. "Abigail Gove Prescott" (death "1751" memorial "7376053") database with digital images, *FindAGrave*, accessed 28 June 2019.
519   William Henry Gove, *The Gove Book: History and Genealogy of the American Family of Gove and Notes of European Goves*, (Salem, MA: Sydney Perley, 1922) p. 50; PDF e-book, https://archive.org/details/govebookhistoryg00gove/page/50 accessed 22 June 2019.
520   "Massachusetts, Town Clerk, Vital and Town Records, 1626-2001." s.v. "Joseph Wilson" (birth "1643" place "Boston"), database with digital images, *FamilySearch*, accessed 28 June 2019.

Massachusetts, but Patience [10-809] sued to have the court release him from that apprenticeship.[521] Joseph married first to Mary Lovejoy [09-405] on July 4, 1670 in Andover, Essex County, Massachusetts.[522]

Mary Lovejoy [09-405] was born on April 11, 1652 in Andover, and was the daughter of John Lovejoy [10-810] and Mary[523] Osgood[524] [10-811]. The children of Joseph Wilson and Mary Lovejoy are listed below:
1. Mary Wilson, born on September 29, 1673. (Probably died before 1675)
2. Mary Wilson, born on February 26, 1674/5.
3. Joseph Wilson [08-202], born on June 6, 1677 and married first to Mary Richardson and second to Rebecah Kimball [08-203].

Mary Lovejoy died almost two weeks after giving birth to Joseph [08-202], dying on June 18, 1677 in Andover. Joseph Wilson [09-404] then married Sarah Lord on April 24, 1678 and had three more children with Sarah. Sarah was imprisoned for witchcraft during the witch-hunts in Massachusetts but was released after they ended. Joseph Wilson [09-404] died on April 2, 1718 in Haverhill, which is also in Essex County, Massachusetts.[525]

[09-406] David Kimball and [09-407] Elizabeth Gage

David Kimball [09-406] was born on July 26, 1671 in Merrimack Village, Essex County, Massachusetts to Benjamin Kimball [10-802] and Mercy Hazeltine [10-803].[526] He married Elizabeth Gage [09-407] about 1694 in Amesbury, Essex County, Massachusetts,[527] although the year is probably an

---

521   William Richard Cutter, ed., *New England Families: Genealogical and Memorial,* (New York: Lewis Historical Publishing Co, 1914), Vol II: p. 576; PDF e-book, https://archive.org/details/newenglandfamili02cutt_1 accessed 10 July 2018.
522   "Massachusetts, Town Clerk, Vital and Town Records, 1626-2001." s.v. "Joseph Wilson" (spouse "Mary Lovejoy" marriage "1670" place "Andover"), database with digital images, *FamilySearch,* accessed 28 June 2019.
523   "Massachusetts, Town Clerk, Vital and Town Records, 1626-2001," Essex County, Andover, Births, marriages, deaths 1651-1700, image 3 of 65, digital images not indexed, *FamilySearch,* accessed 28 June 2019.
524   Lucius Manlius Boltwood, "Marriages in the Town of Andover, MS: from 1647-1700," *The New England Historical and Genealogical Register* Vol 3: p. 65; database with digital images, *American Ancestors,* accessed 30 June 2019.
525   William Richard Cutter, ed., *New England Families: Genealogical and Memorial,* (New York: Lewis Historical Publishing Co, 1914), Vol II: p. 576; PDF e-book, https://archive.org/details/newenglandfamili02cutt_1 accessed 10 July 2018.
526   "Massachusetts Births and Christenings," s.v. David Kimball (birth "1671" place "Merrimack Village"), database with digital images, *FamilySearch,* accessed 4 July 2019.
527   Arthur E Gage, *Some Descendants of John Gage of Ipswich, Mass.,* (Boston: New England Historic Genealogical Company, 1908), p. 4; PDF e-book, https://archive.org/details/somedescendantso00gage accessed May 2017.

estimation due to the original document not having the year written next to their marriage.[528] Elizabeth Gage was born on March 12, 1674/5 in Bradford, Essex County, Massachusetts to Samuel Gage [10-814] and Faith Stickney [10-815].[529] The children of David Kimball and Elizabeth Gage are listed below:

1. Hannah Kimball, born on September 15, 1695 in Bradford and died 18 February 1695/6.
2. Samuel Kimball, born on January 14, 1697/8 in Bradford and died February 14, 1760 in Bradford.
3. Hannah Kimball, born on March 10, 1698 in Bradford and married Jonathan Chadwick on October 25, 1722.
4. David Kimball, born in 1700 in Bradford.
5. Rebecah Kimball [08-203], born August 16, 1703 in Bradford and married Joseph Wilson [08-202] on December 18, 1724 in Bradford.
6. A son with no name, born on November 7, 1705 in Bradford and died November 11, 1705.
7. Jeremiah Kimball, born on October 15, 1707 in Bradford and died in May 1764.
8. Aaron Kimball, born on June 7, 1710 in Haverhill, Essex County, Massachusetts and died on July 30, 1760.
9. Elizabeth Kimball, born on January 14, 1712/3 in Bradford.
10. Abraham Kimball, born on February 18, 1715 in Bradford and died November 26, 1782. He married Judith Hall on December 30, 1736.[530]

Elizabeth [09-407] died before 1717 when David Kimball [09-406] married Ruth. David died on June 14, 1743 in Bradford,[531] and is buried at the Ancient Burial Ground in Bradford.[532]

[09-408] Nathaniel Ayer and [09-409] Esther

Nathaniel Ayer [09-408] was born on November 15, 1676 in Haverhill, Essex County, Massachusetts to Nathaniel Ayer [10-816] and Tamesin Turloar

---

528   "Massachusetts, Town Clerk, Vital and Town Records, 1626-2001," s.v. David Kimball (spouse "Elizabeth Gage" marriage "1690"), database with digital images, *FamilySearch*, accessed 4 July 2019.
529   Arthur E Gage, *Some Descendants of John Gage of Ipswich, Mass.*, (Boston: New England Historic Genealogical Company, 1908), p. 4; PDF e-book, https://archive.org/details/somedescendantso00gage accessed May 2017.
530   Leonard Allison Morrison and Stephen Paschall Sharples, *History of the Kimball Family in America: From 1634 to 1897, and of its Ancestors the Kemballs or Kemboldes of England*, (Boston: Damrell & Upham, 1897), p. 60; PDF e-book, https://archive.org/details/historyofkimball00morr accessed 14 July 2018.
531   Ibid.
532   David Kimball, gravestone, Ancient Burial Ground, Bradford, Essex County, Massachusetts, s.v. "David Kimball" (death "1743" memorial "37886379"), database with digital images, *FindAGrave*, accessed 4 July 2019.

[10-817].[533] However, Cutter gave November 5 as the birthday and spelled the mother's name as Tamsen Thurlow,[534] which appears to be a mistake. Nathaniel Ayer [09-408] married "the wid. Esther Palmer" [09-409] before 1707,[535] who some say is an Esther Wallingford, widow of Joseph Palmer. There are records of an Hester who had children with Joseph Palmer, but I was not able to find records to support any maiden name or ancestry of the widow Esther Palmer [09-409] so her ancestry should not be continued at this time. Esther [09-409] died on August 12, 1743,[536] and Nathaniel Ayer [09-408] died on October 5, 1754 and is buried at Pentucket Cemetery in Haverhill.[537] Their children are listed below:

1. Susannah Ayer, born on August 11, 1707 in Haverhill.
2. Hannah Ayer, born January 24, 1709/10 in Haverhill.
3. David Ayer [08-204], born May 2, 1714 in Haverhill.
4. Sarah Ayer, born on November 23, 1716 in Haverhill.
5. Hannah Ayer, baptized July 3, 1720 in Haverhill.[538]

[09-410] John Shepard and [09-411] Hannah Ayer

John Shepard [09-410] was born on April 21, 1682 in Haverhill, Essex County, Massachusetts to Samuel Shepard [10-820] and Mary[539] Page [10-821]. John Shepard [09-410] married Hannah Ayer [09-411] on February 15, 1704/5 in Haverhill.[540] [541] Hannah Ayer [09-411] was the daughter of Timothy Ayer

---

533   Topsfield Historical Society, *Vital Records of Haverhill Massachusetts: to the End of the Year 1849*, (Topsfield, MA: Topsfield Historical Society, 1911), Vol I: p. 20; PDF e-book, https://archive.org/details/vitalrecordsofha00byuhave/page/1 accessed 25 June 2019.
534   William Richard Cutter, ed., *New England Families: Genealogical and Memorial,* (New York: Lewis Historical Publishing Co, 1913), Vol I: p. 8; PDF e-book, https://archive.org/details/newenglandfamili01cutt_1 accessed 2017.
535   Topsfield Historical Society, *Vital Records of Haverhill Massachusetts: to the End of the Year 1849*, (Topsfield, MA: Topsfield Historical Society, 1911), Vol II: p. 18; PDF e-book, https://archive.org/details/cu31924099427654/page/n8 accessed 25 June 2019.
536   Ibid., Vol II: p. 348.
537   Nathaniel Ayer gravestone, Pentucket Cemetery, Haverhill, Essex County, Massachusetts, s.v. "Nathaniel Ayer" (death "1754" memorial "51715153"), database with digital images, *FindAGrave*, accessed 25 June 2019.
538   Topsfield Historical Society, *Vital Records of Haverhill Massachusetts: to the End of the Year 1849*, (Topsfield, MA: Topsfield Historical Society, 1911), Vol I: pp. 16-20; PDF e-book, https://archive.org/details/vitalrecordsofha00byuhave/page/1 accessed 25 June 2019.
539   Ibid., Vol I: p. 272.
540   "Ayer Genealogy," *The Essex Antiquarian*, Vol. 4: p. 148; database with digital images, *American Ancestors*, accessed 4 July 2019.
541   Topsfield Historical Society, *Vital Records of Haverhill Massachusetts: to the End of the Year 1849*, (Topsfield, MA: Topsfield Historical Society, 1911), Vol II: p.

and [10-822] and Ruth Johnson [10-823], and was born on December 7, 1683 in Haverhill. Hannah died before 1732.[542] The children of John Shepard and Hannah Ayer are listed below:

1. Timothy Shepard, born on November 26, 1706 in Haverhill.
2. Elizabeth Shepard, born on April 5, 1709 in Haverhill.
3. Samuel Shepard, born on September 14, 1711 in Haverhill.
4. Hannah Shepard [08-205], born on April 9, 1714 in Haverhill.[543]

[09-412] John White and [09-413] Lydia Gilman

John White [09-412] was born on March 8, 1663/4 in Haverhill, Essex County, Massachusetts to John White [10-824] and Hannah French [10-825].[544] John White [09-412] was a Deacon and active in the Haverhill community. He was on the board of town officers in 1692, town clerk in 1694, and also owned and commanded a garrison for the defense of the town in 1694. He was Proprietor's Clerk in Haverhill in 1701, and represented Haverhill in the General Court for a total of 8 years. John White [09-412] died on November 20, 1727,[545] and was buried at the Pentucket Cemetery in Haverhill.[546]

John White [09-412] married Lydia Gilman [09-413] on October 24, 1687 in Haverhill.[547] Lydia Gilman was born on December 12, 1668 to John Gilman [10-826] and Elizabeth Treworthy [10-827].[548] (There are multiple spellings of Treworthy, by the way.) The children of John White [09-412] and Lydia

---

284; PDF e-book, https://archive.org/details/cu31924099427654/page/n8 accessed 25 June 2019.

542　"Ayer Genealogy," *The Essex Antiquarian*, Vol. 4: pp. 147-148; database with digital images, *American Ancestors*, accessed 4 July 2019.

543　Topsfield Historical Society, *Vital Records of Haverhill Massachusetts: to the End of the Year 1849*, (Topsfield, MA: Topsfield Historical Society, 1911), Vol I: p. 272; PDF e-book, https://archive.org/details/vitalrecordsofha00byuhave/page/1 accessed 25 June 2019.

544　Ibid, Vol I: p. 311.

545　Daniel Appleton White and Annie Frances Richards, *The Descendants of William White, of Haverhill, Mass.*, (Boston: American Printing and Engraving Company, 1889) pp. 9-11; PDF e-book, https://archive.org/details/descendantswill00richgoog/page/n10 accessed 23 June 2019.

546　John White gravestone, Pentucket Cemetery, Haverhill, Essex County, Massachusetts, s.v. "John White, II" (death "1727" memorial "65747119"), database with digital images, *FindAGrave*, accessed 10 July 2019.

547　Topsfield Historical Society, *Vital Records of Haverhill Massachusetts: to the End of the Year 1849*, (Topsfield, MA: Topsfield Historical Society, 1911), Vol II: p. 328; PDF e-book, https://archive.org/details/cu31924099427654/page/n8 accessed 25 June 2019.

548　James Savage, *A Genealogical Dictionary of the First Settlers of New England: Showing Three Generations of Those Who Came Before May 1692*, (Boston: Little, Brown and Company, 1860), Vol II: p. 257; PDF e-book, http://archive.org/details/genealogicaldic02savarich accessed 17 July 2018.

Gilman [09-413] are listed below:

1. John White, born on September 11, 1688 and died on August 19, 1705.
2. Mary White, born on June 24, 1690 and died in 1777. She married James Ayer of Haverhill on May 10, 1711.
3. Hannah White, born in 1691 and died in 1775. She married Rev. Samuel Phillips of Andover on January 17, 1711/2.
4. William White, born on January 18, 1693/4 and died on December 11, 1737. He married Sarah Phillips on June 12, 1716.
5. Samuel White, born on December 23, 1695 and died on February 1, 1777. He married Ruth Phillips.
6. Nicholas White, born on December 4, 1698 and died in September 1772 in Plaistow, which is now in Rockingham County, New Hampshire. He married Hannah, the daughter of Samuel Ayers.
7. Timothy White, born on November 13, 1700 and died in 1765 in Haverhill. He married Susanna Gardner of Nantucket.
8. Elizabeth White, born on November 16, 1702 and died in January 1776. She married Rev. Amos Main, of Rochester, New Hampshire.
9. James White, born on April 16, 1705 and died on May 1, 1788 in Plaistow. He married first to Abigail Peaslee, and second to Sarah Bailey.
10. John White [08-206], born on September 8, 1707 and died on May 10, 1745. He married Martha Appleton [08-207] before 1732.
11. Joseph White, born on October 21, 1709 and died on April 4, 1713.
12. Abigail White, born on October 21, 1709 and died in December 1792 in Haverhill. She married Moses Hazen on March 5, 1727/8.
13. Lydia White, born on September 11, 1711. She married first to Nathaniel Peaslee on November 16, 1727, and second to a Mr. Flint of Salem.
14. Joanna White, born on March 31, 1714 and died on November 2, 1714.[549]

[09-414] Isaac Appleton and [09-415] Priscilla Baker

Isaac Appleton [09-414] was born in 1664 in Ipswich, Essex County, Massachusetts to Samuel Appleton [10-828] and Mary Oliver [10-829]. Isaac held the title of Major and lived in Ipswich. Maj. Isaac Appleton married Priscilla Baker [09-415],[550] who was born about 1674 based on her age at

---

549   Daniel Appleton White and Annie Frances Richards, *The Descendants of William White, of Haverhill, Mass.*, (Boston: American Printing and Engraving Company, 1889) pp. 11-12; PDF e-book, https://archive.org/details/descendantswill00richgoog/page/n10 accessed 23 June 2019.
550   "Appleton Genealogy," *The Essex Antiquarian*, Vol. 4: p. 3; database with digital images, *American Ancestors*, accessed 10 July 2019.

death.[551] Priscilla was the daughter of Thomas Baker [10-830] of Topsfield[552] and Priscilla Symonds [10-831][553] and was born on December 8, 1674 in Topsfield.[554] Priscilla Baker [09-415] died on May 26, 1731 in Ipswich,[555] and was buried at the Old Burying Ground in Ipswich.[556] Maj. Isaac Appleton died in Ipswich on May 22, 1747,[557] and was also buried at the Old Burying Ground in Ipswich.[558] The children of Isaac Appleton and Priscilla Baker are listed below:

1. Priscilla Appleton, born on March 16, 1697. She married first to Thomas Burnham, and then on May 23, 1734 to Arthur Abbot. She died after June 1774.
2. Isaac Appleton, born on March 21, 1699 in Ipswich and died on July 30, 1700.
3. Mary Appleton, born on October 1, 1701 in Ipswich and married William Osgood of Andover on January 6, 1729/30. She was still living in 1746.
4. Isaac Appleton, born on May 30, 1704 in Ipswich.
5. Rebecca Appleton, born in 1706 in Ipswich and married William Dodge of Wenham on January 9, 1728/9. She was still living in 1746.
6. Elizabeth Appleton, born in 1706 in Ipswich and married Josiah Fairfield on August 4, 1731. She was still living in 1746.
7. Martha Appleton [08-207], who was born on July 30, 1708 in Ipswich and married John White [08-206] on August 4, 1731. She was still living in 1746.
8. Joanna Appleton, who was baptized on November 17, 1717 in Ipswich and married William Storey of Boston on April 11, 1747. She died on

---

551   Priscilla Appleton gravestone, Old Burying Ground, Ipswich, Essex County, Massachusetts, s.v. "Priscilla Baker Appleton" (death "1731" memorial "38222506"), database with digital images, *FindAGrave*, accessed 11 July 2019.
552   James Savage, *A Genealogical Dictionary of the First Settlers of New England: Showing Three Generations of Those Who Came Before May 1692*, (Boston: Little, Brown and Company, 1860), Vol I: p. 60; PDF e-book, https://archive.org/details/genealogicaldic01savarich accessed 17 July 2018.
553   Ibid., Vol I: p. 99.
554   "Massachusetts Births and Christenings, 1639-1915" s.v. "Pricilla Baker" (birth "1674" place "Topsfield"), database, *FamilySearch,* accessed 16 October 2019.
555   "Massachusetts, Town Clerk, Vital and Town Records, 1626-2001," s.v. "Priscilla Appleton" (death "1731" place "Ipswich"), database, *FamilySearch*, accessed 10 July 2019.
556   Priscilla Appleton gravestone, Old Burying Ground, Ipswich, Essex County, Massachusetts, s.v. "Priscilla Baker Appleton" (death "1731" memorial "38222506"), database with digital images, *FindAGrave*, accessed 11 July 2019.
557   "Massachusetts, Town Clerk, Vital and Town Records, 1626-2001," s.v. "Isaac Appleton" (death "1747" place "Ipswich"), database, *FamilySearch,* accessed 10 July 2019.
558   Isaac Appleton gravestone, Old Burying Ground, Ipswich, Essex County, Massachusetts, s.v. "Maj Isaac Appleton" (death "1747" memorial "64416549"), database with digital images, *FindAGrave*, accessed 11 July 2019.

July 16, 1775.[559] [560]

[09-416] Matthias Cowdrey and [09-417] Sarah

Matthias Cowdrey [09-416] was born April 11, 1679 in Reading, Middlesex County, Massachusetts to Nathaniel Cowdrey [10-832] and Mary Bacheldor [10-833]. Matthias also lived in Chelmsford, Middlesex County, Massachusetts and Boston, Suffolk County, Massachusetts. He had at least three children with Sarah [09-417].[561] Some genealogies give Sarah's last name as Fletcher, but I failed to find a marriage record or sourced citation for this last name. Sarah apparently died around 1724 or earlier because Matthias remarried to Susanah Willard on September 3, 1724 in Boston, Suffolk County, Massachusetts.[562] The children of Matthias Cowdrey and Sarah are listed below:

1. Matthias Cowdrey, born 1698 and married Susannah Sherwin in 1725. He died on October 15, 1739 in Chelmsford.
2. Samuel Cowdrey, born on November 18, 1701.
3. John Cowdrey [08-208], born after 1710. He married first to Abigail before about 1731, and then married Hannah Davis on May 30, 1744 in Westford, Middlesex County, Massachusetts. He died about 1760.[563]

559   James Savage, *A Genealogical Dictionary of the First Settlers of New England: Showing Three Generations of Those Who Came Before May 1692*, (Boston: Little, Brown and Company, 1860), Vol I: p. 60; PDF e-book, https://archive.org/details/genealogicaldic01savarich accessed 17 July 2018.
560   "Appleton Genealogy," *The Essex Antiquarian*, Vol. 4: p. 3; database with digital images, *American Ancestors*, accessed 10 July 2019.
561   William Richard Cutter, ed., *Genealogical and Family History of Western New York*, (New York: Lewis Historical Publishing Company, 1912), Vol III: p 1428; PDF e-book, https://archive.org/details/genealogicalfami03incutt accessed 9 July 2018.
562   "Massachusetts Marriages, 1695-1910," s.v. "Matthias Cowdry" and "Susanah Willard" (marriage 1724), database, *FamilySearch*, accessed 21 December 2017.
563   William Richard Cutter, ed., *Genealogical and Family History of Western New York*, (New York: Lewis Historical Publishing Company, 1912), Vol III: p 1428; PDF e-book, https://archive.org/details/genealogicalfami03incutt accessed 9 July 2018.

[09-420] John Parker and [09-421] Sarah

John Parker [09-420] was born on May 14, 1698 in Billerica, Middlesex County, Massachusetts to John Parker [10-840] and Abigail Whittaker [10-841]. He married Sarah [09-421] and had at least one child with her. Not much else is known with certainty about this couple, although there was another John and Sarah Parker at the same time in Reading, Middlesex County, Massachusetts. The son of John Parker [09-420] and Sarah [09-421] was Samuel Parker [08-210], who was born on December 10, 1722 in Billerica and married Anna Tarbell [08-211].[564]

[09-422] John Tarbell and [09-423] Hannah Flint

John Tarbell [09-422] was born on August 9, 1680 in Salem Village (now Danvers), Essex County, Massachusetts to John Tarbell [10-844] and Mary Nurse [10-845].[565] He would have been 12 years old when his grandmother Rebecca (Towne) Nurse [11-1,691] was accused of witchcraft and hung on July 19, 1692 in the Salem Witch Hunt.[566] John married Hannah Flint on August 21, 1705 in Salem, Essex County, Massachusetts.[567] Some sources give 1709 as the marriage date, but they were having children before 1709 so that is probably a transcription error since 5 and 9 are similar in some handwriting. Hannah Flint was born on April 4, 1685 in Salem, Essex County, Massachusetts. Flint gives her parents as John Flint [10-846] and Elizabeth [10-847] but the transcription at FamilySearch gives her parents as Thomas Flint and Elizabeth.[568] [569] This transcription error is due to a misreading of the original record which listed John Flint's children under "Jno Fflint sone to Thomas

---

564   Henry A Hazen, *History of Billerica, Massachusetts: With a Genealogical Register,* (Boston: A Williams and Co, 1883) p. 105 of Genealogical Register; PDF e-book, Internet Archive, https://archive.org/details/historyofbilleri00hazenhe , accessed 9 July 2018.
565   Henry A Hazen, *History of Billerica, Massachusetts: With a Genealogical Register,* (Boston: A Williams and Co, 1883) p. 147 of Genealogical Register; PDF e-book, https://archive.org/details/historyofbilleri00hazenhe accessed 9 July 2018.
566   Charles Henry Wight, "Thomas Tarbell and Some of His Descendants," *The New England Historical and Genealogical Register*, Vol. 61: p 71; database, *American Ancestors*, accessed 12 July 2018.
567"Massachusetts, Town Clerk, Vital and Town Records, 1626-2001," s.v. "John Tarbell" (spouse "Hannah Flint" marriage "1709"). database with digital images, *FamilySearch*, accessed 28 June 2017.
568   John Flint and John H. Stone, compilers, *A Genealogical Register of the Descendants of Thomas Flint of Salem*, (Andover: Warren F. Draper, 1860), p. 11; PDF e-book, https://archive.org/details/genealogicalregi00flin , accessed 12 July 2018.
569   "Massachusetts Births and Christenings, 1639-1915," s.v. "Hannah Flint" (born "1685"), database, *FamilySearch*, accessed 11 July 2017.

Fflint" and added above that line was "+ Eliz his wife".[570]

There were possibly bad feelings about Salem Village, because the children born after 1720 were christened in Lynn, Essex County, Massachusetts even though they were born around Salem. About 1730 John and Hannah finally left Salem Village and moved to Billerica, Middlesex County, Massachusetts.[571] John died in Billerica on February 5, 1757[572] and Hannah died in Billerica on December 14, 1779.[573] The children of John Tarbell and Hannah Flint are listed below:

1. William Tarbell, christened on October 5, 1707 in Danvers (Salem Village).[574]
2. John Tarbell, born July 28, 1707 in Salem.[575]
3. Thomas Tarbell, born on August 5, 1711 in Salem.[576]
4. Hannah Tarbell, born and died on June 19, 1714 in Salem.[577]
5. Anna Tarbell [08-211], born on April 20, 1716 in Salem.[578] She married first to Samuel Parker [08-210] and second to Nathan Crosby.[579]
6. Elizabeth Tarbell, born on August 27, 1718 in Salem.[580] She married John Hosley.[581]

---

570   "Massachusetts, Town Clerk, Vital and Town Records, 1626-2001," not indexed, found in Massachusetts, Essex, County wide, "County court births, marriages, deaths 1654-1795" image 223 of 610; digital images, *FamilySearch*, accessed 8 Aug 2019.

571   Henry A Hazen, *History of Billerica, Massachusetts: With a Genealogical Register,* (Boston: A Williams and Co, 1883) p. 147 of Genealogical Register; PDF e-book, https://archive.org/details/historyofbilleri00hazenhe , accessed 9 July 2018.

572   "Massachusetts, Town Clerk, Vital and Town Records, 1626-2001," s.v. "John Tarbell" (death "1757:). database, *FamilySearch*, accessed 21 December 2017.

573   "Massachusetts, Town Clerk, Vital and Town Records, 1626-2001," s.v. "Hannah Tarbell" (death "1779"), database, *FamilySearch*, accessed 21 December 2017.

574   "Massachusetts Births and Christenings, 1639-1915," s.v. "William Tarbell (birth "1707"), database, *FamilySearch,* accessed 21 December 2017.

575   "Massachusetts Births and Christenings, 1639-1915," s.v. "John Tarbell (birth "1707"), database, *FamilySearch,* accessed 21 December 2017.

576   "Massachusetts Births and Christenings, 1639-1915," s.v. "Thomas Tarbell (birth "1711"), database, *FamilySearch,* accessed 21 December 2017.

577   "Massachusetts Deaths and burials, 1795-1910," s.v. "Hannah Tarbell" (death "1714"), database, *FamilySearch,* accessed 21 December 2017.

578   "Massachusetts Births and Christenings, 1639-1915," s.v. "Anna Tarbell (birth "1716"), database, *FamilySearch,* accessed 21 December 2017.

579   Henry A Hazen, *History of Billerica, Massachusetts: With a Genealogical Register,* (Boston: A Williams and Co, 1883) p. 105 of Genealogical Register; PDF e-book, https://archive.org/details/historyofbilleri00hazenhe , accessed 9 July 2018.

580   "Massachusetts Births and Christenings, 1639-1915," s.v. "Elizabeth Tarbell (birth "1718"), database, *FamilySearch,* accessed 21 December 2017.

581   Henry A Hazen, *History of Billerica, Massachusetts: With a Genealogical Register,* (Boston: A Williams and Co, 1883) p. 147 of Genealogical Register; PDF e-book, https://archive.org/details/historyofbilleri00hazenhe , accessed 9 July 2018.

7. Mary Tarbell, born on February 2, 1720 in Salem.[582]
8. Jonathan Tarbell, born on September 15, 1726 in Salem.[583]
9. David Tarbell, born on September 15, 1726 in Salem.[584] He married Hannah Fitch on August 1, 1751.[585]

[09-424] John Browne and [09-425] Elizabeth Polly

John Brown/Browne was a common name and so it is difficult to trace which John Browne [09-424] to follow in terms of birth date and parents. He married Elizabeth Polly [09-425] on April 22, 1682[586] and there are records of them having five children between 1683 and 1689 in Woburn, Middlesex County, Massachusetts.[587] Elizabeth Polly was born on February 4, 1657 in Woburn to George Polly [10-850] and Elizabeth Winn [10-851].[588] Even though all the children were recorded as being born in Woburn, there is a record of the family being in Billerica, Middlesex County, Massachusetts without approval. On October 31, 1683 John Browne was summoned before the Selectmen of Billerica because he had been staying in town without permission and they had received "an evill report of ye s^d pson." He was ordered to leave or pay a tax to the town. However in Dec 1687 John Browne was reported as not paying the tax.[589] The children of John Browne and Elizabeth Polly are listed below:

1. John Browne, born on March 27, 1683 in Woburn.[590]

---

582   "Massachusetts Births and Christenings, 1639-1915," s.v. "Mary Tarbell (birth "1720"), database, *FamilySearch,* accessed 21 December 2017.
583   "Massachusetts Births and Christenings, 1639-1915," s.v. "Jonathan Tarbell (birth "1726"), database, *FamilySearch,* accessed 21 December 2017.
584   "Massachusetts Births and Christenings, 1639-1915," s.v. "David Tarbell (birth "1726"), database, *FamilySearch,* accessed 21 December 2017.
585   Henry A Hazen, *History of Billerica, Massachusetts: With a Genealogical Register,* (Boston: A Williams and Co, 1883) p. 147 of Genealogical Register; PDF e-book, https://archive.org/details/historyofbilleri00hazenhe , accessed 9 July 2018.
586   Henry A Hazen, *History of Billerica, Massachusetts: With a Genealogical Register,* (Boston: A Williams and Co, 1883) p. 18 of Genealogical Register; PDF e-book, Internet Archive, https://archive.org/details/historyofbilleri00hazenhe , accessed 9 July 2018.
587   "Massachusetts Births and Christenings, 1639-1915," s.v. "John Brown" (birth 1683), "John Brown" (birth 1684/5). "Elizabeth Browne" (birth 1685), "Elizabeth Browne" (birth 1687), "Hannah Browne" (birth 1689), database, *FamilySearch,* accessed 21 Dec 2017.
588   "Massachusetts Births and Christenings, 1639-1915," s.v. "Elizabeth Polly" (birth "1657"), database, *FamilySearch,* accessed 4 June 2017.
589   Henry A Hazen, *History of Billerica, Massachusetts: With a Genealogical Register,* (Boston: A Williams and Co, 1883) p. 18 of Genealogical Register; PDF e-book, Internet Archive, https://archive.org/details/historyofbilleri00hazenhe , accessed 9 July 2018.
590   "Massachusetts Births and Christenings, 1639-1915," s.v. "John Brown"

2. John Brown [08-212], born on January 22, 1684/5 in Woburn.[591] He married Susanna Dutton [08-213] in 1709 in Haverhill, Essex County, Massachusetts.[592]
3. Elizabeth Browne, born on July 6, 1685 in Woburn, and died on July 8, 1685.
4. Elizabeth Browne, born on February 10, 1686/7 in Woburn.
5. Hannah Browne, born on April 27, 1689 in Woburn.[593]

[09-426] Thomas Dutton and [09-427] Rebeckah Brabrooks

Thomas Dutton [09-426] was born on September 14, 1648 in Reading, Middlesex County, Massachusetts to Thomas Dutton [10-852] and Susannah [10-853]. Thomas [09-426] is on record as having land in Billerica, Middlesex County, Massachusetts in 1670, and being part of Sergeant Hill's garrison in 1675.[594] Sgt Hill's garrison was one of twelve garrisons in Billerica for the protection of local residents from Native American raids during King Philip's War.[595] Other military mentions of Thomas Dutton were that in 1677 he was wounded in an expedition to Eastward (what they called Kennebec, Maine at the time), and that he served in the center squadron in 1707.[596]

On January 1, 1678/9 Thomas Dutton [09-426] married Rebeckah Brabrooks [09-427] in Billerica. They had at least five children together but some died young.[597] Rebeckah Brabrooks was the widow of Adam Draper, whom she had married September 15, 1666 in Concord, Middlesex County,

---

(birth "1683"), database, *FamilySearch*, accessed 21 December 2017.

591   "Massachusetts, Town Clerk, Vital and Town Records, 1626-2001," s.v. "John Browne" (spouse "Elizabeth Polly" family group), database with digital images, *FamilySearch*, accessed 21 May 2017.

592   "Massachusetts Marriages, 1695-1910," s.v. "John Browne" (spouse "Susannah Dutton" year "1709"), database, *FamilySearch*, accessed 21 May 2017.

593   "Massachusetts, Town Clerk, Vital and Town Records, 1626-2001," s.v. "John Browne" (spouse "Elizabeth Polly" family group), database with digital images, *FamilySearch*, accessed 21 May 2017.

594   William Richard Cutter, ed., *New England Families: Genealogical and Memorial,* (New York: Lewis Historical Publishing Co, 1913), Vol I: p 195; PDF e-book, https://archive.org/details/genealogicaland01adamgoog , accessed 13 July 2018.

595   *Celebration of the Two Hundredth Anniversary of the Incorporation of Billerica, Massachusetts, May 29th, 1855,* (Lowell, Mass.: S. J. Varney, 1855), p. 34; PDF e-book, https://archive.org/details/celebrationoftwo00bill_0 , accessed 13 July 2018.

596   William Richard Cutter, ed., *New England Families: Genealogical and Memorial,* (New York: Lewis Historical Publishing Co, 1913), Vol I: p 195; PDF e-book, https://archive.org/details/genealogicaland01adamgoog , accessed 13 July 2018.

597   "Massachusetts, Town Clerk, Vital and Town Records, 1626-2001," s.v. "Susanna Dutton" (birth "1689", contains full family group), database with digital images, *FamilySearch,* accessed 13 July 2018.

Massachusetts.[598] There are further online genealogies of Rebeckah Brabrooks but I was not able to verify her parentage. She died on March 16, 1720/1 in Billerica. Thomas Dutton lived to at least 1725, when he married Sarah Convers in Billerica in November of 1725.[599] The children of Thomas Dutton and Rebeckah Brabrooks are listed below:

1. Rebeckah Dutton, born on November 13, 1679 in Billerica.[600] She married Daniel Shed.[601]
2. Thomas Dutton, born on August 2, 1681 in Billerica.
3. John Dutton, born on January 24, 1683/4 in Billerica and died on December 14, 1687.
4. Susanna Dutton, born on April 30, 1687 in Billerica and died on September 3, 1688 in Billerica.
5. Susanna Dutton [08-213], born on November 4, 1689 in Billerica.[602] She married John Brown [08-212] in 1709 in Haverhill, Essex County, Massachusetts.[603]

[09-428] Joseph Kemp and [09-429] Peggy Chamberlain

Joseph Kemp [09-428] was born on September 10, 1699 in Groton, Middlesex County, Massachusetts to Jonathan Kemp [10-856] and Mary [10-857].[604] He married Peggy "Elizabeth" Chamberlain [09-429] on December 20, 1720 in Chelmsford, Middlesex County, Massachusetts.[605] Joseph and Peggy had at least seven children together, between 1725 and 1744 in Billerica,

---

598   "Massachusetts, Town Clerk, Vital and Town Records, 1626-2001," s.v. "Rebeccah Brabrooks" (spouse "Addam Draper" marriage "1666"). database, *FamilySearch*, accessed 21 June 2017.

599   "Massachusetts, Town Clerk, Vital and Town Records, 1626-2001," s.v. "Susanna Dutton" (birth "1689", contains full family group), database with digital images, *FamilySearch*, accessed 13 July 2018.

600   Ibid.

601   Henry A Hazen, *History of Billerica, Massachusetts: With a Genealogical Register,* (Boston: A Williams and Co, 1883) p. 45 of Genealogical Register; PDF e-book, Internet Archive, https://archive.org/details/historyofbilleri00hazenhe , accessed 9 July 2018.

602   "Massachusetts, Town Clerk, Vital and Town Records, 1626-2001," s.v. "Susanna Dutton" (birth "1689", contains full family group), database with digital images, *FamilySearch,* accessed 13 July 2018.

603   "Massachusetts Marriages, 1695-1910," s.v. "Susannah Dutton" (spouse "John Browne" marriage "1709"), database, *FamilySearch*, accessed 21 May 2017.

604   Henry A Hazen, *History of Billerica, Massachusetts: With a Genealogical Register,* (Boston: A Williams and Co, 1883) p. 80 of Genealogical Register; PDF e-book, Internet Archive, https://archive.org/details/historyofbilleri00hazenhe , accessed 9 July 2018.

605   "Massachusetts, Town and Vital Records, 1620-1988," s.v. "Joseph Kemp" (spouse "Peggy Chamberlain" marriage "1720"), database with digital images, *Ancestry.com*, accessed 28 June 2017.

Middlesex County, Massachusetts.[606]

As for Peggy Chamberlain [09-429], there is some disagreement. In the birth records of her children, she is listed as Elizabeth but in the marriage record she is listed as Peggy. I did not find other marriages recorded for Joseph Kemp while he was having children. Hazen and many online trees identify Peggy as the Elizabeth Chamberlain born August 1, 1686 in Cambridge, Massachusetts to Thomas Chamberlain and Elizabeth Hammond. I believe this to be unlikely since Peggy would have been 54 in 1739 when she had David Kemp, and 58 in 1744 when having Oliver Kemp. However, there was a Peggy Chamberlain born on March 12, 1701 in Billerica[607] which is where the children were all born and next to Chelmsford where they married. I believe the Peggy born in Billerica in 1701 is the correct wife of Joseph Kemp instead of the older Elizabeth born in Cambridge in 1686. So Peggy Chamberlain's parents were Clement Chamberlain [10-858] and Mary [10-859]. The children of Joseph Kemp and Peggy Chamberlain are listed below:

1. Jason Kemp [08-214], born on November 11, 1725 in Billerica. He married Hannah Meers [08-215].
2. Joseph Kemp, born on June 20, 1727 in Billerica.
3. Benjamin Kemp, born on June 20, 1731 in Billerica.
4. Sampson Kemp, born on August 29, 1733 in Billerica.
5. Jacob Kemp, born on August 12, 1735 in Billerica.
6. David Kemp, born on June 26, 1739 in Billerica.
7. Oliver Kemp, born on September 9, 1744 in Billerica.[608]

[09-430] Robert Meers and [09-431] Hannah Frost

Robert Meers [09-430] was born on January 6, 1707 in Boston, Suffolk County, Massachusetts to Robert Mears [10-860] and Elizabeth Adams [10-861].[609] He married Hannah Frost [09-431] on April 21, 1726 in Billerica, Middlesex County, Massachusetts.[610] They had at least seven children together,

---

606   Henry A Hazen, *History of Billerica, Massachusetts: With a Genealogical Register,* (Boston: A Williams and Co, 1883) p. 80 of Genealogical Register; PDF e-book, Internet Archive, https://archive.org/details/historyofbilleri00hazenhe , accessed 9 July 2018.
607   "Massachusetts, Town Clerk, Vital and Town Records, 1626-2001," s.v. "Pege Chamberlain" (birth 1701), database with digital images, *FamilySearch,* accessed 13 July 2018.
608   Henry A Hazen, *History of Billerica, Massachusetts: With a Genealogical Register,* (Boston: A Williams and Co, 1883) p. 80 of Genealogical Register; PDF e-book, Internet Archive, https://archive.org/details/historyofbilleri00hazenhe , accessed 9 July 2018.
609   "Massachusetts Births and Christenings, 1639-1915," s.v. "Robert Mires" (birth 1707), database, *FamilySearch,* accessed 21 June 2017.
610   "Massachusetts, Town Clerk, Vital and Town Records, 1626-2001," s.v. "Robert Meers" and "Hannah Frost" (married 1726), database with digital images,

all between 1726/7 and 1736.[611] Hannah Frost was born on May 13, 1702 in Billerica to Samuel Frost, Jr [10-862] and Hannah Mascraft [10-863].[612] The children of Robert Meers [09-430] and Hannah Frost [09-431] are listed below:

1. Abigail Meers, born on January 17, 1726/7 in Billerica.
2. Hannah Meers [08-215], born April 21, 1728 in Billerica.[613] She married Jason Kemp [08-214].[614]
3. Mehittabal Meers, born December 11, 1729 in Billerica.
4. Mary Meers, born July 24, 1731 in Billerica.
5. Roger Meers, born on March 10, 1732/3 in Billerica.
6. Bette Meers, born on March 13, 1734/5 in Billerica.
7. Samuel Meers, born on August 18, 1736 in Billerica.[615]

[10-658] John Tucker

The Tuckers were an early family in Virginia and Barbados, so there were several John Tuckers at this time in Virginia. John Tucker [10-658] was the son of John Tucker [11-1,368], and the mother of his children might have been Rebecca.[616] However, John Tucker's [10-658] will, which was signed on January 11, 1718/9, lists his wife as Mary.[617] I was unable to get more information on when John Tucker married whom. The above mentioned will was probated in Norfolk County, Virginia in September of 1719, possibly on the tenth, so John died in or before September 1719. Four children were mentioned in the will:

1. John Tucker.

FamilySearch, accessed 13 July 2018.
611	"Massachusetts, Town Clerk, Vital and Town Records, 1626-2001," s.v. "Robert Meers" and "Hannah Frost" (married 1726), database with digital images, *FamilySearch*, accessed 13 July 2018.
612	"Massachusetts, Town Clerk, Vital and Town Records, 1626-2001," s.v. "Hannah Frost" (birth 1702), database with digital images, *FamilySearch*, accessed 13 July 2018.
613	"Massachusetts, Town Clerk, Vital and Town Records, 1626-2001," s.v. "Hannah Meers" (birth "1728" shows family group), database with digital images, *FamilySearch*, accessed 21 June 2017.
614	Henry A Hazen, *History of Billerica, Massachusetts: With a Genealogical Register,* (Boston: A Williams and Co, 1883) pp. 19, 80 of Genealogical Register; PDF e-book, Internet Archive, https://archive.org/details/historyofbilleri00hazenhe , accessed 9 July 2018.
615	"Massachusetts, Town Clerk, Vital and Town Records, 1626-2001," s.v. "Hannah Meers" (birth "1728" shows family group), database with digital images, *FamilySearch,* accessed 21 June 2017.
616	Dorothy Wilson Fine, *A Fine Branch of the Family Tree*, (San Jose, CA: El Camino Real Chapter, DAR, 1991), p. 18.
617	"Virginia, Wills and Probate Records, 1652-1983," s.v. "John Tucker" (will "1719"), database with digital images, *Ancestry.com*, accessed 14 Jan 2018.

2.   Thomas Tucker.
3.   Mary Tucker.
4.   Sarah Tucker [09-329][618] who married Henry Netherton [09-328].[619]

[10-768] John Johnson and [10-769] Deborah Ward

John Johnson [10-768] was born about 1629 in Hernhill, Kent, England to Solomon Johnson [11-1,536] and Elinor [11-1,537].[620] [621] By 1657 he was in the American colonies, where he married Deborah Ward [10-769] on November 19, 1657 in Sudbury, Middlesex County, Massachusetts. They had five children together who were recorded being born in Marlborough, Middlesex County, Massachusetts between 1672 and 1680.[622] Deborah Ward was born in England also, in 1637 to William Ward [11-1,538] and Eleanor [11-1,539].[623] Some transcriptions and trees mistakenly place her birth in Massachusetts, but the document itself shows that Deborah was born in England to the first wife of William Ward.

Deborah died on August 9, 1697 in Marlborough,[624] and John was "killed by ye enemy" in Haverhill, Essex County, Massachusetts on August 29, 1708.[625] There is also some confusion over the death of John Johnson [10-768], since another John Johnson died in Haverhill in 1713/4. However, the John Johnson who died in 1713/4 was the wrong age (67 at time of death) and married to someone else. So I believe the 1708 death is correct. The children of John Johnson and Deborah Ward are listed below:

1.   John Johnson, born on January 21, 1672 in Marlborough, and died on December 23, 1676.

---

618   Ibid.

619   Dorothy Wilson Fine, *A Fine Branch of the Family Tree*, (San Jose, CA: El Camino Real Chapter, DAR, 1991), p. 18.

620   Mrs. Ellwood Kimball, "The Solomon Johnson Family," *The New England Historical and Genealogical Register*, Vol 66, p 235; database, *American Ancestors*, accessed 9 July 2018.

621   William W Johnson, *Johnson Genealogy: Records of the Descendants of John Johnson of Ipswich and Andover*, (North Greenfield, Wisconsin: William W Johnson, 1892), p 7; PDF e-book, https://archive.org/details/johnsongenealogy00john , accessed 14 July 2018.

622   Mrs. Ellwood Kimball, "The Solomon Johnson Family," *The New England Historical and Genealogical Register*, Vol 66, p 235; database, *American Ancestors*, accessed 9 July 2018.

623   "Massachusetts, Town Clerk, Vital and Town Records, 1626-2001," s.v. "Deborah Ward" (birth 1637), database with digital images, *FamilySearch*, accessed 14 July 2018.

624   "Massachusetts, Town and Vital Records, 1620-1988," s.v. "Deborah Johnson" (death 1697), database, *Ancestry.com*, accessed 2016.

625   "Massachusetts, Town and Vital Records, 1620-1988," *s.v.* "John Johnson" (death 1708), database, *Ancestry.com*, accessed 2016.

2. Daniel Johnson, [09-384] born on April 5, 1675 in Marlborough. He married Dorothy Lambe [09-385].
3. Elizabeth Johnson, born on July 20, 1677 in Marlborough. She married Joseph Witherby.
4. Deborah Johnson, born on August 22, 1678 in Marlborough.
5. John Johnson, born on February 16, 1680 in Marlborough.[626]

[10-770] Joshua Lambe and [10-771] Mary Alcock

Joshua Lambe [10-770] was born on November 27, 1642 in Roxbury, Suffolk County, Massachusetts to Thomas Lambe [11-1,540] and Dorothy Harbittle [11-1,541].[627] He married Mary Alcock [10-771] in 1675 in Roxbury,[628] and they had at least six children all born between 1674/5 and 1688/9 in Roxbury.[629] Mary Alcock was christened on December 5, 1652 in Roxbury to John Alcock [11-1,542] and Sarah Palsgrave [11-1,543].[630] [631] Joshua Lambe died on September 23, 1690 in Roxbury,[632] and Mary died in 1700.[633] The children of Joshua Lambe and Mary Alcock are listed below:

1. Joshua Lambe, who was born on January 7, 1674/5 in Roxbury.[634]
2. Dorothy Lambe [09-385], who was born on June 8, 1679 in Roxbury.[635]

---

626   Mrs. Ellwood Kimball, "The Solomon Johnson Family," *The New England Historical and Genealogical Register*, Vol 66, p 235; database, *American Ancestors*, accessed 9 July 2018.
627   "Massachusetts, Town Clerk, Vital and Town Records, 1626-2001," s.v. "Joshua Lambe" (birth "1642"), database with digital images, *FamilySearch*, accessed 12 May 2016.
628   Clarence Almon Torrey, *New England Marriages Prior to 1700*, (Baltimore, Maryland: Genealogical Publishing Co., Inc, 2004), p. 448; database with digital images, *Ancestry.com*, accessed 5 May 2016.
629   "Massachusetts, Town and Vital Records, 1620-1988," s.v. "Joshua Lambe" (birth 1674/5), s.v. "Dorothy Lambe" (birth 1679), s.v. "George Lambe" (birth 1681), s.v. "John Lambe" (birth 1684/5), s.v. "Samuel Lambe" (birth 1686), and s.v. "Thomas Lambe" (birth 1688/9), database, *Ancestry.com*, accessed 2016.
630   Clarence Almon Torrey, *New England Marriages Prior to 1700*, (Baltimore, Maryland: Genealogical Publishing Co., Inc, 2004), p. 448; database with digital images, *Ancestry.com*, accessed 5 May 2016.
631   "Massachusetts, Town and Vital Records, 1620-1988," s.v. "Mary Alcock" (birth 1652), database, *Ancestry.com*, accessed 2016.
632   "Massachusetts, Town Clerk, Vital and Town Records, 1626-2001," s.v. "Joshua Lamb" (death 1690), database with digital images, *FamilySearch*, accessed 12 May 2016.
633   Clarence Almon Torrey, *New England Marriages Prior to 1700*, (Baltimore, Maryland: Genealogical Publishing Co., Inc, 2004), p. 448; database with digital images, *Ancestry.com*, accessed 5 May 2016.
634   "Massachusetts, Town and Vital Records, 1620-1988," s.v. "Joshua Lambe" (birth "1674/5"), database, *Ancestry.com*, accessed 2016.
635   "Massachusetts, Town and Vital Records, 1620-1988," s.v. "Dorothy Lambe"

She married Daniel Johnson [09-384] on December 23, 1697 in Framingham, Middlesex County, Massachusetts.[636]

3. George Lambe, who was born on April 27, 1681 in Roxbury.[637]
4. John Lambe, who was born on February 3, 1684/5 in Roxbury.[638]
5. Samuel Lambe, who was born on April 9, 1686 in Roxbury.[639]
6. Thomas Lambe, who was born on March 23, 1688/9 in Roxbury.[640]

[10-772] Nathaniel Richardson and [10-773] Mary

Nathaniel Richardson [10-772] was born January 2, 1650/1 in Woburn, Middlesex County, Massachusetts to Thomas Richardson [11-1,544] and Mary [11-1,545]. He married Mary, but I could not verify her surname. On December 19, 1675 Nathaniel was wounded in the "Great Swamp Fight" during King Philip's War. He survived to be made a freeman in Woburn in 1690, and died on December 4, 1714. Mary died on December 22, 1719.[641] The children of Nathaniel Richardson and Mary are listed below:

1. Nathaniel Richardson, who was born before August 27, 1673 in Woburn. He married Abigail Reed.
2. James Richardson, who was born on February 26, 1675/6 in Woburn. He married first to Rebecca Eaton, and then to Elizabeth Arnold.
3. Mary Richardson, who was born on March 10, 1679/80 in Woburn. She married first to Thomas Wyman, and second to Joseph Winn.
4. Joshua Richardson, who was born on June 3, 1681 in Woburn. He married Hannah.
5. Martha Richardson, who was born in 1683 in Woburn.
6. John Richardson, who was born on January 25, 1684/5 in Woburn. He married Abigail.
7. Thomas Richardson [09-386], who was born on April 15, 1687 in Woburn, and married Elizabeth Green [09-387].

(birth "1679"), database, *Ancestry.com,* accessed 2016.

636   "Massachusetts, Town Clerk, Vital and Town Records, 1626-2001," s.v. "Daniel Johnson" (spouse "Dorothia Lamb" marriage "1697"), database with digital images, *FamilySearch,* accessed 3 May 2016.

637   "Massachusetts, Town and Vital Records, 1620-1988," s.v. "George Lambe" (birth "1681"), database, *Ancestry.com,* accessed 2016.

638   "Massachusetts, Town and Vital Records, 1620-1988," s.v. "John Lambe" (birth "1684/5"), database, *Ancestry.com,* accessed 2016.

639   "Massachusetts, Town and Vital Records, 1620-1988," s.v. "Samuel Lambe" (birth "1686"), database, *Ancestry.com,* accessed 2016.

640   "Massachusetts, Town and Vital Records, 1620-1988," s.v. "Dorothy Lambe" (birth "1688/89"), database, *Ancestry.com,* accessed 2016.

641   John Adams Vinton, *The Richardson Memorial: Comprising a Full History and Genealogy of the Posterity of the Three Brothers,* (Portland, Maine: Brown Thurston and Co, 1876), p. 509-510; PDF e-book, https://archive.org/details/richardsonmemori00vint , accessed 10 July 2018.

8. Hannah Richardson, who was born on May 6, 1689 in Woburn. She married first to Timothy Baldwin and second to John Vinton.

9. Samuel Richardson, who was born on September 24, 1691 in Woburn and married Sarah.

10. Phinehas Richardson, who was born in February 1693/4 in Woburn.

11. Phebe Richardson, who was born on March 4, 1695/6 in Woburn. She married David Wyman.

12. Amos Richardson, who was born on August 10, 1698 in Woburn and married Abigail.

13. Benjamin Richardson, who was born on August 27, 1700 in Woburn and died on September 5, 1700.[642]

[10-774] Samuel Green and [10-775] Elizabeth Upham

Samuel Green [10-774] was born August 5, 1670 in Malden, Middlesex County, Massachusetts to Thomas Green [11-1,548] and Rebecca Hills [11-1,549].[643] He married Elizabeth Upham [10-775] on October 28, 1691 in Malden, Middlesex County, Massachusetts[644] and they had at least eight children together. Samuel held the title of Captain, and in 1717 was one of the original founders of Leicester, Worcester County, Massachusetts. He died on January 2, 1735/6.[645]

Elizabeth Upham [10-775] is more difficult to trace. In the source by Greene in the footnotes, it is supposed that Elizabeth is the daughter of Deacon Phineas Upham. However the Massachusetts birth and christenings database at FamilySearch show that Elizabeth, daughter of Phineas Upham, was born in 1699. So the Elizabeth Upham who married Samuel Green in 1691 could not have been the daughter of Deacon Phineas Upham. Other internet trees and *NEHGR* assign this Elizabeth Upham to Lt. Phineas Upham, who was the father of Deacon Phineas Upham.[646] I believe Lt. Phineas Upham [11-1,550] was the correct father for this Elizabeth Upham, and Ruth Wood [11-1,551] was her mother. As for the death of Elizabeth (Upham) Green [10-775], there

---

642   John Adams Vinton, *The Richardson Memorial: Comprising a Full History and Genealogy of the Posterity of the Three Brothers,* (Portland, Maine: Brown Thurston and Co, 1876), p. 509-510; PDF e-book, https://archive.org/details/richardsonmemori00vint , accessed 10 July 2018.

643   "Massachusetts Births and Christenings, 1639-1915," s.v. "Samuel Green" (birth "1670"), database, *FamilySearch*, accessed 13 July 2017.

644   "Massachusetts, Town Clerk, Vital and Town Records, 1626-2001," s.v. "Samuel Green" (spouse "Elizabeth Upham" marriage "1691"), database with digital images, *FamilySearch*, accessed 13 July 2017.

645   Samuel S. Greene, *A Genealogical Sketch of the Descendants of Thomas Green of Malden, Mass.*, (Boston: Henry W. Dutton & Son, 1858), pp. 12-13; PDF e-book, https://archive.org/details/genealogicalsket00gree , accessed 10 July 2018.

646   "Upham Genealogy," *The New England Historical and Genealogical Register,* Vol 23: p. 34; database, *American Ancestors,* accessed 21 July 2018.

were multiple Elizabeth Greens who died in the 1700's in Massachusetts so I could not verify which death was hers. The children of Samuel Green and Elizabeth Upham are listed below:

1. Elizabeth Green [09-387], who was born on April 4, 1693 in Malden. She married Thomas Richardson [09-386].
2. Rebecca Green, who was born on April 4, 1695 in Malden, and married Samuel Baldwin.
3. Ruth Green, who married Joshua Nichols.
4. Thomas Green, who was born in 1699 in Malden, and married Martha Lynde on January 13, 1725/6 in Malden.
5. Lydia Green, who first married Abiathar Vinton on April 30, 1723 in Malden, and then married Samuel Stower on January 15, 1746.
6. Barsheby Green, who married Elisha Nevins.
7. Abigail Green, who married Henry King.
8. Annie Green, who married Ebenezer Lamb.[647]

[10-776] William Merrick and [10-777] Abigail Hopkins

William Merrick [10-776] was born on September 15, 1643 in Eastham, Barnstable County, Massachusetts to William Merrick [11-1,552] and Rebecca Tracy [11-1,553]. He married Abigail Hopkins [10-777] on May 23, 1667, and they had at least nine children together between 1668 and 1684. Abigail was born in October 1644 to Giles Hopkins [11-1,554] and Catherine Wheldon [11-1,555], and lived until at least 1684 when her last known child was born. At some point after 1684, William Merrick [10-776] had a second marriage to a woman named Elizabeth.

William Merrick [10-776] became a legal voter in Eastham in 1675, but had moved to Hardwick, Worcester County, Massachusetts by 1719 when he represented Hardwick in the General Assembly. In 1722, William was the Surveyor of Roads for Hardwick. William held the rank of Ensign and died October 30, 1732.[648] The children of William Merrick [10-776] and Abigail Hopkins [10-777] are listed below:

1. Rebecca Merrick, who was born on November 28, 1668 and married a Mr. Sparrow.
2. William Merrick, who was born on August 1, 1670 and died on March 20, 1671.
3. Stephen Merrick, who was born on March 26, 1673.

---

647   Samuel S. Greene, *A Genealogical Sketch of the Descendants of Thomas Green of Malden, Mass.*, (Boston: Henry W. Dutton & Son, 1858), pp. 12-13; PDF e-book, https://archive.org/details/genealogicalsket00gree , accessed 10 July 2018.
648   George Byron Merrick, *Genealogy of the Merrick-Mirick-Myrick Family of Massachusetts: 1636-1902*, (Madison, WI: Tracy, Gibbs & Co, 1902), p. 14; PDF e-book, *Internet Archive*, https://archive.org/details/genealogymerric00merrgoog , accessed 9 July 2018.

4. Nathaniel Merrick [09-388], who was born in 1675 in Eastham. He married Alice Freeman [09-389].
5. Hannah Merrick, who married John Snow.
6. Benjamin Merrick.
7. John Merrick, who married Anna Sears.
8. Ruth Merrick, who was born in 1684 and married first to Samuel Sears on November 4, 1710. Then she married Chillingworth Foster. Ruth died on February 13, 1766.[649]

[10-778] Samuel Freeman and [10-779] Mercy Southworth

Samuel Freeman [10-778] was born on May 11, 1638 in Watertown, Middlesex County, Massachusetts to Samuel Freeman [11-1,556] and Apphia Quick [11-1,557].[650] [651] He married Mercy Southworth [10-779] on May 12, 1658 in Eastham, Barnstable County, Massachusetts and they had at least nine children, but due to transcription errors some marriage record transcriptions give March instead of May, or Mary or Marcy instead of Mercy, or Southern instead of Southworth.[652] [653] In 1676 Samuel Freeman became a deacon of the Eastham church,[654] and was buried in the Cove Burying Ground of Eastham after dying November 20, 1712.[655]

Mercy Southworth [10-779] was the daughter of Constant Southworth [11-1,558] and Elizabeth Collier [11-1,559],[656] or Collins according to one source.[657]

---

649   Ibid.
650   "Massachusetts, Town Clerk, Vital and Town Records, 1626-2001," s.v. "Samuel Freeman" (birth 1638), database with digital images, *FamilySearch*, accessed 19 January 2018.
651   William Richard Cutter, ed., *Genealogical and Personal Memoirs: Relating to the Families of Boston and Eastern Massachusetts*, (New York: Lewis Historical Publishing Company, 1908), Vol II: p. 848; PDF e-book, https://archive.org/details/genealogicaland01cuttgoog , accessed 10 July 2018.
652   "Massachusetts Marriages, 1695-1910," s.v. "Samuel Freeman" and "Mary Southern" (marriage 1658), database, *FamilySearch*, accessed 19 January 2018.
653   William Richard Cutter, ed., *Genealogical and Personal Memoirs: Relating to the Families of Boston and Eastern Massachusetts*, (New York: Lewis Historical Publishing Company, 1908), Vol II: p. 848; PDF e-book, https://archive.org/details/genealogicaland01cuttgoog , accessed 10 July 2018.
654   Ibid.
655   Samuel Freeman, grave marker, Cove Burying Ground, Eastham, Barnstable County, Massachusetts, digital image, s.v. "Samuel Freeman" (death 1712, memorial 6023850), database with digital images, *FindAGrave*, accessed 19 January 2018.
656   William Richard Cutter, ed., *Genealogical and Personal Memoirs: Relating to the Families of Boston and Eastern Massachusetts*, (New York: Lewis Historical Publishing Company, 1908), Vol II: p. 848; PDF e-book, https://archive.org/details/genealogicaland01cuttgoog , accessed 10 July 2018.
657   George Byron Merrick, *Genealogy of the Merrick-Mirick-Myrick Family of Massachusetts: 1636-1902*, (Madison, WI: Tracy, Gibbs & Co, 1902), p. 19; PDF e-

Mercy's death is not known due to her gravestone breaking and becoming unreadable, but she is also buried at the Cove Burying Ground of Eastham.[658] The children of Samuel Freeman and Mercy Southworth are listed below:

1. Apphia Freeman, who was born on December 11, 1659 and died on February 19, 1660 in Eastham.
2. Samuel Freeman, who was born on March 26, 1662 in Eastham. He married first to Elizabeth Sparrow on February 5, 1684, and then Bathsheba Smith about 1693.
3. Apphia Freeman, who was born on January 1, 1666 in Eastham. She married Isaac Pepper on October 17, 1685.
4. Constant Freeman, who was born on March 31, 1669 and married Jane Treat on October 11, 1694.
5. Elizabeth Freeman, who was born on June 26, 1671 in Eastham. She married first to Abraham Remich, and then a Mr. Merrick.
6. Edward Freeman, who died young.
7. Mary Freeman.
8. Alice Freeman [09-389], who married Nathaniel Merrick [09-388].
9. Mercy Freeman.[659]

[10-780] John Freeman and [10-781] Sarah Merrick

John Freeman [10-780] was born in December, 1651 in Eastham, Barnstable County, Massachusetts to John Freeman [11-1,560] and Mercy Prence [11-1,561].[660] His first marriage was to Sarah Merrick [10-781], on December 18, 1672,[661] and they had at least eleven children together.[662] Sarah Merrick was

---

book, *Internet Archive*, https://archive.org/details/genealogymerric00merrgoog , accessed 9 July 2018.

658   Mercy Southworth, grave marker remnants, Cove Burying Ground, Eastham, Barnstable County, Massachusetts, digital image, s.v. "Mercy Southworth" (memorial 54241927), database, *FindAGrave*, accessed 19 January 2018.

659   William Richard Cutter, ed., *Genealogical and Personal Memoirs: Relating to the Families of Boston and Eastern Massachusetts*, (New York: Lewis Historical Publishing Company, 1908), Vol II: p. 848; PDF e-book, https://archive.org/details/genealogicaland01cuttgoog , accessed 10 July 2018.

660   William Richard Cutter, ed., *New England Families: Genealogical and Memorial*, (New York: Lewis Historical Publishing Company, 1914), Vol II: p. 854; PDF e-book, https://archive.org/details/newenglandfamili02cutt_1 accessed 10 July 2018.

661   George Byron Merrick, *Genealogy of the Merrick-Mirick-Myrick Family of Massachusetts: 1636-1902*, (Madison, WI: Tracy, Gibbs & Co, 1902), p 14; PDF e-book, *Internet Archive*, https://archive.org/details/genealogymerric00merrgoog , accessed 9 July 2018.

662   William Richard Cutter, ed., *New England Families: Genealogical and Memorial*, (New York: Lewis Historical Publishing Company, 1914), Vol II: p. 854; PDF e-book, https://archive.org/details/newenglandfamili02cutt_1 accessed 10 July

born on August 1, 1654 to William Merrick [11-1,562] and Rebecca Tracy [11-1,563].[663] Sarah died on April 21, 1696, so John Freeman married Marcy [10-783], the widow of Elkanah Watson [10-782]. By October 17, 1700 John moved to Harwich, Barnstable County, Massachusetts where he was one of the eight original members of the Harwich church. He died on July 27, 1721[664] and was buried at the Old Burying Ground in Brewster, Barnstable County, Massachusetts.[665] The children of John Freeman and Sarah Merrick are listed below:

1. John Freeman, born September 3, 1674 and died in 1674 in Eastham.
2. Sarah Freeman, who was born in September 1676.
3. John Freeman [09-390], who was born in July 1678 in Eastham. He married Mercy Watson [09-391] about 1701.
4. Rebecca Freeman, who was born on January 28, 1680/1.
5. Nathaniel Freeman, who was born on March 17, 1682/3 in Eastham.
6. Benjamin Freeman, who was born in July 1685.
7. Mercy Freeman, who was born on August 3, 1687 in Eastham.
8. Patience Freeman.
9. Susanna Freeman.
10. Elizabeth Freeman.
11. Mary Freeman.[666]

[10-782] Elkanah Watson and [10-783] Marcy Hedge

Elkanah Watson was born on February 25, 1655/6 to George Watson [11-1,564] and Phebe Hicks [11-1,565].[667] He married Marcy Hedge in 1676[668] and

---

2018.

663   George Byron Merrick, *Genealogy of the Merrick-Mirick-Myrick Family of Massachusetts: 1636-1902*, (Madison, WI: Tracy, Gibbs & Co, 1902), p 14; PDF e-book, *Internet Archive*, https://archive.org/details/genealogymerric00merrgoog , accessed 9 July 2018.

664   William Richard Cutter, ed., *New England Families: Genealogical and Memorial*, (New York: Lewis Historical Publishing Company, 1914), Vol II: p. 854; PDF e-book, https://archive.org/details/newenglandfamili02cutt_1 accessed 10 July 2018.

665   "John Freeman," grave marker, Old Burying Ground, Brewster, Barnstable County, Massachusetts, digital image s.v. "John Freeman" (death 1721, memorial 51252114), database with digital images, *FindAGrave*, accessed 19 January 2018.

666   William Richard Cutter, ed., *New England Families: Genealogical and Memorial*, (New York: Lewis Historical Publishing Company, 1914), Vol II: p. 854; PDF e-book, https://archive.org/details/newenglandfamili02cutt_1 accessed 10 July 2018.

667   Henry Cole Quinby, ed., "The Watsons," *New England Family History*, Vol III: p 469; PDF e-book, https://archive.org/details/newenglandfamily03quin accessed 10 July 2018.

668   Clarence Almon Torrey, *New England Marriages Prior to 1700*, (Baltimore,

they had at least four children together.[669]   Elkanah drowned at Plymouth Harbor on February 8, 1689/90.[670][671]

Marcy Hedge [10-783] was born in 1659 to William Hedge [11-1,566].[672] There is some dispute about whether she was a Hedge or Bradford, but the marriage transcription says she was a Hedge. Also, sometimes her name is given as Mercy, but her gravestone and father's will says Marcy. Sometime after April of 1696, she married John Freeman [10-780] since her first husband Elkanah Watson [10-782] had died.[673]   Marcy died on September 27, 1721[674] and is buried at the Old Burying Ground in Brewster, Barnstable County, Massachusetts.[675]   The children of Elkanah Watson [10-782] and Marcy Hedge [10-783] are listed below:

1. John Watson, who was born in 1679 and died on September 9, 1731. He married first to Sarah Rogers on January 26, 1715, and second to Priscilla Thomas on July 8, 1729.

2. Phebe Watson, who was born in 1681 and married Edmund Freeman about 1703.[676]

3. Mercy Watson [09-391], who was born in October 1683 in

Maryland: Genealogical Publishing Co., Inc, 2004); s.v. "Elkanah Watson" and "Mercy Hedge" (marriage 1676), database with digital images, *Ancestry.com,* accessed 5 May 2016.

669   Henry Cole Quinby, ed., "The Watsons," *New England Family History*, Vol III: p 469; PDF e-book, https://archive.org/details/newenglandfamily03quin accessed 10 July 2018.

670   William Richard Cutter, ed., *New England Families: Genealogical and Memorial,* (New York: Lewis Historical Publishing Company, 1914), Vol II: p. 854; PDF e-book, https://archive.org/details/newenglandfamili02cutt_1 accessed 10 July 2018.

671   Henry Cole Quinby, ed., "The Watsons," *New England Family History*, Vol III: p 469; PDF e-book, https://archive.org/details/newenglandfamily03quin accessed 10 July 2018.

672   Clarence Almon Torrey, *New England Marriages Prior to 1700,* (Baltimore, Maryland: Genealogical Publishing Co., Inc, 2004); s.v. "Elkanah Watson" and "Mercy Hedge" (marriage 1676), database with digital images, *Ancestry.com,* accessed 5 May 2016.

673   Henry Cole Quinby, ed., "The Watsons," *New England Family History*, Vol III: p 469; PDF e-book, https://archive.org/details/newenglandfamily03quin accessed 10 July 2018.

674   Henry Cole Quinby, ed., "The Watsons," *New England Family History*, Vol III: p 470; PDF e-book, https://archive.org/details/newenglandfamily03quin accessed 10 July 2018.

675   Marcy Freeman, grave marker, Old Burying Ground, Brewster, Barnstable County, Massachusetts, digital image, s.v. "Marcy Hedge Watson Freeman" (death 1721, memorial 35900289), database with digital images, *FindAGrave,* accessed 22 January 2018.

676   Henry Cole Quinby, ed., "The Watsons," *New England Family History*, Vol III: p 469; PDF e-book, https://archive.org/details/newenglandfamily03quin accessed 10 July 2018.

Plymouth,[677] now in Plymouth County, Massachusetts. She married John Freeman [09-390] about 1701.[678]

4. Mary Watson, who was born in 1688 and married Nathaniel Freeman on October 24, 1706.[679]

[10-800] John Carleton and [10-801] Hannah Jewett

John Carleton [10-800] was born about 1635 in England to Edward Carleton [11-1,600] and Ellen Newton [11-1,601].[680] [681] There is some dispute about whether his mother was a Denton or Newton, but modern research indicates that she was a Newton as will be explained in the section for Edward Carleton [11-1,600] and Ellen Newton [11-1,601]. By 1661 John Carleton was in Haverhill, Essex County, Massachusetts, where he married Hannah Jewett [10-801].[682] John and Hannah had at least three children until John Carleton died on January 22, 1668 in Haverhill.[683]

Hannah Jewett [10-801] was born June 15, 1641 in a part of Rowley which is now Georgetown in Essex County, Massachusetts to Joseph Jewett [11-1,602] and Mary Mallinson [11-1,603].[684] (Some transcriptions will incorrectly give April as her birth month because the document says it was the fourth month, but that is an error due to the different calendar in use at the time. In the Julian calendar of the time, the fourth month of the year is actually June.) After her first husband John Carleton died, Hannah married Christopher Babbage.

---

677   "Massachusetts Births and Christenings, 1639-1915," s.v. "Mercy Watson" (birth "1683"), database, *FamilySearch*, accessed 17 December 2017.
678   William Richard Cutter, ed., *New England Families: Genealogical and Memorial*, (New York: Lewis Historical Publishing Company, 1914), Vol II: p. 854; PDF e-book, https://archive.org/details/newenglandfamili02cutt_1 accessed 10 July 2018.
679   Henry Cole Quinby, ed., "The Watsons," *New England Family History*, Vol III: p 469; PDF e-book, https://archive.org/details/newenglandfamily03quin accessed 10 July 2018.
680   William Richard Cutter, ed., *New England Families: Genealogical and Memorial*, (New York: Lewis Historical Publishing Co, 1913), Vol II: p 509; PDF e-book, https://archive.org/details/newenglandfamili02cutt , accessed 14 July 2018.
681   Frederick Lewis Weis, *Ancestral Roots of Certain American Colonists Who Came to America before 1700*, 8 ed., (Baltimore: Genealogical Publishing Company, 2008), p. 7, line 2-42.
682   "Massachusetts Marriages, 1695-1910," s.v. "John Carleton" and "Hanah Jewet" (marriage 1661), database, *FamilySearch*, accessed 22 January 2018.
683   William Richard Cutter, ed., *New England Families: Genealogical and Memorial*, (New York: Lewis Historical Publishing Co, 1913), Vol II: p 509; PDF e-book, https://archive.org/details/newenglandfamili02cutt , accessed 14 July 2018.
684   "Massachusetts, Town Clerk, Vital and Town Records, 1626-2001," not indexed (Essex County>Georgetown>Births, Marriages 1636-1888>image 78 of 263), digital images, *FamilySearch*, accessed 29 August 2019.

She died September 25, 1723 in Bradford, Essex County, Massachusetts.[685] The children of John Carleton [10-800] and Hannah Jewett [10-801] are listed below:

1. Joseph Carleton, who was born March 21, 1662/3 in Haverhill.[686]
2. Edward Carleton [09-400], who was born on March 22, 1664/5 in a part of Haverhill[687] once known as Bradford, and married Elizabeth Kimball [09-401] before 1699 in Haverhill.[688]
3. Thomas Carleton, who was born on November 1, 1667 in Haverhill.[689]

[10-802] Benjamin Kimball and [10-803] Mercy Hazeltine

Benjamin Kimball [10-802] was born in 1637 in Ipswich, Essex County, Massachusetts to Richard Kimball [11-1,604] and Ursula Scott [11-1,605].[690] [691] Benjamin married Mercy Hazeltine [10-803] on April 16, 1660 in Salisbury, Essex County, Massachusetts.[692] The transcription for the marriage records the location as Amesbury, Essex County, Massachusetts, but the document itself says the location is Salisbury, which is three miles away from Amesbury. Benjamin and Mercy had at least ten children between 1661 and 1684.[693]

Mercy Hazeltine [10-803] was born on October 16, 1642 in Rowley, Essex

685   William Richard Cutter, ed., *New England Families: Genealogical and Memorial,* (New York: Lewis Historical Publishing Co, 1913), Vol II: p 509; PDF e-book, https://archive.org/details/newenglandfamili02cutt , accessed 14 July 2018.
686   Topsfield Historical Society, *Vital Records of Haverhill Massachusetts: to the End of the Year 1849,* (Topsfield, MA: Topsfield Historical Society, 1911), Vol I: p. 55; PDF e-book, https://archive.org/details/vitalrecordsofha00byuhave/page/1 accessed 25 June 2019.
687   Ibid., Vol I: p. 54.
688   Ibid., Vol II: p. 54.
689   Ibid., Vol I: p. 55.
690   Leonard Allison Morrison and Stephen Paschall Sharples, *History of the Kimball Family in America: From 1634 to 1897, and of its Ancestors the Kemballs or Kemboldes of England,* (Boston: Damrell & Upham, 1897), p. 34; PDF e-book, https://archive.org/details/historyofkimball00morr , accessed 14 July 2018.
691   Benjamin Kimball, grave marker, Ancient Burial Ground, Bradford, Essex County, Massachusetts, digital image, s.v. "Benjamin Kimball" (death 1696, memorial 34271250), database with digital images, *FindAGrave,* accessed 15 July 2017.
692   "Massachusetts, Town Clerk, Vital and Town Records, 1626-2001," s.v. "Benjamin Kimball" and "Mary Hazeltine" (marriage 1660), database with digital images, *FamilySearch,* accessed 15 July 2017.
693   Leonard Allison Morrison and Stephen Paschall Sharples, *History of the Kimball Family in America: From 1634 to 1897, and of its Ancestors the Kemballs or Kemboldes of England,* (Boston: Damrell & Upham, 1897), p. 45; PDF e-book, https://archive.org/details/historyofkimball00morr , accessed 14 July 2018.

County, Massachusetts to Robert Hazelton [11-1,606] and Ann [11-1,607].[694] [695] [696] She has also been recorded as Mary or Marcy but her gravestone says Mercy. Mercy died on January 5, 1707/8 and is buried at the Ancient Burial Ground in Bradford, Essex County, Massachusetts.[697] The children of Benjamin Kimball [10-802] and Mercy Hazeltine [10-803] are listed below:

1. Anna Kimball, who was born on December 22, 1661. She married Richard Barker on April 21, 1682.
2. Mercy Kimball, who was born on December 27, 1663, and died on February 5, 1663/4.
3. Richard Kimball, who was born on December 3, 1664 and died on January 10, 1710/1. He married Mehitable Day.
4. Elizabeth Kimball [09-401], who was born on July 24, 1669, and married Edward Carleton [09-400].
5. David Kimball [09-406], who was born on July 26, 1671, and died June 14, 1743.[698] He married Elizabeth Gage [09-407].
6. Jonathan Kimball, who was born on November 26, 1673 in Bradford, and died on September 30, 1749. He first married Lydia Day on July 15, 1696, and then the widow Jane Plummer on November 3, 1739.[699]
7. Robert Kimball, who was born on March 6, 1675/6 in Bradford, and died on February 24, 1743/4. He married Susanna Atwood.
8. Abraham Kimball, who was born on March 24, 1677 in Bradford[700] and died on February 26, 1707/8. He married Mary Green.
9. Samuel Kimball, who was born on March 28, 1680 in Bradford, and died in 1739. He married Eunice Chadwick.
10. Ebenezer Kimball, who was born on June 20, 1684 in Bradford, and died on January 23, 1715. He married Ruth Eaton.[701]

---

694   "Massachusetts Births and Christenings, 1639-1915," s.v. "Mercy Hazeltine" (birth 1642), database, *FamilySearch*, accessed 16 July 2017.
695   William Richard Cutter, ed., *Genealogical and Personal Memoirs: Relating to the Families of the State of Massachusetts*, (New York: Lewis Historical Publishing Company, 1910), Vol IV: p 2344; https://archive.org/details/genealogicaland01adamgoog accessed 9 July 2018.
696   Mercy Kimball, grave marker, Ancient Burial Ground, Bradford, Essex County, Massachusetts, digital image, s.v. "Mercy Haseltine Kimball" (death 1707/8, memorial 18505527), database with digital images, *FindAGrave*, accessed 15 July 2017.
697   Mercy Kimball, grave marker, Ancient Burial Ground, Bradford, Essex County, Massachusetts, digital image, s.v. "Mercy Haseltine Kimball" (death 1707/8, memorial 18505527), database with digital images, *FindAGrave*, accessed 15 July 2017.
698   Leonard Allison Morrison and Stephen Paschall Sharples, *History of the Kimball Family in America: From 1634 to 1897, and of its Ancestors the Kemballs or Kemboldes of England*, (Boston: Damrell & Upham, 1897), p. 45; PDF e-book, https://archive.org/details/historyofkimball00morr , accessed 14 July 2018.
699   Ibid., p. 60.
700   Ibid., p. 61.
701   Ibid., p. 62.

[10-804] Samuel Dalton and [10-805] Mehitable

Samuel Dalton [10-804] was born about 1629 in England, based on his age at immigration to New England in 1635.[702]   He was the son of Philemon Dalton [11-1,608] and Anne Cole [11-1,609].[703]   In 1658, Samuel was the town clerk of Hampton, which is now in Rockingham County, New Hampshire, and from 1662 to 1674 he was a representative.[704]   Samuel Dalton died on August 22, 1681 in Hampton.[705]

As for the wife of Samuel Dalton [10-804], there are some discrepancies. Savage said that Samuel Dalton had two or three marriages, and married Mehitable Palmer about 1676. So Samuel's sons Philemon [09-402], Timothy, and Samuel were all from a prior marriage.[706]   However Torrey said that Samuel Dalton married Mehitable Palmer on February 6, 1650,[707] which would make her the mother of Philemon Dalton [09-402].   The birth record transcription (made in 1906) for Philemon Dalton [09-402] recorded "Mehetable" as the mother of Philemon Dalton in 1664, but did not give Mehitable's surname.[708]   Also, Philemon Dalton testified in probate court in 1711 that Mehitable Palmer was his mother,[709] but he might have called his stepmother his mother since she helped raise him as a teenager. So due to discrepancies I will not connect the Palmer line (which is covered anyway due

---

702   James Savage, *A Genealogical Dictionary of the First Settlers of New England,* (Boston: Little, Brown and Company, 1860) Vol II: p. 3; PDF e-book, http://archive.org/details/genealogicaldic02savarich accessed 17 July 2018.
703   George F Sanborn, Jr. and Melinde Lutz Sanborn, "The Dalton Cluster: Timothy Dalton, Philemon Dalton, Richard Everard, and Deborah (Everard) Blake," *The New England Historical and Genealogical Register,* Vol 154: p. 283; database with digital images, *American Ancestors,* accessed 20 October 2019.
704   James Savage, *A Genealogical Dictionary of the First Settlers of New England,* (Boston: Little, Brown and Company, 1860) Vol II: p. 3; PDF e-book, http://archive.org/details/genealogicaldic02savarich accessed 17 July 2018.
705   "New Hampshire, Town Clerk, Vital and Town Records, 1636-1947," not indexed, Rockingham>Hampton>Town Records 1645-1832 Vol 1>image 299 of 316 "Samuel Dalton", digital images, *FamilySearch,* accessed 1 September 2019.
706   James Savage, *A Genealogical Dictionary of the First Settlers of New England,* (Boston: Little, Brown and Company, 1860) Vol 2: p. 3; PDF e-book, http://archive.org/details/genealogicaldic02savarich accessed 17 July 2018.
707   Clarence Almon Torrey, "U.S., New England Marriages Prior to 1700," s.v. "Samuel Dalton" (spouse "Mehitable Palmer" marriage "1650"), database with digital images, *Ancestry.com,* accessed 2 September 2019.
708   "New Hampshire Birth Records, Early to 1900," s.v. "Philemon Dalton" (birth "1664"), database with digital images, *FamilySearch,* accessed 28 June 2019.
709   Albert Stillman Batchellor, ed., *Probate Records of the Province of New Hampshire,* (Concord, NH: Rumford Printing Co, 1907) Vol I: p. 244: PDF e-book, https://archive.org/details/newhampshireprov31none/page/n3 accessed 5 September 2019.

to her sister Elizabeth Palmer [11-1,645] also being in this tree), since it is not certain whether Savage was right about multiple marriages or whether Torrey was right about Mehitable Palmer's marriage to Samuel Dalton in 1650.

[10-806] Edward Gove and [10-807] Hannah Titcomb

Edward Gove [10-806] was born about 1636[710] in London, England, based on his age at death recorded on his gravestone, even though some say he was born about 1630. Edward Gove was the son of John Gove [11-1,612].[711] There would be some confusion about who was Edward Gove's mother if he was born about 1630, because there is a record of a "John Goaue" and "Mary Shard" getting married in London, England on February 6, 1630/1.[712] So since Edward Gove was born about 1636 according to his gravestone, it is clear that Mary Shard [11-1,613] was his mother.

Edward Gove [10-806] had a residence in Salisbury, Essex County, Massachusetts as early as April 16, 1657, and in 1660 he married Hannah[713] Titcomb[714] [10-807]. There is a theory, which many including the Gove Book follow, in which Hannah was really Hannah Partridge based on her being mentioned in some New Hampshire wills, even though the marriage record put her as Hannah Titcomb. I failed to find a Hannah Partridge marrying any Titcomb in Salisbury before 1660, but it is possible that she was a widow who was born with the maiden name of Partridge. Unfortunately, I did not find strong enough evidence to clear up the discrepancy regarding her maiden name, so I will not follow her ancestry further.

After March 1665 Edward Gove moved his residence to Hampton, Rockingham County, New Hampshire. He made freeman status in 1678 in Hampton, and in 1680 was a representative for New Hampshire. On January

---

710   Edward Gove, grave marker, Pine Grove Cemetery, Hampton, Rockingham County, New Hampshire, digital image, s.v. "Edward Gove" (death "1691" memorial "7376023"), database with digital images, *FindAGrave*, accessed 11 September 2019.
711   William Henry Gove, *The Gove Book: History and Genealogy of the American Family of Gove and Notes of European Goves*, (Salem, MA: Sydney Perley, 1922) pp. 11-13; PDF e-book,
https://archive.org/details/govebookhistoryg00gove/page/50 accessed 22 June 2019.
712   "London, England, Church of England Baptisms, Marriages and Burials, 1538-1812," entry not indexed, City of London>St Nicholas, Cole Abbey>1538-1651, "John Goaue" 6 Feb 1630 marriage, digital images, *Ancestry.com*, accessed 11 September 2019.
713   William Henry Gove, *The Gove Book: History and Genealogy of the American Family of Gove and Notes of European Goves*, (Salem, MA: Sydney Perley, 1922) pp. 13-14; PDF e-book,
https://archive.org/details/govebookhistoryg00gove/page/50 accessed 22 June 2019
714   "Massachusetts, Town Clerk, Vital and Town Records, 1626-2001," s.v. "Edward Gove" (spouse "Hannah Titcomb" marriage "1660"), database, *FamilySearch*, accessed 8 September 2019.

27, 1682/3, Edward tried to lead a revolt against the appointed governor, and was arrested. He was in the Tower of London between June 6, 1683 and April 9, 1686.[715] Edward died at the age of 55 on July 29, 1691 and is buried at the Pine Grove Cemetery in Hampton, New Hampshire.[716] Hannah died after 1712.[717] The children of Edward Gove and Hannah Titcomb are listed below:

1. John Gove, born on September 19, 1661 in Salisbury and married Sarah, who was the widow of William Russell, in 1686. John died on October 15, 1737.
2. William Gove, born on October 21, 1662 and died March 1, 1663, both in Salisbury.
3. Hannah Gove, born on March 5, 1664 in Salisbury, and married Abraham Clement on May 10, 1683.
4. Mary Gove, born on April 4, 1666 in Hampton. She married first to Joseph Sanborn, and second to a Mr. Morrill.
5. Abigail Gove, born on July 23, 1667 in Hampton and died on August 23, 1667.
6. Penuel Gove, born on July 10, 1668 in Hampton and died on August 1, 1671.
7. Abigail Gove [09-403], born on April 17, 1670 in Hampton. She married first to Philemon Dalton [09-402] on September 25, 1690 in Hampton, second to Deacon Benjamin Sanborn on November 24, 1724, and third to James Prescott on June 17, 1746.
8. Ebenezer Gove, born on May 23, 1671 in Hampton. He married Judith Sanborn on December 20, 1692, and died on April 16, 1758 in Hampton.
9. Edward Gove, born on May 13, 1673 in Hampton and died on November 12, 1675.
10. Jeremiah Gove, born on October 13, 1674 in Hampton and died on September 9, 1692.
11. Rachel Gove, born on January 29, 1676 and died soon after.
12. Ann Gove, born on January 9, 1677 in Hampton and married Jeremiah Conner on July 3, 1696. She died on February 12, 1722/3 in Exeter, Rockingham County, New Hampshire.
13. Sarah Gove, born on July 8, 1678 in Hampton and married Samuel

---

715   William Henry Gove, *The Gove Book: History and Genealogy of the American Family of Gove and Notes of European Goves,* (Salem, MA: Sydney Perley, 1922) pp. 14-45; PDF e-book, https://archive.org/details/govebookhistoryg00gove/page/50 accessed 22 June 2019

716   "Massachusetts, Town Clerk, Vital and Town Records, 1626-2001," s.v. "Edward Gove" (spouse "Hannah Titcomb" marriage "1660"), database, *FamilySearch,* accessed 8 September 2019.

717   William Henry Gove, *The Gove Book: History and Genealogy of the American Family of Gove and Notes of European Goves,* (Salem, MA: Sydney Perley, 1922) p. 48; PDF e-book, https://archive.org/details/govebookhistoryg00gove/page/50 accessed 22 June 2019

Dearborn on December 10, 1698.[718]

[10-808] William Wilson and [10-809] Patience Grindall

William Wilson [10-808] was baptized on May 13, 1610 in Donington on Bain, Lincolnshire, England to William Wilson [11-1,616] and Alice [11-1,617].[719] There are documents linking William Wilson to his parents, in which he leased out his land near them in Donington on Bain.[720] On October 6, 1634 at St Botolphe Parish in Boston, Lincolnshire, England, William Wilson [10-808] married Patience Grindall [10-809],[721] who was the widow of James Trustrome.[722] Soon after the marriage, William Wilson and Patience Grindall crossed to New England, where William was admitted to the church in Boston, Suffolk County, Massachusetts on September 6, 1635. William's occupation was joiner at the time, and he made freeman on May 25, 1636. He was a deputy marshal and prison keeper in 1642, and Savage incorrectly gave his death as 1646.[723] Their fifth child was born in 1648, so William died sometime before May 1653 when his widow Patience was involved in a lawsuit.[724]

Patience Grindall [10-809] was christened on October 23, 1603 in Hareby, Lincolnshire, England to William Grindall [11-1,618],[725] who had married Bridgitt Richard [11-1,619] in 1600.[726] The children of William Wilson and Patience Grindall are listed below:

---

718   Ibid., pp. 49-51.
719   "England Births and Baptisms 1538-1975" s.v. "William Wilson" (baptized "1610" place "Donington on Bain, England"), database online, *FindMyPast,* accessed 29 June 2019.
720   William Richard Cutter, ed., *New England Families: Genealogical and Memorial,* (New York: Lewis Historical Publishing Company, 1914), Vol II: p. 576; PDF e-book, https://archive.org/details/newenglandfamili02cutt_1 accessed 10 July 2018.
721   "Lincolnshire Marriages," s.v. "William Wilson" (spouse "Patience Trustram" year "1634"), database with digital images, *FindMyPast,* accessed 28 June 2019.
722   "Lincolnshire Marriages," s.v. "Patience Grindall" (spouse "James Trustrome" year "1627"), database with digital images, *FindMyPast,* accessed 28 June 2019.
723   James Savage, *A Genealogical Dictionary of the First Settlers of New England: Showing Three Generations of Those Who Came Before May 1692,* (Boston: Little, Brown and Company, 1860), Vol IV: pp. 589-590; PDF e-Book, http://archive.org/details/genealogicaldic04savarich accessed 17 July 2018.
724   William Richard Cutter, ed., *New England Families: Genealogical and Memorial,* (New York: Lewis Historical Publishing Company, 1914), Vol II: p. 576; PDF e-book, https://archive.org/details/newenglandfamili02cutt_1 accessed 10 July 2018.
725   "England Births and Christenings, 1538-1975," s.v. "Patience Grindall" (christened "1603" place "Hareby"), database, *FamilySearch,* accessed 29 June 2019.
726   "England Marriages, 1538-1973," s.v. "William Grundall" (spouse "Bridgitt Richard" year "1600" place "Bolingbroke"), database, *FamilySearch,* accessed 29 June 2019.

1. Shoreborne Wilson, who was born on August 6, 1635 near Boston, Massachusetts.[727]
2. Mary Wilson, born on January 11, 1637 in Boston, Massachusetts.[728]
3. John Wilson, born in January 1639 in Boston, Massachusetts.[729]
4. Joseph Wilson [09-404], born on November 10, 1643 in Boston, Massachusetts.[730]
5. Newgrade Wilson, born and died in 1648.[731]

[10-810] John Lovejoy and [10-811] Mary Osgood

There are two genealogies for John Lovejoy [10-810]. It is known through court records that he was born about 1622. So one places him as being from London, England since there is a record of a John Lovejoy being born to a Rowland Lovejoy in London in 1622, but there is no evidence that the John Lovejoy who came to Massachusetts was the same John Lovejoy born in London. The other genealogy for John Lovejoy establishes that a "John Lougie" or "Lowgie" was a servant on the passenger list of the ship *Confidence* that came to Massachusetts in 1638. This John Lougie (the letter u was sometimes used or mistaken for v in records of the time) was 16 years old and from Caversham, which was in Oxfordshire at the time but is now in Berkshire, England. There is a record of a John Lovejoy being born to a William Lovejoy [11-1,620] in Caversham on July 14, 1622.[732] I believe the Caversham genealogy is correct.

John Lovejoy [10-810] married Mary Osgood [10-811] on June 1, 1651. Mary Osgood was the daughter of Christopher Osgood [11-1,622][733] and Mary

---

727   "Massachusetts Births and Christenings, 1639-1915," s.v. "Shoreborne Wilson" (born "1635" place "Boston"), database, *FamilySearch,* accessed 30 September 2019.
728   "Massachusetts Births and Christenings, 1639-1915," s.v. "Mary Wilson" (born "1637" place "Boston"), database, *FamilySearch,* accessed 30 September 2019.
729   "Massachusetts Births and Christenings, 1639-1915," s.v. "John Wilson" (born "1639" place "Boston"), database, *FamilySearch,* accessed 30 September 2019.
730   "Massachusetts Births and Christenings, 1639-1915," s.v. "Joseph Wilson" (born "1643" place "Boston"), database, *FamilySearch,* accessed 28 June 2019.
731   William Richard Cutter, ed., *New England Families: Genealogical and Memorial,* (New York: Lewis Historical Publishing Company, 1914), Vol II: p. 576; PDF e-book, https://archive.org/details/newenglandfamili02cutt_1 accessed 10 July 2018.
732   James R Henderson, "English Origins of John Lovejoy of Andover, Massachusetts," *The New England Historical and Genealogical Register,* Vol 163: p. 28; database, *American Ancestors,* accessed 30 June 2019.
733   James Savage, *A Genealogical Dictionary of the First Settlers of New England: Showing Three Generations of Those Who Came Before May 1692,* (Boston: Little, Brown and Company, 1860), Vol III: p. 122; PDF e-Book, http://archive.org/details/genealogicaldic04savarich accessed 17 July 2018.

Everatt [11-1,623].[734] John Lovejoy [10-810] made freeman status in 1673, but his wife Mary [10-811] died on July 15, 1675. John married Naomi, the daughter of John Hoyt of Salisbury, on March 23, 1678, and lived about 12 more years. John Lovejoy died on November 7, 1690.[735]

The children of John Lovejoy and Mary Osgood are listed below:

1. Mary Lovejoy [09-405], who married Joseph Wilson [09-404] in 1670.
2. Christopher Lovejoy, who was born about 1659. He married Sarah Russ on May 26, 1685 and died in 1737.
3. Ebenezer Lovejoy, who was born about 1673. He married Mary Foster on July 11, 1693, and died in 1759.
4. Nathaniel Lovejoy, who was born about 1674. He married Dorothy Hoyt on March 21, 1694, and died in 1758.
5. Benjamin Lovejoy, who was a soldier and died at "Pemaquid" in 1689.
6. John Lovejoy.
7. William Lovejoy.
8. Joseph Lovejoy.
9. Sarah Lovejoy, who married William Johnson on May 23, 1678.
10. Ann Lovejoy, who married Jonathan Blanchard on May 26, 1685.
11. Abigail Lovejoy, who married Nehemiah Abbot on April 9, 1691.[736]

[10-814] Samuel Gage and [10-815] Faith Stickney

Samuel Gage [10-814] was born about 1638 and was the son of John Gage [11-1,628] and Amy [11-1,629]. Samuel reached freeman status on May 31, 1671 in Haverhill, Essex County, Massachusetts, and married Faith Stickney [10-815] on June 10, 1674[737] in Bradford, Essex County, Massachusetts.[738] Faith Stickney [10-815] was born on February 4, 1641/2 and was the daughter of William Stickney [11-1,630] and Elizabeth [11-1,631]. Samuel Gage [10-814] and Faith Stickney [10-815] had one surviving child, Elizabeth Gage [09-

---

734   Osgood Field, "A Contribution to the History of the Family of Osgood," *The New England Historical and Genealogical Register,* Vol 20: p. 27; database, *American Ancestors,* accessed 24 October 2019.

735   James Savage, *A Genealogical Dictionary of the First Settlers of New England: Showing Three Generations of Those Who Came Before May 1692,* (Boston: Little, Brown and Company, 1860), Vol III: p. 122; PDF e-Book, http://archive.org/details/genealogicaldic04savarich accessed 17 July 2018.

736   Ibid., Vol III: p. 122.

737   Arthur E. Gage, *Some Descendants of John Gage of Ipswich, Mass.,* (Boston: New England Historic Genealogical Company, 1908), p. 4; PDF e-book, https://archive.org/details/somedescendantso00gage , accessed 9 July 2018.

738   "Massachusetts, Town Clerk, Vital and Town Records, 1626-2001," s.v. "Samuell Gage" (spouse "Faith Stickney" marriage "1674"); database, *FamilySearch,* accessed 4 October 2019.

407] before Samuel Gage [10-814] died on July 20, 1676[739] in Bradford.[740]

[10-816] Nathaniel Ayer and [10-817] Tamesin Turloar

There is some confusion about Nathaniel Ayer's parents, because John and Nathaniel were names that were often repeated in this large family. Many place this Nathaniel as the one born in 1654/5 to John Ayer, Jr and Sarah Williams, but that is in the wrong generation since Nathaniel Ayer [10-816] married Tamesin Turloar [10-817] on May 10, 1670 in Haverhill, Essex County, Massachusetts.[741] At that time and place, a male getting married at 15 did not seem very common. So I believe Whitmore is right in writing that Nathaniel Ayer [10-816] was the son of John Ayer [11-1,632] and Hannah [11-1,633].[742] Others give a year and place for the birth of Nathaniel as 1638 England, but I have found no evidence to support this. Likewise, some place Tamesin Turloar [10-817] as being born in Cornwall, England in 1640, but I found found no evidence establishing the origin of the Tamesin Turloar who married Nathaniel Ayer. So a girl born in Cornwall at the right time with a similar name could be a coincidence, and more evidence is needed. Tamesin Turloar [10-817] died on December 13, 1700, and Nathaniel Ayer [10-816] died on November 17, 1717.[743] Their children are listed below:

1. Hannah Ayer, who was born on June 2, 1671 in Haverhill and probably died young.
2. Hannah Ayer, who was born on December 19, 1672 in Haverhill.
3. Elizabeth Ayer, who was born on August 19, 1674 in Haverhill.[744]
4. Nathaniel Ayer [09-408], who was born on November 15, 1676 in

---

739   Arthur E. Gage, *Some Descendants of John Gage of Ipswich, Mass.*, (Boston: New England Historic Genealogical Company, 1908), p. 4; PDF e-book, https://archive.org/details/somedescendantso00gage , accessed 9 July 2018.
740   "Massachusetts Deaths and Burials, 1795-1910," s.v. "Samuel Gage" (year "1676" place "Bradford"); database, *FamilySearch,* accessed 4 October 2019.
741   Topsfield Historical Society, *Vital Records of Haverhill Massachusetts: to the End of the Year 1849,* (Topsfield, Massachusetts: Topsfield Historical Society, 1911), Vol II: p 18; PDF e-book, https://archive.org/details/cu31924099427654 accessed 9 July 2018.
742   W.H. Whitmore, "The Ayres and Ayer Families," *The New England Historical and Genealogical Register,* (Boston: New England Historic Genealogical Society, 1847-) Vol 17: p. 307; PDF e-book, https://archive.org/details/newenglandhistorv17wate/page/n669 accessed 6 October 2019.
743   Ibid., Vol 17: p. 308.
744   Topsfield Historical Society, *Vital Records of Haverhill Massachusetts: to the End of the Year 1849,* (Topsfield, Massachusetts: Topsfield Historical Society, 1911), Vol I: p. 17; PDF e-book, https://archive.org/details/vitalrecordsofha00byuhave/page/1 accessed 25 June 2019.

Haverhill.[745] He married the widow Esther Palmer [09-409].[746]

5.   Abiah Ayer, born on February 5, 1678 in Haverhill.
6.   Obadiah Ayer, born on January 20, 1680 in Haverhill.
7.   Ruth Ayer, who was born on December 30, 1681 in Haverhill.
8.   Unnamed child who died young, born on September 5, 1683 in Haverhill.
9.   Benjamin Ayer, who was born on August 9, 1684 in Haverhill.
10. Mary Ayer, who was born on September 9, 1687 in Haverhill.
11. Ruth Ayer, who was born on May 12, 1689 in Haverhill.[747]

[10-820] Samuel Shepard and [10-821] Mary Page

Samuel Shepard [10-820] married Mary Page [10-821] on July 14, 1673 in Haverhill, Essex County, Massachusetts, but she was referred to as the widow Mary Dow.[748] Mary had married John Dow in her first marriage on October 23, 1665 in Haverhill.[749] Mary Page [10-821] was baptized on May 3, 1646 to John Page [11-1,642] and Mary Marsh [11-1,643].[750] As for the parents of Samuel Shepard [10-820], I could not find any evidence regarding his birth or parents. Samuel died on June 13, 1707 in Salisbury, Essex County, Massachusetts.[751] The children of Samuel Shepard [10-820] and Mary Page [10-821] are listed below:

1.   Mary Shepard, born on July 28, 1674 in Haverhill.
2.   Bethia Shepard, born on April 28, 1677 in Haverhill.
3.   Samuel Shepard, born on January 15, 1679 in Haverhill.
4.   John Shepard [09-410], born on April 21, 1682 in Haverhill.
5.   Israel Shepard, born on July 3, 1684 in Haverhill.
6.   Sarah Shepard, born on January 30, 1686 in Haverhill, but died young.
7.   Sarah Shepard, born on August 11, 1689 in Haverhill.[752]

---

745   Ibid., Vol I: p. 20.
746   Ibid., Vol II: p. 18.
747   Ibid., Vol I: pp. 15-21.
748   Topsfield Historical Society, *Vital Records of Haverhill Massachusetts: to the End of the Year 1849*, (Topsfield, Massachusetts: Topsfield Historical Society, 1911), Vol II: p. 285; PDF e-book, https://archive.org/details/cu31924099427654 accessed 9 July 2018.
749   Ibid., Vol II: p. 93.
750   William Richard Cutter, ed., *Genealogical and Personal Memoirs: Relating to the Families of Boston and Eastern Massachusetts*, (New York: Lewis Historical Publishing Company, 1908), Vol I: pp. 560-1; PDF e-book, https://archive.org/details/genealogicalpers00cutt accessed 20 July 2018.
751   "Massachusetts Deaths and Burials, 1795-1910," s.v. "Samuell Shepard" (death "1707" place "Salisbury"), database, *FamilySearch*, accessed 6 October 2019.
752   Topsfield Historical Society, *Vital Records of Haverhill Massachusetts: to the End of the Year 1849*, (Topsfield, Massachusetts: Topsfield Historical Society, 1911), Vol I: p. 272; PDF e-book, https://archive.org/details/vitalrecordsofha00byuhave/page/

[10-822] Timothy Ayer and [10-823] Ruth Johnson

Timothy Ayer [10-822] was born on October 2, 1659 in Haverhill, Essex County, Massachusetts[753] to Robert Ayer [11-1,644] and Elizabeth Palmer [11-1,645].[754] Timothy married Ruth Johnson [10-823] on November 24, 1682. Ruth Johnson [10-823] was from Hampton, Rockingham County, New Hampshire,[755] and the only record of a Ruth Johnson being born in Hampton between 1650 and 1668 was on July 13, 1666 to Peter Johnson [11-1,646] and Ruth[756] Moulton [11-1,647]. (Even though the transcription says May, the document said "5 mo." which was July in the Julian calendar.)[757] Timothy Ayer (10-822] died on August 14, 1689,[758] and Ruth Johnson [10-823] then married Samuel Dow on May 5, 1691. She died on July 25, 1751.[759] The children of Timothy Ayer [10-822] and Ruth Johnson [10-823] are listed below:
1. Hannah Ayer [09-411], born on December 7, 1683 in Haverhill. She married Samuel Shepard [09-410] on February 15, 1704/5, and died before 1732.
2. Ruth Ayer, who was born on April 3, 1686 in Haverhill, and died on January 27, 1686/7.
3. Mary Ayer, who was born on July 16, 1688.[760]

[10-824] John White and [10-825] Hannah French

John White [10-824] was the son of William White [11-1,648] and Mary [11-1,649].[761] Some say Mary was the Mary Ware who traveled in the same ship as William White to Massachusetts, but that is not conclusive evidence that she married him. John White [10-824] was born about 1639 based on his

---

1 accessed 25 June 2019.
753   "Ayer Genealogy," *The Essex Antiquarian,* Vol 4: p. 147; database with digital images, *American Ancestors,* accessed 4 July 2019.
754   Ibid., Vol 4: p. 145.
755   Ibid., Vol 4: p. 147.
756   "New Hampshire Birth Records, Early to 1900," s.v. "Ruth Johnson" (year "1666" place "Hampton"), database, *FamilySearch,* accessed 7 October 2019.
757   "New Hampshire Marriage Records, 1637-1947," s.v. "Peter Jonson" (spouse "Ruth Moulton" year "1660"), database, *FamilySearch,* accessed 7 October 2019.
758   "Ayer Genealogy," *The Essex Antiquarian,* Vol 4: p. 147; database with digital images, *American Ancestors,* accessed 4 July 2019.
759   Ibid., Vol 4: p. 148.
760   Ibid.
761   Daniel Appleton White and Annie Frances Richards, *The Descendants of William White, of Haverhill, Mass.,* (Boston: American Printing and Engraving Company, 1889) p. 7; PDF e-book, https://archive.org/details/descendantswill00richgoog/page/n10 accessed 23 June 2019.

age at death, and married Hannah French [10-825] in 1662.

There might have been two ceremonies, because the marriage is mentioned as being on November 25, 1662 in Salem, Essex County, Massachusetts in one source,[762] and as being on November 26, 1662 in Salisbury, Essex County, Massachusetts according to another source.[763] The town clerk record of the marriage confuses some people, because it says the 9th month. So some put it as being in September, but the 9th month of the Julian calendar in use at the time was actually November.

Hannah French [10-825] was the daughter of Edward French [B11-1,650].[764] [765] I was not able to find good evidence for the name of Hannah's mother. John White [10-824] and Hannah French [10-825] were not married for many years, because John White [10-824] died on January 1, 1668/9 in Haverhill, Essex County, Massachusetts.[766] He was buried at Pentucket Cemetery in Haverhill.[767] Hannah French [10-825] then married Thomas Philbrick in 1669. The care of the child of John White [10-824] and Hannah French [10-825], who was also named John White [09-412], went to the grandfather William White [11-1,648].[768]

[10-826] John Gilman and [10-827] Elizabeth Treworthy

John Gilman [10-826] was christened on May 23, 1626 in Hingham, Norfolk, England, and his parents were Edward Gilman [B11-1,652] and Mary Clark [11-1,653]. John Gilman immigrated with his family to Boston, Suffolk County, Massachusetts in 1638 in the ship *Diligent*.[769] By about 1648, John

---

762   Ibid., p. 8.
763   "Massachusetts, Town Clerk, Vital and Town Records, 1626-2001," s.v. "John White" (spouse "Hannah French" marriage "1662"), database with digital images, *FamilySearch*, accessed 9 October 2019.
764   James Savage, *A Genealogical Dictionary of the First Settlers of New England: Showing Three Generations of Those Who Came Before May 1692*, (Boston: Little, Brown and Company, 1860) Vol II: p. 205; PDF e-book, http://archive.org/details/genealogicaldic02savarich accessed 17 July 2018.
765   Daniel Appleton White and Annie Frances Richards, *The Descendants of William White, of Haverhill, Mass.*, (Boston: American Printing and Engraving Company, 1889) p. 8; PDF e-book, https://archive.org/details/descendantswill00richgoog/page/n10 accessed 23 June 2019.
766   Ibid., p. 9.
767   John White, grave marker, Pentucket Cemetery, Haverhill, Essex County, Massachusetts, digital image, s.v. "John White, I" (death "1668" memorial "87201698"), database with digital images, *FindAGrave*, accessed 9 October 2019.
768   Daniel Appleton White and Annie Frances Richards, *The Descendants of William White, of Haverhill, Mass.*, (Boston: American Printing and Engraving Company, 1889) p. 9; PDF e-book, https://archive.org/details/descendantswill00richgoog/page/n10 accessed 23 June 2019.
769   James Savage, *A Genealogical Dictionary of the First Settlers of New England: Showing Three Generations of Those Who Came Before May 1692*, (Boston:

Gilman was in Exeter, Rockingham County, New Hampshire, where he was in the lumber and milling business. In 1652, he was elected as a selectman for Exeter, and later became a judge.[770] Then, on June 30, 1657, John Gilman [10-826] married Elizabeth Treworthy [10-827] in Exeter.[771] Elizabeth Treworthy [10-827] was the daughter of James Treworthy [11-1,654] and Catherine Shapleigh [11-1,655].[772]

In 1693, John Gilman [10-826] became speaker of the house.[773] He died on July 24, 1708 in Exeter, and was 84 according to his death record[774] which would have made his birth about 1624. Elizabeth Treworthy [10-827] died on September 8, 1719 in Exeter.[775] Even though it is suspiciously long, I have no evidence to the contrary so the recorded children of John Gilman and Elizabeth Treworthy are listed below:

1. Mary Gilman, born on September 10, 1658 and who married Jonathan Thing.
2. James Gilman, born on February 6, 1660.
3. Elizabeth Gilman, born on August 16, 1661. She married first to Nathaniel Ladd in 1678, then second to Henry Wadleigh on December 3, 1693.
4. John Gilman, born on October 6, 1663 and died young.
5. Catharine Gilman, born on March 16, 1665 and died about 1684.
6. Sarah Gilman, born on February 25, 1667 and married Stephen Dudley on December 24, 1684.
7. Lydia Gilman [09-413], born on December 12, 1668 and married John

---

Little, Brown and Company, 1860) Vol II: p. 257; PDF e-book, http://archive.org/details/genealogicaldic02savarich accessed 17 July 2018.

770   Arthur Gilman, *The Gilman Family: Traced in the Line of Hon. John Gilman, of Exeter, N.H., with an Account of Many Other Gilmans, in England and America,* (Albany, NY: Joel Munsell, 1869) p. 40; PDF e-book, https://ia600200.us.archive.org/33/items/gilmanfamilytrac00gilm/gilmanfamilytrac00gilm.pdf accessed 11 October 2019.

771   "New Hampshire Marriage Records, 1637-1947," s.v. "John Gilman" (spouse "Elizabeth Treworthy" year "1657"), database, *FamilySearch,* accessed 11 October 2019.

772   James Savage, *A Genealogical Dictionary of the First Settlers of New England: Showing Three Generations of Those Who Came Before May 1692,* (Boston: Little, Brown and Company, 1860) Vol IV: p. 330; PDF e-book, http://archive.org/details/genealogicaldic04savarich accessed 17 July 2018.

773   Arthur Gilman, *The Gilman Family: Traced in the Line of Hon. John Gilman, of Exeter, N.H., with an Account of Many Other Gilmans, in England and America,* (Albany, NY: Joel Munsell, 1869) p. 40; PDF e-book, https://ia600200.us.archive.org/33/items/gilmanfamilytrac00gilm/gilmanfamilytrac00gilm.pdf accessed 11 October 2019.

774   "New Hampshire Deaths and Burials, 1784-1949," s.v. "John Gilman" (death "1708"), database, *FamilySearch,* accessed 11 October 2019.

775   "New Hampshire Deaths and Burials, 1784-1949," s.v. "Elizabeth Gilman" (spouse "John Gilman" death "1719"), database, *FamilySearch,* accessed 11 October 2019.

White [09-412].

8. Samuel Gilman, born on March 30, 1671 and died about 1691.
9. Nicholas Gilman, born on December 26, 1672.
10. Abigail Gilman, born on November 3, 1674 and married Samuel Thing.
11. John Gilman, born on January 19, 1677.
12. Deborah Gilman, born on April 30, 1679 and died about 1680.
13. Joanna Gilman, born on April 30, 1679. She married first to Robert Coffin, and second to Henry Dyer.
14. Joseph Gilman, born on October 25, 1680.
15. Alice Gilman, born on May 23, 1683 and married James Leavitt.
16. Catharine Gilman, born on November 27, 1684. She married first to Peter Folsom II, and second to Richard Calley of Stratham.[776]

[10-828] Samuel Appleton and [10-829] Mary Oliver

Samuel Appleton [10-828] was born about 1625 in Little Waldingfield, Suffolk, England to Samuel Appleton [11-1,656] and Judith Everard [11-1,657].[777] However, Savage gives 1624 for his christening and says the mother was Mary Everard.[778] This confusion appears to be because Judith [11-1,657] died in England and then Samuel Appleton [11-1,656] married a lady named Martha. When Samuel Appleton [10-828] about 10 in 1635, his father brought him to Massachusetts. Samuel Appleton [10-828] married Hannah Paine of Boston on April 2, 1651, but his second marriage was to Mary Oliver [10-829][779] on December 8, 1656 in Newbury, Essex County, Massachusetts.[780] Mary Oliver [10-829] was born on June 7, 1640 in Newbury[781] to John Oliver [11-1,658] and Joanna Goodale [11-1,659].[782]

---

776   James Savage, *A Genealogical Dictionary of the First Settlers of New England: Showing Three Generations of Those Who Came Before May 1692*, (Boston: Little, Brown and Company, 1860) Vol II: pp. 257-8; PDF e-book, http://archive.org/details/genealogicaldic02savarich accessed 17 July 2018.
777   "Appleton Genealogy," *The Essex Antiquarian*, Vol. 4: p. 1; database with digital images, *American Ancestors*, accessed 10 July 2019.
778   James Savage, *A Genealogical Dictionary of the First Settlers of New England: Showing Three Generations of Those Who Came Before May 1692*, (Boston: Little, Brown and Company, 1860) Vol I: p. 60; PDF e-book, https://archive.org/details/genealogicaldic01savarich accessed 17 July 2018.
779   "Appleton Genealogy," *The Essex Antiquarian*, Vol. 4: pp. 1-2; database with digital images, *American Ancestors*, accessed 10 July 2019.
780   "Massachusetts, Town Clerk, Vital and Town Records, 1626-2001," s.v. "Samuell Aplton" (spouse "Mary Oliver" marriage "1656"), database with digital images, *FamilySearch*, accessed 16 October 2019.
781   "Massachusetts, Town Clerk, Vital and Town Records, 1626-2001," s.v. "Mary Olliver" (birth "1640" place "Newbury"), database with digital images, *FamilySearch*, accessed 16 October 2019.
782   James Savage, *A Genealogical Dictionary of the First Settlers of New*

Samuel Appleton [10-828] was an officer in the King Philip's War in 1676, and owned a saw mill in Ipswich, Essex County, Massachusetts where he had all his children. From 1692 to about 1696 he was a Judge of the Inferior Court of Common Pleas, and made a will in 1695. Samuel Appleton [10-828] died on May 15, 1696 in Ipswich.[783] He was buried at the Old Burying Ground in Ipswich.[784] His widow Mary died within a year later, on February 15, 1697 and was also buried at the Old Burying Ground in Ipswich.[785] The children of Samuel Appleton [10-828] and Mary Oliver [10-829] are listed below:

1. John Appleton, who was born in 1660 in Ipswich.
2. Isaac Appleton [09-414], who was born in 1664 in Ipswich.
3. Joanna Appleton, who married Matthew Whipple before 1696.
4. Joseph Appleton, who was born on June 5, 1674 in Ipswich and died in 1689.
5. Oliver Appleton, who died on June 30, 1676.
6. Mary Appleton, who died on June 9, 1676.
7. Oliver Appleton, born in 1677 in Ipswich.
8. Mary Appleton, born on October 20, 1679 in Ipswich and died in 1689.[786]

[10-830] Thomas Baker and [10-831] Priscilla Symonds

Thomas Baker [10-830] was christened on September 18, 1636 in the parish of St. Peter Mancroft in Norwich, Norfolk, England to John Baker [11-1,660] and Elizabeth [11-1,661].[787] Within a year, on April 8, 1637, there is a record of the family going through the process of emigrating to Massachusetts.[788] In 1665, Thomas Baker [10-830] made freeman status, and married Priscilla

England: Showing Three Generations of Those Who Came Before May 1692, (Boston: Little, Brown and Company, 1860) Vol III: p. 309; PDF e-book, http://archive.org/details/genealogicaldic03savarich accessed 17 July 2018.

783   "Appleton Genealogy," The Essex Antiquarian, Vol. 4: pp. 1-2; database with digital images, American Ancestors, accessed 10 July 2019.

784   Samuel Appleton, gravestone, Old Burying Ground, Ipswich, Essex County, Massachusetts, s.v. "Col Samuel Appleton, Jr" (year "1696" memorial "38222231"), database with digital images, FindAGrave, accessed 16 October 2019.

785   Mary Appleton, gravestone, Old Burying Ground, Ipswich, Essex County, Massachusetts, s.v. "Mary Oliver Appleton" (death "1697" memorial "38222119"), database with digital images, FindAGrave, accessed 16 October 2019.

786   "Appleton Genealogy," The Essex Antiquarian, Vol. 4: p. 2; database with digital images, American Ancestors, accessed 10 July 2019.

787   William S. Appleton, Ancestry of Priscilla Baker, Who Lived 1674-1731, and Was the Wife of Isaac Appleton, of Ipswich, (Cambridge: Press of John Wilson and Son, 1870) p. 5; PDF e-book, https://archive.org/details/ancestrypriscil00applgoog/page/n16 accessed 16 October 2019.

788   Ibid., p. 3.

Symonds [10-831][789] on March 26, 1672/3 in Topsfield, Essex County, Massachusetts.[790] Priscilla Symonds was born about 1648, based on the age at death on her gravestone,[791] and her parents were Samuel Symonds [11-1,662] and Martha Read [11-1,663].[792]

Thomas Baker [10-830] was a militia officer, and was a representative in 1686, 1689, and 1690.[793] He died on March 18, 1717/8 and was buried at Pine Grove Cemetery in Topsfield.[794] His widow Priscilla [10-831] died on January 2, 1733/4 and was buried at the Old Burying Ground in Ipswich, Essex County, Massachusetts.[795] The children of Thomas Baker and Priscilla Symonds are listed below:

1. Priscilla Baker [09-415], who was born on December 8, 1674 in Topsfield.[796]
2. Martha Baker, who was born on October 14, 1682 in Topsfield.[797]
3. Rebecka Baker, who was born on November 16, 1685 in Topsfield.[798]
4. Thomas Baker, born on February 17, 1688 in Topsfield.[799]

---

789   James Savage, *A Genealogical Dictionary of the First Settlers of New England: Showing Three Generations of Those Who Came Before May 1692*, (Boston: Little, Brown and Company, 1860) Vol I: p. 99; PDF e-book, https://archive.org/details/genealogicaldic01savarich accessed 17 July 2018.
790   "Massachusetts Marriages, 1695-1910," s.v. "Thomas Baker" (spouse "Pricilla Symonds" year "1672"), database, *FamilySearch,* accessed 16 October 2019.
791   Priscilla Symonds Baker, gravestone, Old Burying Ground, Ipswich, Essex County, Massachusetts, s.v. "Priscilla Symonds Baker" (death "1733" memorial "64327729"), database with digital images, *FindAGrave,* accessed 16 October 2019.
792   William S. Appleton, *Ancestry of Priscilla Baker, Who Lived 1674-1731, and Was the Wife of Isaac Appleton, of Ipswich,* (Cambridge: Press of John Wilson and Son, 1870) p. 62; PDF e-book, https://archive.org/details/ancestrypriscil00applgoog/page/n16 accessed 16 October 2019.
793   James Savage, *A Genealogical Dictionary of the First Settlers of New England: Showing Three Generations of Those Who Came Before May 1692*, (Boston: Little, Brown and Company, 1860) Vol I: p. 99; PDF e-book, https://archive.org/details/genealogicaldic01savarich accessed 17 July 2018.
794   Thomas Baker, Pine Grove Cemetery, Topsfield, Essex County, Massachusetts, s.v. "Capt Thomas Baker" (death "1718" memorial "10750511"), database with digital images, *FindAGrave,* accessed 16 October 2019.
795   Priscilla Symonds Baker, gravestone, Old Burying Ground, Ipswich, Essex County, Massachusetts, s.v. "Priscilla Symonds Baker" (death "1733" memorial "64327729"), database with digital images, *FindAGrave,* accessed 16 October 2019.
796   "Massachusetts Births and Christenings, 1639-1915" s.v. "Pricilla Baker" (birth "1674" place "Topsfield"), database, *FamilySearch,* accessed 16 October 2019.
797   "Massachusetts Births and Christenings, 1639-1915" s.v. "Martha Baker" (birth "1682" place "Topsfield"), database, *FamilySearch,* accessed 16 October 2019.
798   "Massachusetts Births and Christenings, 1639-1915" s.v. "Rebecka Baker" (birth "1685" place "Topsfield"), database, *FamilySearch,* accessed 16 October 2019.
799   "Massachusetts Births and Christenings, 1639-1915" s.v. "Tho. Baker" (birth "1688" place "Topsfield"), database, *FamilySearch,* accessed 16 October 2019.

5.   John Baker, born on January 6, 1690 in Topsfield.[800]

[10-832] Nathaniel Cowdrey and [10-833] Mary Bacheldor

Nathaniel Cowdrey [10-832] was the son of William Cowdrey [11-1,664] and Joanna [11-1,665].[801] His first marriage was to Elizabeth on November 22, 1654 in Reading, Middlesex County, Massachusetts.[802] [803] She probably died before 1660, and on November 22, 1660 he married Mary Bacheldor [10-833] in Reading.[804] [805] Nathaniel and Mary had at least eight children between 1661 and 1679.[806] Mary was born in 1635 to John Batchelder [11-1,666] and Rebecca [11-1,667]. Nathaniel was Deacon at the First Congregational Church in Reading, and after 1687 was the town clerk of Reading. He died on June 16, 1690 in Reading and Mary died on February 27, 1729.[807] The children of Nathaniel Cowdrey [10-832] and Mary Bacheldor [10-833] are listed below:

1.   Nathaniel Cowdrey, born in 1661.
2.   Rebecca Cowdrey,[808] born on October 25, 1663 in Reading.[809]
3.   William Cowdrey, born on March 31, 1666 in Reading.[810]

---

800   "Massachusetts Births and Christenings, 1639-1915" s.v. "John Baker" (birth "1690" place "Topsfield"), database, *FamilySearch,* accessed 16 October 2019.
801   William Richard Cutter, ed., *Genealogical and Family History of Western New York,* (New York: Lewis Historical Publishing Company, 1912), Vol III: p 1427; PDF e-book, https://archive.org/details/genealogicalfami03incutt accessed 9 July 2018.
802   "Massachusetts Marriages, 1695-1910," s.v. "Nathanoll Cowdry" and "Elizeboth" (marriage 1654), database, *FamilySearch,* accessed 25 January 2018.
803   William Richard Cutter, ed., *Genealogical and Family History of Western New York,* (New York: Lewis Historical Publishing Company, 1912), Vol III: p 1428; PDF e-book, https://archive.org/details/genealogicalfami03incutt accessed 9 July 2018.
804   "Massachusetts Marriages, 1695-1910," s.v. "Nathanell Cowdry" and "Mary Basholler" (marriage 1660) database, *FamilySearch,* accessed 25 January 2018.
805   William Richard Cutter, ed., *Genealogical and Family History of Western New York,* (New York: Lewis Historical Publishing Company, 1912), Vol III: p 1428; PDF e-book, https://archive.org/details/genealogicalfami03incutt accessed 9 July 2018.
806   Frederick Clifton Pierce, *Batchelder, Batcheller, Genealogy,* (Chicago: W B Conkey Company, 1898), p 353; PDF e-book, https://archive.org/details/batchelderbatche1898pier accessed 15 July 2018.
807   William Richard Cutter, ed., *Genealogical and Family History of Western New York,* (New York: Lewis Historical Publishing Company, 1912), Vol III: p 1428; PDF e-book, https://archive.org/details/genealogicalfami03incutt accessed 9 July 2018.
808   Frederick Clifton Pierce, *Batchelder, Batcheller, Genealogy,* (Chicago: W B Conkey Company, 1898), p 353; PDF e-book, https://archive.org/details/batchelderbatche1898pier accessed 15 July 2018.
809   "Massachusetts, Town Clerk, Vital and Town Records, 1626-2001," s.v. "Rebeccah Cowdrey" (birth "1663") database with digital images, *FamilySearch,* accessed 25 January 2018.
810   "Massachusetts, Town Clerk, Vital and Town Records, 1626-2001," s.v. "Willm. Cowdrey" (birth "1666") database with digital images, *FamilySearch,* accessed

4. Mary Cowdrey, born on August 7, 1668 in Reading.[811]
5. Joanna Cowdrey, born in 1673.
6. Susana Cowdrey, born in 1676.
7. Nathaniel Cowdrey, born in 1679.
8. Matthias Cowdrey [09-416],[812] born on April 11, 1679 in Reading.[813]

[10-840] John Parker and [10-841] Abigail Whittaker

John Parker [10-840] was born on March 17, 1667/8 in Billerica, Middlesex County, Massachusetts to Benjamin Parker [11-1,680] and Sarah Hartwell [11-1,681].[814] [815] John married Abigail Whittaker on December 15, 1696 in Billerica[816] and they had one child before John died on January 1, 1698/9 in Billerica.[817] [818] Abigail was the daughter of John Whittaker [Bu11-1,682] and Elizabeth [Bu11-1,683],[819] and she was born on May 14, 1671 in Watertown, Middlesex County, Massachusetts.[820] After her first husband John died, she

---

25 January 2018.

811   "Massachusetts, Town Clerk, Vital and Town Records, 1626-2001," s.v. "Mary Cowdrey" (birth "1668") database with digital images, *FamilySearch,* accessed 25 January 2018.

812   Frederick Clifton Pierce, *Batchelder, Batcheller, Genealogy,* (Chicago: W B Conkey Company, 1898), p 353; PDF e-book, https://archive.org/details/batchelderbatche1898pier accessed 15 July 2018.

813   "Massachusetts, Town Clerk, Vital and Town Records, 1626-2001," s.v. "Matthias Cowdry" (birth "1679") database with digital images, *FamilySearch,* accessed 16 October 2019.

814   Henry A Hazen, *History of Billerica, Massachusetts: With a Genealogical Register,* (Boston: A Williams and Co, 1883) p. 105 of Genealogical Register; PDF e-book, Internet Archive, https://archive.org/details/historyofbilleri00hazenhe , accessed 9 July 2018.

815   "Massachusetts, Town Clerk, Vital and Town Records, 1626-2001," s.v. "John Parker (birth March 1667/8), database with digital images, *FamilySearch,* accessed 25 January 2018.

816   "Massachusetts Marriages, 1695-1910," s.v. "John Parker" and "Abigail Whittaker" (marriage 1696), database, *FamilySearch,* accessed 25 January 2018.

817   Henry A Hazen, *History of Billerica, Massachusetts: With a Genealogical Register,* (Boston: A Williams and Co, 1883) p. 105 of Genealogical Register; PDF e-book, Internet Archive, https://archive.org/details/historyofbilleri00hazenhe , accessed 9 July 2018.

818   "Massachusetts, Town Clerk, Vital and Town Records, 1626-2001," s.v. "John Parker" (birth 1698). database with digital images, *FamilySearch,* accessed 25 January 2018.

819   Henry A Hazen, *History of Billerica, Massachusetts: With a Genealogical Register,* (Boston: A Williams and Co, 1883) p. 105 of Genealogical Register; PDF e-book, Internet Archive, https://archive.org/details/historyofbilleri00hazenhe , accessed 9 July 2018.

820   "Massachusetts, Town Clerk, Vital and Town Records, 1626-2001," s.v.

married Simon Crosby on March 16, 1702 in Billerica.[821] [822] The child of John Parker [10-840] and Abigail Whittaker [10-841] was John Parker [09-420], who was born on May 14, 1698 in Billerica.[823]

[10-844] John Tarbell and [10-845] Mary Nurse

John Tarbell [10-844] was born about 1654 to Thomas Tarbell [11-1,688] and Mary [11-1,689], probably in Watertown, Middlesex County, Massachusetts. Before 1678 John enlisted as a soldier during King Philip's War, and he held the rank of Ensign at some point before his death.[824] On October 25, 1678 John Tarbell married Mary Nurse [10-845] in Danvers (then named Salem Village), Essex County, Massachusetts.[825] Mary Nurse was born about 1659 to Francis Nurse [11-1,690] and Rebecca Towne [11-1,691].[826] John Tarbell died March 25, 1715 in Danvers and is buried at the Nurse Homestead Cemetery in Danvers.[827] Mary died on June 28, 1749.[828] The children of John Parker [10-844] and Mary Nurse [10-845] are listed below:

1. John Tarbell [09-422], born on August 9, 1680 in Danvers (Salem Village).
2. Mary Tarbell, born on April 3, 1688 in Danvers and married Abraham

---

"Abigall Whitacar" (birth 1671), database with digital images, *FamilySearch*, accessed 4 May 2018.

821 "Massachusetts, Town Clerk, Vital and Town Records, 1626-2001," s.v. "Abigail Whittaker" and "Simon Crosbey" (marriage 1702), database, *FamilySearch*, accessed 25 January 2018.

822 Henry A Hazen, *History of Billerica, Massachusetts: With a Genealogical Register*, (Boston: A Williams and Co, 1883) p. 105 of Genealogical Register; PDF e-book, Internet Archive, https://archive.org/details/historyofbilleri00hazenhe , accessed 9 July 2018.

823 "Massachusetts, Town Clerk, Vital and Town Records, 1626-2001," s.v. "John Parker" (birth "1698"), database with digital images, *FamilySearch*, accessed 25 January 2018.

824 Charles Henry Wight, "Thomas Tarbell and Some of His Descendants," *The New England Historical and Genealogical Register*, Vol 61: p 70; database, *American Ancestors*, accessed 15 July 2018.

825 "Massachusetts, Town Clerk, Vital and Town Records, 1626-2001," s.v. "John Tarbell" and "Mary Nurse" (marriage 1678), database with digital images, *FamilySearch*, accessed 15 July 2018.

826 Charles Henry Wight, "Thomas Tarbell and Some of His Descendants," *The New England Historical and Genealogical Register*, Vol 61: p 70; database, *American Ancestors*, accessed 15 July 2018.

827 John Tarbell, grave marker, Nurse Homestead Cemetery, Danvers, Essex County, Massachusetts, digital images s.v. "John Tarbell" (death 1715, memorial 22271995), database with digital images, *FindAGrave*, accessed 25 January 2018.

828 Charles Henry Wight, "Thomas Tarbell and Some of His Descendants," *The New England Historical and Genealogical Register*, Vol 61: p 70; database, *American Ancestors*, accessed 15 July 2018.

Goodale on June 23, 1725.
3. Cornelius Tarbell, born on March 25, 1690 in Danvers.
4. Jonathan Tarbell, born on February 21, 1691 in Danvers and died between 1715 and 1718.
5. Elizabeth Tarbell, born on March 23, 1693/4 in Danvers and married Obed Abbot of Bedford. She died on May 29, 1752 in Bedford, Middlesex County, Massachusetts.
6. Sarah Tarbell, born on October 2, 1696 in Danvers and married Benjamin Hutchinson on February 7, 1715. She died on April 12, 1767 in Bedford.[829]

[10-850] George Polly and [10-851] Elizabeth Winn

I have not been able to verify the parents of George Polly [10-850] or where he came from. He married Elizabeth Winn [10-851] on May 24, 1649 in Woburn, Middlesex County, Massachusetts and they had at least seven children between 1650 and 1663.[830] [831] Elizabeth [10-851] was the daughter of Edward Winn [11-1,702] and Joanna [11-1,703] and most likely was born in Britain. George Polly [10-850] was a carpenter and in 1665 became surveyor of fences in Woburn.[832] He died on December 22, 1683 in Woburn,[833] and Elizabeth died on May 2, 1695.[834] Known children for George Polly [10-850] and Elizabeth Winn [10-851] are listed below:
1. John Polly, born on December 16, 1650.
2. Joseph Polly, born on December 25, 1652.[835]
3. George Polly, born on January 4, 1656 in Woburn.[836]

---

829   Ibid.
830   Horace Gillette Cleveland, *A Genealogy of Benjamin Cleveland*, (Chicago: n.p., 1879), p. 77; PDF e-book, https://archive.org/details/genealogyofbenja00clev accessed 15 July 2018.
831   "Massachusetts, Town Clerk, Vital and Town Records, 1626-2001," s.v. "George Polly" and "Elizabeth Winn" (marriage 1649), database with digital images, *FamilySearch*, accessed 15 July 2018.
832   Horace Gillette Cleveland, *A Genealogy of Benjamin Cleveland*, (Chicago: n.p., 1879), p. 77; PDF e-book, https://archive.org/details/genealogyofbenja00clev accessed 15 July 2018.
833   "Massachusetts, Town Clerk, Vital and Town Records, 1626-2001," s.v. "George Polly" (death 1683), database with digital images, *FamilySearch*, accessed 4 June 2017.
834   Horace Gillette Cleveland, *A Genealogy of Benjamin Cleveland*, (Chicago: n.p., 1879), p. 77; PDF e-book, https://archive.org/details/genealogyofbenja00clev accessed 15 July 2018.
835   Ibid.
836   "Massachusetts, Town Clerk, Vital and Town Records, 1626-2001," s.v. "George Polly" (birth "1656" place "Woburn"), database with digital images, *FamilySearch*, accessed 4 June 2017.

4. Elizabeth Polly [09-425], born on February 4, 1657 in Woburn.[837]
5. Samuel Polly, born on January 24, 1661 and died in February 1661.
6. Hannah Polly, born on April 6, 1662 and died the same day.
7. Hannah Polly, born on June 28, 1663.[838]

[10-852] Thomas Dutton and [10-853] Susannah

Thomas Dutton [10-852] was born about 1620 in Cheshire, England to John Dutton [11-1,704].[839] He was about ten years old when his father brought him to the colonies and apparently lived in Reading, Middlesex County, Massachusetts before 1669.[840] It was probably there that he married Susannah and had at least some of his nine children with her. On November 22, 1669 Thomas was accepted as an inhabitant of Billerica, Middlesex County, Massachusetts,[841] and Susannah died in Billerica on August 27, 1684.[842] Thomas then married Ruth Hooper in Billerica on September 10, 1684.[843] I could not verify when Thomas Dutton died.

Some genealogies give Susannah [10-853] the last name of Palmer based on a reference that Susannah Dutton was a Palmer cousin. However I could not verify that this Susannah was born with the last name of Palmer. She was born about 1626 though, because her death record said she was fifty-eight years old at death in 1684.[844] The known children of Thomas Dutton [10-852] and Susannah [10-853] are listed below:

1. Thomas Dutton [09-426], born September 14, 1648 in Reading.[845]

---

837   "Massachusetts, Town Clerk, Vital and Town Records, 1626-2001," s.v. "Elizabeth Polly" (birth "1657" place "Woburn"), database with digital images, *FamilySearch*, accessed 4 June 2017.

838   Horace Gillette Cleveland, *A Genealogy of Benjamin Cleveland*, (Chicago: n.p., 1879), p. 77; PDF e-book, https://archive.org/details/genealogyofbenja00clev accessed 15 July 2018.

839   William Richard Cutter, ed., *New England Families: Genealogical and Memorial*, (New York: Lewis Historical Publishing Co, 1913), Vol I: p 195; PDF e-book, https://archive.org/details/newenglandfamili01cutt_1 , accessed 10 July 2018.

840   John W. Jordan, ed., *Genealogical and Personal History of Western Pennsylvania*, (New York: Lewis Historical Publishing Company, 1915), Vol I: p 137; PDF e-book https://archive.org/details/genealogicalpers01injord accessed 15 July 2018.

841   Ibid.

842   "Massachusetts, Town Clerk, Vital and Town Records, 1626-2001," s.v. "Susanna Dutton" (death 1684), database with digital images, *FamilySearch*, accessed 26 January 2018.

843   "Massachusetts, Town Clerk, Vital and Town Records, 1626-2001," s.v. "Thomas Dutton" and "Ruth Hooper" (marriage 1684), database with digital images, *FamilySearch*, accessed 26 January 2018.

844   "Massachusetts, Town Clerk, Vital and Town Records, 1626-2001," s.v. "Susanna Dutton" (death 1684), database with digital images, *FamilySearch*, accessed 26 January 2018.

845   William Richard Cutter, ed., *New England Families: Genealogical and*

2. Mary Dutton, born November 14, 1651.
3. Susannah Dutton, born on February 27, 1654.
4. John Dutton, born on March 2, 1656.
5. Elizabeth Dutton, born on January 28, 1659.
6. Joseph Dutton, born on January 25, 1661 in Woburn. He first married Rebecca Fitch in 1685, and second Mary Smith in 1693. He died in 1733 in East Haddam, Middlesex County, Massachusetts.
7. Sarah Dutton, born on March 5, 1662.
8. James Dutton, born on August 25, 1665.
9. Benjamin Dutton, born on February 19, 1669.[846]

[10-856] Jonathan Kemp and [10-857] Mary

Jonathan Kemp [10-856] was born on April 6, 1668 in Groton, Middlesex County to Samuel Kemp [11-1,712] and Sarah Foster [11-1,713].[847][848] His first marriage was to Mary [10-857],[849] probably near Groton before 1699 but I could not find a marriage record to verify Mary's last name. They had at least four children together between 1699 and 1714 based on transcriptions at *FamilySearch*. On November 19, 1718 Jonathan married Sarah Gilson in Groton and he had at least three more children with her.[850] The known children for Jonathan Kemp [10-856] and Mary [10-857] are listed below:
1. Joseph Kemp [09-428], born on September 10, 1699 in Groton.[851]
2. Mary Kemp, born on May 27, 1702 in Groton.[852]

Memorial, (New York: Lewis Historical Publishing Co, 1913), Vol I: p 195; PDF e-book, https://archive.org/details/newenglandfamili01cutt_1 , accessed 10 July 2018.
846   John W. Jordan, ed., *Genealogical and Personal History of Western Pennsylvania,* (New York: Lewis Historical Publishing Company, 1915), Vol I: p 137; PDF e-book https://archive.org/details/genealogicalpers01injord accessed 15 July 2018.
847   Henry A Hazen, *History of Billerica, Massachusetts: With a Genealogical Register,* (Boston: A Williams and Co, 1883) p. 80 of Genealogical Register; PDF e-book, Internet Archive, https://archive.org/details/historyofbilleri00hazenhe , accessed 9 July 2018.
848   "Massachusetts, Town Clerk, Vital and Town Records, 1626-2001," s.v. "Jonathan Kemp" (birth 1668), database with digital images, *FamilySearch*, accessed 27 January 2018.

849   Henry A Hazen, *History of Billerica, Massachusetts: With a Genealogical Register,* (Boston: A Williams and Co, 1883) p. 80 of Genealogical Register; PDF e-book, Internet Archive, https://archive.org/details/historyofbilleri00hazenhe , accessed 9 July 2018.
850   "Massachusetts Marriages, 1695-1910," s.v. "Jonathan Kemp" (marriage 1718, spouse "Sarah Gilson"), database, *FamilySearch*, accessed 27 January 2018.
851   "Massachusetts Births and Christenings, 1639-1915" s.v. "Joseph Keemp" (birth "1699" place "Groton"), database, *FamilySearch*, accessed 27 January 2018.
852   "Massachusetts Births and Christenings, 1639-1915" s.v. "Mary Kemp" (birth "1702" place "Groton"), database, *FamilySearch*, accessed 27 January 2018.

3. Josiah Kemp, born on March 8, 1708 in Chelmsford, Middlesex County, Massachusetts.[853]
4. John Kemp, born on September 26, 1714 in Chelmsford.[854]

[10-858] Clement Chamberlain and [10-859] Mary

Clement Chamberlain [10-858] was born on May 30, 1669 in Billerica, Middlesex County, Massachusetts to William Chamberlain [11-1,716] and Rebecca [11-1,717].[855] [856] His wife was Mary [10-859] and they had at least eight children together between 1693 and 1708, who are listed below:[857]

1. Mary Chamberlain, born on January 20, 1692/3 in Billerica,[858] and married Jonathan Cram of Wilmington on December 1, 1732.
2. Clement Chamberlain, born in 1694 and married Elizabeth. He died on January 21, 1754.
3. Joseph Chamberlain, born in November 1696 and married Mary Johnson.[859]
4. John Chamberlain, born on June 8, 1699 in Billerica[860] and died on June 1716.[861]

---

853   "Massachusetts Births and Christenings, 1639-1915" s.v. "Josiah Keymp" (birth "1708" place "Chelmsford"), database, *FamilySearch*, accessed 27 January 2018.
854   "Massachusetts Births and Christenings, 1639-1915" s.v. "John Kemp" (birth "1714" place "Chelmsford"), database, *FamilySearch*, accessed 27 January 2018.
855   Henry A Hazen, *History of Billerica, Massachusetts: With a Genealogical Register,* (Boston: A Williams and Co, 1883) p. 23 of Genealogical Register; PDF e-book, Internet Archive, https://archive.org/details/historyofbilleri00hazenhe , accessed 9 July 2018.
856"   Massachusetts, Town Clerk, Vital and Town Records, 1626-2001," s.v. "Clement Chamberlain" (birth 1669), database with digital images, *FamilySearch*, accessed 27 January 2018.
857   Henry A Hazen, *History of Billerica, Massachusetts: With a Genealogical Register,* (Boston: A Williams and Co, 1883) p. 23 of Genealogical Register; PDF e-book, Internet Archive, https://archive.org/details/historyofbilleri00hazenhe , accessed 9 July 2018.
858   "Massachusetts Births and Christenings, 1639-1915," s.v. "Mary Chamberlain" (birth "1692" place "Billerica"), database, *FamilySearch*, accessed 27 January 2018.
859   Henry A Hazen, *History of Billerica, Massachusetts: With a Genealogical Register,* (Boston: A Williams and Co, 1883) p. 23 of Genealogical Register; PDF e-book, Internet Archive, https://archive.org/details/historyofbilleri00hazenhe , accessed 9 July 2018.
860   "Massachusetts Births and Christenings, 1639-1915," s.v. "John Chamberlain" (birth "1699" place "Billerica"), database, *FamilySearch*, accessed 27 January 2018.
861   Henry A Hazen, *History of Billerica, Massachusetts: With a Genealogical Register,* (Boston: A Williams and Co, 1883) p. 23 of Genealogical Register; PDF e-book, Internet Archive, https://archive.org/details/historyofbilleri00hazenhe , accessed 9 July 2018.

5. Peggy "Elizabeth" Chamberlain [09-429], born on March 12, 1701 in Billerica.[862]
6. William Chamberlain, born on March 3, 1703/4 and married Esther.
7. Rebecca Chamberlain, born on April 14, 1705.[863]
8. Anna Chamberlain, born on May 29, 1708 in Billerica.[864]

[10-860] Robert Mears and [10-861] Elizabeth Adams

Robert Mears [10-860] (or Mires) was born on January 29, 1671/2 in Boston, Suffolk County, Massachusetts to James Mears [11-1,720] and Elizabeth Mellowes [11-1,721].[865] [866] His first marriage was to Elizabeth Adams [10-861], on July 30, 1706 in Boston,[867] and there are records of them having two children between 1707 and 1710.[868] I could not verify who Elizabeth's parents were, or what happened to her. Robert Mears [10-860] married again on May 2, 1733, to Mary Dresser.[869] The known children for Robert Mears [10-860] and Elizabeth Adams [10-861] are listed below:

1. Robert Meers [09-430], born on January 6, 1707 in Boston.[870]
2. John Mears, born on January 8, 1710 in Boston.[871]

---

862   "Massachusetts, Town Clerk, Vital and Town Records, 1626-2001," s.v. "Pege Chamberlain" (birth "1701" place "Billerica") database with digital images, *FamilySearch,* accessed 7 January 2018.

863   Henry A Hazen, *History of Billerica, Massachusetts: With a Genealogical Register,* (Boston: A Williams and Co, 1883) p. 23 of Genealogical Register; PDF e-book, Internet Archive, https://archive.org/details/historyofbilleri00hazenhe , accessed 9 July 2018.

864   "Massachusetts Births and Christenings, 1639-1915," s.v. "Anna Chamberlain" (birth "1708" place "Billerica"), database, *FamilySearch,* accessed 27 January 2018.

865   William Richard Cutter, ed., *Genealogical and Personal Memoirs: Relating to the Families of Boston and Eastern Massachusetts,* (New York: Lewis Historical Publishing Company, 1908), Vol III: p 1480; PDF e-book, https://archive.org/details/genealogicaland00cuttgoog accessed 15 July 2018.

866   "Massachusetts Births and Christenings, 1639-1915," s.v. "Robert Meers" (birth "1671"), database, *FamilySearch,* accessed 27 January 2018.

867   "Massachusetts, Compiled Marriages, 1633-1850," s.v. "Robert Meers" (marriage "1706" spouse "Elizabeth Adams"), database, *Ancestry.com,* accessed 11 July 2017.

868   William Richard Cutter, ed., *Genealogical and Personal Memoirs: Relating to the Families of Boston and Eastern Massachusetts,* (New York: Lewis Historical Publishing Company, 1908), Vol III: p 1480; PDF e-book, https://archive.org/details/genealogicaland00cuttgoog accessed 15 July 2018.

869   Ibid.

870   "Massachusetts Births and Christenings, 1639-1915," s.v. "Robert Mires" (birth "1707" place "Boston"), database, *FamilySearch,* accessed 11 July 2017.

871   William Richard Cutter, ed., *Genealogical and Personal Memoirs: Relating to the Families of Boston and Eastern Massachusetts,* (New York: Lewis Historical

[10-862] Samuel Frost and [10-863] Hannah Mascraft

Samuel Frost [10-862] was born on February 28, 1669/70 in Billerica, Middlesex County, Massachusetts to James Frost [11-1,724] and Elizabeth Foster [11-1,725].[872] [873] He married Hannah Mascraft [10-863] on July 15, 1701 in Roxbury, Suffolk County, Massachusetts[874] and they had at least six children together between 1702 and 1714.[875] Hannah Mascraft was born on May 6, 1677 in Roxbury to Daniel Mascroft [11-1,726] and Mary Gorton [11-1,727].[876] Hannah died on December 25, 1753 in Billerica, and Samuel died on December 7, 1755 in Tewksbury, Middlesex County, Massachusetts.[877] The known children for Samuel Frost [10-862] and Hannah Mascraft [10-863] are listed below:

1. Hannah Frost [09-431], born on May 13, 1702 in Billerica.
2. Samuel Frost, born on November 26, 1703 in Billerica.
3. Daniel Frost, born on June 9, 1705 in Billerica.
4. Abigail Frost, born on June 18, 1710 in Billerica.
5. John Frost, born on April 30, 1712 in Billerica.
6. Elizabeth Frost, born on August 16, 1714 in Billerica.[878]

Publishing Company, 1908), Vol III: p 1480; PDF e-book, https://archive.org/details/genealogicaland00cuttgoog accessed 15 July 2018.

872   Henry A Hazen, *History of Billerica, Massachusetts: With a Genealogical Register,* (Boston: A Williams and Co,   1883)   p. 62 of Genealogical Register; PDF e-book, Internet Archive,   https://archive.org/details/historyofbilleri00hazenhe , ...accessed 9 July 2018.

873   "Massachusetts, Town Clerk, Vital and Town Records, 1626-2001," s.v. "Samuel Frost" (birth "1669/70"), database with digital images, *FamilySearch,* accessed 27 January 2018.

874   "Massachusetts, Town Clerk, Vital and Town Records, 1626-2001," s.v. "Samuel Frost" (marriage 1701, spouse "Hannah Mascraft"), database with digital images, *FamilySearch,* accessed 12 July 2017.

875   "Massachusetts, Town Clerk, Vital and Town Records, 1626-2001," s.v. "Hannah Frost" (birth 1702), database with digital images, *FamilySearch,* accessed 11 July 2017.

876   "Massachusetts, Town Clerk, Vital and Town Records, 1626-2001," s.v. "Hannah Marscroft" (birth 1677), database with digital images, *FamilySearch,* accessed 12 July 2017.

877   Henry A Hazen, *History of Billerica, Massachusetts: With a Genealogical Register,* (Boston: A Williams and Co, 1883)   p. 62 of Genealogical Register; PDF e-book, Internet Archive,   https://archive.org/details/historyofbilleri00hazenhe , ...accessed 9 July 2018.

878   "Massachusetts, Town Clerk, Vital and Town Records, 1626-2001," Samuel and Hannah Frost family group s.v. "Hannah Frost" (birth "1702" place "Billerica"), database with digital images, *FamilySearch,* accessed 11 July 2017.

[11-1,536] Solomon Johnson

Solomon Johnson [11-1,536] was born about 1601 in Hernhill, Kent, England.[879] [880] Even though some online genealogies trace Solomon's ancestry further, I was not able to find strong evidence connecting him to his parents. Solomon's probable first marriage was in England and he had children there, including Solomon Jr with whom he is sometimes confused. Then in 1638 Solomon [11-1,536] married Elinor in England[881] and had more children with her after emigrating to New England in 1639.[882] By February 3, 1639, Solomon lived in Sudbury, Middlesex County, Massachusetts and he was made freeman there in 1645. By 1660 Solomon had moved to Marlborough, Middlesex County, Massachusetts where he was a selectman from 1661 to 1665 and constable from 1663 to 1664. Solomon [11-1,536] was a tailor by trade, and also served as a deacon in church. He died in June of 1687 in Marlborough.[883] The known children of Solomon Johnson [11-1,536] with his first wife were:

1. Solomon Johnson, born about 1627 in England, and died August 26, 1690 in Sudbury. He married first to Hannah, and second to Hannah Crefts of Natomy on February 1, 1687 in Watertown, Middlesex County, Massachusetts.
2. John Johnson [10-768], born about 1629 in Hernhill, Kent, England. He married Deborah Ward [10-769] on November 19, 1657 in Sudbury, and was killed on August 29, 1708 in Haverhill.[884]

[11-1,538] William Ward and [11-1,539] Eleanor

William Ward [11-1,538] was born in 1603 in England.[885] [886] It is not clear

---

879   William W Johnson, *Johnson Genealogy: Records of the Descendants of John Johnson of Ipswich and Andover*, (North Greenfield, Wisconsin: William W Johnson, 1892), p 7; PDF e-book, https://archive.org/details/johnsongenealogy00john , accessed 14 July 2018.
880   "US and International Marriage Records, 1560-1900," s.v. "Solomon Johnson" (marriage 1638, spouse "Elinor"), database, *Ancestry.com*, accessed 2016.
881   "US and International Marriage Records, 1560-1900," s.v. "Solomon Johnson" (marriage 1638, spouse "Elinor"), database, *Ancestry.com*, accessed 2016.
882   "US and Canada, Passenger and Immigration Lists Index, 1500s-1900s" s.v. "Solomon Johnson" (immigration 1639), database, *Ancestry.com*, accessed 28 January 2018.
883   Mrs. Ellwood Kimball, "The Solomon Johnson Family," *The New England Historical and Genealogical Register*, Vol 66, p 234; database, *American Ancestors*, accessed 9 July 2018.
884   Ibid., Vol 66, pp. 234-5.
885   Clarence Almon Torrey, *New England Marriages Prior to 1700*, (Baltimore, Maryland: Genealogical Publishing Co.,   Inc, 2004), p. 779; database with digital images, *Ancestry.com*, accessed 12 May 2016.
886   Andrew Henshaw Ward, *Ward Family: Descendants of William Ward, who*

about the names of his parents or where he was born, although a hint might be that the Ward family arms in Massachusetts matched those of the Wards in Durham, England.[887]   By 1626, William [11-1,538] was in Newton, Cambridgeshire, England where he married his first wife, Eleanor [11-1,539].[888] They had six known children together in England, between 1626 and 1639. Some say the children were born in Sudbury, Middlesex County, Massachusetts, but the original document listing all of William's children says these children from the first marriage were born in England.[889]   Not much is known about Eleanor [11-1,539], but she probably died before 1639 when William [11-1,538] married his second wife Elizabeth Storey in England. Also in 1639, William took his new wife and children from his first marriage to Massachusetts.[890] William had eight more children with Elizabeth, from 1640 to 1658, all in Sudbury.[891] Then in 1660 William Ward moved to Marlborough, Middlesex County, Massachusetts.[892] In Marlborough William held the title of Deacon and died on 10 Aug 1687.[893] William Ward is buried at Spring Hill Cemetery in Marlborough.[894] The known children of William Ward [11-1,538] and Eleanor [11-1,539] are listed below:

1. John Ward, born in 1626 in England.
2. Joanna Ward, born in 1628 in England.
3. Obadiah Ward, born in 1632 in England.
4. Richard Ward, born in 1635 in England.
5. Deborah Ward [10-769], born in 1637 in England.
6. Hannah Ward, born in 1639 in England.[895]

---

settled in Sudbury, Mass, in 1639, (Boston, MA: Samuel Drake, 1851), p. VI; PDF e-book, https://archive.org/details/wardfamilydesce00wardgoog accessed 17 July 2018.

887   Ibid.

888   Clarence Almon Torrey, *New England Marriages Prior to 1700*, (Baltimore, Maryland: Genealogical Publishing Co., Inc, 2004), p. 779; database with digital images, *Ancestry.com*, accessed 12 May 2016.

889   "Massachusetts, Town Clerk, Vital and Town Records," s.v. "Deborah Ward" (birth 1637, in William Ward family on image), database with digital images, *FamilySearch*, accessed 6 May 2016.

890   "US and Canada, Passenger and Immigration Lists Index, 1500s-1900s," s.v. "William Ward" (immigration 1639), database, *Ancestry.com*, accessed 2016.

891   "Massachusetts, Town Clerk, Vital and Town Records," s.v. "Deborah Ward" (birth 1637, in William Ward family on image), database with digital images, *FamilySearch,* accessed 6 May 2016.

892   Andrew Henshaw Ward, *Ward Family: Descendants of William Ward, who settled in Sudbury, Mass, in 1639*, (Boston, MA: Samuel Drake, 1851), p. VII; PDF e-book, https://archive.org/details/wardfamilydesce00wardgoog accessed 17 July 2018.

893   "Massachusetts, Town and Vital Records, 1620-1988," s.v. "William Ward" (death 1687), database, *Ancestry.com,* accessed 2016.

894   William Ward, grave marker, Spring Hill Cemetery, Marlborough, Middlesex County, Massachusetts, digital image, *FindAGrave*, s.v. "William Ward" (death 1687, memorial 6190756), accessed 28 January 2018.

895   "Massachusetts, Town Clerk, Vital and Town Records," William Ward family group s.v. "Deborah Ward" (birth "1637"), database with digital images, *FamilySearch,*

[11-1,540] Thomas Lambe and [11-1,541] Dorothy Harbittle

Thomas Lambe [11-1,540] was a merchant in London before arriving in Massachusetts in 1630 with his first wife Elizabeth. It is not clear when he was born, so his ancestry can not accurately be traced further back without further information. Thomas had at least six children with Elizabeth, of which two were born in England before 1630. Then on May 18, 1631, Thomas became a freeman in Roxbury, which is now in Boston, Suffolk County, Massachusetts. About 1634 he is mentioned as having 37 acres of land. Then Elizabeth died in 1639 due to complications from childbirth.[896]

On July 16, 1640 Thomas Lambe [11-1,540] married Dorothy Harbittle [11-1,541] (sometimes spelled Harbottle) in Roxbury, [897] Dorothy was a "maide servant".   Thomas and Dorothy had at least three children together, born in Roxbury between 1641 and 1644. Then Thomas died on January 28, 1646 of a feverish delirium from a bad cold in Roxbury. About 1651 or 1652 Dorothy [11-1,541] married Thomas Hawley.[898]   I could not find when Dorothy died. The known children of Thomas Lambe [11-1,540] and Dorothy Harbittle [11-1,541] are listed below:
1. Caleb Lambe, born on April 9, 1641 in Roxbury.[899]
2. Joshua Lambe [10-770], born on November 27, 1642 in Roxbury.[900]
3. Mary Lambe, born on September 29, 1644 in Roxbury.[901]

[11-1,542] John Alcock and [11-1,543] Sarah Palsgrave

John Alcock [11-1,542] was christened on January 21, 1626/7 at St Margaret's Church in Leicester, Leicestershire, England to George Alcock [12-

accessed 6 May 2016.
896   Charles Francis Lamb, *Nathan Lamb of Leicester, Massachusetts: His Ancestors and Descendants*, (Madison, Wisconsin: n.p., 1930), pp. 22-24; e-book, https://archive.org/details/nathanlamboffeic00lamb accessed 17 July 2018.
897   Clarence Almon Torrey, *New England Marriages Prior to 1700*, (Baltimore, Maryland: Genealogical Publishing Co., Inc, 2004), p. 448; database with digital images, *Ancestry.com*, accessed 5 May 2016.
898   Charles Francis Lamb, *Nathan Lamb of Leicester, Massachusetts: His Ancestors and Descendants*, (Madison, Wisconsin: n.p., 1930), pp. 22-24; e-book, https://archive.org/details/nathanlamboffeic00lamb accessed 17 July 2018.
899   "Massachusetts Births and Christenings, 1639-1915," s.v. "Caleb Lambe" (birth "1641" place "Roxbury"), database, *FamilySearch*, accessed 28 January 2018.
900   "Massachusetts, Town Clerk, Vital and Town Records, 1626-2001," s.v. "Joshua Lambe" (birth "1642" place "Roxbury"), database, *FamilySearch*, accessed 12 May 2016.
901   "Massachusetts Births and Christenings, 1639-1915," s.v. "Mary Lambe" (birth "1644" place "Roxbury"), database, *FamilySearch*, accessed 28 January 2018.

3,084] and the sister [12-3,085] of Reverend Thomas Hooker, possibly Anne.[902] [903] [904] As a three year old child in 1630, John came with his family in the fleet of Governor Winthrop to Massachusetts.[905] [906] John graduated from Harvard University in Cambridge, Middlesex County, Massachusetts in 1646 at the age of nineteen, then taught school in 1647 in Hartford, Connecticut. About 1648, John was back in Roxbury where he married Sarah Palsgrave [11-1,543].[907] [908] Sarah Palsgrave was born about 1621[909] in England to Richard Palgrave [12-3,086] and Ann [12-3,087], and her family came over to Massachusetts in 1630 with the Winthrop fleet also. About 1652, John was a physician in Roxbury, and became a freeman there on November 22, 1652. Sarah died on November 29, 1665 in Roxbury and John died on March 27, 1667, also in Roxbury.[910] The known children of John Alcock [11-1,542] and Sarah Palsgrave [11-1,543] are listed below:

1. Sarah Alcock, christened on May 26, 1650 in Roxbury.[911]
2. Anna Alcock, christened on May 26, 1650 in Roxbury.[912]

---

902   Clarence Almon Torrey, *New England Marriages Prior to 1700*, (Baltimore, Maryland: Genealogical Publishing Co., Inc, 2004), p. 7; database with digital images, *Ancestry.com,* accessed 5 May 2016.
903   John Langdon Sibley, *Biographical Sketches of Graduates of Harvard University: in Cambridge, Massachusetts,* (Cambridge, Massachusetts: University Bookstore, 1873), Vol I: p. 124; PDF e-book, https://archive.org/details/biographicalsket01sibluoft accessed 17 July 2018.
904   "England Births and Christenings, 1538-1975," s.v. "Johannes Alcocke" (birth 1626), database, *FamilySearch,* accessed 28 January 2018.
905   "US and Canada, Passenger and Immigration Lists Index, 1500s-1900s," s.v. "John Alcock" (immigration 1630), database, accessed 13 May 2016.
906   James Savage, *A Genealogical Dictionary of the First Settlers of New England: Showing Three Generations of Those Who Came Before May 1692,* (Boston: Little, Brown and Company, 1860), Vol I: p. 21; PDF e-book, http://archive.org/details/genealogicaldic01savarich accessed 17 July 2018.
907   John Langdon Sibley, *Biographical Sketches of Graduates of Harvard University: in Cambridge, Massachusetts,* (Cambridge, Massachusetts: University Bookstore, 1873), Vol I: p. 126; PDF e-book, https://archive.org/details/biographicalsket01sibluoft accessed 17 July 2018.
908   Clarence Almon Torrey, *New England Marriages Prior to 1700*, (Baltimore, Maryland: Genealogical Publishing Co., Inc, 2004), p. 7; database with digital images, *Ancestry.com,* accessed 5 May 2016.
909   Clarence Almon Torrey, *New England Marriages Prior to 1700*, (Baltimore, Maryland: Genealogical Publishing Co., Inc, 2004), p. 7; database with digital images, *Ancestry.com,* accessed 5 May 2016.
910   John Langdon Sibley, *Biographical Sketches of Graduates of Harvard University: in Cambridge, Massachusetts,* (Cambridge, Massachusetts: University Bookstore, 1873), Vol I: pp. 123-126; PDF e-book, https://archive.org/details/biographicalsket01sibluoft accessed 17 July 2018.
911   "Massachusetts, Town Clerk, Vital and Town Records, 1626-2001," s.v. "Sarah Alcock" (birth "1650" place "Roxbury"), database with digital images, *FamilySearch*, accessed 28 January 2018.
912   "Massachusetts, Town Clerk, Vital and Town Records, 1626-2001," s.v.

3. Mary Alcock [10-771], born in 1652 in Roxbury.[913]
4. George Alcock, christened on March 25, 1655 in Roxbury.[914]
5. John Alcock, christened on January 15, 1656 in Roxbury.[915]
6. Elizabeth Alcock, christened on January 27, 1659 in Roxbury.[916]
7. Palsgrave Alcock, christened on May 20, 1662 in Roxbury.[917]

[11-1,544] Thomas Richardson and [11-1,545] Mary

Thomas Richardson [11-1,544] was christened on July 3, 1608 in Westmill, Hertfordshire, England to Thomas Richardson [12-3,088] and Katherine Duxford [12-3,089].[918] By 1638 he was in Massachusetts, where there is a record of him on February 18, 1637/8 joining the church in Charlestown, which is now part of Boston, Suffolk County, Massachusetts. Thomas was made freeman on May 2, 1638 in Charlestown. He married Mary before 1638 (she had already joined the Charlestown church on 21 Feb 1635/6) and they had at least seven children together, between 1638 and 1651.[919] Some say Mary's surname was Baldwin, but I have found no evidence to support any surname or ancestry for her. Thomas died on August 28, 1651 in Woburn, Middlesex County, Massachusetts[920] and Mary later married Michael Bacon on October

---

"Anna Alcock" (birth "1650" place "Roxbury"), database with digital images, *FamilySearch*, accessed 28 January 2018.

913   "Massachusetts, Town and Vital Records, 1620-1988," s.v. "Mary Alcock" (birth "1652"), database, *Ancestry.com*, accessed 2016.

914   "Massachusetts, Town Clerk, Vital and Town Records, 1626-2001," s.v. "George Alcock" (birth "1655" place "Roxbury"), database with digital images, *FamilySearch*, accessed 28 January 2018.

915   "Massachusetts, Town Clerk, Vital and Town Records, 1626-2001," s.v. "John Alcock" (birth "1656" place "Roxbury"), database with digital images, *FamilySearch*, accessed 28 January 2018.

916   "Massachusetts, Town Clerk, Vital and Town Records, 1626-2001," s.v. "Elisabeth Alcocke" (birth "1662" place "Roxbury"), database with digital images, *FamilySearch*, accessed 28 January 2018.

917   "Massachusetts, Town Clerk, Vital and Town Records, 1626-2001," s.v. "Palsgrave Alcocke" (birth "1650" place "Roxbury"), database with digital images, *FamilySearch*, accessed 28 January 2018.

918   William Richard Cutter, ed., *New England Families: Genealogical and Memorial,* (New York: Lewis Historical Publishing Co, 1913), Vol IV: p. 1931; PDF e-book, https://archive.org/details/XNewEnglandFamiliesGenealogicalAndMemorialARecordO fHerPeopleInTheMakingOfCommonw accessed 10 July 2018.

919   John Adams Vinton, *The Richardson Memorial: Comprising a Full History and Genealogy of the Posterity of the Three Brothers,* (Portland, Maine: Brown Thurston and Co, 1876), pp. 509-510; PDF e-book, https://archive.org/details/richardsonmemori00vint , accessed 10 July 2018.

920   Ibid., p. 505.

26, 1655 in Woburn. Mary died on May 19, 1670.[921] The known children of Thomas Richardson [11-1,544] and Mary [11-1,545] are listed below:

1. Mary Richardson, christened on November 17, 1638 in Charlestown, and married John Baldwin on May 16, 1655.
2. Sarah Richardson, christened on November 22, 1640 in Charlestown, and married Michael Bacon, Jr on March 22, 1660.
3. Isaac Richardson, born on May 14, 1643 in Woburn, and married Deborah Fuller.
4. Thomas Richardson, born on October 4, 1645 in Woburn. He married first to Mary Stimpson, and later to Sarah Patten.
5. Ruth Richardson, born on April 14, 1647 in Woburn.
6. Phebe Richardson, born on January 24, 1648/9 in Woburn.
7. Nathaniel Richardson [10-772], born on January 2, 1650/1 in Woburn and died on December 4, 1714. He married Mary [10-773].[922]

[11-1,548] Thomas Green and [11-1,549] Rebecca Hills

There is some disagreement about the birthplace of Thomas Green [11-1,548]. One source speculates he was from Leicestershire,[923] but another cites a ship certificate giving the birthplace as St. Albans, Hertfordshire, England about 1620 and I find this likely.[924] Thomas Green's parents were Thomas Green [12-3,096] and Elizabeth[925] Harvy [12-3,097].[926]

Thomas Green [11-1,548] immigrated to Massachusetts in 1635 from England at the age of 15,[927] and about 1653 married Rebecca Hills [11-1,549].[928] Rebecca was the daughter of Joseph Hills [12-3,098] and Rose

---

921   Ibid., p. 506.
922   Ibid.
923   Samuel S. Greene, *A Genealogical Sketch of the Descendants of Thomas Green of Malden, Mass.*, (Boston: Henry W. Dutton & Son, 1858), p. 9; PDF e-book, https://archive.org/details/genealogicalsket00gree , accessed 10 July 2018.

924   William Richard Cutter, ed., *Genealogical and Personal Memoirs: Relating to the Families of the State of Massachusetts*, (New York: Lewis Historical Publishing Company, 1910), Vol IV: p. 2313; PDF e-book, https://archive.org/details/genealogicaland01adamgoog accessed 9 July 2018.
925   Samuel S. Greene, *A Genealogical Sketch of the Descendants of Thomas Green of Malden, Mass.*, (Boston: Henry W. Dutton & Son, 1858), p. 8; PDF e-book, https://archive.org/details/genealogicalsket00gree , accessed 10 July 2018.
926   "England Marriages, 1538-1973," s.v. "Thomas Greene" (spouse "Elizabeth Harvy" year "1618"), database, *FamilySearch*, accessed 14 May 2018.
927   William Richard Cutter, ed., *Genealogical and Personal Memoirs: Relating to the Families of the State of Massachusetts*, (New York: Lewis Historical Publishing Company, 1910), Vol IV: p. 2313; PDF e-book, https://archive.org/details/genealogicaland01adamgoog accessed 9 July 2018.
928   Samuel S. Greene, *A Genealogical Sketch of the Descendants of Thomas Green of Malden, Mass.*, (Boston: Henry W. Dutton & Son, 1858), p. 9; PDF e-book,

Clarke [12-3,099], and was baptized in Maldon, Essex, England on April 20, 1634.[929] Thomas and Rebecca had at least five children together, between 1654 and 1670. Then Thomas died on Feb 13, 1671/2, followed by Rebecca on June 6, 1674.[930] The known children of Thomas Green [11-1,548] and Rebecca Hills [11-1,549] are listed below:

1. Rebecca Green, born in 1654 and died on May 25, 1726. She married Thomas Newell of Lynn in 1674.
2. Thomas Green, who was born in February 1655/6 and died on April 15, 1674.
3. Hannah Green, who was born on October 16, 1658 in Malden, and died on March 25, 1659.
4. Hannah Green, who was born on February 24, 1659/60 in Malden, and married John Vinton on August 26, 1677.
5. Samuel Green [10-774], who was born on Aug 5, 1670 in Malden, married Elizabeth Upham [10-775], and died on January 2, 1735/6.[931]

[11-1,550] Phineas Upham and [11-1,551] Ruth Wood

Phineas Upham [11-1,550] was christened on September 21, 1634 in Exeter, Devon, England. His parents were John Upham [12-3,100] and Elizabeth Webb [12-3,101].[932] As for Elizabeth's surname, there is some disagreement but it was likely Webb at birth according to a reference in a will.[933]

Since Phineas Upham's parents came to Massachusetts in 1635,[934] Phineas would have been still an infant when he immigrated. He married Ruth Wood [11-1,551] on April 14, 1658 in Malden, Middlesex County, Massachusetts.[935] Based on her age at death, Ruth Wood would have been born around 1636.[936]

---

https://archive.org/details/genealogicalsket00gree , accessed 10 July 2018.

929 William Sandford Hills, *Genealogical Data Relating to the Ancestry and Descendants of William Hills and of Joseph Hills,* (Boston: Hills Family Genealogical and Historical Association, 1902), p. 72; PDF e-book, https://archive.org/details/genealogicaldata00hill accessed 17 July 2018.

930 Samuel S. Greene, *A Genealogical Sketch of the Descendants of Thomas Green of Malden, Mass.,* (Boston: Henry W. Dutton & Son, 1858), p. 9; PDF e-book, https://archive.org/details/genealogicalsket00gree , accessed 10 July 2018.

931 Ibid., pp. 9-13.

932"England Births and Christenings, 1538-1975," s.v. "Phinees Uppam" (birth 1634), database, *FamilySearch,* accessed 22 July 2018.

933 F K Upham, *Upham Genealogy: the Descendants of John Upham, of Massachusetts,* (Albany, NY: Joel Munsell's Sons, 1892), p. 34; PDF e-book, https://archive.org/details/uphamgenealogyde00upha accessed 22 July 2018.

934 Ibid., p. 33.

935 "Massachusetts, Town Clerk, Vital and Town Records, 1626-2001," s.v. "Ruth Woods" (marriage 1658, spouse "Phineas Upham"), database, *FamilySearch,* accessed 22 July 2018.

936 "Upham Genealogy," *The New England Historical and Genealogical Register,*

There is some disagreement about the parents of Ruth Wood, and I was not able to find much evidence to determine the identity of the actual parents.

Phineas Upham was a Lieutenant in King Philip's War, and was wounded in a battle against the Indians in a frozen swamp during a snowstorm in the winter of 1675.[937] He never recovered and died in October 1676.[938] His grave is at Bell Rock Cemetery in Malden.[939] Ruth died in 1696/7 and was also buried at Bell Rock Cemetery.[940] The known children of Phineas Upham [11-1,550] and Ruth Wood [11-1,551] are listed below:

1. Phineas Upham, born in 1659. He married Mary Mellins and died in October 1720.
2. Nathaniel Upham, born in 1661 and died on November 11, 1717. He married Sarah.
3. Ruth Upham, born in 1664 and died about 1676.
4. John Upham, born in 1666 and died in 1733. He married first to Abigail Haywood in 1688, and second to Tamzen Ong in 1717/8.
5. Elizabeth Upham [10-775]
6. Thomas Upham, who married first to Elizabeth Hovey in 1693, second to Mary Brown on October 2, 1704, and finally to Ruth Cutler, the widow of John Smith. Thomas died on November 28, 1735.
7. Richard Upham, who married Abigail Hovey on May 19, 1698. He died on May 18, 1734.[941]

Vol 23: p. 34; database, *American Ancestors,* accessed 21 July 2018.

937   F K Upham, *Upham Genealogy: the Descendants of John Upham, of Massachusetts,* (Albany, NY: Joel Munsell's Sons, 1892), pp. 59-67; PDF e-book, https://archive.org/details/uphamgenealogyde00upha accessed 22 July 2018.

938   F K Upham, *Upham Genealogy: the Descendants of John Upham, of Massachusetts,* (Albany, NY: Joel Munsell's Sons, 1892), p. 34; PDF e-book, https://archive.org/details/uphamgenealogyde00upha accessed 22 July 2018.

939   Phineas Upham, grave marker, Bell Rock Cemetery, Middlesex County, Massachusetts, digital image s.v. "Lieut Phineas Upham" (death 1676, memorial 36215389), database with digital images, *FindAGrave,* accessed 22 July 2018.

940   Ruth Upham, grave marker, Bell Rock Cemetery, Middlesex County, Massachusetts, digital image s.v. "Ruth Wood Upham" (death 1696/7, memorial 36215403), database with digital images, *FindAGrave,* accessed 22 July 2018.

941   "Upham Genealogy," *The New England Historical and Genealogical Register,* Vol 23: p. 34; database, *American Ancestors,* accessed 21 July 2018.

[11-1,552] William Merrick and [11-1,553] Rebecca Tracy

William Merrick [11-1,552] was born about 1603 in Wales. Some ancestries give the parents of William as John Meyrick and Dorothy Bishop in Pembrokeshire, Wales, but I have not seen any solid evidence that this was the same William Merrick who emigrated to New England. William [11-1,552] arrived in Charlestown, now part of Boston, Suffolk County, Massachusetts, in 1636 on the ship "James". In Massachusetts, William was a Lieutenant in the Colonial Militia from 1636 to 1642.

William Merrick [11-1,552] married Rebecca Tracy [11-1,553] in 1642 and they had at least ten children together, between 1643 and 1665.[942] Rebecca was born before 1627 in Plymouth, Plymouth County, Massachusetts to Stephen Tracy [12-3,106] and Tryphosa Lee [12-3,107].[943] William Merrick became a legal voter in Eastham, Barnstable County, Massachusetts on May 22, 1655 and Rebecca died in Eastham in 1668.[944] William died before March 6, 1688/9, since that is when his will was probated.[945] The known children of William Merrick [11-1,552] and Rebecca Tracy [11-1,553] are listed below:

1. William Merrick [10-776], born on September 15, 1643 in Eastham. He married first to Abigail Hopkins [10-777], and second to Elizabeth. William died on October 30, 1732.
2. Stephen Merrick, born on May 12, 1646.
3. Rebecca Merrick, born on July 28, 1648.
4. Mary Merrick, born on November 4, 1650, and married Stephen Hopkins.
5. Ruth Merrick, born on May 15, 1652, and married Edmund Freeman in January 1677.
6. Sarah Merrick [10-781], born on August 1, 1654 and died April 21, 1696. She married John Freeman [10-780] on December 18, 1672.
7. John Merrick, born on January 15, 1656/7.
8. Isaac Merrick, born on January 6, 1660/1.
9. Joseph Merrick, born on June 1, 1662.
10. Benjamin Merrick, born on February 1, 1664/5.[946]

---

942   George Byron Merrick, *Genealogy of the Merrick-Mirick-Myrick Family of Massachusetts: 1636-1902*, (Madison, WI: Tracy, Gibbs & Co, 1902), p 13; PDF e-book, *Internet Archive*, https://archive.org/details/genealogymerric00merrgoog , accessed 9 July 2018.
943   James Savage, *A Genealogical Dictionary of the First Settlers of New England: Showing Three Generations of Those Who Came Before May 1692*, (Boston: Little, Brown and Company, 1860), Vol IV: p. 321; PDF e-book, http://archive.org/details/genealogicaldic04savarich accessed 17 July 2018.
944   George Byron Merrick, *Genealogy of the Merrick-Mirick-Myrick Family of Massachusetts: 1636-1902*, (Madison, WI: Tracy, Gibbs & Co, 1902), p 13; PDF e-book, *Internet Archive*, https://archive.org/details/genealogymerric00merrgoog , accessed 9 July 2018.
945   Ibid., p. 14.
946   Ibid.

[11-1,554] Giles Hopkins and [11-1,555] Catherine Wheldon

Giles Hopkins [11-1,554] was christened in Hursley, Hampshire, England on January 30, 1607 with the father listed as Stephen Hopkins [12-3,108].[947] His mother's name was Mary [12-3,109], but she died in 1613[948] before the family came to what is now Plymouth, Plymouth County, Massachusetts in 1620 on the "Mayflower".[949] So Giles was in Massachusetts from the beginning.

On October 9, 1639, Giles married Catherine Wheldon [11-1,555] in Plymouth, now in Plymouth County, Massachusetts.[950] Catherine was the daughter of Gabriel Wheldon [12-3,110].[951] Giles Hopkins and Catherine Wheldon had at least ten children together, born between 1640 and 1664.[952] Catherine died on March 5, 1688,[953] and Giles was buried in 1690 at the Cove Burying Ground in Eastham, Barnstable County, Massachusetts.[954] The known children of Giles Hopkins and Catherine Wheldon [11-1,555] are listed below:

1. Mary Hopkins, born in 1640.
2. Stephen Hopkins, born in September 1642.
3. John Hopkins, born and died in 1643.
4. Abigail Hopkins [10-777], born in October 1644.
5. Deborah Hopkins, born in Jun 1648.

---

947   "England Births and Christenings, 1538-1975," s.v. "Ediginus Hopkyns" (birth 1607)," database, *FamilySearch,* accessed 30 January 2018.

948   Caleb Johnson, "The True Origin of Stephen Hopkins of the Mayflower: With Evidence of His Earlier Presence in Virginia," *The American Genealogist,* Vol 73: p. 163; database, *American Ancestors,* accessed 23 July 2018.

949   James Savage, *A Genealogical Dictionary of the First Settlers of New England: Showing Three Generations of Those Who Came Before May 1692,* (Boston: Little, Brown and Company, 1860), Vol. II: p. 462; PDF e-book, http://archive.org/details/genealogicaldic02savarich accessed 17 July 2018.

950   Jan Porter and Daniel F. Stramara, Jr, "The Origin of Gabriel Wheldon of Yarmouth and Malden, Massachusetts," *The New England Historical and Genealogical Register,* Vol. 163, p. 260, database, *American Ancestors,* accessed 17 July 2018.

951   Jan Porter and Daniel F. Stramara, Jr, "The Origin of Gabriel Wheldon of Yarmouth and Malden, Massachusetts," *The New England Historical and Genealogical Register,* Vol. 163, p. 254, database, *American Ancestors,* accessed 17 July 2018.

952   James Savage, *A Genealogical Dictionary of the First Settlers of New England: Showing Three Generations of Those Who Came Before May 1692,* (Boston: Little, Brown and Company, 1860), Vol. II: p. 462; PDF e-book, http://archive.org/details/genealogicaldic02savarich accessed 17 July 2018.

953   Jan Porter and Daniel F. Stramara, Jr, "The Origin of Gabriel Wheldon of Yarmouth and Malden, Massachusetts," *The New England Historical and Genealogical Register,* Vol. 163, p. 260, database, *American Ancestors,* accessed 17 July 2018.

954   Giles Hopkins, grave marker, Cove Burying Ground, Eastham, Barnstable County, Massachusetts, digital image, s.v. "Giles Hopkins" (death 1690, memorial 8635), database with digital images, *FindAGrave,* accessed 29 January 2018.

6. Caleb Hopkins, born in January 1651.
7. Ruth Hopkins, born in June 1653.
8. Joshua Hopkins, born in June 1657.
9. William Hopkins, born on January 9, 1661.
10. Elisabeth Hopkins, born in November 1664 and died young.[955]

[11-1,556] Samuel Freeman and [11-1,557] Apphia Quick

I was not able to convincingly trace the parents of Samuel Freeman [11-1,556]. He married Apphia Quick [11-1,557] in St. Ann Blackfriars Parish in London, England on July 14, 1624.[956] Apphia Quick was the daughter of William Quicke [12-3,114] of London, who was a grocer and who sold medicine.[957]

Samuel Freeman [11-1,556] was admitted as a member of the Honourable Artillery Company of London on April 3, 1627.[958] Then Samuel and Apphia arrived in Massachusetts in 1630 in Governor Winthrop's fleet, and stayed at Watertown, Middlesex County, Massachusetts.[959] After 1631, Samuel Freeman returned to England due to legal troubles, and was imprisoned in the fleet until 1634 when the charges were proven false. By December 5, 1637, Samuel was back in Massachusetts, and was admitted as a freeman of Watertown on May 27, 1639. Samuel Freeman died before October 15, 1646,[960] after which Apphia Quick was said to have married Governor Thomas Prence. Apphia died before Aug 1, 1668.[961] The known children of Samuel Freeman [11-1,556] and Apphia Quick [11-1,557] are listed below:

---

955   James Savage, *A Genealogical Dictionary of the First Settlers of New England: Showing Three Generations of Those Who Came Before May 1692*, (Boston: Little, Brown and Company, 1860), Vol. II: p. 462; PDF e-book, http://archive.org/details/genealogicaldic02savarich accessed 17 July 2018.
956   "London, England, Church of England Baptisms, Marriages and Burials, 1538-1812," s.v. "Samuel Freeman" (marriage 1624, spouse "Apphia Quick") database with digital images, *Ancestry.com,* accessed 13 July 2017.
957   Willis Freeman, "The Ancestry of Samuel Freeman of Watertown," *The American Genealogist,* Vol 11: p. 178; database, *American Ancestors,* accessed 17 July 2018.
958   Ibid., Vol 11: p. 178.
959   William Richard Cutter, ed., *Genealogical and Personal Memoirs: Relating to the Families of Boston and Eastern Massachusetts,* (New York: Lewis Historical Publishing Company, 1908), Vol II: p. 848; PDF e-book, https://archive.org/details/genealogicaland01cuttgoog , accessed 10 July 2018.
960   Willis Freeman, "The Ancestry of Samuel Freeman of Watertown," *The American Genealogist,* Vol 11: p. 178; database, *American Ancestors,* accessed 17 July 2018.
961   Willis Freeman, "The Ancestry of Samuel Freeman of Watertown," *The American Genealogist,* Vol 11: p. 179; database, *American Ancestors,* accessed 17 July 2018.

1. Henry Freeman, who married first to Hannah Stearns on December 25, 1650, and second to Mary Sherman on November 27, 1656.
2. Apphia Freeman.
3. Samuel Freeman [10-778], who married Mercy Southworth [10-779], and died in 1712.[962]

[11-1,558] Constant Southworth and [11-1,559] Elizabeth Collier

Constant Southworth [11-1,558] was born in 1615 in Leiden, South Holland, Netherlands to Edward Southworth [12-3,116] and Alice Carpenter [12-3,117].[963] [964] They were an English family in exile in Holland due to their Puritan religious beliefs. Edward [12-3,116] died in 1621 in England, so Alice [12-3,117] took the children to Massachusetts on the ship "Anne" in 1623 and eventually married Governor Bradford. Constant [11-1,558] grew up in Massachusetts and was admitted as a freeman in 1636/7. He fought against the Native Americans in 1637, and was in a council of war in 1653. Between 1659 and 1673 Constant was deputy of the general court and Massachusetts Assistant Treasurer.[965] Constant died on March 11, 1679 in Freetown, Bristol County, Massachusetts.[966] [967]

On November 2, 1637, Constant [11-1,558] married Elizabeth Collier[968]

---

962   William Richard Cutter, ed., *Genealogical and Personal Memoirs: Relating to the Families of Boston and Eastern Massachusetts*, (New York: Lewis Historical Publishing Company, 1908), Vol II: p. 848; PDF e-book, https://archive.org/details/genealogicaland01cuttgoog , accessed 10 July 2018.
963   William Richard Cutter, ed., *New England Families: Genealogical and Memorial,* (New York: Lewis Historical Publishing Co, 1913), Vol III: p. 1201, PDF e-book, https://archive.org/details/newenglandfamili03will accessed 10 July 2018.
964   George Byron Merrick, *Genealogy of the Merrick-Mirick-Myrick Family of Massachusetts: 1636-1902*, (Madison, WI: Tracy, Gibbs & Co, 1902), p 19; PDF e-book, *Internet Archive*, https://archive.org/details/genealogymerric00merrgoog , accessed 9 July 2018.
965   William Richard Cutter, ed., *New England Families: Genealogical and Memorial,* (New York: Lewis Historical Publishing Co, 1913), Vol III: p. 1201, PDF e-book, https://archive.org/details/newenglandfamili03will accessed 10 July 2018.
966   "Massachusetts Deaths and Burials, 1795-1910", s.v. "Constant Southworth" (death 1679), database, *FamilySearch*, accessed 31 January 2018.
967   James Savage, *A Genealogical Dictionary of the First Settlers of New England: Showing Three Generations of Those Who Came Before May 1692*, (Boston: Little, Brown and Company, 1860), Vol IV: p. 143; PDF e-book, http://archive.org/details/genealogicaldic04savarich accessed 17 July 2018.
968   James Savage, *A Genealogical Dictionary of the First Settlers of New England: Showing Three Generations of Those Who Came Before May 1692*, (Boston: Little, Brown and Company, 1860), Vol I: p. 433; PDF e-book, http://archive.org/details/genealogicaldic01savarich accessed 17 July 2018.

[11-1,559] and they had at least eight children together.[969]   Even though one source gave her last name as Collins,[970] another source gives the last name as Collier.[971]   So apparently the original documents were difficult to read. Elizabeth was the daughter of William Collier [12-3,118] and Jane Clark [12-3,119].[972] [973]   The children of Constant Southworth [11-1,558] and Elizabeth Collier [11-1,559] are listed below:

1. Edward Southworth, who married Mary Peabody on November 16, 1669.
2. Nathaniel Southworth, born in 1648 and married Desire Gray on January 10, 1672.
3. William Southworth, born in 1659.
4. Mercy Southworth [10-779], who married Samuel Freeman [10-778] on May 12, 1658.
5. Alice Southworth, who married Benjamin Church on December 26, 1667.
6. Mary Southworth, who married David Alden.
7. Elizabeth Southworth, who married William Fobes.
8. Priscilla Southworth.[974]

[11-1,560] John Freeman and [11-1,561] Mercy Prence

John Freeman [11-1,560] was born in 1621[975] in England to Edmund

969   James Savage, *A Genealogical Dictionary of the First Settlers of New England: Showing Three Generations of Those Who Came Before May 1692*, (Boston: Little, Brown and Company, 1860), Vol IV: p. 143; PDF e-book, http://archive.org/details/genealogicaldic04savarich accessed 17 July 2018.
970   George Byron Merrick, *Genealogy of the Merrick-Mirick-Myrick Family of Massachusetts: 1636-1902*, (Madison, WI: Tracy, Gibbs & Co, 1902), p 19; PDF e-book, *Internet Archive*, https://archive.org/details/genealogymerric00merrgoog , accessed 9 July 2018.
971   William Richard Cutter, ed., *New England Families: Genealogical and Memorial,* (New York: Lewis Historical Publishing Co, 1913), Vol III: p. 1201, PDF e-book, https://archive.org/details/newenglandfamili03will accessed 10 July 2018.
972   George Byron Merrick, *Genealogy of the Merrick-Mirick-Myrick Family of Massachusetts: 1636-1902*, (Madison, WI: Tracy, Gibbs & Co, 1902), p 19; PDF e-book, *Internet Archive*, https://archive.org/details/genealogymerric00merrgoog , accessed 9 July 2018.
973   Clarence Almon Torrey, *New England Marriages Prior to 1700*, (Baltimore, Maryland: Genealogical Publishing Co., Inc, 2004), Third Supplement p. 62; database with digital images, *Ancestry.com,* accessed 31 January 2018.
974   James Savage, *A Genealogical Dictionary of the First Settlers of New England: Showing Three Generations of Those Who Came Before May 1692*, (Boston: Little, Brown and Company, 1860), Vol IV: p. 143; PDF e-book, http://archive.org/details/genealogicaldic04savarich accessed 17 July 2018.
975   John Freeman, grave marker, Cove Burying Ground, Eastham, Barnstable County, Massachusetts, digital image, s.v. "John Freeman" (death 1719, memorial

Freeman [12-3,120] and Bennett Hodsoll [12-3,121].[976] One source says 1627 but the gravestone says he was born in 1621. John married Mercy Prence [11-1,561] on February 13 or 14, 1650 in Sandwich, Barnstable County, Massachusetts.[977] Mercy was born about 1631[978] to Thomas Prence [12-3,122] and Patience Brewster [12-3,123].[979]

From 1654 to 1662 John Freeman [11-1,560] was a deputy in Eastham, Barnstable County, Massachusetts. Then he was a selectman in Eastham from 1663 to 1673. At the age of 72 on December 7, 1692 John was appointed to the bench of common pleas in Eastham. He also fought in wars with the Native Americans. Mercy [11-1,561] died on September 28, 1711[980] [981]and was buried at Cove Burying Ground in Eastham.[982] John [11-1,560] died on October 28, 1719[983] and was also buried at Cove Burying Ground.[984] The known children of John Freeman [11-1,560] and Mercy Prence [11-1,561] are listed below:

1. John Freeman, born on February 2, 1650 and died the same year.
2. John Freeman [10-780], born in December 1651 in Eastham. He married first to Sarah Merrick [10-781], and second to Mercy, the

<hr>

7301580), database with digital images, *FindAGrave*, accessed 1 February 2018.
976   William Richard Cutter, ed., *New England Families: Genealogical and Memorial*, (New York: Lewis Historical Publishing Company, 1914), Vol II: p. 853; PDF e-book, https://archive.org/details/newenglandfamili02cutt_1 accessed 10 July 2018.
977   James Savage, *A Genealogical Dictionary of the First Settlers of New England: Showing Three Generations of Those Who Came Before May 1692*, (Boston: Little, Brown and Company, 1860), Vol III: p. 477; PDF e-book, http://archive.org/details/genealogicaldic03savarich accessed 17 July 2018.
978   William Richard Cutter, ed., *New England Families: Genealogical and Memorial*, (New York: Lewis Historical Publishing Company, 1914), Vol II: p. 853; PDF e-book, https://archive.org/details/newenglandfamili02cutt_1 accessed 10 July 2018.
979   "Connecticut Deaths and Burials, 1772-1934," s.v. "Mercy Prince" (death 1711), database, FamilySearch, accessed 1 February 2018.
980   William Richard Cutter, ed., *New England Families: Genealogical and Memorial*, (New York: Lewis Historical Publishing Company, 1914), Vol II: p. 853; PDF e-book, https://archive.org/details/newenglandfamili02cutt_1 accessed 10 July 2018.
981   "Connecticut Deaths and Burials, 1772-1934," s.v. "Mercy Prince" (death 1711), database, FamilySearch, accessed 1 February 2018.
982   Marcy Freeman, grave marker, Cove Burying Ground, Eastham, Barnstable County, Massachusetts, digital image s.v. "Mercy Prence Freeman" (death 1711, memorial 6023848), database with digital images, *FindAGrave*, accessed 1 February 2018.
983   William Richard Cutter, ed., *New England Families: Genealogical and Memorial*, (New York: Lewis Historical Publishing Company, 1914), Vol II: p. 853; PDF e-book, https://archive.org/details/newenglandfamili02cutt_1 accessed 10 July 2018
984   John Freeman, grave marker, Cove Burying Ground, Eastham, Barnstable County, Massachusetts, digital image, s.v. "John Freeman" (death 1719, memorial 7301580), database with digital images, *FindAGrave*, accessed 1 February 2018.

widow of Elkanah Watson after April 1696. He died on July 27, 1721.

3. Thomas Freeman, born in September 1653.
4. Patience Freeman, who married Lt. Samuel Paine on January 31, 1682/3.
5. Hannah Freeman, who married John Mayo on April 14, 1681.
6. Edmund Freeman, born in June 1657.
7. Mercy Freeman, born in July 1659.
8. William Freeman, born about 1660.
9. Prince Freeman, born on February 3, 1665/6.
10. Nathaniel Freeman, born on March 20, 1670/1.
11. Bennet Freeman, born on March 7, 1672.[985]

[11-1,564] George Watson and [11-1,565] Phebe Hicks

George Watson [11-1,564] was born in 1603 in England to Robert Watson [12-3,128] and Elizabeth [12-3,129].[986] As George Watson was not an uncommon name, I had difficulty tracing where in England he was born because of multiple possibilities. George Watson came to Plymouth about 1632 with his parents, his older brother Robert, and his younger brother Thomas.

In 1633, George Watson [11-1,564] lived in Plymouth County, Massachusetts,[987] and about 1635 George married Phebe Hicks [11-1,565] in Plymouth, Plymouth County, Massachusetts.[988] Phebe was the daughter of Robert Hicks [12-3,130] and Margaret [12-3,131],[989] and was christened at St. Mary Magdalen in Bermondsey, Southwark, London, England on March 15, 1614/5.[990] Phebe came to Massachusetts at a young age in 1623 in the ship "Anne" with her mother and three siblings.[991]

---

985   William Richard Cutter, ed., *New England Families: Genealogical and Memorial*, (New York: Lewis Historical Publishing Company, 1914), Vol II: p. 853; PDF e-book, https://archive.org/details/newenglandfamili02cutt_1 accessed 10 July 2018

986   Henry Cole Quinby, ed., "The Watsons," *New England Family History*, Vol III: p 468; PDF e-book, https://archive.org/details/newenglandfamily03quin accessed 10 July 2018.

987   Ibid., p. 468.

988   Clarence Almon Torrey, *New England Marriages Prior to 1700*, (Baltimore, Maryland: Genealogical Publishing Co., Inc, 2004), p. 785; database with digital images, *Ancestry.com*, accessed 2 February 2018.

989   Henry Cole Quinby, ed., "The Watsons," *New England Family History*, Vol III: p 468; PDF e-book, https://archive.org/details/newenglandfamily03quin accessed 10 July 2018.

990   Robert Charles Anderson, *The Great Migration Begins: Immigrants to New England 1620-1633*, (Boston: New England Historic Genealogical Society, 1995), Vol II: p. 927; database with digital images, *Ancestry.com*, accessed 30 June 2018.

991   James Savage, *A Genealogical Dictionary of the First Settlers of New*

In 1637, George Watson [11-1,564] was made freeman in Plymouth County, where he may have stayed the rest of his life.[992] Phebe [11-1,565] died on May 22, 1663, and George died on January 31, 1689 in Plymouth.[993] [994] The known children for George Watson [11-1,564] and Phebe Hicks [11-1,565] are listed below:

1. Phebe Watson, who married Jonathan Shaw on January 22, 1656/7.
2. Mary Watson, born about 1641. She married Thomas Leonard of Taunton on August 21, 1662, and died on December 1, 1723.
3. John Watson, died young.
4. Samuel Watson, born on January 18, 1647/8.
5. Elizabeth Watson, born on January 18, 1647/8, and married Joseph Williams of Taunton on November 28, 1667.
6. Jonathan Watson, born on March 9, 1651/2, died young.
7. Elkanah Watson [10-782], born on February 25, 1655/6 and drowned on February 8, 1689/90.[995]

[11-1,566] William Hedge

William Hedge [11-1,566] was born about 1613 in England to Elisha Hedge [12-3,132] and Anne Ward [12-3,133]. Then name of William's earlier wife who mothered his children is unknown but she must have died before 1667, since William [11-1,566] married Blanche after 1667.[996] William Hedge appeared on the Massachusetts records on May 14, 1634 when he was made freeman in Lynn, Essex County, Massachusetts. He also lived at some point in Sandwich, Barnstable County, Massachusetts,[997] and before 1643 he moved to

England: Showing Three Generations of Those Who Came Before May 1692, (Boston: Little, Brown and Company, 1860), Vol II: p. 410; PDF e-book, http://archive.org/details/genealogicaldic02savarich accessed 17 July 2018.

992   Henry Cole Quinby, ed., "The Watsons," *New England Family History*, Vol III: p 468; PDF e-book, https://archive.org/details/newenglandfamily03quin accessed 10 July 2018.

993   Henry Cole Quinby, ed., "The Watsons," *New England Family History*, Vol III: p 469; PDF e-book, https://archive.org/details/newenglandfamily03quin accessed 10 July 2018.

994   "Massachusetts Deaths and Burials, 1795-1910," s.v. "George Watson" (death 1689), database, FamilySearch, accessed 2 February 2018.

995   Henry Cole Quinby, ed., "The Watsons," *New England Family History*, Vol III: p 469; PDF e-book, https://archive.org/details/newenglandfamily03quin accessed 10 July 2018.

996   Matthew Hovious, "The Hedge, Ward, and Taylor Ancestry of Captain William Hedge of Yarmouth, Massachusetts," *The New England Historical and Genealogical Register*, Vol 167: p. 170; database, *American Ancestors*, accessed 25 July 2018.

997   James Savage, *A Genealogical Dictionary of the First Settlers of New England: Showing Three Generations of Those Who Came Before May 1692*, (Boston:

Yarmouth, Barnstable County, Massachusetts. In Yarmouth, William Hedge became Captain of the militia in 1659.[998] In his Will of June 30, 1670 in Plymouth County, Massachusetts, William Hedge [11-1,566] mentioned having eight children who are listed below:

1. Abraham Hedge
2. Elisha Hedge
3. John Hedge
4. Elemuel Hedge
5. Sarah Hedge, who married a Matthews.
6. Elizabeth Hedge, who married Jonathan Barnes.
7. Mary Hedge, who married a Sturgis.
8. Marcy Hedge [10-873] [999]

[11-1,600] Edward Carleton and [11-1,601] Ellen Newton

There is some disagreement about the birth of Edward Carleton [11-1,600]. Cutter used an 1800's Carleton family genealogy to trace Edward Carleton's birth to London, England in 1605 to Erasmus and Elizabeth Carleton.[1000] However, christening records in London show that Edward being christened in 1620, which would have made him young to be married before emigrating to Massachusetts in 1638/9. It is still plausible though. The newer research goes with an Edward christened in Beeford, East Riding of Yorkshire, England on October 20, 1610 to Walter Carleton [12-3,200] and Jane Gibbon [12-3,201].[1001] The age of the Yorkshire Edward is more likely and he married an Ellen which is the name listed as the mother of the Massachusetts Edward. So evidence supports the newer research fitting better than the 1800's genealogy.

Edward Carleton [11-1,600] of Yorkshire as mentioned in the preceding paragraph, married Ellen Newton [11-1,601] on November 3, 1636 at St. Martin cum Gregory's Church (Micklegate) in York, North Yorkshire,

---

Little, Brown and Company, 1860), Vol II: p. 400, PDF e-book, http://archive.org/details/genealogicaldic02savarich accessed 17 July 2018.

998   Matthew Hovious, "The Hedge, Ward, and Taylor Ancestry of Captain William Hedge of Yarmouth, Massachusetts," *The New England Historical and Genealogical Register*, Vol 167: p. 170; database, *American Ancestors*, accessed 25 July 2018.

999   "Massachusetts, Plymouth County, Probate Records, 1633-1967," s.v. "William Hedge" (will 1670), database with digital images, *FamilySearch*, accessed 22 January 2018.

1000   William Richard Cutter, ed., *New England Families: Genealogical and Memorial*, (New York: Lewis Historical Publishing Co, 1913), Vol II: p 509; PDF e-book, https://archive.org/details/newenglandfamili02cutt accessed 10 July 2018.

1001   Tracy Elliot Hazen, "The English Ancestry of Edward Carleton of Rowley, Mass.," *The New England Historical and Genealogical Register*, Vol. 93: p. 40; database, *American Ancestors*, accessed 18 July 2018.

England.[1002] [1003] Ellen Newton [11-1,601] was the daughter of Lancelot Newton [12-3,202] and Mary Lee [12-3,203], and was christened in Hedon, East Riding of Yorkshire, England on September 4, 1614.[1004] (In the christenings of Edward Carleton and Ellen Newton, the sources differ as to the month they were born so I went with the transcriptions.) Edward [11-1,600] and Ellen [11-1,601] had one child in England, came over to Massachusetts in 1638 with the Ezekiel Rogers group, and then had three more children in Massachusetts.[1005]

Edward Carleton [11-1,600] was made freeman in Rowley, Essex County, Massachusetts in 1643, then was a member of the general court in Rowley from 1644 to 1647. Edward was then a trial justice from 1648 to 1650 in Rowley. However, about 1651 he emigrated back to England where he died about 1661.[1006] The known children of Edward Carleton [11-1,600] and Ellen Newton [11-1,601] are listed below:

1. John Carleton [10-800], born about 1636 in England and married Hannah Jewett [10-801]. He died on January 22, 1668 in Haverhill.
2. Edward Carleton, born on August 28, 1639 in Rowley.
3. Mary Carleton, born after 1639 in Rowley.
4. Elizabeth Carleton, born after 1639 in Rowley.[1007]

[11-1,602] Joseph Jewett and [11-1,603] Mary Mallinson

Joseph Jewett [11-1,602] was christened on December 31, 1609 in Bradford, West Yorkshire, England as the son of Edward Jewett [12-3,204] and Mary Taylor [12-3,205].[1008] [1009] He married Mary Mallinson [11-1,603] on October 1, 1634 in England and they had at least six children together.[1010] Mary Mallinson

---

1002   "England Marriages, 1538-1973," s.v. "Ed. Carlton" (marriage 1636, spouse "Ellenar Newton"), database, *FamilySearch,* accessed 6 February 2018.
1003   Tracy Elliot Hazen, "The English Ancestry of Edward Carleton of Rowley, Mass.," *The New England Historical and Genealogical Register,* Vol. 93: p. 40; database, *American Ancestors,* accessed 18 July 2018.
1004   "England Births and Christenings, 1538-1975," s.v. "Ellen Newton" (christened 1614), database, *FamilySearch,* accessed 6 February 2018.
1005   William Richard Cutter, ed., *New England Families: Genealogical and Memorial,* (New York: Lewis Historical Publishing Co, 1913), Vol II: p 509; PDF e-book, https://archive.org/details/newenglandfamili02cutt accessed 10 July 2018.
1006   Ibid., Vol II: p 509.
1007   Ibid.
1008   William Richard Cutter, ed., *Genealogical and Personal Memoirs: Relating to the Families of Boston and Eastern Massachusetts,* (New York: Lewis Historical Publishing Company, 1908), Vol II: p. 941; PDF e-book, https://archive.org/details/genealogicaland01cuttgoog , accessed 10 July 2018.
1009   Joseph Jewett, grave marker, Rowley Burial Ground, Rowley, Essex County, Massachusetts, digital image, s.v. "Joseph Jewett" (death 1661, memorial 6910127), database with digital images, *FindAGrave,* accessed 6 February 2018.
1010   William Richard Cutter, ed., *Genealogical and Personal Memoirs: Relating to*

[11-1,603] was christened on May 29, 1606 in Bradford, with Richard Mallinson [12-3,206] and Sara Waterhouse [12-3,207] as her parents.[1011]

Joseph Jewett [11-1,602] and Mary Mallinson [11-1,603] emigrated to Massachusetts in the Ezekiel Rogers group of 1638-9. Joseph was made freeman in Rowley, Essex County, Massachusetts on May 2, 1639. Mary was buried on April 12, 1652 in Massachusetts, so Joseph [11-1,602] married again on May 13, 1653 to the widow Ann Allen in Boston, Suffolk County, Massachusetts.[1012] Joseph died in early 1661 and was buried on February 26, 1660/1 in the Rowley Burial Ground of Rowley.[1013] [1014] The known children of Joseph Jewett [11-1,602] and Mary Mallinson [11-1,603] are listed below:

1. Jeremiah Jewett, born about 1637 in England and married Sarah Dickinson on May 1, 1661. He died on May 20, 1714.
2. Sarah Jewett, who married Captain Philip Nelson on June 24, 1657.
3. Hannah Jewett [10-801], born in 1641. She married first to John Carleton [10-800] in 1661, and second to Christopher Babbage after 1668. She died on September 25, 1723 in Bradford.
4. Nehemiah Jewett, born in February, 1643.
5. Faith Jewett, born on March 5, 1645 and died young.
6. Patience Jewett, born on March 5, 1645 and married Shubael Walker of Bradford on May 29, 1666.[1015]

[11-1,604] Richard Kimball and [11-1,605] Ursula Scott

Richard Kimball [11-1,604] was born in Rattlesden, Suffolk, England before 1595.[1016] Some genealogies give the parents of Richard Kimball as Henry

the Families of Boston and Eastern Massachusetts, (New York: Lewis Historical Publishing Company, 1908), Vol II: p. 941; PDF e-book, https://archive.org/details/genealogicaland01cuttgoog , accessed 10 July 2018.

1011   Tracy Elliot Hazen, "Two Founders of Rowley, Mass.," The New England Historical and Genealogical Register, Vol 94: p. 112; database, American Ancestors, accessed 30 July 2018.

1012   William Richard Cutter, ed., Genealogical and Personal Memoirs: Relating to the Families of Boston and Eastern Massachusetts, (New York: Lewis Historical Publishing Company, 1908), Vol II: p. 941; PDF e-book, https://archive.org/details/genealogicaland01cuttgoog , accessed 10 July 2018.

1013   "Massachusetts Deaths and Burials, 1795-1910," s.v. "Joseph Jewett" (death 1660/1), database, FamilySearch, accessed 6 February 2018.

1014   Joseph Jewett, grave marker, Rowley Burial Ground, Rowley, Essex County, Massachusetts, digital image, s.v. "Joseph Jewett" (death 1661, memorial 6910127), database with digital images, FindAGrave, accessed 6 February 2018.

1015   William Richard Cutter, ed., Genealogical and Personal Memoirs: Relating to the Families of Boston and Eastern Massachusetts, (New York: Lewis Historical Publishing Company, 1908), Vol II: p. 941; PDF e-book, https://archive.org/details/genealogicaland01cuttgoog , accessed 10 July 2018.

1016   Leonard Allison Morrison and Stephen Paschall Sharples, History of the

Kimball and Johanna Eysley, but there is no direct evidence I have seen to link Richard to them. There is a record of them having a child in Rattlesden in 1589, so it is possible Richard could have been their child. However there is no record of Henry and Johanna having a child named Richard, so I will stop here.

Richard Kimball [11-1,604] and Ursula Scott [11-1,605] apparently got married in England, and had several children there before emigrating to Massachusetts in 1634 on the ship "Elizabeth".[1017] Ursula was christened in Rattlesden on February 14, 1598, and her parents were Henry Scott [12-3,210] and Martha Whatlocke [12-3,211].[1018] [1019]

Richard [11-1,604] became a freeman on May 6, 1635 in Watertown, Middlesex County, Massachusetts and as of 1637 he was a wheelwright in Ipswich, Middlesex County, Massachusetts. Ursula [11-1,605] probably died before 1661, and on October 23, 1661 Richard married the widow Margaret Dow.[1020] Richard Kimball died in Ipswich on June 22, 1675.[1021] [1022] The known children of Richard Kimball [11-1,604] and Ursula Scott [11-1,605] are listed below:

1. Abigail Kimball, born in Rattlesden and died on June 17, 1658 in Salisbury.
2. Henry Kimball, born on August 12, 1615 in Rattlesden.
3. Elizabeth Kimball, born in 1621 in Rattlesden, and still living in 1675.
4. Richard Kimball, born in 1623 in Rattlesden, and died on May 26, 1676 in Wenham, Essex County, Massachusetts.
5. Mary Kimball, born in 1625 Rattlesden, and married Robert Dutch.
6. Martha Kimball, born in 1629 in Rattlesden, and married Joseph Fowler.
7. John Kimball, born in 1631 in Rattlesden, and died on May 6, 1698.
8. Thomas Kimball, born in 1633 in Rattlesden, and married Mary Smith.

Kimball Family in America: From 1634 to 1897, and of its Ancestors the Kemballs or Kemboldes of England, (Boston: Damrell & Upham, 1897), p. 32; PDF e-book, https://archive.org/details/historyofkimball00morr , accessed 14 July 2018.

1017   Ibid., p. 27.

1018   "England Births and Christenings, 1538-1975," s.v. "Urslaye Scoote" (birth 1598), database, *FamilySearch,* accessed 16 July 2017.

1019   J. R. Olorenshaw, *Notes on the History of the Church and Parish of Rattlesden, in the County of Suffolk,* (Peterborough: Geo. C. Caster, Market Place, 1900), p. 240; PDF e-book, https://dcms.lds.org/delivery/DeliveryManagerServlet?from=fhd&dps_pid=IE3997643 accessed 31 July 2018.

1020   Leonard Allison Morrison and Stephen Paschall Sharples, *History of the Kimball Family in America: From 1634 to 1897, and of its Ancestors the Kemballs or Kemboldes of England,* (Boston: Damrell & Upham, 1897), p. 29; PDF e-book, https://archive.org/details/historyofkimball00morr , accessed 14 July 2018.

1021   "Massachusetts Deaths and Burials, 1795-1910," s.v. "Richard Kemball" (death 1675), database, *FamilySearch,* accessed 7 February 2018.

1022   Leonard Allison Morrison and Stephen Paschall Sharples, *History of the Kimball Family in America: From 1634 to 1897, and of its Ancestors the Kemballs or Kemboldes of England,* (Boston: Damrell & Upham, 1897), p. 32; PDF e-book, https://archive.org/details/historyofkimball00morr , accessed 14 July 2018.

He died on May 3, 1676 in a raid by natives.

9. Sarah Kimball, born in 1635 in Watertown, and married Edward Allen on November 24, 1658. She died on June 12, 1690.
10. Benjamin Kimball [10-802], born in 1637 in Ipswich.
11. Caleb Kimball, born in 1639 in Ipswich, and died in 1682.[1023]

[11-1,606] Robert Hazelton and [11-1,607] Ann

There is some dispute about the ancestry of Robert Hazelton [11-1,606] (or Haseltine). However, since he was part of the Ezekiel Rogers congregation which came over to Massachusetts in 1638,[1024] Robert would have been from the vicinity of Rowley, East Riding of Yorkshire, England. So I consider it very likely that he was the Robert christened on January 2, 1610 in Howden, East Riding of Yorkshire, England, and his father was Robert Haseltine [12-3,212].[1025] I do not have access to records which would confirm the name of his mother.

Robert Hazelton [11-1,606] married Ann [11-1,607] in Rowley, Essex County, Massachusetts on October 23, 1639.[1026] I have not seen convincing evidence for Ann's surname. Robert and Ann had at least ten children, between 1640 and 1662.[1027]

Robert Hazelton [11-1,606] was made freeman in Rowley on May 13, 1640. Then in 1649 he was among the first settlers of Bradford, Essex County, Massachusetts. Robert established the first ferry between Bradford and Haverhill, Essex County, Massachusetts. He died on August 27, 1674 and Ann [11-1,607] died on July 26, 1684.[1028] The children of Robert Hazelton [11-1,606] and Ann [11-1,607] are listed below:

1. Anna Hazelton, born January 2, 1640 and married Caleb Kimball in 1660.
2. Mercy Hazeltine [10-803], born on October 16, 1642.
3. David Hazelton.
4. Mary Hazelton, born on December 14, 1646.

1023   Ibid., pp. 32-34.
1024   William Richard Cutter, ed., *Genealogical and Personal Memoirs: Relating to the Families of the State of Massachusetts*, (New York: Lewis Historical Publishing Company, 1910), Vol IV, p. 2344; PDF e-book,
https://archive.org/details/genealogicaland01adamgoog accessed 9 July 2018.
1025   "England Births and Christenings, 1538-1975," s.v. "Robart Haseltine" (birth 1610), database, *FamilySearch*, accessed March 2018.

1026   William Richard Cutter, ed., *Genealogical and Personal Memoirs: Relating to the Families of the State of Massachusetts*, (New York: Lewis Historical Publishing Company, 1910), Vol IV, p. 2344; PDF e-book,
https://archive.org/details/genealogicaland01adamgoog accessed 9 July 2018.
1027   Ibid., Vol IV, p. 2344.
1028   Ibid., Vol IV, p. 2344.

5. Abraham Hazelton, born on March 3, 1648 and married Elizabeth Langley on October 4, 1671. He died on April 28, 1711.
6. Deliverance Hazelton, born in January 1651 and died young.
7. Elizabeth Hazelton, born on January 15, 1652/3 and died young.
8. Deliverance Hazelton, born in 1655 and married Nathaniel Dane of Andover.
9. Robert Hazelton, born on September 7, 1657 and married Elizabeth Jewett in 1680.
10. Gershom Hazelton, born on January 31, 1661/2 and married Abiah Dalton in 1690.

[11-1,608] Philemon Dalton and [11-1,609] Anne Cole

Philemon Dalton [11-1,608] was born about 1590, based on his age at immigration to Massachusetts,[1029] and was the son of George Dalton [12-3,216]. Philemon was a linen weaver and married Anne Cole [11-1,609] on October 11,1625 in Dennington, Suffolk, England.[1030] They came over to Massachusetts in 1635 in the ship *Increase*. Philemon was made a freeman on March 3, 1636, and they moved to Dedham, Norfolk County, Massachusetts about 1637. They moved again to Hampton, Rockingham County, New Hampshire in 1640.[1031] At some point before Philemon Dalton [11-1,608] wrote his will in November 1656, Anne Cole [11-1,609] died since he mentioned his new wife Dorothy in the will.[1032] Then on June 4, 1662, he died from a falling tree. Savage said the death was in Ipswich, Essex County, Massachusetts,[1033] but the death record

---

1029   James Savage, *A Genealogical Dictionary of the First Settlers of New England: Showing Three Generations of Those Who Came Before May 1692*, (Boston: Little, Brown and Company, 1860), Vol II: p. 3; PDF e-book, http://archive.org/details/ genealogicaldic02savarich accessed 17 July 2018.
1030   George F Sanborn, Jr. and Melinde Lutz Sanborn, "The Dalton Cluster: Timothy Dalton, Philemon Dalton, Richard Everard, and Deborah (Everard) Blake," *The New England Historical and Genealogical Register*, Vol 154: p. 283; database with digital images, *American Ancestors*, accessed 20 October 2019.
1031   James Savage, *A Genealogical Dictionary of the First Settlers of New England: Showing Three Generations of Those Who Came Before May 1692*, (Boston: Little, Brown and Company, 1860), Vol II: p. 3; PDF e-book, http://archive.org/details/ genealogicaldic02savarich accessed 17 July 2018.
1032   George F Sanborn, Jr. and Melinde Lutz Sanborn, "The Dalton Cluster: Timothy Dalton, Philemon Dalton, Richard Everard, and Deborah (Everard) Blake," *The New England Historical and Genealogical Register*, Vol 154: p. 283; database with digital images, *American Ancestors*, accessed 20 October 2019.
1033   James Savage, *A Genealogical Dictionary of the First Settlers of New England: Showing Three Generations of Those Who Came Before May 1692*, (Boston: Little, Brown and Company, 1860), Vol II: p. 3; PDF e-book, http://archive.org/details/ genealogicaldic02savarich accessed 17 July 2018.

was for Hampton.[1034] The known child for Philemon Dalton [11-1,608] and Hannah [11-1,609] was Samuel Dalton [10-804], who also immigrated on the *Increase* with the family.[1035]

[11-1,612] John Gove and [11-1,613] Mary Shard

John Gove [11-1,612] was born about 1604 in England,[1036] and married Mary Shard [11-1,613] at St. Nicholas, Cole Abbey Parish, London, London, England on February 6, 1630/1.[1037] Some say John Gove had two marriages, and that the first marriage was to Sarah Mott in 1625,[1038] however the evidence is weak so I don't think it is clear whether he married Sarah Mott or not. John Gove died on February 28, 1647/8 in Charlestown, which is now in Boston, Suffolk County, Massachusetts. The son of John Gove [11-1,612] and Mary Shard [11-1,613] was Edward Gove [10-806], who was born in England but not in 1630 as the Gove book said.[1039] It would have been about 1636 based on his gravestone.[1040]

[11-1,616] William Wilson and [11-1,617] Alice

William Wilson [11-1,616] lived in Donington on Bain, Lincolnshire,

---

1034   "New Hampshire Death Records, 1654-1947," s.v. "Philemon Dalton" (year "1662" place "Hampton"), database with digital images, *FamilySearch,* accessed 19 October 2019.
1035   James Savage, *A Genealogical Dictionary of the First Settlers of New England: Showing Three Generations of Those Who Came Before May 1692*, (Boston: Little, Brown and Company, 1860), Vol II: p. 3; PDF e-book, http://archive.org/details/genealogicaldic02savarich accessed 17 July 2018.
1036   William Henry Gove, *The Gove Book: History and Genealogy of the American Family of Gove and Notes of European Goves* (Salem, MA: Sydney Perley, 1922) p. 9; PDF e-book, https://archive.org/details/govebookhistoryg00gove/page/50 accessed 22 June 2019.
1037   City of London Corporation Libraries, Archives, London, England, Church of England Baptisms, Marriages and Burials, 1538-1812 Burials, 1538-1812 database," not indexed s.v. City of London>St Nicholas, Cole Abbey>1538-1651 "John Goaue" (spouse "Mary Shard" marriage "1630"), archive with digital images, *Ancestry.com,* accessed 11 September 2019.
1038   William Henry Gove, *The Gove Book: History and Genealogy of the American Family of Gove and Notes of European Goves* (Salem, MA: Sydney Perley, 1922) p. 9; PDF e-book, https://archive.org/details/govebookhistoryg00gove/page/50 accessed 22 June 2019.
1039   Ibid.
1040   Edward Gove, grave marker, Pine Grove Cemetery, Hampton, Rockingham County, New Hampshire, digital image, s.v. "Edward Gove" (death "1691" memorial "7376023"), database with digital images, *FindAGrave,* accessed 11 September 2019.

England, where his son William Wilson [10-808] was born about 1610.[1041] William Wilson [11-1,616] had died by October 24, 1638, when his son William [10-808] arranged to sell the land in Donington on Bain for William's [11-1,616] debts to be paid and for his mother Alice [11-1,617] to be brought to New England.[1042] It is not clear whether Alice actually came to New England.

[11-1,618] William Grindall and [11-1,619] Bridgitt Richard

William Grindall [11-1,618] married Bridgitt Richard [11-1,619] in Old Bolingbroke, Lincolnshire, England on June 19, 1600.[1043] They had two children who I found in the databases and are below:
1. William Grindall, christened on March 29, 1601 in Hareby, Lincolnshire, England.[1044]
2. Patience Grindall [10-809], christened on October 23, 1603 in Hareby.[1045]

[11-1,620] William Lovejoy

Not much is known of William Lovejoy [11-1,620]. He was listed as the father in the birth record for when his son John Lovejoy [10-810] was born on July 14, 1622 in Caversham, which is in Reading, Berkshire, England. However there were possibly multiple men by the name of William Lovejoy in Berkshire at the time, so it is difficult to sort out details for each of them.[1046]

[11-1,622] Christopher Osgood and [11-1,623] Mary Everatt

Christopher Osgood [11-1,622] was christened on April 17, 1606 in Newton

---

1041   "England Births and Baptisms 1538-1975," s.v. "William Wilson" (birth "1610" place "Donington on Bain") database, *FindMyPast*, accessed 29 June 2019.
1042   Robert Charles Anderson, *The Great Migration: Immigrants to New England, 1634-1635. T-Y.* (Boston: New England Historic Genealogical Society, 2011) Vol VII: p. 452; database with digital images, *American Ancestors*, accessed 28 June 2019.
1043   "England Marriages, 1538-1973," s.v. "William Grundall" (spouse "Bridgitt Richard" year "1600" place "Bolingbroke"), database, *FamilySearch*, accessed 29 June 2019.
1044   "Lincolnshire Baptisms," s.v. "William Grindal" (birth "1601" place "Hareby"), database with digital images, *FindMyPast*, accessed 21 October 2019.
1045   "England Births and Christenings, 1538-1975," s.v. "Patience Grindall" (birth "1603" place "Hareby"), database, *FamilySearch*, accessed 29 June 2019.
1046   James R Henderson, "English Origins of John Lovejoy of Andover, Massachusetts," *The New England Historic and Genealogical Register,* Vol 163: p. 28; database with digital images, *American Ancestors*, accessed 30 June 2019.

Tony, Wiltshire, England to Thomas Osgood [12-3,244] and Margaret Skeat [12-3,245].[1047] Christopher Osgood had two marriages, which has confused some sources. His first marriage was to Mary Everatt [11-1,623], on April 21, 1632 in St. Mary's Parish, Marlborough, Wiltshire, England. There were multiple christenings in Wiltshire for girls named Mary Everatt (or something similar) in the early 1600's, so more information will be needed to trace her lineage further. Mary Everatt [11-1,623] had one child with Christopher Osgood [11-1,622], who was christened in St. Mary's Parish of Marlborough, Wiltshire, England on March 17, 1632/3. The daughter's name was Mary Osgood [10-811], and then Mary Everatt [11-1,623] was buried a month after her only child's birth, on April 21, 1633 in St. Mary's Parish. After his first wife died, Christopher Osgood [11-1,622] married Margaret Fowler on July 28, 1633 in St. Mary's Parish,[1048] then they went to Massachusetts in 1634. Christopher was made a freeman on May 6, 1635, and died in 1650.[1049]

[11-1,628] John Gage and [11-1,629] Amy

John Gage was born about 1604 in England. Some sources identify this John Gage as the son of Sir John Gage in Suffolk, but that John Gage married a Mary Baker and died childless.[1050] This John Gage married a woman recorded as Amee sometime before 1638 when they started having children in New England.[1051] Some online ancestries give Amy's surname as Wilford, but I have not found any strong evidence to support this surname.

John Gage arrived in New England before 1630, and he signed the covenant roll of the First Church of Boston, Suffolk County, Massachusetts on August 27, 1630.[1052] He was a farmer and carpenter, who made freeman on March 4, 1633 in Ipswich, Essex County, Massachusetts. By 1639, he was a Corporal in the militia.[1053] Amy died in June of 1658,[1054] and John married the widow Sarah

---

1047   Jane Fletcher Fiske, "New Light on the English background of the Osgoods of Essex County, Massachusetts," *The American Genealogist,* Vol 83: p. 53; database with digital images, *American Ancestors,* accessed 24 October 2019.

1048   Osgood Field, "A Contribution to the History of the Family of Osgood," *The New England Historic and Genealogical Register,* Vol 20: p. 27; database with digital images, *American Ancestors,* accessed 21 October 2019.

1049   James Savage, *A Genealogical Dictionary of the First Settlers of New England: Showing Three Generations of Those Who Came Before May 1692,* (Boston: Little, Brown and Company, 1860), Vol III: p. 320; PDF e-book, http://archive.org/details/genealogicaldic03savarich accessed 17 July 2018.

1050   Arthur E. Gage, *Some Descendants of John Gage of Ipswich, Mass.,* (Boston: New England Historic Genealogical Company, 1908), p. 3; PDF e-book, https://archive.org/details/somedescendantso00gage , accessed 9 July 2018.

1051   Ibid., p. 4.

1052   Ibid., p. 3.

1053   Ibid., p. 3.

1054   "Massachusetts Deaths and Burials, 1795-1910," s.v. "Amy Gage" (death

Keyes on November 7, 1658 in Ipswich. By 1661 John lived in Bradford, Essex County, Massachusetts, where he was a Sergeant in the militia by 1670. John Gage died on March 24, 1672/3 in Bradford.[1055] [1056] The children of John Gage [11-1,628] and Amy [11-1,629] are listed below:

1. Samuel Gage [10-814], born in 1638 and married Faith Stickney [10-815]. He died on July 20, 1676.
2. Daniel Gage, born in 1639 and married Sarah Kimball on May 3, 1674. He died on November 8, 1705.
3. Benjamin Gage, who married first to Mary Keyes on February 16, 1663 and second to Prudence Leaver on October 11, 1671. He died on October 10, 1672.
4. Nathaniel Gage, born in 1645 and married the widow Mary (Weeks) Green. Nathaniel died on April 30, 1728.
5. Jonathan Gage, born in 1645 and married Hester Chandler on November 12, 1667. He died on March 15, 1675/6.
6. Josiah Gage, born in 1647 and married first to Lydia Ladd. His second marriage was to Martha Dow, and he died on July 5, 1717.[1057]

[11-1,630] William Stickney and [11-1,631] Elizabeth

Many people believe that William Stickney [11-1,630] was from Hull in Yorkshire, or from Lincolnshire, or both. One theory is that he was born in Lincolnshire and then the family moved to Hull in Yorkshire, England, which is where it is believed he left for Massachusetts. Even though there was a William Stickney born around 1600 in Lincolnshire parish records, I am skeptical about the lack of evidence saying this is the same William Stickney [11-1,630] who emigrated to Massachusetts. It might have been a coincidence of two babies being christened with the same name in different places, especially since a search of records at the *FamilySearch* database shows that there was at least one Stickney family having children around 1600 in Yorkshire when William Stickney [11-1,630] might have been born. So I believe more evidence is needed to trace this family further.

William Stickney [11-1,630] was married to Elizabeth [11-1,631], possibly in England. Some say her last name was Dawson due to a Yorkshire record of a William Stickney who married Elizabeth Dawson in 1628, but more evidence

---

1658), database, *FamilySearch*, accessed 20 February 2018.

1055   Arthur E. Gage, *Some Descendants of John Gage of Ipswich, Mass.*, (Boston: New England Historic Genealogical Company, 1908), p. 3; PDF e-book, https://archive.org/details/somedescendantso00gage , accessed 9 July 2018.

1056   "Massachusetts Deaths and Burials, 1795-1910," s.v. "John Gage" (death 1672/3), database, *FamilySearch*, accessed 20 February 2018.

1057   Arthur E. Gage, *Some Descendants of John Gage of Ipswich, Mass.*, (Boston: New England Historic Genealogical Company, 1908), pp. 4-5; PDF e-book, https://archive.org/details/somedescendantso00gage , accessed 9 July 2018.

is needed to determine where the William Stickney who went to Massachusetts came from in England in order to accept Dawson since there is a possibility he came from somewhere else. There is evidence of William Stickney [11-1,630] in Massachusetts in 1639, when he was admitted to the church in Boston, Suffolk County, Massachusetts on January 6. Then on November 24, 1639, William Stickney [11-1,630] was in a group dismissed from the Boston church to establish a church in Rowley, Essex County, Massachusetts. He made freeman status on October 7, 1640,[1058] and apparently lived in the part of Rowley that later split off to become Georgetown, Essex County, Massachusetts since the birth record transcriptions say Georgetown instead of Rowley. William Stickney [11-1,630] was buried on January 25, 1664/5 in Rowley[1059] and the known children of William Stickney [11-1,630] and Elizabeth [11-1,631] are listed below, but please note that even though transcriptions give the dates as birth dates, I suspect they are actually christening dates due to the number of "twins":

1. John Stickney, born or christened January 14, 1640 in Georgetown.[1060]
2. Faith Stickney [10-815], born February 4, 1641/2 and married Samuel Gage [10-814].[1061]
3. Andrew Stickney, born or christened on March 11, 1644 in Georgetown.[1062]
4. Thomas Stickney, born or christened on January 3, 1646 in Georgetown.[1063]
5. Elizabeth Stickney, born or christened on January 3, 1646 in Georgetown.[1064] She was buried in Rowley on September 7, 1659.[1065]

1058   James Savage, *A Genealogical Dictionary of the First Settlers of New England: Showing Three Generations of Those Who Came Before May 1692*, (Boston: Little, Brown, and Company, 1860), Vol IV: p. 192; PDF e-book, http://archive.org/details/genealogicaldic04savarich accessed 17 July 2018.
1059   "Massachusetts, Town Clerk, Vital and Town Records, 1626-2001," s.v. "William Stickney" (death "1664" place "Rowley"), database with digital images, *FamilySearch*, accessed 25 October 2019.
1060   "Massachusetts Births and Christenings, 1639-1915," s.v. "John Stickney" (birth "1640" place "Georgetown"), database, *FamilySearch*, accessed 25 October 2019.
1061   Arthur E Gage, *Some Descendants of John Gage of Ipswich, Mass.,* (Boston: New England Historic Genealogical Company, 1908), p. 4; PDF e-book, https://archive.org/details/somedescendantso00gage accessed May 2017.
1062   "Massachusetts Births and Christenings, 1639-1915," s.v. "Andrew Stickney" (birth "1644" place "Georgetown"), database, *FamilySearch*, accessed 25 October 2019.
1063   "Massachusetts Births and Christenings, 1639-1915," s.v. "Thomas Stickney" (birth "1646" place "Georgetown"), database, *FamilySearch*, accessed 25 October 2019.
1064   "Massachusetts Births and Christenings, 1639-1915," s.v. "Elizabeth Stickney" (birth "1646" place "Georgetown"), database, *FamilySearch*, accessed 25 October 2019.
1065   "Massachusetts Deaths and Burials, 1795-1910," s.v. "Elizabeth Stickny"

6. Mercy Stickney, born or christened on November 14, 1648 in Georgetown.[1066] She was buried in Rowley on January 14, 1676.[1067]
7. Adding Stickney, born or christened on November 14, 1648 in Georgetown.[1068] Adding was marked as a male in the birth transcription but as a female in the death transcription, which was for September 17, 1660 in Rowley.[1069]
8. Amos Stickney.
9. Samuel Stickney.
10. Mary Stickney.[1070]

[11-1,632] John Ayer and [11-1,633] Hannah

John Ayer [11-1,632] was present in Salisbury, Essex County, Massachusetts by 1640. About 1647, he moved to Haverhill, Essex County, Massachusetts.[1071] I found no evidence to support where in England he came from, so more information will be needed to narrow down possibilities and further trace his ancestry. John Ayer [11-1,632] died on March 31, 1657 in Haverhill,[1072] and his will was probated on October 6, 1657.[1073] His wife Hannah [11-1,633] outlived him, and might have died in 1688 according to some sources. However, she was also mentioned in a land deed in 1692[1074] so there was probably more than one Hannah Ayer at the time getting confused with each other. The known children of John Ayer [11-1,632] and Hannah [11-1,633] are listed below:

1. John Ayer, who married first to Sarah Williams on May 5, 1646, and

(death "1659" place "Rowley") database, *FamilySearch*, accessed 25 October 2019.
1066   "Massachusetts Births and Christenings, 1639-1915," s.v. "Mercy Stickney" (birth "1648" place "Georgetown"), database, *FamilySearch*, accessed 25 October 2019.
1067   "Massachusetts Deaths and Burials, 1795-1910," s.v. "Mercy Stickney" (death "1676" place "Rowley") database, *FamilySearch*, accessed 25 October 2019.
1068   "Massachusetts Births and Christenings, 1639-1915," s.v. "Adding Stickney" (birth "1648" place "Georgetown"), database, *FamilySearch*, accessed 25 October 2019.
1069   "Massachusetts Deaths and Burials, 1795-1910," s.v. "Adding Stickny" (death "1660" place "Rowley") database, *FamilySearch*, accessed 25 October 2019.
1070   James Savage, *A Genealogical Dictionary of the First Settlers of New England: Showing Three Generations of Those Who Came Before May 1692*, (Boston: Little, Brown, and Company, 1860), Vol IV: p. 192; PDF e-book, http://archive.org/details/genealogicaldic04savarich accessed 17 July 2018.
1071   "Ayer Genealogy," *The Essex Antiquarian*, Vol 4: p. 145; database with digital images, *American Ancestors*, accessed 4 July 2019.
1072   Ibid.
1073   W. H. Whitmore, "The Ayres and Ayer Families," *The New England Historical and Genealogical Register*, Vol 17: p. 307; database with digital images, *American Ancestors*, accessed 25 October 2019.
1074   Ibid.

second to Mary Wooddam on March 26, 1663.

2. Robert Ayer [11-1,644], born about 1625. He married Elizabeth Palmer [11-1,645] on February 27, 1650/1 and died sometime between 1713 and 1723.
3. Thomas Ayer, who married Elizabeth Hutchins on April 1, 1656 and died on November 9, 1686.
4. Peter Ayer, born about 1633 and married Hannah Allen on November 1, 1659. He died on January 2, 1698/9 in Boston, Suffolk County, Massachusetts.
5. Obadiah Ayer, who married Hannah Pike on March 19, 1660/1 and died on November 14, 1694.
6. Nathaniel Ayer [10-816], who married Tamesin Turloar [10-817] on May 10, 1670 in Haverhill. He died on November 17, 1717.
7. Hannah Ayer, who was born on December 21, 1644 in Salisbury, Essex County, Massachusetts and married Stephen Webster on March 24, 1662/3.[1075]
8. Rebecca Ayer, who married John Aslet on October 8, 1648.
9. Mary Ayer.[1076]

[11-1,642] John Page and [11-1,643] Mary Marsh

Based on age at death, John Page [11-1,642] was born about 1614.[1077] He has not been found on passenger lists showing where he came from, so some speculate that since he first showed up in records for Hingham, which is now in Plymouth County, Massachusetts, he might have been a servant who came over in the group from Hingham, Norfolk, England. While possible, it is still speculation. More information is needed to trace him, especially since there are multiple births at the time in England with the name John Page in the record databases at *FamilySearch*.

John Page [11-1,642] married Mary Marsh [11-1,643] probably in Massachusetts before 1641 when their first child was christened in Hingham, Massachusetts.[1078] Mary Marsh [11-1,643] was the daughter of George Marsh

1075 "Ayer Genealogy," *The Essex Antiquarian,* Vol 4: pp. 145-6; database with digital images, *American Ancestors,* accessed 4 July 2019.
1076 W. H. Whitmore, "The Ayres and Ayer Families," *The New England Historical and Genealogical Register,* Vol 17: p. 307; database with digital images, *American Ancestors,* accessed 25 October 2019.
1077 Topsfield Historical Society, V*ital Records of Haverhill Massachusetts: to the End of the Year 1849* (Topsfield, Massachusetts: Topsfield Historical Society, 1911) Vol II: p. 453; PDF e-book, https://archive.org/details/cu31924099427654/page/n8 accessed 25 June 2019.
1078 William Richard Cutter, ed., *Genealogical and Personal Memoirs: Relating to the Families of Boston and Eastern Massachusetts* (New York: Lewis Historical Publishing Company, 1908) Vol I: p. 560; PDF e-book, https://archive.org/details/genealogicalpers00cutt accessed 20 July 2018.

[12-3,286] and Elizabeth [12-3,287].[1079] John Page died on November 23, 1687 in Haverhill, Essex County, Massachusetts,[1080] and Mary Marsh died on February 15, 1696/7 in Haverhill.[1081] The children of John Page [11-1,642] and Mary Marsh [11-1,643] are listed below:

1. John Page, christened on July 11, 1641 in Hingham, Plymouth County, Massachusetts. He married Sarah Davis on June 14, 1663 in Hingham.
2. Onesiphorus Page, christened on November 6, 1643 in Hingham, Massachusetts. He married first to Mary Hauxworth on November 22, 1664, and second to the widow Sarah Rowell on July 31, 1695.
3. Benjamin Page, christened on July 14, 1644 and married Mary Whittier on September 21, 1666. He died on June 28, 1736 in Salisbury, Essex County, Massachusetts.
4. Mary Page [10-821], christened on May 3, 1646. She married first to John Dow on October 23, 1665, and second to Samuel Shepard [10-820] on July 14, 1673.
5. Joseph Page, christened on March 5, 1647/8. He married first to Judith Guile on January 21, 1671 in Hingham, and second to Martha Heath on December 2, 1673.[1082]
6. Abraham Page, born on February 27, 1648/9 in Haverhill.[1083]
7. Cornelius Page, christened on July 15, 1649. He married first to Martha Clough on November 13, 1674, and second to Mary Marsh on January 16, 1684. Cornelius died before July 18, 1698.
8. Sarah Page, christened on July 18, 1651 and married James Sanders on January 14, 1669.
9. Elizabeth Page, born on June 4, 1653 in Haverhill and died on July 3, 1653 in Haverhill.
10. Mercy Page, born on April 1, 1655 in Haverhill, and married John Clough on November 13, 1674.
11. An unnamed child, birth date uncertain, died on March 26, 1658 in Haverhill.
12. Ephraim Page, born on February 27, 1658/9 in Haverhill and died on

---

1079   "The Great Migration: Immigrants to New England, 1634-1635, Vol V, M-P," p. 25, database with digital images, *American Ancestors*, accessed 26 October 2019.

1080   Topsfield Historical Society, *Vital Records of Haverhill Massachusetts: to the End of the Year 1849* (Topsfield, Massachusetts: Topsfield Historical Society, 1911) Vol II: p. 453; PDF e-book, https://archive.org/details/cu31924099427654/page/n8 accessed 25 June 2019.

1081   Ibid., Vol II: p. 455.

1082   William Richard Cutter, ed., *Genealogical and Personal Memoirs: Relating to the Families of Boston and Eastern Massachusetts* (New York: Lewis Historical Publishing Company, 1908) Vol I: p. 561; PDF e-book, https://archive.org/details/genealogicalpers00cutt accessed 20 July 2018.

1083   Topsfield Historical Society, Vital Records of Haverhill Massachusetts: to the End of the Year 1849 (Topsfield, Massachusetts: Topsfield Historical Society, 1911) Vol I: p. 236; PDF e-book, https://archive.org/details/vitalrecordsofha00byuhave/page/ 1 accessed 25 June 2019.

July 22, 1659 in Haverhill.[1084]

[11-1,644] Robert Ayer and [11-1,645] Elizabeth Palmer

Robert Ayer [11-1,644] was born about 1625 to John Ayer [11-1,632] and Hannah [11-1,633]. He married Elizabeth Palmer [11-1,645] on February 27, 1650/1,[1085] and Elizabeth was the daughter of Henry Palmer [12-3,290][1086] and his wife Elizabeth[1087] Masy [12-3,291].[1088] Elizabeth Palmer [11-1,645] had been christened on June 23, 1633 in Frampton, Dorset, England.[1089] In May of 1666, Robert Ayer [11-1,644] made freeman, and in 1671 he became the constable. He was also described as a yeoman or plowman. Elizabeth Palmer [11-1,645] died on April 24, 1705 at the age of 71, but Robert Ayer [11-1,644] was still living as of 1711.[1090] The known children of Robert Ayer [11-1,644] and Elizabeth Palmer [11-1,645] are listed below:

1. Elizabeth Ayer, born on November 10, 1652 in Haverhill, Essex County, Massachusetts. She married first to John Clement on February 22, 1676 and second to Samuel Watts on March 8, 1696/7.
2. Samuel Ayer, born on November 11, 1654 in Haverhill. He married Mary Johnson on December 14, 1681 and was killed by the French and Native Americans who attacked Haverhill on August 29, 1708.
3. Mehitable Ayer, born on September 14, 1656 in Haverhill.
4. Timothy Ayer [10-822], born on October 2, 1659 in Haverhill. He married Ruth Johnson [10-823] on November 24, 1682, and died on August 14, 1689.

1084   William Richard Cutter, ed., *Genealogical and Personal Memoirs: Relating to the Families of Boston and Eastern Massachusetts* (New York: Lewis Historical Publishing Company, 1908) Vol I: p. 561; PDF e-book, https://archive.org/details/genealogicalpers00cutt accessed 20 July 2018.
1085   "Ayer Genealogy," *The Essex Antiquarian,* Vol 4: p. 145, database with digital images, *American Ancestors,* accessed 28 October 2019.
1086   James Savage, *A Genealogical Dictionary of the First Settlers of New England: Showing Three Generations of Those Who Came Before May 1692* (Boston: Little, Brown and Company, 1860) Vol III: p. 340; PDF e-book, http://archive.org/details/genealogicaldic03savarich accessed 17 July 2018.
1087   Topsfield Historical Society, *Vital Records of Haverhill Massachusetts: to the End of the Year 1849* (Topsfield, Massachusetts: Topsfield Historical Society, 1911) Vol II: p. 455; PDF e-book, https://archive.org/details/cu31924099427654/page/n8 accessed 25 June 2019.
1088   "England, Dorset, Parish Registers, 1538-2001," s.v. "Henry Palmer" (spouse "Elizabeth Masy" marriage "1632"), database, *FamilySearch,* accessed 8 November 2019.
1089   "England, Dorset, Parish Registers, 1538-2001," s.v. "Elizabeth Palmer" (birth "1633"), database, *FamilySearch,* accessed 8 November 2019.
1090   "Ayer Genealogy," *The Essex Antiquarian,* Vol 4: p. 145, database with digital images, *American Ancestors,* accessed 28 October 2019.

5. An unnamed daughter, who died on July 9, 1662 in Haverhill.
6. Hannah Ayer, born on January 26, 1663 in Haverhill and died on March 10, 1675/6.
7. Mary Ayer, born on January 15, 1667 in Haverhill and died on April 14, 1668.[1091]

[11-1,646] Peter Johnson and [11-1,647] Ruth Moulton

Peter Johnson [11-1,646] was christened in 1639 in "Winnicunnet," which later became Hampton, Rockingham County, New Hampshire, to Edmond Johnson [12-3,292] and Mary [12-3,293]. On April 3, 1660, he married Ruth Moulton [11-1,647] in Hampton.[1092] (Note that the original documents at Hampton used the month number in the Julian calendar, so many transcriptions at *FamilySearch* for this family are off by two months due to not being aware of the difference in calendars. For example, the transcription at *FamilySearch* incorrectly gives February 3, 1660[1093] for the marriage at the time of this writing.) Ruth Moulton was christened on May 7, 1640 in Hampton to John Moulton [12-3,294] and Ann[1094] Grene[1095] [12-3,295]. I found four children for Peter Johnson [11-1,646] and Ruth Moulton [11-1,647], and they are listed below:

1. Mary Johnson, born on April 7, 1663 in Hampton.[1096]
2. Ruth Johnson [10-823], born on 13 July 1666 in Hampton.[1097]
3. Edmond Johnson, born on July 8, 1671 in Hampton.[1098]

1091   Ibid., Vol 4: pp. 145-7.

1092   Robert Charles Anderson, "Great Migration: Immigrants to New England, 1634-1635, Volume IV, I-L" p. 62, database with digital images, *American Ancestors*, accessed 28 October 2019.

1093   "New Hampshire Marriage Records, 1637-1947," s.v. "Peter Jonson" (spouse "Ruth Moulton" year "1660"), database with digital images, *FamilySearch,* accessed 7 October 2019.

1094   James Savage, *A Genealogical Dictionary of the First Settlers of New England: Showing Three Generations of Those Who Came Before May 1692*, (Boston: Little, Brown, and Company, 1860) Vol III: p. 248; PDF e-book, http://archive.org/details/genealogicaldic03savarich accessed 17 July 2018.

1095   Joy Wade Moulton, "Some Doubts about the English Background of the Moulton Family," *The New England Historical and Genealogical Register,* Vol 144: p. 261, database with digital images, *American Ancestors*, accessed 28 October 2019.

1096   "New Hampshire Birth Records, Early to 1900," s.v. "Mary Johnson" (birth "1663" place "Hampton") database with digital images, *FamilySearch,* accessed 29 October 2019.

1097   "New Hampshire Birth Records, Early to 1900," s.v. "Ruth Johnson" (birth "1666" place "Hampton") database with digital images, *FamilySearch,* accessed 29 October 2019.

1098   "New Hampshire Birth Records, Early to 1900," s.v. "Edmond Johnson" (birth "1671" place "Hampton") database with digital images, *FamilySearch,* accessed 29 October 2019.

4. Peter Johnson, born on November 25, 1674 in Hampton.[1099]

[11-1,648] William White and [11-1,649] Mary

William White [11-1,648] was born about 1610, based on his age at death. Very little can be proven at this time about where he came from in England or even when he arrived in Massachusetts due several people in Massachusetts at that time having the same name of William White. They are often mixed up together. William White [11-1,648] was in Massachusetts by 1639, which is about when he married Mary Ware [11-1,649]. In 1642, William became a freeman in Newbury, Essex County, Massachusetts, but moved to Haverhill, Essex County, Massachusetts soon after. Mary Ware [11-1,649] died on February 22, 1681/2 in Haverhill, and William White [11-1,648] married the widow Sarah Foster on September 21, 1682. He died on September 28, 1690 in Haverhill. Although they probably had more children, evidence is weak. It can be proven through original documents that John White [10-824] was the son of William White [11-1,648] and Mary Ware [11-1,649].[1100]

[11-1,650] Edward French

Edward French [11-1,650] was in Ipswich, Essex County, Massachusetts by 1636 and was an early inhabitant of Salisbury, Essex County, Massachusetts. He died on December 28, 1674, and his will mentioned four children and his wife Ann.[1101] However, it is not certain if Ann was the mother of the children. The known children of Edward French [11-1,650] are listed below:
1. Joseph French
2. John French
3. Samuel French
4. Hannah French [10-825].[1102]

1099   "New Hampshire Birth Records, Early to 1900," s.v. "Peter Johnson" (birth "1674" place "Hampton") database with digital images, *FamilySearch*, accessed 29 October 2019.
1100   Robert Charles Anderson, "Great Migration: Immigrants to New England, 1634-1635, Volume VII, T-Y," p. 348, database with digital images, *American Ancestors*, accessed 29 Oct 2019.
1101   James Savage, *A Genealogical Dictionary of the First Settlers of New England: Showing Three Generations of Those Who Came Before May 1692*, (Boston: Little, Brown, and Company, 1860) Vol II: p. 205; PDF e-book, http://archive.org/details/genealogicaldic02savarich accessed 17 July 2018.
1102   Ibid.

[11-1,652] Edward Gilman and [11-1,653] Mary Clark

Edward Gilman [11-1,652] was born about 1587 in Norfolk, England, and reported in a deposition that his father was also named Edward Gilman [12-3,304]. Edward Gilman [11-1,652] married Mary Clark [11-1,653] in Hingham, Norfolk, England on June 3, 1614.[1103] Some speculate that Mary Clark's parents were John Clark and Elizabeth because they appear in the Hingham parish records as having children around 1600, but I do not find that convincing enough to trace them as her parents.

In 1638, Edward Gilman [11-1,652] and Mary Clark [11-1,653] from Hingham in England on the ship *Diligent* with their children and servants. They arrived in Boston, Suffolk County, Massachusetts, and Edward made freeman status on March 13, 1639. They lived in Rehoboth, Bristol County, Massachusetts in 1643, but were in Ipswich, Essex County by 1647. By 1652 they were in Exeter, Rockingham County, New Hampshire, which is where Edward Gilman [11-1,652] is said to have died.[1104] Mary Clark [11-1,653] died in Hingham, Plymouth County, Massachusetts on June 22, 1681.[1105] The known children for Edward Gilman [11-1,652] and Mary Clark [11-1,653] are listed below:

1. Mary Gilman, christened on August 6, 1615 in Norfolk, England.
2. Edward Gilman, christened on December 26, 1617 in Norfolk, England.
3. Sarah Gilman, christened on January 19, 1622 in Norfolk, England.
4. John Gilman [10-826], christened on May 23, 1626 in Norfolk, England, and married Elizabeth Treworthy [10-827].
5. Moses Gilman, christened on March 11, 1630 in Norfolk, England.[1106]

1103   Clarence Almon Torrey, "English Origin of Edward Gilman," *The American Genealogist* Vol 11: p. 137; database with digital images, *American Ancestors,* accessed 30 October 2019.

1104   James Savage, *A Genealogical Dictionary of the First Settlers of New England: Showing Three Generations of Those Who Came Before May 1692,* (Boston: Little, Brown, and Company, 1860) Vol II: p. 257; PDF e-book, http://archive.org/details/genealogicaldic02savarich accessed 17 July 2018.

1105   "Massachusetts, Town Clerk, Vital and Town Records, 1626-2001," s.v. "Mary Gillman" (death "1681" place "Hingham") database with digital images, *FamilySearch,* accessed 30 October 2019.

1106   James Savage, *A Genealogical Dictionary of the First Settlers of New England: Showing Three Generations of Those Who Came Before May 1692,* (Boston: Little, Brown, and Company, 1860) Vol II: p. 257; PDF e-book, http://archive.org/details/genealogicaldic02savarich accessed 17 July 2018.

[11-1,654] James Treworthy and [11-1,655] Catherine Shapleigh

A genealogist known for faking sources, known under the pseudonym Gustave Anjou, researched this family so extra skepticism is needed for any sources cited for them. More information is available, but if I couldn't verify it with a more reputable source then I didn't include it. So James Treworthy [11-1,654], or Treworgye, was possibly from Cornwall,[1107] but he married Catherine Shapleigh [11-1,655] in Kingswear, Devonshire, England on March 16, 1616.[1108] Catherine was the daughter of Alexander Shapleigh [12-3,310], who was a merchant. James Treworthy acted as an agent for his father-in-law and others, and was in Kittery, York County, Maine by 1636.[1109] The known children of James Treworthy [11-1,654] and Catherine Shapleigh [11-1,655] are listed below:
1. Elizabeth Treworthy [10-827], who married John Gilman [10-826].
2. Joanna Treworthy, who married John Ameridith. Or his last name might have been Meridith or Merryday.
3. Lucy Treworthy, who married first to Humphrey Chadbourne, and second to Thomas Wells of Kittery.[1110]

[11-1,656] Samuel Appleton and [11-1,657] Judith Everard

Samuel Appleton [11-1,656] was born about 1586 in Little Waldingfield, Suffolk, England to Thomas Appleton [12-3,312] and Mary Isaacke [12-3,313]. Samuel married Judith Everard [11-1,657] on January 24, 1616 in Preston St Mary, Suffolk, England.[1111] Judith Everard was the daughter of John Everard [12-3,314] and Judith Bourne [12-3,315].[1112]

1107   James Savage, *A Genealogical Dictionary of the First Settlers of New England: Showing Three Generations of Those Who Came Before May 1692*, (Boston: Little, Brown, and Company, 1860) Vol IV: p. 330; PDF e-book, http://archive.org/details/genealogicaldic04savarich accessed 17 July 2018.
1108   "Devon Marriages and Banns," s.v. "Catheryn Shapleigh" (spouse "James Treworgye" year "1616"), database with digital images, *FindMyPast,* accessed 30 October 2019.
1109   James Savage, *A Genealogical Dictionary of the First Settlers of New England: Showing Three Generations of Those Who Came Before May 1692*, (Boston: Little, Brown, and Company, 1860) Vol IV: p. 330; PDF e-book, http://archive.org/details/genealogicaldic04savarich accessed 17 July 2018.
1110   Ibid.
1111   Joseph James Muskett, ed., *Suffolk Manorial Families: Being the County Visitations and Other Pedigrees* (Exeter: William Pollard & Co., 1900) Vol I: p. 329; PDF e-book, https://archive.org/details/bub_gb_ZxANnBnHKBQC/page/n335 accessed 15 October 2019.
1112   Leslie Mahler, "Confirmation of the Parentage of Judith Everard, Wife of Samuel Appleton o f Ipswich, Massachusetts," *The New England Historical and*

Judith Everard [11-1,657] died before about 1633, when Samuel Appleton [11-1,656] married Martha.[1113] Then Samuel Appleton [11-1,656] took his family to Massachusetts about 1635. [1114] He died in 1670 and was buried in June in Rowley, Essex County, Massachusetts.[1115] The known children of Samuel Appleton [11-1,656] and Judith Everard [11-1,657] are listed below:

1. Mary Appleton, christened in 1616 in Little Waldingfield.
2. Judith Appleton, christened in 1618 in Little Waldingfield and died in 1629 in Reydon, Suffolk, England.
3. Martha Appleton, christened in Little Waldingfield and married Richard Jacob of Ipswich, Massachusetts.
4. John Appleton, christened in 1622 in Little Waldingfield. He married Priscilla Glover in 1651, and died in 1699 in Ipswich, Massachusetts.
5. Samuel Appleton, [10-828] christened in 1625 in Little Waldingfield. He first married Hannah Paine in 1651, and married second to Mary Oliver [10-829] in 1656.
6. Sarah Appleton, christened in 1629 in Reydon, Suffolk, England and married Reverend Samuel Phillips of Rowley, Massachusetts.[1116]

[11-1,658] John Oliver and [11-1,659] Joanna Goodale

This John Oliver [11-1,658] who lived in Newbury, Essex County, Massachusetts, is sometimes confused with a John Oliver who lived in Boston, Massachusetts and was the son of Thomas Oliver. John Oliver [11,658] of Newbury was a linen draper who reported in a 1640 deposition that he was from Bristol, England and aged 27. This John Oliver [11-1,658] showed up in Newbury around April 9, 1639 and became a freeman in Newbury on May13, 1640. He married Joanna Goodale[1117] [11-1,659] around 1639, as indicated by

Genealogical Register, Vol 160: p. 109; database with digital images, *American Ancestors,* accessed 31 October 2019.

1113   "Appleton Genealogy," *The Essex Antiquarian,* Vol 4: p. 2; database with digital images, *American Ancestors,* accessed 31 October 2019.

1114   Joseph James Muskett, ed., *Suffolk Manorial Families: Being the County Visitations and Other Pedigrees* (Exeter: William Pollard & Co., 1900) Vol I: p. 330; PDF e-book, https://archive.org/details/bub_gb_ZxANnBnHKBQC/page/n335 accessed 15 October 2019.

1115   "Appleton Genealogy," *The Essex Antiquarian,* Vol 4: p. 2; database with digital images, *American Ancestors,* accessed 31 October 2019.

1116   Joseph James Muskett, ed., *Suffolk Manorial Families: Being the County Visitations and Other Pedigrees* (Exeter: William Pollard & Co., 1900) Vol I: p. 330; PDF e-book, https://archive.org/details/bub_gb_ZxANnBnHKBQC/page/n335 accessed 15 October 2019.

1117   Charles Henry Pope, *The Pioneers of Massachusetts, A Descriptive List, Drawn from the Records of the Colonies, Towns, and Churches, and other Contemporaneous Documents* (Boston: Charles H. Pope, 1900) p. 335; PDF e-book, https://archive.org/details/pioneersofmassac00pope/page/8 accessed 1 November 2019.

the birth of their child in June 1640.[1118]

Joanna Goodale [11-1,659] was the daughter of ----- Goodale [12-3,318] and Elizabeth [12-3,319], who came from Yarmouth, Norfolk, England. After John Oliver [11-1,658] died, which was about 1642, his widow Joanna [11-1,659] was granted administration of his estate on June 14, 1642. She later married William Gerrish on April 17, 1645.[1119] The child of John Oliver [11-1,658] and Joanna Goodale [11-1,659] is below:

1.   Mary Oliver [10-829], born on June 7, 1640 in Newbury.[1120]

[11-1,660] John Baker and [11-1,661] Elizabeth

John Baker [11-1,660] was born about 1598 based on his age at emigration from England. He was a grocer from Norwich, Norfolk, England, and his wife was Elizabeth [11-1,661]. Elizabeth was born about 1606, based on age at emigration. In 1637 they were examined in England for permission to go to Charlestown, which is now in Boston, Suffolk County, Massachusetts, but they appeared in Ipswich, Essex County, Massachusetts in 1638.[1121]

John Baker [11-1,660] made freeman status in Ipswich on June 2, 1641 and showed up frequently in town records. He was authorized to sell wine in Ipswich on November 13, 1644 and also brewed and sold beer until losing his license to brew beer on September 28, 1652 because he was suspected of not putting in enough malt in the beer.[1122] Elizabeth was still living in 1666,[1123] and John Baker was living in Topsfield, Essex County, Massachusetts in 1680.[1124]

1118   "Massachusetts, Town Clerk, Vital and Town Records, 1626-2001," s.v. "Mary Olliver" (birth "1640" place "Newbury"), database with digital images, *FamilySearch*, accessed 16 Oct 2019.

1119   Charles Henry Pope, *The Pioneers of Massachusetts, A Descriptive List, Drawn from the Records of the Colonies, Towns, and Churches, and other Contemporaneous Documents* (Boston: Charles H. Pope, 1900) pp. 191, 335; PDF e-book, https://archive.org/details/pioneersofmassac00pope/page/8 accessed 1 November 2019.

1120   "Massachusetts, Town Clerk, Vital and Town Records, 1626-2001," s.v. "Mary Olliver" (birth "1640" place "Newbury"), database with digital images, *FamilySearch*, accessed 16 Oct 2019.

1121   William S. Appleton, *Ancestry of Priscilla Baker, Who Lived 1674-1731, and Was the Wife of Isaac Appleton, of Ipswich* (Cambridge: Press of John Wilson and Son, 1870) p. 5; PDF e-book, https://archive.org/details/ancestrypriscil00applgoog/page/n16 accessed 16 October 2019.

1122   Ibid., pp. 5-6.

1123   Charles Henry Pope, *The Pioneers of Massachusetts, A Descriptive List, Drawn from the Records of the Colonies, Towns, and Churches, and other Contemporaneous Documents* (Boston: Charles H. Pope, 1900) p. 28; PDF e-book, https://archive.org/details/pioneersofmassac00pope/page/8 accessed 1 November 2019.

1124   William S. Appleton, *Ancestry of Priscilla Baker, Who Lived 1674-1731, and Was the Wife of Isaac Appleton, of Ipswich* (Cambridge: Press of John Wilson and

The children of John Baker [11-1,660] and Elizabeth [11-1,661] are listed below:

1.   Elizabeth Baker, born in 1633 in Norwich, England.
2.   John Baker, born in 1634 in Norwich, England. He married Katherine, daughter of Rev. William Perkins on May 13, 1667, and died in 1718.
3.   Thomas Baker [10-830], born on September 13, 1636 in Norwich, England.
4.   Martha Baker, born in Ipswich, Massachusetts. She married first to Obadiah Antrim of Salem, and second to Thomas Andrews on June 22, 1670 in Topsfield, Massachusetts.[1125]

[11-1,662] Samuel Symonds and [11-1,663] Martha Read

Samuel Symonds [11-1,662] was born in Essex, England to Richard Symonds [12-3,324] of Yeldham and Elizabeth Plume [12-3,325].[1126] The first marriage of Samuel Symonds was to Dorothy Harlakendon, with whom he had multiple children. Then before about 1638, Samuel Symonds [11-1,662] married Martha Read [11-1,663], and they were in Ipswich, Essex County, Massachusetts by March of 1637/8. Samuel Symonds became the Deputy Governor of Massachusetts.[1127]

Martha Read [11-1,663] was born on July 13, 1602 in North Benfleet, Essex, England and was the daughter of Edmund Reade[1128] [12-3,326] and Elizabeth Cooke[1129] [12-3,327]. Her first marriage was to Daniel Epes, so she was a widow when she married Samuel Symonds [11-1,662]. She died about 1662, after an apparent mental illness or dementia.[1130] Samuel Symonds then

---

Son, 1870) p. 6; PDF e-book, https://archive.org/details/ancestrypriscil00applgoog/page/n16 accessed 16 October 2019.

1125   Ibid., p. 7.

1126   Walter Charles Metcalfe, ed., *The Visitations of Essex by Hawley, 1552; Hervey, 1558; Cooke, 1570; Raven, 1612; and Owen and Lilly, 1634. To which Are Added Miscellaneous Essex Pedigrees from Various Harleian Manuscripts: and an Appendix Containing Berry's Essex Pedigrees.*, (London: Mitchell and Hughes, 1878) p. 495; PDF e-book, https://archive.org/details/visitationsofess1314metc/page/n8 accessed 3 November 2019.

1127   Charles Henry Pope, *The Pioneers of Massachusetts, A Descriptive List, Drawn from the Records of the Colonies, Towns, and Churches, and other Contemporaneous Documents* , (Boston: Charles H. Pope, 1900) p. 445; PDF e-book, https://archive.org/details/pioneersofmassac00pope/page/8 accessed 1 November 2019.

1128   "Notes," *The New England Historical and Genealogical Register,* Vol 84: p. 113; database with digital images, *American Ancestors,* Accessed 3 November 2019.

1129   Henry F. Waters, "Genealogical Gleanings in England," *The New England Historical and Genealogical Register,* Vol 47: pp. 128-9; database with digital images, *American Ancestors,* Accessed 3 November 2019.

1130   William S. Appleton, *Ancestry of Priscilla Baker, Who Lived 1674-1731, and*

had a third marriage, to Rebecca, the widow of John Hall of Salisbury. He died before November 6, 1678 when his will was probated.[1131] Samuel Symonds [11-1,662] had about ten children with his first wife Dorothy Harlakendon, but other than the children listed below, with some of the children it is not clear which are from his second wife, Martha Read [11-1,663].[1132]

1. Martha Symonds.
2. Ruth Symonds.
3. Priscilla Symonds [10-831].[1133]

[11-1,664] William Cowdrey and [11-1,665] Joanna

William Cowdrey [11-1,664] was born in 1602 in Weymouth, Dorset, England,[1134] but I could not verify the identity of his parents. He emigrated in 1630 from Southampton, England to Lynn, Essex County, Massachusetts. One possibility for when he married his first wife Joanna [11-1,665] is in Lynn in 1638.[1135] However, some people believe that the marriage record of a "Wm Cowdrye" and "Joanna Licence" in 1626 in Buckinghamshire, England is for this couple. Since William Cowdrey was from Dorset, and not Buckinghamshire, and since other sources indicate he married later in Massachusetts, I do not believe the Buckinghamshire marriage record is a likely match.

William Cowdrey [11-1,664] was a representative to the general assembly of the colonies for Lynn before 1644. Then in 1644 he was one of the first settlers of Reading, Middlesex County, Massachusetts, where he was town clerk and a Selectman from 1644 to 1687. In 1654, William received a license to sell alcohol to the Native Americans at his discretion.[1136]

William Cowdrey [11-1,664] and Joanna [11-1,665] had at least three

---

Was the Wife of Isaac Appleton, of Ipswich, (Cambridge: Press of John Wilson and Son, 1870) p. 70; PDF e-book,
https://archive.org/details/ancestrypriscil00applgoog/page/n16 accessed 16 October 2019.
1131   Charles Henry Pope, *The Pioneers of Massachusetts, A Descriptive List, Drawn from the Records of the Colonies, Towns, and Churches, and other Contemporaneous Documents* , (Boston: Charles H. Pope, 1900) p. 445; PDF e-book, https://archive.org/details/pioneersofmassac00pope/page/8 accessed 1 November 2019.
1132   James Savage, *A Genealogical Dictionary of the First Settlers of New England: Showing Three Generations of Those Who Came Before May 1692* , (Boston: Little, Brown and Company, 1860) Vol IV: p. 246; PDF e-book,
http://archive.org/details/genealogicaldic04savarich accessed 17 July 2018.
1133   Ibid.
1134   William Richard Cutter, ed., *Genealogical and Family History of Western New York*, (New York: Lewis Historical Publishing Company, 1912), Vol III: p 1427; PDF e-book, https://archive.org/details/genealogicalfami03incutt accessed 9 July 2018.
1135   Ibid., Vol III: p. 1427.
1136   Ibid., Vol III: p. 1427.

children together[1137] before Joanna died on May 6, 1666. After Joanna died, William married Alse (Alice) on December 5, 1666. William died on November 10, 1687 in Reading.[1138] The children of William Cowdrey [11-1,664] and Joanna [11-1,665] are listed below:

1. Nathaniel Cowdrey [10-832].
2. Matthias Cowdrey.
3. Bethia Cowdrey.[1139]

[11-1,666] John Batchelder and [11-1,667] Rebecca

John Batchelder [11-1,666] was born in England and was the son of Joshua Batcheller (12-3,332).[1140] John married Rebecca[1141] [11-1,667] before 1635, and had at least five children after 1635.[1142] He showed up in Watertown, Middlesex County, Massachusetts by 1636, where he was a selectman and received six lots of land. By 1651, John was in Reading, Middlesex County, Massachusetts where he was a selectman from 1651 to 1666. Rebecca [11-1,667] died on March 9, 1662 in Reading,[1143] although the *FamilySearch* transcription says 1655.[1144] Then in 1666 John Batchelder became a Puritan minister.[1145] John had a will in 1670, in which he mentions some children

---

1137   James Savage, *A Genealogical Dictionary of the First Settlers of New England: Showing Three Generations of Those Who Came Before May 1692*, (Boston: Little, Brown and Company, 1860), Vol I: p. 466; PDF e-book, http://archive.org/details/genealogicaldic01savarich accessed 17 July 2018.
1138   William Richard Cutter, ed., *Genealogical and Family History of Western New York*, (New York: Lewis Historical Publishing Company, 1912), Vol III: p 1427; PDF e-book, https://archive.org/details/genealogicalfami03incutt accessed 9 July 2018.
1139   James Savage, *A Genealogical Dictionary of the First Settlers of New England: Showing Three Generations of Those Who Came Before May 1692*, (Boston: Little, Brown and Company, 1860), Vol I: p. 466; PDF e-book, http://archive.org/details/genealogicaldic01savarich accessed 17 July 2018.
1140   Frederick Clifton Pierce, *Batchelder, Batcheller, Genealogy*, (Chicago: W B Conkey Company, 1898), p 347; PDF e-book, https://archive.org/details/batchelderbatche1898pier accessed 15 July 2018.
1141   Ibid., p. 352.
1142   William Richard Cutter, ed., *Genealogical and Family History of Western New York*, (New York: Lewis Historical Publishing Company, 1912), Vol III: p 1428; PDF e-book, https://archive.org/details/genealogicalfami03incutt accessed 9 July 2018.
1143   James Savage, *A Genealogical Dictionary of the First Settlers of New England: Showing Three Generations of Those Who Came Before May 1692*, (Boston: Little, Brown and Company, 1860), Vol I: p. 88; PDF e-book, http://archive.org/details/genealogicaldic01savarich accessed 17 July 2018.
1144   "Massachusetts Deaths and Burials, 1795-1910," s.v. "Robocka Bachellor" (death 1655), database, *FamilySearch*, accessed 2 May 2018.
1145   Frederick Clifton Pierce, *Batchelder, Batcheller, Genealogy*, (Chicago: W B Conkey Company, 1898), p 353; PDF e-book, https://archive.org/details/batchelderbatche1898pier accessed 15 July 2018.

including Mary "Cowdery" (B12-161f).[1146] John Batchelder died on March 3, 1676,[1147] although the *FamilySearch* transcription says May[1148] possibly due to difficulty reading the handwriting of the original document. The children of John Batchelder [11-1,666] and Rebecca [11-1,667] are listed below:
1. Mary Bacheldor [10-833], born about 1635 and who married Nathaniel Cowdrey [10-832].
2. Samuel Bacheldor, born in 1639 and died in 1662.
3. David Bacheldor, born in 1643 and married Hannah Plummer.
4. Jonathan Bacheldor, born in 1643 and died in 1653.
5. John Bacheldor, who married first to Sarah, second to Hannah, and third to Hannah.[1149]

[11-1,680] Benjamin Parker and [11-1,681] Sarah Hartwell

Benjamin Parker [11-1,680] was born in June 1636 in Cambridge, Middlesex County, Massachusetts to Robert Parker [12-3,360] and Judith [12-3,361].[1150] [1151] By 1660, Benjamin was in Billerica, Middlesex County, Massachusetts, where he married Sarah Hartwell [11-1,681] on April 18, 1661. Then Benjamin Parker [11-1,680] died on January 17, 1671/2, and his wife Sarah Hartwell [11-1,681] died a few years later on July 8, 1674.[1152] The children of Benjamin Parker and Sarah Hartwell are listed below:
1. Benjamin Parker, born on June 29, 1662 in Billerica.
2. John Parker, born on December 3, 1663 in Billerica and died on December 8, 1663.

1146   "Probate records 1648-1924 (Middlesex County, Massachusetts)," s.v. "John Batchhelder" (will 1670), database with digital images, *FamilySearch*, accessed 25 January 2018.
1147   Frederick Clifton Pierce, *Batchelder, Batcheller, Genealogy*, (Chicago: W B Conkey Company, 1898), p 353; PDF e-book, https://archive.org/details/batchelderbatche1898pier accessed 15 July 2018.
1148   "Massachusetts Deaths and Burials, 1795-1910," s.v. "John Bachellor" (death 1676), database, *FamilySearch*, accessed 2 May 2018.
1149   Frederick Clifton Pierce, *Batchelder, Batcheller, Genealogy*, (Chicago: W B Conkey Company, 1898), p 353; PDF e-book, https://archive.org/details/batchelderbatche1898pier accessed 15 July 2018.
1150   Henry A Hazen, *History of Billerica, Massachusetts: With a Genealogical Register,* (Boston: A Williams and Co, 1883) p. 105 of Genealogical Register; PDF e-book, Internet Archive, https://archive.org/details/historyofbilleri00hazenhe , accessed 9 July 2018.
1151"Massachusetts Births and Christenings, 1639-1915," s.v. "Benjamin Parker" (birth 1636), database, *FamilySearch*, accessed 2 May 2017.
1152   Henry A Hazen, *History of Billerica, Massachusetts: With a Genealogical Register,* (Boston: A Williams and Co, 1883) p. 105 of Genealogical Register; PDF e-book, Internet Archive, https://archive.org/details/historyofbilleri00hazenhe , accessed 9 July 2018.

3. Samuel Parker, born on November 19, 1664 in Billerica and died in 1664.
4. John Parker [10-840], born on March 17, 1667/8 in Billerica. He married Abigail Whittaker [10-841] and died on January 1, 1698/9 in Billerica.
5. Samuel Parker, born on September 26, 1670 in Billerica, and died on December 1, 1670.[1153]

[11-1,682] John Whittaker and [11-1,683] Elizabeth

According to court records, John Whittaker [11-1,682] was born about 1641.[1154] Since there were multiple children born in England around 1641 with a name similar to John Whittaker, it would be difficult to trace his parents any further without supporting evidence. There is also confusion about who he married, because there was a court case where John promised to marry Mary Linfield but married Elizabeth [11-1,683] instead.[1155] Elizabeth was born about 1642 according to court records.[1156]

Some people speculate that Mary and Elizabeth were the same person, but I have not seen the evidence to support that theory. Whatever the case, John married Elizabeth before about 1661 when their first child was born.[1157] The children of John Whittaker [11-1,682] and Elizabeth [11-1,683] are listed below:

1. Elizabeth Whittaker, born in 1661.[1158]
2. John Whittaker, born on August 23, 1662 in Watertown, Middlesex County, Massachusetts.[1159]
3. Jonathan Whittaker, born on October 8, 1664 in Watertown.[1160]

1153   Ibid.
1154   Henry A Hazen, *History of Billerica, Massachusetts: With a Genealogical Register,* (Boston: A Williams and Co, 1883) p. 162 of Genealogical Register; PDF e-book, Internet Archive, https://archive.org/details/historyofbilleri00hazenhe , accessed 9 July 2018.
1155   James Savage, *A Genealogical Dictionary of the First Settlers of New England: Showing Three Generations of Those Who Came Before May 1692*, (Boston: Little, Brown and Company, 1860), Vol IV: p. 507; PDF e-book, http://archive.org/details/genealogicaldic04savarich accessed 17 July 2018.
1156   Henry A Hazen, *History of Billerica, Massachusetts: With a Genealogical Register,* (Boston: A Williams and Co, 1883) p. 162 of Genealogical Register; PDF e-book, Internet Archive, https://archive.org/details/historyofbilleri00hazenhe , accessed 9 July 2018.
1157   Ibid., pp. 105, 162 of the Genealogical Register.
1158   Ibid., p 162 of the Genealogical Register.
1159   "Massachusetts, Town Clerk, Vital and Town Records, 1626-2001," s.v. "John Whittacar" (birth "1662"), database with digital images, *FamilySearch*, accessed 4 May 2018.
1160   "Massachusetts, Town Clerk, Vital and Town Records, 1626-2001," s.v.

4. Sary Whittaker, born on June 12, 1666 in Watertown.[1161]
5. Hannah Whittaker, born on May 14, 1669 in Watertown.[1162]
6. Abigail Whittaker [10-841], born on May 14, 1671 in Watertown.[1163]
7. John Whittaker, born in 1663.[1164]
8. Daniel Whittaker, born on May 10, 1679 in Billerica.[1165] Some say March due to a transcription error with the Julian calendar.

[11-1,688] Thomas Tarbell and [11-1,689] Mary

Thomas Tarbell [11-1,688] first appeared in the records of Watertown, Middlesex County, Massachusetts about 1647. They moved to Groton, Middlesex County, Massachusetts after March 30, 1663, where Mary [11-1,689] died on April 29, 1674.[1166] After Native Americans destroyed Groton in 1676, Thomas moved to Charlestown which is now part of Boston, Suffolk County, Massachusetts. In Charlestown, Thomas married Susanna, the widow of John Lawrence on August 15, 1676.[1167] There is some confusion about the location of the 2nd marriage and the death of Thomas, with some sources placing them in Groton. However since Groton was destroyed earlier in 1676, the location is more likely to have been Charlestown. Thomas died in Charlestown on April 27, 1678 of small pox.[1168] The children of Thomas

"Jonathan Whittacar" (birth "1664"), database with digital images, *FamilySearch*, accessed 4 May 2018.

1161   "Massachusetts, Town Clerk, Vital and Town Records, 1626-2001," s.v. "Sary Whittacar" (birth "1666"), database with digital images, *FamilySearch*, accessed 4 May 2018.

1162   "Massachusetts, Town Clerk, Vital and Town Records, 1626-2001," s.v. "Hannah Whittacar" (birth "1669"), database with digital images, *FamilySearch*, accessed 4 May 2018.

1163   "Massachusetts, Town Clerk, Vital and Town Records, 1626-2001," s.v. "Abigail Whitacar" (birth "1671"), database with digital images, *FamilySearch*, accessed 4 May 2018.

1164   Henry A Hazen, *History of Billerica, Massachusetts: With a Genealogical Register,* (Boston: A Williams and Co, 1883) p. 162 of Genealogical Register; PDF e-book, Internet Archive, https://archive.org/details/historyofbilleri00hazenhe , accessed 9 July 2018.

1165   "Massachusetts, Town Clerk, Vital and Town Records, 1626-2001," s.v. "Daniel Whittaker" (birth "1679"), database with digital images, *FamilySearch*, accessed 4 May 2018.

1166   Charles Henry Wight, "Thomas Tarbell and Some of His Descendants," *The New England Historical and Genealogical Register*, Vol 61: p 70; database, *American Ancestors*, accessed 15 July 2018.

1167   James Savage, *A Genealogical Dictionary of the First Settlers of New England: Showing Three Generations of Those Who Came Before May 1692*, (Boston: Little, Brown and Company, 1860), Vol IV: p. 256; PDF e-book, http://archive.org/details/genealogicaldic04savarich accessed 17 July 2018.

1168   "Massachusetts, Town Clerk, Vital and Town Records, 1626-2001," s.v.

Tarbell [11-1,688] and Mary [11-1,689] are listed below:
1.   Thomas Tarbell
2.   Mary Tarbell, who married Jonathan Sawtell of Groton on July 3, 1665 and died on April 26, 1676.
3.   Sarah Tarbell, born about 1648 and married Cornelius Church before May 31, 1680. She died in 1715 in Salem, Essex County, Massachusetts.
4.   Abigail Tarbell, who married Joshua Whitney in 1672.
5.   John Tarbell [10-844], born about 1654 in Watertown. He married Mary Nurse [10-845] and died in 1715 in Salem Village, which was later renamed to Danvers, Essex County, Massachusetts.
6.   Elizabeth Tarbell, born on January 5, 1656/7 and married James Bennett on February 4, 1680/1. She died on July 25, 1684.
7.   William Tarbell, born on February 26, 1658/9.
8.   Martha Tarbell, who married Thomas Mitchell on May 18, 1685 in Salem.[1169]

[11-1,690] Francis Nurse and [11-1,691] Rebecca Towne

Francis Nurse [11-1,690] was born on January 18, 1618 in England,[1170] and married Rebecca Towne [11-1,691] on August 24, 1644.[1171] Rebecca Towne was the daughter of William Towne [12-3,382] and Joan Blessing [12-3,383] and was christened on February 21, 1621 in Yarmouth, Norfolk, England.[1172]

Francis Nurse lived in Salem Village by 1647,[1173] which is now known as Danvers in Essex County, Massachusetts. He was a skilled woodworker, and made trays and utensils from wood for the town. The Nurse family was influential at the time, and Francis was a deacon at First Church in Salem

---

"Thomas Tarball" (death 1678), database with digital images, *FamilySearch*, accessed 6 May 2018.

1169   Charles Henry Wight, "Thomas Tarbell and Some of His Descendants," *The New England Historical and Genealogical Register*, Vol 61: p 70; database, *American Ancestors*, accessed 15 July 2018.

1170   William Richard Cutter, ed., *Genealogical and Personal Memoirs: Relating to the Families of Boston and Eastern Massachusetts*, (New York: Lewis Historical Publishing Company, 1908), Vol III: p. 1489; PDF e-book, https://archive.org/details/genealogicaland00cuttgoog accessed 10 July 2018.

1171   Ibid., Vol III: p. 1490.

1172   Charles W. Upham, *Salem Witchcraft: With an Account of Salem Village, and a History of Opinions on Witchcraft and Kindred Subjects*, (Boston: Wiggin and Lunt, 1867), Vol II: p 60; PDF e-book, https://archive.org/details/salemwitchcraftw02upha_0 accessed 20 July 2018.

1173   William Richard Cutter, ed., *Genealogical and Personal Memoirs: Relating to the Families of Boston and Eastern Massachusetts*, (New York: Lewis Historical Publishing Company, 1908), Vol III: p. 1489; PDF e-book, https://archive.org/details/genealogicaland00cuttgoog accessed 10 July 2018.

Village.[1174] Some speculate that the wealth and influence of the Nurse family led to Rebecca being accused of witchcraft. Rebecca was executed for witchcraft in Salem Village on July 19, 1692, even though the jury found her not guilty.[1175] Francis died a few years later on November 22, 1695 in Salem Village.[1176] The children of Francis Nurse [11-1,690] and Rebecca Towne [11-1,691] are listed below:

1. John Nurse, who was born in 1645. His first marriage was to Elizabeth Smith on November 1, 1672, and second to Elizabeth Verry on August 17, 1677. He died in 1715.
2. Rebecca Nurse, born in 1647 and who married Thomas Preston on April 15, 1669.
3. Samuel Nurse, born on February 3, 1649 and died on July 15, 1715.
4. Mary Nurse [10-845], who was born about 1659 and married John Tarbell [10-844] on October 25, 1678. She died on June 28, 1749.
5. Francis Nurse, who died on February 5, 1716.
6. Sarah Nurse, who was born in 1663 and married in July 1700 to a Michael ____.
7. Elizabeth Nurse, who was born on January 9, 1665 and married William Russell.
8. Benjamin Nurse, who was born on January 22, 1666 and died in 1748.[1177]

[11-1,702] Edward Winn and [11-1,703] Joanna

Edward Winn [11-1,702] was recorded being in Charlestown, which is now part of Boston, Suffolk County, Massachusetts, as early as December 1640.[1178] As to where in Britain he was born, or the surname for his first wife, Joanna [11-1,703], I was not able to verify the information conclusively. They were in Woburn, Middlesex County, Massachusetts in 1641, where Edward was made a freeman on May 10, 1643.[1179]

Joanna [11-1,703] had at least four children with Edward Winn [11-1,702]

1174   Ibid., Vol III: p. 1490.
1175   Charles Henry Wight, "Thomas Tarbell and Some of His Descendants," *The New England Historical and Genealogical Register*, Vol 61: p 70; database, *American Ancestors*, accessed 15 July 2018.
1176   William Richard Cutter, ed., *Genealogical and Personal Memoirs: Relating to the Families of Boston and Eastern Massachusetts*, (New York: Lewis Historical Publishing Company, 1908), Vol III: p. 1489; PDF e-book, https://archive.org/details/genealogicaland00cuttgoog accessed 10 July 2018.
1177   Ibid., Vol III: p. 1490.
1178   James Savage, *A Genealogical Dictionary of the First Settlers of New England: Showing Three Generations of Those Who Came Before May 1692*, (Boston: Little, Brown and Company, 1860), Vol IV: p. 596; PDF e-book, http://archive.org/details/genealogicaldic04savarich accessed 17 July 2018.
1179   Ibid., Vol IV: p. 596.

before dying on March 8, 1649 in Woburn.[1180] [1181]   So Edward married Sarah Beall on August 10, 1649 in Woburn.[1182]   Then he had a third marriage to Ann or Hannah Wood, the widow of Nicholas Wood, after March 1680 when Sarah died.   On September 5, 1682, Edward Winn died in Woburn.[1183]   The children of Edward Winn [11-1,702] and Joanna [11-1,703] are listed below:

1. Joseph Winn, who married Rebekah Reed about 1664.
2. Ann Winn, who married Moses Cleveland on September 26, 1648 in Woburn.
3. Elizabeth Winn [10-851], who married George Polly [10-850] and died on May 2, 1695.
4. Increase Winn, who was born on December 5, 1641 in Woburn and married Hannah Sawtell on July 13, 1665 in Woburn.[1184]

[11-1,704] John Dutton

About all that is known about John Dutton [11-1,704] is that he came from Chester, England and arrived in Dorchester, which is now in Boston, Suffolk County, Massachusetts, in 1630 with his son Thomas Dutton [10-852], who had been born about 1620.[1185]   There was an aristocratic family of Dutton's in Cheshire at that time and it is likely he was connected somehow. However, the connection has not been conclusively established at this time, and there is disagreement.

[11-1,712] Samuel Kemp and [11-1,713] Sarah Foster

Samuel Kemp [11-1,712] married Sarah Foster [11-1,713] on May 23, 1662 in Billerica, Middlesex County, Massachusetts.[1186]   Samuel and Sarah moved

---

1180   Horace Gillette Cleveland, *A Genealogy of Benjamin Cleveland*, (Chicago: n.p., 1879), p. 77; PDF e-book, https://archive.org/details/genealogyofbenja00clev accessed 15 July 2018.

1181   "Massachusetts, Town Clerk, Vital and Town Records, 1626-2001," s.v. "Joanna Winn" (death 1649), database with digital images, *FamilySearch*, accessed 6 May 2018.

1182"Massachusetts, Town Clerk, Vital and Town Records, 1626-2001," s.v. "Edward Winn" (marriage 1649, spouse "Sarah Beall"), database with digital images, *FamilySearch*, accessed 6 May 2018.

1183   Horace Gillette Cleveland, *A Genealogy of Benjamin Cleveland*, (Chicago: n.p., 1879), p. 77; PDF e-book, https://archive.org/details/genealogyofbenja00clev accessed 15 July 2018.

1184   Ibid., pp. 77-78.

1185   John W. Jordan, ed., *Genealogical and Personal History of Western Pennsylvania*, (New York: Lewis Historical Publishing Company, 1915), Vol I: p 137; PDF e-book https://archive.org/details/genealogicalpers01injord accessed 15 July 2018.

1186   Henry A Hazen, *History of Billerica, Massachusetts: With a Genealogical*

around, partly due to pressure from the Native Americans. Not much else can be established for certain.

Some genealogies have Edward Kemp as the father for Samuel Kemp [11-1,712]. However, the 1669 will of Edward Kemp lists Samuel Kemp [11-1,712] as a kinsman, not a son. So other genealogies place Robert Kemp of Dedham as the father of Samuel Kemp [11-1,712].[1187] [1188] To further complicate things, there was an English birth record in the right time and place listing Richard Kemp as the father of a Samuel Kemp. So I stopped at Samuel Kemp [11-1,712] as of 2018 to avoid error. Likewise, the genealogy of Sarah Foster [11-1,713] is also in dispute, with Hazen saying perhaps she was the daughter of Thomas Foster of Braintree.[1189] The children of Samuel Kemp [11-1,712] and Sarah Foster [11-1,713] are listed below:

1. Samuel Kemp, born on February 23, 1662/3 in Billerica.
2. Abigail Kemp, born on March 27, 1664/5 in Billerica.[1190]
3. Jonathan Kemp [10-856], born on April 6, 1668 in Groton, Middlesex County, Massachusetts.[1191]
4. Ann Kemp, born in May 1671 in Andover, Essex County, Massachusetts.[1192]
5. Mehitable Kemp, born on January 4, 1673 in Groton.[1193]
6. Zerubbabel Kemp, born on May 23, 1677 in Andover.[1194]
7. Sarah Kemp, born on April 18, 1679 in Andover.[1195]
8. Bethiah Kemp, born on July 9, 1683 in Groton.[1196]

Register, (Boston: A Williams and Co, 1883) p. 80 of Genealogical Register; PDF e-book, https://archive.org/details/historyofbilleri00hazenhe , accessed 9 July 2018.
1187   Henry A Hazen, *History of Billerica, Massachusetts: With a Genealogical Register,* (Boston: A Williams and Co, 1883) p. 80 of Genealogical Register; PDF e-book, https://archive.org/details/historyofbilleri00hazenhe , accessed 9 July 2018.
1188   William Richard Cutter, ed., *Genealogical and Personal Memoirs: Relating to the Families of the State of Massachusetts*, (New York: Lewis Historical Publishing Company, 1910), Vol IV: p. 2171; PDF e-book,
https://archive.org/details/genealogicaland01adamgoog accessed 9 July 2018.
1189   Henry A Hazen, *History of Billerica, Massachusetts: With a Genealogical Register,* (Boston: A Williams and Co, 1883) p. 54 of Genealogical Register; PDF e-book, https://archive.org/details/historyofbilleri00hazenhe , accessed 9 July 2018.
1190   Ibid.
1191   "Massachusetts, Town Clerk, Vital and Town Records, 1626-2001," s.v. "Jonathan Kemp" (birth "1668"), database with digital images, *FamilySearch*, accessed 27 January 2018.
1192   "Massachusetts Births and Christenings, 1639-1915," s.v. "An Kemp" (birth "1671"), database, *FamilySearch*, accessed 7 May 2018.
1193   Henry A Hazen, *History of Billerica, Massachusetts: With a Genealogical Register,* (Boston: A Williams and Co, 1883) p. 80 of Genealogical Register; PDF e-book, https://archive.org/details/historyofbilleri00hazenhe , accessed 9 July 2018.
1194   "Massachusetts Births and Christenings, 1639-1915," s.v. "Zerubbabel Kemp" (birth "1677"), database, *FamilySearch*, accessed 7 May 2018.
1195   "Massachusetts Births and Christenings, 1639-1915," s.v. "Sarah Kemp" (birth "1679"), database, *FamilySearch*, accessed 7 May 2018.
1196   Henry A Hazen, *History of Billerica, Massachusetts: With a Genealogical*

[11-1,716] William Chamberlain and [11-1,717] Rebecca

William Chamberlain [11-1,716] was born about 1619. Sometime before 1649, William [11-1,716] married Rebecca [11-1,717]. Rebecca died in prison on September 26, 1692 in Cambridge, Middlesex County, Massachusetts. She was accused of witchcraft. William died on May 31, 1705 in Billerica, Middlesex County, Massachusetts.[1197] I was not able to verify Rebecca's surname, nor could I verify William's further ancestry. The children of William Chamberlain [11-1,716] and Rebecca [11-1,717] are listed below:

1. Timothy Chamberlain, born on August 13, 1649 in Woburn, Middlesex County, Massachusetts.[1198]
2. Isaac Chamberlain, born on October 1, 1650 in Woburn.[1199]
3. Sarah Chamberlain, born on May 20, 1655 in Billerica. She married John Shed.
4. Jacob Chamberlain, born on January 18, 1657/8 in Billerica.
5. Thomas Chamberlain, born on February 20, 1659/60 in Billerica, but the date might be in error due to proximity to the next child's birth.
6. Edmond Chamberlain, born on July 15, 1660 in Billerica. He married first to the widow Mercy Abbot, and second to Sarah Forbush of Reading.
7. Rebecca Chamberlain, born on February 23, 1662/3 in Billerica. She married Thomas Stearns.
8. Abraham Chamberlain, born on January 6, 1664/5 in Billerica.
9. Ann Chamberlain, born on March 3, 1665/6 in Billerica.
10. Clement Chamberlain [10-858], born on May 30, 1669 in Billerica. He married Mary [10-859].
11. Daniel Chamberlain, born on September 27, 1671 in Billerica. He married Mary.[1200]

Register, (Boston: A Williams and Co, 1883) p. 80 of Genealogical Register; PDF e-book, https://archive.org/details/historyofbilleri00hazenhe , accessed 9 July 2018.

1197   Henry A Hazen, *History of Billerica, Massachusetts: With a Genealogical Register,* (Boston: A Williams and Co, 1883) p. 23 of Genealogical Register; PDF e-book, https://archive.org/details/historyofbilleri00hazenhe , accessed 9 July 2018.

1198   "Massachusetts Births and Christenings, 1639-1915," s.v. "Timothy Chamberlain" (birth "1649"), database, *FamilySearch,* accessed 27 January 2018.

1199   "Massachusetts Births and Christenings, 1639-1915," s.v. "Isaac Chamberlain" (birth "1650"), database, *FamilySearch,* accessed 27 January 2018.

1200   Henry A Hazen, *History of Billerica, Massachusetts: With a Genealogical Register,* (Boston: A Williams and Co, 1883) p. 23 of Genealogical Register; PDF e-book, https://archive.org/details/historyofbilleri00hazenhe , accessed 9 July 2018.

[11-1,720] James Mears and [11-1,721] Elizabeth Mellowes

James Mears was born on March 9, 1644 in Boston, Suffolk County, Massachusetts to Robert Mears [12-3,440] and Elizabeth Johnson [12-3,441]. James was a felt-maker,[1201] and married Elizabeth Mellowes [11-1,721] sometime before their first child was born in 1667.[1202] Elizabeth Mellowes was born on January 5, 1643 in Charlestown, which is now part of Boston. Her parents were Edward Mellowes [12-3,442] and Hannah Smith [12-3,443].[1203] [1204] James died on October 6, 1712 in Boston.[1205] The children of James Mears [11-1,720] and Elizabeth Mellowes [11-1,721] are listed below:

1. James Mears, born on August 1, 1667 in Boston.
2. Elizabeth Mears, born on August 1, 1668 in Boston.
3. Edward Mears, born on March 22, 1669/70 in Boston.
4. Robert Mears [10-860], who was born on January 29, 1671/2 in Boston. He married first to Elizabeth Adams [10-861] on July 30, 1706 in Boston, and second to Mary Dresser on May 2, 1733.
5. Oliver Mears, born on December 3, 1673 in Boston.
6. Hannah Mears, born on June 28, 1676/7 in Boston and died in 1678.
7. Hannah Mears, born on June 2, 1678 in Boston.
8. John Mears, born on May 11, 1680 in Boston. He married Sarah Trask on June 17, 1714.
9. Nathaniel Mears, born on October 7, 1681 in Boston.
10. Nathaniel Mears, born on September 26, 1683 in Boston.
11. Stephen Mears, born on May 15, 1690 in Boston.[1206]

1201   William Richard Cutter, ed., *Genealogical and Family History of Western New York*, (New York: Lewis Historical Publishing Company, 1912), Vol III: p 1480; PDF e-book, https://archive.org/details/genealogicalfami03incutt accessed 9 July 2018.
1202   Clarence Almon Torrey, *New England Marriages Prior to 1700*, (Baltimore, Maryland: Genealogical Publishing Co., Inc, 2004), s.v. "James Mears" (spouse "Elizabeth Mellowes"), database with digital images, *Ancestry.com,* accessed 27 January 2018.
1203   "Massachusetts, Town Clerk, Vital and Town Records, 1626-2001," s.v. "Elisabeth Mellowes" (birth 1643).database, *FamilySearch*, accessed 27 January 2018.
1204   William Richard Cutter, ed., *Genealogical and Personal Memoirs: Relating to the Families of Boston and Eastern Massachusetts*, (New York: Lewis Historical Publishing Company, 1908), Vol II: p. 906; PDF e-book, https://archive.org/details/genealogicaland01cuttgoog accessed 10 July 2018.
1205   "Massachusetts, Town and Vital Records, 1620-1988," s.v. "James Meers" (death 1712), database, *Ancestry.com*, accessed 27 January 2018.
1206   William Richard Cutter, ed., *Genealogical and Personal Memoirs: Relating to the Families of Boston and Eastern Massachusetts*, (New York: Lewis Historical Publishing Company, 1908), Vol III: p. 1480; PDF e-book, https://archive.org/details/genealogicaland00cuttgoog accessed 10 July 2018.

[11-1,724] James Frost and [11-1,725] Elizabeth Foster

James Frost [11-1,724] was born on April 9, 1643 to Edmund Frost [12-3,448] and Thomasine [12-3,449].[1207] James [11-1,724] first married Rebecca Hamlet on December 7, 1664 in Billerica, Middlesex County, Massachusetts, but she died on July 20, 1666. So then he married Elizabeth Foster [11-1,725] on January 22, 1666/7 in Billerica.[1208] [1209] Elizabeth Foster was the daughter of Thomas Foster [12-3,450] of Braintree, and her mother may have been Elizabeth but it is not certain. James was a deacon, and died on August 12, 1711 in Billerica. Elizabeth died in 1726 in Billerica.[1210] The children of James Frost and Elizabeth Foster are listed below:

1. Thomas Frost, born on October 18, 1667 in Billerica. He married first to Rebecca Farley on December 12, 1695 in Billerica, second to Hannah Richardson of Woburn on March 28, 1706 in Billerica, and third to Deborah. He died on March 6, 1742 in Billerica.
2. John Frost, born on November 14, 1668 in Billerica, and died on March 3, 1668/9 in Billerica.
3. Samuel Frost [10-862], born on February 28, 1669/70 in Billerica and married Hannah Mascraft [10-863]. He died on December 7, 1755 in Tewksbury, Middlesex County, Massachusetts.
4. Elizabeth Frost, born on November 6, 1672 in Billerica and married Peter Corneal.
5. Edmond Frost, born on May 14 1673 in Billerica and died on May 18, 1673 in Billerica.
6. Mary Frost, born on May 6, 1676 in Billerica and married John Walker.
7. Sarah Frost, born on July 15, 1678 in Billerica and married Nathaniel Howard.
8. Hannah Frost, born on January 31, 1680/1 in Billerica.
9. Joseph Frost, born on March 21, 1682/3 in Billerica. He married first to Sarah (French) Flint on April 5, 1710 in Billerica, and second to Rebecca Frost on December 8, 1718 in Billerica. He died on December 28, 1737 in Tewksbury.
10. Abigail Frost, born on August 23, 1685 in Billerica, and married

---

1207   James Savage, *A Genealogical Dictionary of the First Settlers of New England: Showing Three Generations of Those Who Came Before May 1692*, (Boston: Little, Brown and Company, 1860), Vol II: p. 211; PDF e-book, http://archive.org/details/genealogicaldic02savarich accessed 17 July 2018.
1208   Henry A Hazen, *History of Billerica, Massachusetts: With a Genealogical Register,* (Boston: A Williams and Co, 1883) p. 61 of Genealogical Register; PDF e-book, https://archive.org/details/historyofbilleri00hazenhe , accessed 9 July 2018.
1209   "Massachusetts, Town Clerk, Vital and Town Records, 1626-2001," s.v. "James Ffrost" (marriage 1667 "Elizabeth Ffoster"), database, *FamilySearch*, accessed 2018.
1210   Henry A Hazen, *History of Billerica, Massachusetts: With a Genealogical Register,* (Boston: A Williams and Co, 1883) p. 61 of Genealogical Register; PDF e-book, https://archive.org/details/historyofbilleri00hazenhe , accessed 9 July 2018.

Ephraim Kidder.

11. Benjamin Frost, born on March 8, 1687/8 in Billerica. He married first to Mary Stearns on December 21, 1710 in Billerica, and second to the widow Hannah Richardson on February 15, 1725/6 in Billerica. He died on March 24, 1753 in Billerica.[1211]

[11-1,726] Daniel Mascroft and [11-1,727] Mary Gorton

Daniel Mascroft [11-1,726] (sometimes spelled differently) married Mary Gorton [11-1,727] on May 23, 1665 in Roxbury, which is now part of Boston, Suffolk County, Massachusetts.[1212] Not much else is known about Daniel Mascroft, except that he had at least five children and died before Mary Gorton.[1213] Mary Gorton was born on September 3, 1648 in Roxbury to John Gorton [12-3,454] and Mary [12-3,455],[1214] and died on June 30, 1703.[1215] The children of Daniel Mascroft [11-1,726] and Mary Gorton [11-1,727] are listed below:

1. Elizabeth Mascroft, who married Samuel Spencer on March 18, 1700 in Roxbury.
2. Hannah Mascraft [10-863], who married Samuel Frost [10-862].
3. Samuel Mascroft, who was christened on February 3, 1684.
4. Mehitable Mascroft, who was born on February 28, 1683.
5. Mary Mascroft, who died on June 3, 1688.[1216]

[12-3,084] George Alcock and [12-3,085] Anne (?) Hooker

George Alcock [12-3,084]was born in England sometime before 1610, and enrolled at Oxford University in 1622. [1217] George Alcock came to Roxbury,

1211   Ibid.
1212   "Massachusetts, Town Clerk, Vital and Town Records, 1626-2001," s.v. "Daniel Mascroft" (marriage 1665, spouse "Mary Gorton"), database, *FamilySearch*, accessed 27 January 2018.
1213   James Savage, *A Genealogical Dictionary of the First Settlers of New England: Showing Three Generations of Those Who Came Before May 1692*, (Boston: Little, Brown and Company, 1860), Vol III: p. 159; PDF e-book, http://archive.org/details/genealogicaldic03savarich accessed 17 July 2018.
1214   "Massachusetts Births and Christenings, 1639-1915," s.v. "Mary Gorton" (birth 1648), database, *FamilySearch*, accessed 11 May 2018.
1215   James Savage, *A Genealogical Dictionary of the First Settlers of New England: Showing Three Generations of Those Who Came Before May 1692*, (Boston: Little, Brown and Company, 1860), Vol III: p. 159; PDF e-book, http://archive.org/details/genealogicaldic03savarich accessed 17 July 2018.
1216   Ibid.
1217   G Andrews Moriarty, "The Alcocks of Roxbury, Mass.," *The New England Historical and Genealogical Register,* Vol 97: p. 11; database, *American Ancestors,*

which is now part of Boston, Suffolk County, Massachusetts, in 1630.[1218] He had children by two different wives, but the mother of John Alcock [11-1,542] was a sister of Rev. Thomas Hooker, possibly the sister named Anne. The Rev. Thomas Hooker and his sister were children of Thomas Hooker [13-6,170] who might have come from Leicestershire. She died in her first winter in Massachusetts in 1630. George Alcock [12-3,084] was the first deacon of the Roxbury Church in Roxbury, which is now part of Boston, Suffolk County, Massachusetts;[1219] and was still deacon when he died on December 22, 1640.[1220] He was buried on December 30, 1640 in Roxbury.[1221]

There is a possible connection between the Alcock family that came to Massachusetts and the Alicock family of Sibertoft mentioned in *The Visitations of Northamptonshire*, since the Alcock brothers who came to Massachusetts were Thomas and George, and they had a sister Elizabeth Whitehouse in England.[1222] However the Thomas Alicock of Sibertoft had different wives than the Massachusetts Thomas Alcock, so I doubt this is a match.

The child of George Alcock[12-3,084] and ___ Hooker [12-3,085] was John Alcock [11-1,542], who married Sarah Palsgrave [11-1,543].[1223]

[12-3,086] Richard Palgrave and [12-3,087] Anne

Richard Palgrave [12-3,086] was born about 1580 in Wymondham, Norfolk, England to Edward Palgrave [13-6,172].   [1224] The Palgrave family tree

<hr>

accessed 21 July 2018.
1218   James Savage, *A Genealogical Dictionary of the First Settlers of New England: Showing Three Generations of Those Who Came Before May 1692*, (Boston: Little, Brown and Company, 1860), Vol I: p. 21; PDF e-book, http://archive.org/details/ genealogicaldic01savarich accessed 17 July 2018.
1219   G Andrews Moriarty, "The Alcocks of Roxbury, Mass.," *The New England Historical and Genealogical Register,* Vol 97: p. 11; database, *American Ancestors*, accessed 21 July 2018.
1220   John Langdon Sibley, *Biographical Sketches of Graduates of Harvard University: in Cambridge, Massachusetts*, (Cambridge, Massachusetts: University Bookstore, 1873), Vol I: p. 123; PDF e-book, https://archive.org/details/biographicalsket01sibluoft accessed 17 July 2018.
1221   "Massachusetts, Town Clerk, Vital and Town Records, 1626-2001," s.v. "George Alcock" (burial 1640), database, *FamilySearch*, accessed 28 January 2018.
1222   G Andrews Moriarty, "The Alcocks of Roxbury, Mass.," *The New England Historical and Genealogical Register,* Vol 97: p. 11; database, *American Ancestors*, accessed 21 July 2018.
1223   John Langdon Sibley, *Biographical Sketches of Graduates of Harvard University: in Cambridge, Massachusetts*, (Cambridge, Massachusetts: University Bookstore, 1873), Vol I: p. 126; PDF e-book, https://archive.org/details/biographicalsket01sibluoft accessed 17 July 2018.
1224   Gary Boyd Roberts, *English Origins of New England Families*, (Baltimore, MD: Genealogical Publishing Co, Inc, 1984), Vol III: p. 70; database, *Ancestry.com*, accessed 13 May 2018.

continues back to royalty,[1225] but there is not enough space in this volume to cover them. Richard was a physician about 1620 in Wymondham and then immigrated to Charlestown, which is now part of Boston, Suffolk County, Massachusetts, in 1630. Richard Palgrave was made freeman in Charlestown on May 18, 1631,[1226] and was still a resident of Charlestown as late as 1648.[1227]

At some point before 1618 when his first child was born, Richard Palgrave [12-3,086] married Anne [12-3,087]. Anne was born about 1594, and had at least ten children with Richard. Richard died in 1651 in Middlesex County, Massachusetts, and Anne may have gone to London, England by March 17, 1655/6 for a while. However when she died in 1669, Anne was back in Roxbury.[1228] The children of Richard Palgrave [12-3,086] and Anne [12-3,087] are listed below:

1. Mary Palgrave, born about 1618 in England and died on March 11, 1697/8.
2. Benjamin Palgrave, born about 1620/1 in Wymondham, and died on February 22, 1622/3 in Wymondham.[1229]
3. Sarah Palsgrave [11-1,543], born about 1621 and married John Alcock [11-1,542] about 1648.[1230]
4. Benjamin Palgrave, born in 1623/4 in Wymondham and died in 1629/30.
5. Elizabeth Palgrave, born in 1626 in Wymondham and died in 1707 in Massachusetts.
6. Hannah Palgrave, born in 1628 in Barnham Broom, Norfolk, England.
7. Rebecca Palgrave, born in 1631 in Boston, Massachusetts.
8. John Palgrave, born in 1634 in Massachusetts and died before 1660.
9. Lydia Palgrave, born in 1635 in Massachusetts.
10. Bethia Palgrave, born in 1638 in Massachusetts and died on August 21, 1638 in Massachusetts.[1231]

1225   Frederick Lewis Weis, *Ancestral Roots of Certain American Colonists Who Came to America before 1700*, 8 ed., (Baltimore: Genealogical Publishing Company, 2008), p. 22, line 15-39.
1226   Gary Boyd Roberts, *English Origins of New England Families*, (Baltimore, MD: Genealogical Publishing Co, Inc, 1984), Vol III: p. 70; database, *Ancestry.com*, accessed 13 May 2018.
1227   John Langdon Sibley, *Biographical Sketches of Graduates of Harvard University: in Cambridge, Massachusetts*, (Cambridge, Massachusetts: University Bookstore, 1873), Vol I: p. 126; PDF e-book, https://archive.org/details/biographicalsket01sibluoft accessed 17 July 2018.
1228   Gary Boyd Roberts, *English Origins of New England Families*, (Baltimore, MD: Genealogical Publishing Co, Inc, 1984), Vol III: p. 70; database, *Ancestry.com*, accessed 13 May 2018.
1229   Ibid.
1230   Clarence Almon Torrey, *New England Marriages Prior to 1700*, (Baltimore, MD: Genealogical Publishing Co., Inc, 2004) p. 7; database with digital images, *Ancestry.com*, accessed 5 May 2016.
1231   Gary Boyd Roberts, *English Origins of New England Families*, (Baltimore, MD: Genealogical Publishing Co, Inc, 1984), Vol III: p. 70; database, *Ancestry.com*,

[12-3,088] Thomas Richardson and [12-3,089] Katherine Duxford

Thomas Richardson [12-3,088] married Katherine Duxford [12-3,089] on August 21, 1590 in Hertfordshire, England. They had at least seven children together, between 1593 and 1608. Thomas was a farmer. Katherine was buried in Hertfordshire on March 10, 1631, and Thomas was buried in Westmill, Hertfordshire, England on January 8, 1633.[1232]

I was not able to find any birth records for Katherine Duxford in Hertfordshire, and there were multiple children named Thomas Richardson born in Hertfordshire in the late 1500's to early 1600's. So I do not believe Thomas Richardson can be traced further at this time. However, Katherine Duxford [12-3,089] was named in a 1618 will as the daughter of Richard Duxford [13-6,178], who died before April 27, 1622 when his will was probated.[1233]

The children of Thomas Richardson [12-3,088] and Katherine Duxford [12-3,089] are listed below:

1. Elizabeth Richardson, who was christened at Westmill on January 13, 1593.
2. Ezekiel Richardson.
3. John Richardson.
4. James Richardson, who was christened on April 6, 1600 at Westmill.
5. Samuel Richardson, who was christened at Westmill on December 22, however it is not clear if it was 1602 or 1604.
6. Margaret Richardson, who was christened at Westmill on April 19, 1607.
7. Thomas Richardson [11-1,544], who was christened on July 3, 1608 at Westmill.[1234]

---

accessed 13 May 2018.

1232   William Richard Cutter, ed., *New England Families: Genealogical and Memorial,* (New York: Lewis Historical Publishing Co, 1913), Vol IV: p. 1931; PDF e-book, https://archive.org/details/XNewEnglandFamiliesGenealogicalAndMemorialARecordO fHerPeopleInTheMakingOfCommonw accessed 10 July 2018.

1233   John B Threlfall, "The Duxford Ancestry of the Richardsons and Wymans," *The New England Historical and Genealogical Register,* Vol 139: p. 147; database with digital images, *American Ancestors*, accessed 21 July 2018.

1234   William Richard Cutter, ed., *New England Families: Genealogical and Memorial,* (New York: Lewis Historical Publishing Co, 1913), Vol IV: p. 1931; PDF e-book, https://archive.org/details/XNewEnglandFamiliesGenealogicalAndMemorialARecordO fHerPeopleInTheMakingOfCommonw accessed 10 July 2018.

[12-3,096] Thomas Green and [12-3,097] Elizabeth Harvy

Thomas Green [12-3,096] was said to be born about 1606 in England,[1235] but he must have been born around 1600 or earlier due to his age at marriage. He married Elizabeth Harvy [12-3,097] on September 30, 1618 in St. Michael's Church in Bishops Stortford, Hertfordshire, England.[1236] Since their son Thomas Green [11-1,548] reported in 1635 at emigration being from Hertfordshire, England,[1237] I believe Thomas Green and Elizabeth were also most likely from Hertfordshire. However, since both of the names Thomas Green and Elizabeth Harvy with spelling variations were used more than once in Hertfordshire between 1600 and 1608, I do not believe they can be accurately traced any further without more information to narrow their field of possible ancestors down.

Thomas Green [12-3,096] and Elizabeth Harvy [12-3,097] had at least ten children in England and Massachusetts, between about 1620 and 1653. Elizabeth died on August 22, 1658 in Malden, Middlesex County, Massachusetts, where Thomas was a selectman at the time. Then on September 5, 1659, Thomas Green married Francis, the widow of Richard Cook, in Malden.[1238] [1239] Thomas Green died on December 19, 1667 in Malden.[1240] [1241] The children of Thomas Green [12-3,096] and Elizabeth Harvy [12-3,097] are listed below:

1. Thomas Green [11-1,548], born about 1620 and married Rebecca Hills [11-1,549] about 1653. He died on February 13, 1671/2.
2. Elizabeth Green, born about 1628 in England.
3. John Green, born about 1632 in England and married Sarah Wheeler on

---

1235   Samuel S. Greene, *A Genealogical Sketch of the Descendants of Thomas Green of Malden, Mass.*, (Boston: Henry W. Dutton & Son, 1858), p. 8; PDF e-book, https://archive.org/details/genealogicalsket00gree , accessed 10 July 2018.
1236   "England Marriages, 1538-1973," s.v. "Thomas Greene" (marriage 1618, spouse "Elizabeth Harvy"), database, *FamilySearch*, accessed 14 May 2018.
1237   William Richard Cutter, ed., *Genealogical and Personal Memoirs: Relating to the Families of the State of Massachusetts*, (New York: Lewis Historical Publishing Company, 1910), Vol IV: p. 2313; PDF e-book, https://archive.org/details/genealogicaland01adamgoog accessed 9 July 2018.
1238   Samuel S. Greene, *A Genealogical Sketch of the Descendants of Thomas Green of Malden, Mass.*, (Boston: Henry W. Dutton & Son, 1858), p. 8; PDF e-book, https://archive.org/details/genealogicalsket00gree , accessed 10 July 2018.
1239   "Massachusetts, Town Clerk, Vital and Town Records, 1626-2001," s.v. "Thomas Green" (marriage 1659, spouse "Frances Cook"), database, *FamilySearch*, accessed 11 May 2018.
1240   Samuel S. Greene, *A Genealogical Sketch of the Descendants of Thomas Green of Malden, Mass.*, (Boston: Henry W. Dutton & Son, 1858), p. 8; PDF e-book, https://archive.org/details/genealogicalsket00gree , accessed 10 July 2018.
1241   "Massachusetts Deaths and Burials, 1795-1910," s.v. "Thomas Green" (death 1667), database, *FamilySearch*, accessed 11 May 2018.

December 18, 1660.

4. Mary Green, born about 1633 in England and married Captain John Waite before 1656.
5. William Green, born about 1635. He married Elizabeth Wheeler first, and second to Isabel (Farmer) Blood.
6. Henry Green, who was born about 1638 and married Esther Hasse on January 11, 1671/2.
7. Samuel Green, born in March 1645 and married first to Mary Cook in 1666, and second to Susanna.
8. Hannah Green, born about 1647 and married Joseph Richardson of Woburn on November 5, 1666. She died on May 20, 1721.
9. Martha Green, born about 1650.
10. Dorcas Green, born on May 1, 1653 in Malden. She married James Barrett of Malden on January 11, 1671/2 and died in 1682.[1242]

[12-3,098] Joseph Hills and [12-3,099] Rose Clarke

Joseph Hills [12-3,098] was the son of George Hills [13-6,196] and Mary [12-6,197], who was the widow of William Symonds. Joseph was christened on March 3, 1602 in Great Burstead, Essex, England. On July 22, 1624, Joseph Hills [12-3,098] married Rose Clarke [12-3,099] in Great Burstead, where they lived until 1631 or 1632. Rose Clarke is sometimes misnamed Rose Dunster because a will mentions the wife of Joseph Hills as being a sister of a Dunster. However, that must refer to a later wife of Joseph because Rose was already dead by the time of the will in question. The marriage record says Rose's surname was Clarke.[1243]

In 1631 or 1632, Joseph Hills and Rose moved their family to Maldon, Essex, England, where they lived until 1638. On July 17, 1638, Joseph Hills arrived in Boston, Massachusetts in the *Susan and Ellen*, in which he had worked as the undertaker. The Hills family stayed in Charlestown, which is now part of Boston, and were among the first to settle what was then known as Mystic Side. Joseph later named Mystic Side as Malden. He was influential in Malden, serving as a selectman, a representative to the colony legislature, and a deputy.[1244]

Joseph Hills had at least ten children with Rose until she died on March 24, 1650 in Malden. Joseph then married Hannah Smith, who was the widow of

---

1242   Samuel S. Greene, *A Genealogical Sketch of the Descendants of Thomas Green of Malden, Mass.*, (Boston: Henry W. Dutton & Son, 1858), pp. 8-9; PDF e-book, https://archive.org/details/genealogicalsket00gree , accessed 10 July 2018.
1243   William Sandford Hills, *Genealogical Data Relating to the Ancestry and Descendants of William Hills and of Joseph Hills,* (Boston: Hills Family Genealogical and Historical Association, 1902), p. 69; PDF e-book, https://archive.org/details/genealogicaldata00hill accessed 17 July 2018.
1244   Ibid., p. 70.

Edward Mellows, on June 24, 1651 in Malden. After Hannah died, Joseph married Helen Atkinson in January 1656 in Malden. Then Helen died, and Joseph married Ann, the widow of Henry Lunt, on March 8, 1665 in Newbury, Essex County, Massachusetts. He stayed in Newbury until his death on February 5, 1688, having been blind since about 1678.[1245] The children of Joseph Hills [12-3,098] and Rose Clarke [12-3,099] are listed below:

1. Mary Hills, who was christened on November 13, 1625 at Great Burstead and married Captain John Waite. She died on November 25, 1674 in Malden, Massachusetts.
2. Elizabeth Hills, who was christened on October 21, 1627 in Great Burstead and married George Blanchard. She died in Malden, Massachusetts.
3. Joseph Hills, who was christened on August 2, 1629 in Great Burstead and married Hannah Smith. He died on April 19, 1674 in Malden, Massachusetts.
4. James Hills, who was christened on March 6, 1631 in Great Burstead.
5. John Hills, who was christened on March 21, 1632 in Maldon, England, and died on July 28, 1652 in Malden, Massachusetts.
6. Rebecca Hills [11-1,549], who was christened on April 20, 1634 in Maldon, England. She married Thomas Green [11-1,548] and died on June 6, 1674 in Malden, Massachusetts.
7. Steven Hills, christened on May 1, 1636 in Maldon, England and died before 1638 in Maldon, England.
8. Sarah Hills, who was christened on August 14, 1637 in Maldon, England and died the same day.
9. Gershom Hills, who was born on July 27, 1639 in Charlestown and married Elizabeth Chadwick on November 11, 1667. He died after 1710 in Malden, Massachusetts.
10. Mehitable Hills, who was born on January 1, 1641 in Malden, Massachusetts, and died in July 1652 in Malden, Massachusetts.[1246]

[12-3,100] John Upham and [12-3,101] Elizabeth Webb

Based on age at death, John Upham [12-3,100] was born around 1598 in England,[1247] and his wife was Elizabeth Webb [12-3,101]. There is some disagreement about Elizabeth's last name, but she was probably born a Webb. The notes in her apparent brother Richard Webb's will refer to John Upham as the uncle of Richard Webb's son. Since there is no record of Richard Webb marrying a sister of John Upham, that leaves the likelihood of Richard Webb

---

1245   Ibid., pp. 71-72.
1246   Ibid., p. 72.
1247   "Upham Genealogy," *The New England Historical and Genealogical Register*, Vol 23: p. 33; database with digital images, *American Ancestors*, accessed 21 July 2018.

being Elizabeth's brother and the conclusion that her surname was Webb.[1248]

John [12-3,100] and Elizabeth [12-3,101] immigrated to Massachusetts in 1635 with the Hull Colony.[1249] On September 2, 1635, John was made a freeman of Weymouth in what is now Norfolk County, Massachusetts.[1250] He was active in local government[1251] and in 1642 helped to negotiate with the Native Americans to purchase the land that Weymouth was located on so there would be a clear title to the land.[1252]

By 1648 John [12-3,100] and Elizabeth [12-3,101] moved to Malden in what is now Middlesex County, Massachusetts.[1253] Elizabeth probably died there before 1671, since John Upham married Catherine Holland in August of 1671.[1254] John died of smallpox at the age of about eighty-four on February 25, 1681/2[1255] and was buried at Bell Rock Cemetery in Malden.[1256] The children of John Upham [12-3,100] and Elizabeth Webb [12-3,101] are listed below:

1. John Upham, who died in 1640 in Weymouth.
2. Mary Upham, who married John Whittemore. She died on June 27, 1677.
3. Elizabeth Upham, who married Thomas Welch. She died on January 12, 1705/6.
4. Nathaniel Upham, who married Elizabeth Stedman in 1661/2 and died the same year.
5. Phineas Upham [11-1,550], who married Ruth Wood [11-1,551] and died in October 1676.
6. Priscilla Upham, who married Thomas Croswell. She died in 1717.[1257]

1248   F K Upham, *Upham Genealogy: the Descendants of John Upham, of Massachusetts*, (Albany, NY: Joel Munsell's Sons, 1892), p. 34; PDF e-book, https://archive.org/details/uphamgenealogyde00upha accessed 22 July 2018.
1249   Ibid., p. 33.
1250   Ibid., p. 34.
1251   Ibid., p. 40.
1252   Ibid., p. 42.
1253   Ibid., p. 42.
1254   "Upham Genealogy," *The New England Historical and Genealogical Register*, Vol 23: p. 33; database with digital images, *American Ancestors*, accessed 21 July 2018.
1255   F K Upham, *Upham Genealogy: the Descendants of John Upham, of Massachusetts*, (Albany, NY: Joel Munsell's Sons, 1892), p. 48; PDF e-book, https://archive.org/details/uphamgenealogyde00upha accessed 22 July 2018.
1256   John Upham, grave marker, Bell Rock Cemetery, Malden, Middlesex County, Massachusetts, digital image s.v. "John Upham" (death 1681, memorial 36215381), database with digital images, *FindAGrave*, accessed 22 July 2018.
1257   "Upham Genealogy," *The New England Historical and Genealogical Register*, Vol 23: p. 33; database with digital images, *American Ancestors*, accessed 21 July 2018.

[12-3,106] Stephen Tracy and [12-3,107] Tryphosa Lee

Stephen Tracy [12-3,106] was christened on December 28, 1596 in Great Yarmouth, Norfolk, England, and was the son of Stephen Tracy [13-6,212] and Agnes Erdley [13-6,213].[1258] [1259] [1260] There is another, older, genealogy for Stephen Tracy[1261] but I found the evidence for the modern genealogy to be compelling enough to dismiss the older genealogy. Original sources and Stephen's being of Great Yarmouth support the modern research.

Stephen Tracy [12-3,106] was among the Puritans who left England for Holland before coming to the Massachusetts colony. In Leiden, now part of South Holland, the Netherlands, Stephen married Tryphosa Lee [12-3,107] on January 3, 1621. I was not able to verify the ancestry of Tryphosa Lee. Stephen Tracy [12-3,106] immigrated to Massachusetts in the ship *Anne* in 1623. Tryphosa may have stayed in Holland for a couple more years, but was in Plymouth, Plymouth County, Massachusetts by 1627 for the birth of their second child. At some point Stephen Tracy returned to England, and made a will in London, England on March 20, 1654/5. He died not long afterwards, and Tryphosa was apparently already dead since she was not mentioned in the will.[1262] The children of Stephen Tracy [12-3,106] and Tryphosa Lee [12-3,107] are listed below:

1. Sarah Tracy, born about January 1623 in Leiden and married George Partridge in November 1638 in Plymouth County, Massachusetts.
2. Rebecca Tracy [11-1,553], born before 1627 in Plymouth and married William Merrick [11-1,552][1263] in 1642 in Eastham, Barnstable County, Massachusetts. She died in 1668 in Eastham.[1264]
3. Ruth Tracy, born about 1628.
4. Mary Tracy, born about 1630.
5. John Tracy, born about 1632 and married Mary Prence about 1661.[1265]

1258   Robert Charles Anderson, *The Great Migration Begins: Immigrants to New England 1620-1633*, (Boston: New England Historic Genealogical Society, 1995), Vol III: p. 1833; database with digital images, *Ancestry.com*, accessed 29 January 2018.
1259   "England Births and Christenings, 1538-1975," s.v. "Stephen Trace" (birth 1596). database, *FamilySearch*, accessed 29 January 2018.
1260   "England Marriages, 1538-1973," s.v. "Stephen Trass" (marriage 1586 spouse "Agnes Erdley"), database, *FamilySearch*, accessed 15 May 2018.
1261   William Richard Cutter, ed., *New England Families: Genealogical and Memorial*, (New York: Lewis Historical Publishing Co, 1913), Vol I: p. 137; PDF e-book, https://archive.org/details/newenglandfamili01cutt_1 accessed 10 July 2018.
1262   Robert Charles Anderson, *The Great Migration Begins: Immigrants to New England 1620-1633*, (Boston: New England Historic Genealogical Society, 1995), Vol III: pp. 1832-3; database with digital images, *Ancestry.com*, accessed 29 January 2018.
1263   Ibid.
1264   George Byron Merrick, *Genealogy of the Merrick-Mirick-Myrick Family of Massachusetts: 1636-1902* (Madison, WI: Tracy, Gibbs & Co, 1902) p. 13; PDF e-book, https://archive.org/details/genealogymerric00merrgoog accessed 26 June 2017.
1265   Robert Charles Anderson, *The Great Migration Begins: Immigrants to New England 1620-1633*, (Boston: New England Historic Genealogical Society, 1995), Vol

[12-3,108] Stephen Hopkins and [12-3,109] Mary

Stephen Hopkins [12-3,108] was said to be of London,[1266] but I was not able to verify any birth records for him nor any marriage records for his first wife. Stephen's first wife was Mary [12-3,109].[1267] At least three of his children from Mary were born in Hursley, Hampshire, England.[1268] [1269] [1270] Stephen Hopkins was probably the same person who was shipwrecked in Bermuda in the *Sea Adventure* in 1609, and got into trouble with the authorities. The shipwreck survivors were stranded almost two years until they built two small ships to carry them to Virginia, and Stephen Hopkins probably returned to England soon afterwards.[1271]

While Stephen was overseas, Mary had died and was buried on May 9, 1613.[1272] Then Stephen married Elizabeth Fisher in 1617 as his second wife,[1273] and by 1620 Stephen brought his family over to Massachusetts in the *Mayflower*.[1274] Stephen died before July 27, 1644 in Plymouth, Plymouth County, Massachusetts.[1275] The children of Stephen Hopkins [12-3,108] and

III: p. 1833; database with digital images, *Ancestry.com*, accessed 29 January 2018.
1266   B F De Costa, "Stephen Hopkins of the Mayflower," *The New England Historical and Genealogical Register*, Vol 33: p. 300; database, *American Ancestors*, accessed 20 July 2018.
1267   Caleb Johnson, "The True Origin of Stephen Hopkins of the Mayflower: With Evidence of His Earlier Presence in Virginia," *The American Genealogist*, Vol 73: p. 163; database, *American Ancestors*, accessed 23 July 2018.
1268   "England Births and Christenings, 1538-1975," s.v. "Constancia Hopkyns" (birth 1606), database, *FamilySearch*, accessed 30 January 2018.
1269   "England Births and Christenings, 1538-1975," s.v. "Ediginus Hopkyns" (birth 1607), database, *FamilySearch*, accessed 30 January 2018.
1270   Caleb Johnson, "The True Origin of Stephen Hopkins of the Mayflower: With Evidence of His Earlier Presence in Virginia," *The American Genealogist*, Vol 73: p. 163; database, *American Ancestors*, accessed 23 July 2018.
1271   B F De Costa, "Stephen Hopkins of the Mayflower," *The New England Historical and Genealogical Register*, Vol 33: p. 300-1; database, *American Ancestors*, accessed 20 July 2018.
1272   Caleb Johnson, "The True Origin of Stephen Hopkins of the Mayflower: With Evidence of His Earlier Presence in Virginia," *The American Genealogist*, Vol 73: p. 163; database, *American Ancestors*, accessed 23 July 2018.
1273   Timothy Hopkins, "Stephen Hopkins of the Mayflower and Some of His Descendants," *The New England Historical and Genealogical Register,* Vol 102: p. 46; database, *American Ancestors,* accessed 20 July 2018.
1274   James Savage, *A Genealogical Dictionary of the First Settlers of New England: Showing Three Generations of Those Who Came Before May 1692*, (Boston: Little, Brown and Company, 1860), Vol II: p. 462; PDF e-book, http://archive.org/details/genealogicaldic02savarich accessed 17 July 2018.
1275   Timothy Hopkins, "Stephen Hopkins of the Mayflower and Some of His Descendants," *The New England Historical and Genealogical Register,* Vol 102: p. 46;

Mary [12-3,109] are listed below:
1. Elizabeth Hopkins, christened on May 13, 1604 in Hursley.
2. Constance Hopkins, christened on May 11, 1606 in Hursley[1276] and married Nicholas Snow before 1628. She died in 1670.[1277]
3. Giles Hopkins [11-1,554], christened on January 30, 1607 in Hursley.[1278]

[12-3,110] Gabriel Wheldon

Gabriel Wheldon [12-3,110] might have been the son of Henry Wheldon but that is only an inference based on a will.[1279] I don't believe this inference is strong enough to continue Gabriel's genealogy. Gabriel was a blacksmith in 1617 in Old Basford, which is now in Nottingham, Nottinghamshire, England.[1280] He was active in his church in Old Basford, and became a churchwarden at St. Leodegarius Church in 1622.[1281] Gabriel married Jane before 1637, but it is not clear if she was the mother of his children.[1282] By 1637 he was a farmer.[1283]

Gabriel Wheldon immigrated to Massachusetts sometime between 1637 and June of 1639, when he was mentioned being in Yarmouth, which is now in Barnstable County, Massachusetts. Sometime after 1639, Gabriel married Margaret, and then by 1648 he had moved to Malden, which is now in Middlesex County, Massachusetts.[1284]

On October 21, 1653, Gabriel sold his property in Arnold, Nottinghamshire, England to William Crofts of Lynn, in what is now Massachusetts.[1285] This sale was the evidence used to trace Gabriel back to Nottinghamshire. The next year,

---

database, *American Ancestors,* accessed 20 July 2018.
1276   Caleb Johnson, "The True Origin of Stephen Hopkins of the Mayflower: With Evidence of His Earlier Presence in Virginia," *The American Genealogist,* Vol 73: p. 163; database, *American Ancestors,* accessed 23 July 2018.
1277   Timothy Hopkins, "Stephen Hopkins of the Mayflower and Some of His Descendants," *The New England Historical and Genealogical Register,* Vol 102: p. 47; database, *American Ancestors,* accessed 20 July 2018.
1278   Caleb Johnson, "The True Origin of Stephen Hopkins of the Mayflower: With Evidence of His Earlier Presence in Virginia," *The American Genealogist,* Vol 73: p. 163; database, *American Ancestors,* accessed 23 July 2018.
1279   Jan Porter and Daniel F. Stramara, Jr., "The Origin of Gabriel Wheldon of Yarmouth and Malden, Massachusetts," *The New England Historical and Genealogical Register,* Vol 163: p. 256; database, *American Ancestors,* accessed 23 July 2018.
1280   Ibid., Vol 163: p. 256.
1281   Ibid., Vol 163: p. 255.
1282   Ibid., Vol 163, p. 260.
1283   Ibid., Vol 163: p. 256.
1284   Ibid., Vol 163: p. 256.
1285   Ibid., Vol 163: p. 254.

on February 11, 1654, Gabriel made his will,[1286] and died in Malden before April 4, 1654.[1287] The children of Gabriel Wheldon [12-3,110] are listed below:

1. Thomas Wheldon, christened on February 1, 1611/2 at St. Leodegarius Church and buried there on April 15, 1614.
2. Catherine Wheldon [11-1,555], christened on March 6, 1616/7 at St. Leodegarius Church.[1288] She married Giles Hopkins [11-1,554] in 1639 and died after March 5, 1688/9.[1289]
3. Henry Wheldon, christened on February 21, 1618/9 at St. Leodegarius Church.
4. Mary Wheldon, christened on December 23, 1621 at St. Leodegarius Church.
5. Martha Wheldon, christened on December 23, 1621 at St. Leodegarius Church.
6. John Wheldon, christened on November 5, 1623 at St. Leodegarius Church.
7. Ruth Wheldon, christened on July 5, 1626 at St. Leodegarius Church.
8. John Wheldon, christened on October 4, 1630 at St. Leodegarius Church.[1290]

[12-3,114] William Quicke

William Quicke [12-3,114] was a grocer and apothecary (pharmacist) in London, England.[1291] Almost all I could find of William was from his will of October 26, 1614. He had a wife named Elizabeth, but it is not certain that she was the mother of any of his children. William also had a brother Nicholas Quicke, and three daughters. His will was proved on January 21, 1614/5, so he died before then.[1292] The three daughters of William Quicke are mentioned below:

1. Apphia Quicke [11-1,557].

1286   James Savage, *A Genealogical Dictionary of the First Settlers of New England: Showing Three Generations of Those Who Came Before May 1692*, (Boston: Little, Brown and Company, 1860), Vol IV, p. 504; PDF e-book, http://archive.org/details/genealogicaldic04savarich accessed 17 July 2018.
1287   Jan Porter and Daniel F. Stramara, Jr., "The Origin of Gabriel Wheldon of Yarmouth and Malden, Massachusetts," *The New England Historical and Genealogical Register*, Vol 163: pp. 253-4; database, *American Ancestors*, accessed 23 July 2018.
1288   Ibid., Vol 163: p. 254.
1289   Ibid., Vol 163: p. 260.
1290   Ibid., Vol 163: p. 254.
1291   Willis Freeman, "The Ancestry of Samuel Freeman of Watertown," *The American Genealogist*, Vol 11: p. 178; database, *American Ancestors*, accessed 23 July 2018.
1292   Henry F. Waters, "Genealogical Gleanings in England," *The New England Historical and Genealogical Register*, Vol 38: p. 60; database, *American Ancestors*,, accessed 25 July 2018.

2. Elizabeth Quicke.
3. Deborah Quicke.[1293]

[12-3,116] Edward Southworth and [12-3,117] Alice Carpenter

Edward Southworth [12-3,116] was born about 1590 in England and emigrated to Leiden in now South Holland, Netherlands due to religious persecution.[1294]   He was the son of Thomas Southworth [13-6,232] and Rosamond Lister [13-6,233],[1295] who were impoverished aristocrats due to religious persecution.   Some people doubt the connection between Edward Southworth and these parents, but the preponderance of evidence makes the connection very likely. The Edward Southworth who went to Leiden and the Edward Southworth who was the London aristocrat were both born about 1590, died about 1621 in London, were short of cash but of high standing, lived in an upper class neighborhood in London, had a brother named Thomas, and were both Protestant.[1296] So the connection is very strong. The Southworth line goes back to royalty[1297] and will need to be continued in another volume.

Edward Southworth [12-3,116] was a silk worker in Leiden, and married Alice Carpenter [12-3,117] while living there. Alice was also born about 1590 and was the daughter of Alexander Carpenter [13-6,234].[1298] They had at least two sons in Holland[1299] before Edward Southworth returned to England and died in 1621. Alice came to Massachusetts in the ship *Anne* in 1623 and married Governor Bradford, but her sons came to Massachusetts later. Alice died on March 26, 1670 in Massachusetts.[1300]   The children of Edward

---

1293   Ibid.
1294   William Richard Cutter, ed., *New England Families: Genealogical and Memorial,* (New York: Lewis Historical Publishing Co, 1913), Vol III: p. 1202; PDF e-book, https://archive.org/details/newenglandfamili03will accessed 10 July 2018.
1295   Frederick Lewis Weis, *The Ancestry of Ensign Constant and Captain Thomas Southworth of Plymouth and Duxbury, Massachusetts,* (Dublin, New Hampshire: n.p., 1958), p. 32; PDF e-book, https://dcms.lds.org/delivery/DeliveryManagerServlet? dps_pid=IE6282139 accessed 22 July 2018.
1296   Ibid., pp. 39-40.
1297   Frederick Lewis Weis, *Ancestral Roots of Certain American Colonists Who Came to America before 1700,* 8 ed., (Baltimore: Genealogical Publishing Company, 2008), p. 14, line 9-41.
1298   William Richard Cutter, ed., *New England Families: Genealogical and Memorial,* (New York: Lewis Historical Publishing Co, 1913), Vol III: p. 1202; PDF e-book, https://archive.org/details/newenglandfamili03will accessed 10 July 2018.
1299   James Savage, *A Genealogical Dictionary of the First Settlers of New England: Showing Three Generations of Those Who Came Before May 1692,* (Boston: Little, Brown and Company, 1860), Vol IV: p. 143; http://archive.org/details/genealogicaldic04savarich accessed 17 July 2018.
1300   William Richard Cutter, ed., *New England Families: Genealogical and*

Southworth [12-3,116] and Alice Carpenter [12-3,117] are listed below:
1. Constant Southworth [11-1,558], born in 1615 and married Elizabeth Collier [11-1,559] in 1637. He died in 1679.
2. Thomas Southworth, married Elizabeth Reynor in December 1641 and died on December 8, 1669.[1301]

[12-3,118] William Collier and [12-3,119] Jane Clark

William Collier was born about 1585[1302] and may have been christened on March 14, 1585 as the son of Mathew Collyver in Westminster, London, England.[1303] Some internet genealogies place William Collier's birth elsewhere with different parents for some reason, but that does not fit the known facts of his age and that he was from London. Due to uncertainty, I will stop with William for now. William Collier married Jane Clark in St. Olave's Church, Southwark, London, England on May 16, 1611.[1304] Not much is verified about Jane Clark. William was a London merchant who aided the Massachusetts colonies until he arrived in Plymouth, Plymouth County, Massachusetts in 1633.[1305] Jane died after 1653, and William died in 1670 in Plymouth.[1306] [1307] The children of William Collier [12-3,118] and Jane Clark [12-3,119] are listed below:
1. Sarah Collier, who married Love Brewster in 1634.
2. Rebecca Collier, who married Job Cole in 1634.
3. Mary Collier, who married Thomas Prence on April 1, 1635.

Memorial, (New York: Lewis Historical Publishing Co, 1913), Vol III: p. 1202; PDF e-book, https://archive.org/details/newenglandfamili03will accessed 10 July 2018.
1301   James Savage, *A Genealogical Dictionary of the First Settlers of New England: Showing Three Generations of Those Who Came Before May 1692,* (Boston: Little, Brown and Company, 1860), Vol IV: p. 143; http://archive.org/details/genealogicaldic04savarich accessed 17 July 2018.
1302   Clarence Almon Torrey, *New England Marriages Prior to 1700,* (Baltimore, Maryland: Genealogical Publishing Co., Inc, 2004), 3rd Supplement p. 62; database with digital images, *Ancestry.com,* accessed 31 January 2018.
1303   "England Births and Christenings, 1538-1975," s.v. "William Collyver" (christened 1585), database, *FamilySearch,* accessed 11 June 2018.
1304   Clarence Almon Torrey, *New England Marriages Prior to 1700,* (Baltimore, Maryland: Genealogical Publishing Co., Inc, 2004), 3rd Supplement p. 62; database with digital images, *Ancestry.com,* accessed 31 January 2018.
1305   William Richard Cutter, ed., *New England Families: Genealogical and Memorial,* (New York: Lewis Historical Publishing Co, 1913), Vol III: p. 1201; PDF e-book, https://archive.org/details/newenglandfamili03will accessed 10 July 2018.
1306   Clarence Almon Torrey, *New England Marriages Prior to 1700,* (Baltimore, Maryland: Genealogical Publishing Co., Inc, 2004), 3rd Supplement p. 62; database with digital images, *Ancestry.com,* accessed 31 January 2018.
1307   William Richard Cutter, ed., *New England Families: Genealogical and Memorial,* (New York: Lewis Historical Publishing Co, 1913), Vol III: p. 1201; PDF e-book, https://archive.org/details/newenglandfamili03will accessed 10 July 2018.

4. Elizabeth Collier [11-1,559], who married Constant Southworth [11-1,558] on November 2, 1637.[1308]
5. William Collier, christened on April 29, 1629 in London, England.[1309]

[12-3,120] Edmund Freeman and [12-3,121] Bennett Hodsoll

Edmund Freeman [12-3,120] was said to have been born about 1590.[1310] [1311] He was christened, however, on July 25, 1596 in Pulborough, West Sussex, England as the son of Edmund Freeman [13-6,240][1312] and Alice Cowles [13-6,241].[1313] Edmund Freeman [12-3,120] married Bennett Hodsoll [12-3,121] in Cowfold, West Sussex, England on June 16, 1617.[1314]

Bennett Hodsoll [12-3,121] was the daughter of John Hodsoll [13-6,242] and Anne Maundy [13-6,243], and was christened on August 23, 1596 in the All Hallows Barking Parish of the city of London, England.[1315] The Hodsoll family of Sussex and Kent Counties in England is very old, but is difficult to trace more than two generations past Bennett Hodsoll. John Hodsoll [13-6,242] was born about 1555 in England to John Hodsoll of Kent [14-12,484] and supplied wood for the Royal Navy. He also was an investor in the Virginia Colony. John Hodsoll [13-6,242] was buried on November 20, 1617 in Cowfold.[1316] His first wife Anne Maundy [13-6,243] was born about 1560 to John Maundy [14-12,486] and Alice Temple [14-12,487]. John Maundy [14-12,486] was buried on December 8, 1568 in All Hallows Barking, London,

---

1308   James Savage, A Genealogical Dictionary of the First Settlers of New England: Showing Three Generations of Those Who Came Before May 1692, (Boston: Little, Brown and Company, 1860), Vol I: p. 433; http://archive.org/details/genealogicaldic01savarich accessed 17 July 2018.
1309   "England Births and Christenings, 1538-1975," s.v. "William Collier" (birth "1621" place "London"), database, *FamilySearch*, accessed 25 June 2018.
1310   William Richard Cutter, ed., *New England Families: Genealogical and Memorial*, (New York: Lewis Historical Publishing Company, 1914), Vol II: p. 853; PDF e-book, https://archive.org/details/newenglandfamili02cutt_1 accessed 10 July 2018.
1311   Edmond Freeman, grave marker, Saddle and Pillion Cemetery, Sagamore, Bourne, Barnstable County, Massachusetts, digital image, s.v. "Edmond Freeman" (death 1682, memorial 6127309), database with digital images, *FindAGrave,* accessed 1 February 2018.
1312   "England, Sussex Parish Registers, 1538-1910," s.v. "Edmund Freeman" (christening 1596), database, *FamilySearch,* accessed 27 June 2018.
1313   "England Marriages, 1538-1973," s.v. "Edmonde Freeman" (year "1591" spouse "Alice Cowles"), database, *FamilySearch,* accessed 27 June 2018.
1314   "England, Sussex Parish Registers, 1538-1910," s.v. "Edmund Freeman" (year "1617" spouse "Bennet Hodsoll"), database, *FamilySearch,* accessed 27 June 2018.
1315   Richard L. Bush, English Ancestry of Bennett Hodsoll, First Wife of Edmond Freeman of Sandwich, Massachusetts," *The New England Historical and Genealogical Register*, Vol 164: pp. 109-110; database, *American Ancestors*, accessed 24 July 2018.
1316   Ibid., pp. 108-9.

England. Alice [14-12,487] then married Hugh Pope on November 13, 1569 in All Hallows Barking Parish of London.[1317]

Bennett Hodsoll [12-3,121] was buried on April 12, 1630 in Pulborough, West Sussex, England.[1318] Edmund Freeman [12-3,120] went on to marry Elizabeth Raymer on August 10, 1632 in Shipley, West Sussex, England.[1319] In 1635 Edmund came to Massachusetts in the ship *Abigail*, probably with extended family and perhaps a couple of his children.[1320] Edmund Freeman died in Sandwich, Barnstable County, Massachusetts in 1682[1321] and is buried at Saddle and Pillion Cemetery in Sandwich.[1322] The children of Edmund Freeman [12-3,120] and Bennett Hodsoll [12-3,121] are listed below:

1. Alice Freeman, christened on June 9, 1619 at Pulborough.[1323]
2. Edmond Freeman, christened on November 26, 1620 in Billingshurst, West Sussex, England.[1324]
3. Bennett Freeman.
4. Elizabeth Freeman.
5. John Freeman [11-1,560].
6. Nathaniel Freeman.[1325]

[12-3,122] Thomas Prence and [12-3,123] Patience Brewster

Thomas Prence [12-3,122] was born about 1601 in England and was the son of Thomas Prence of Lechlade [13-6,244]. Thomas [12-3,122] came to Massachusetts in 1621 in the ship *Fortune*, and stayed in Plymouth, Plymouth

1317   Ibid., pp. 106-108.
1318   Ibid., pp. 104-5.
1319   "England Marriages, 1538-1973," s.v. "Edmundus Freiman" (marriage "1632" spouse "Elisabetha Raymer"), database, *FamilySearch*, accessed 27 June 2018.
1320   James Savage, *A Genealogical Dictionary of the First Settlers of New England: Showing Three Generations of Those Who Came Before May 1692*, (Boston: Little, Brown and Company, 1860), Vol II: p. 203; PDF e-book, http://archive.org/details/genealogicaldic02savarich accessed 17 July 2018.
1321   William Richard Cutter, ed., *New England Families: Genealogical and Memorial*, (New York: Lewis Historical Publishing Company, 1914), Vol II: p. 853; PDF e-book, https://archive.org/details/newenglandfamili02cutt_1 accessed 10 July 2018.
1322   Edmond Freeman, grave marker, Saddle and Pillion Cemetery, Sagamore, Bourne, Barnstable County, Massachusetts, digital image, s.v. "Edmond Freeman" (death 1682, memorial 6127309), database with digital images, *FindAGrave*, accessed 1 February 2018.
1323   "England, Sussex Parish Registers, 1538-1910," s.v. "Alice Freeman" (year "1619"), database, *FamilySearch*, accessed 27 June 2018.
1324   "England, Sussex Parish Registers, 1538-1910," s.v. "Edmond Freeman" (year "1620"), database, *FamilySearch*, accessed 27 June 2018.
1325   Richard L. Bush, English Ancestry of Bennett Hodsoll, First Wife of Edmond Freeman of Sandwich, Massachusetts," *The New England Historical and Genealogical Register*, Vol 164: pp. 109-110; database, *American Ancestors*, accessed 24 July 2018.

County, Massachusetts until about 1634. He married Patience Brewster [12-3,123] on August 5, 1624.[1326]

Patience Brewster [12-3,123] was the daughter of William Brewster [13-6,246] and Mary [13-6,247], and had come over on the ship *Ann* in 1623.[1327] Thomas and Patience had at least five children together until she died in 1634. After Patience died, Thomas moved to Duxbury, Plymouth County, Massachusetts and married Mary Collier on April 1, 1635.[1328] The children of Thomas Prence [12-3,122] and Patience Brewster [12-3,123] are listed below:

1. Thomas Prence.
2. Rebecca Prence, who married Edmund Freeman on April 22, 1646.
3. Hannah Prence, who married first to Nathaniel Mayo on February 13, 1650, and second to Jonathan Sparrow.
4. Mercy Prence [11-1,561], who married John Freeman on February 14, 1649/50.
5. Sarah Prence, who married Jeremiah Howe of Yarmouth in 1650.[1329]

In 1635 Thomas Prence [12-3,122] became Governor of the colony. He varied between Governor and Assistant until 1658. After 1645, Thomas moved to Eastham, Barnstable County, Massachusetts until after he had his third marriage, to Mary, the widow of Samuel Freeman, in 1662. Then they moved back to Plymouth, where he died on March 29, 1673.[1330]

William Brewster [13-6,246] was born about 1567 to William Brewster [14-12,492]. William [13-6,246] went to Cambridge University in 1580, then in 1587 became assistant to the William Davison, Secretary of State to Queen Elizabeth. After the fall of William Davison from his position, William Brewster [13-6,246] became postmaster before 1607. In 1607, William [13-6,246] and other Pilgrims tried to flee to Holland to escape religious persecution but were caught and imprisoned. They succeeded in 1608 in escaping England for Holland, but then William Brewster [13-6,246] went on the *Mayflower* in 1620 to Massachusetts. Mary [13-6,247], who had been born about 1569 and married William Brewster [13-6,246] after 1587, brought the children over to Massachusetts in the *Ann* in 1623. She died in 1627 in Plymouth, and William died in 1644 in Plymouth.[1331]

1326   James Savage, *A Genealogical Dictionary of the First Settlers of New England: Showing Three Generations of Those Who Came Before May 1692*, (Boston: Little, Brown and Company, 1860), Vol III: p. 477; PDF e-book, http://archive.org/details/genealogicaldic03savarich accessed 17 July 2018.
1327   James Savage, *A Genealogical Dictionary of the First Settlers of New England: Showing Three Generations of Those Who Came Before May 1692*, (Boston: Little, Brown and Company, 1860), Vol I: p. 246; PDF e-book, http://archive.org/details/genealogicaldic01savarich accessed 17 July 2018.
1328   James Savage, *A Genealogical Dictionary of the First Settlers of New England: Showing Three Generations of Those Who Came Before May 1692*, (Boston: Little, Brown and Company, 1860), Vol III: p. 477; PDF e-book, http://archive.org/details/genealogicaldic03savarich accessed 17 July 2018.
1329   Ibid.
1330   Ibid.
1331   Lucy Hall Greenlaw, "Early Generations of the Brewster Family," *The New*

[12-3,128] Robert Watson and [12-3,129] Elizabeth

Robert Watson [12-3,128] and his wife Elizabeth [12-3,129] had at least five children. I was not able to verify birth information on this couple, although they were said to have been from London, England before moving to Massachusetts. About 1632 the family came to Plymouth, Plymouth County, Massachusetts.[1332] The children of Robert Watson [12-3,128] and Elizabeth [12-3,129] are listed below:
1. Robert Watson, born in England and married Mary Rockwell in 1646.
2. George Watson [11-1,564], born in 1603 in England.
3. Samuel Watson, born in England.
4. Frances Watson, who married John Rogers.
5. Thomas Watson.[1333]

[12-3,130] Robert Hicks and [12-3,131] Margaret

Robert Hicks [12-3,130] was a leather worker in London, England and may have been the son of James Hicks and Phoebe Hicks.[1334] However modern research has failed to confirm a connection to that family, so I am not including it. Sometime before 1603, Robert [12-3,130] married Margaret [12-3,131]. There are records of at least eight children christened for them at St. Mary Magdalene Church in Bermondsey, Southwark, London, England, and another child born in Plymouth, Plymouth County, Massachusetts.[1335] Robert Hicks arrived in Massachusetts in 1621 in the ship *Fortune*, and Margaret followed with the children in 1623 in the ship *Ann*.[1336] Robert Hicks died on May 24, 1647 in Plymouth, and Margaret died before March 6, 1665/6, when her will

England Historical and Genealogical Register, Vol 53: pp. 109-10; database, *American Ancestors*, accessed 25 July 2018.

1332   Henry Cole Quinby, ed., "The Watsons," *New England Family History*, Vol III: p 467; PDF e-book, https://archive.org/details/newenglandfamily03quin accessed 10 July 2018.

1333   Ibid.

1334   William Richard Cutter, ed., *Genealogical and Personal Memoirs: Relating to the Families of the State of Massachusetts*, (New York: Lewis Historical Publishing Company, 1910), Vol IV: p. 2685; PDF e-book, https://archive.org/details/genealogicaland01adamgoog accessed 9 July 2018.

1335   Robert Charles Anderson, *The Great Migration Begins: Immigrants to New England 1620-1633*, (Boston: New England Historic Genealogical Society, 1995), Vol II: p. 927; database with digital images, *Ancestry.com*, accessed 30 June 2018.

1336   James Savage, *A Genealogical Dictionary of the First Settlers of New England: Showing Three Generations of Those Who Came Before May 1692*, (Boston: Little, Brown and Company, 1860), Vol II: p. 410; PDF e-book, http://archive.org/details/genealogicaldic02savarich accessed 17 July 2018.

was probated in Plymouth.[1337]   The children of Robert Hicks [12-3,130] and Margaret [12-3,131] are listed below:

1. Thomas Hicks, christened on February 19, 1603/4 at Bermondsey, and buried April 23, 1604.
2. John Hicks, christened on October 12, 1605 at Bermondsey.
3. Sara Hicks, christened on October 25, 1607 at Bermondsey, and buried on February 24, 1617/8.
4. Richard Hicks, christened on September 17, 1609 at Bermondsey.
5. Samuel Hicks, christened on August 18, 1611 at Bermondsey. He married Lydia Doane on September 11, 1645 in Plymouth, Massachusetts.
6. Lydia Hicks, christened on September 6, 1612 at Bermondsey. She married Edward Bangs before 1633.
7. Phebe Hicks [11-1,565], christened on March 15, 1614/5 in Bermondsey. She married George Watson [11-1,564].
8. Mary Hicks, christened on May 11, 1617 in Bermondsey, and buried on September 14, 1619.
9. Ephraim Hicks, born about 1625 in Plymouth, Massachusetts. He married Elizabeth Howland on September 13, 1649 and died on December 12, 1649.[1338]

[12-3,132] Elisha Hedge and [12-3,133] Anne Ward

Elisha Hedge [12-3,132] was born about 1585 to Thomas Hedge [13-6,264]. On July 12, 1610, Elisha Hedge [12-3,132] married Anne Ward [12-3,133] in Middleton Cheney, Northamptonshire, England, and they had at least three children.[1339] Anne Ward [12-3,133] was born about 1590 to Thomas Ward [13-6,266] and Frances Taylor [13-6,267].[1340] Anne died before 1621 in England, but Elisha was still alive in 1645 when he was recorded as living in Adstone, Northamptonshire, England.[1341] The children of Elisha Hedge [12-3,132] and Anne Ward [12-3,133] are listed below:

1. Thomas Hedge, born about 1611 in England. He married Elizabeth, and died in 1670 in Adstone.
2. William Hedge [11-1,566], born about 1613 in England.

1337   Robert Charles Anderson, *The Great Migration Begins: Immigrants to New England 1620-1633*, (Boston: New England Historic Genealogical Society, 1995), Vol II: p. 927; database with digital images, *Ancestry.com*, accessed 30 June 2018.
1338   Ibid.
1339   Matthew Hovious, "The Hedge, Ward, and Taylor Ancestry of Captain William Hedge of Yarmouth, Massachusetts," *The New England Historical and Genealogical Register*, Vol 167: p. 169; database, *American Ancestors*, accessed 26 July 2018.
1340   Ibid., Vol 167: p. 176.
1341   Ibid., Vol 167: p. 169.

3.   Rebecca Hedge, alive between 1620 and 1670.[1342]

Elisha's [12-3,132] father Thomas Hedge [13-6,264] was born about 1560, and was a merchant tailor in London, England. He married Alice but it is not known if Alice was Elisha's mother. Thomas [13-6,264] died on March 9, 1622/3 in Adstone. The father of Thomas Hedge [13-6,264] was also named Thomas Hedge [14-12,528]. The senior Thomas Hedge [14-12,528] was buried on April 10, 1602 in Newnham, Northamptonshire, England.[1343] There is a further genealogy on the internet that has the Hedges come from Northumberland, but I have not seen any evidence connecting the Hedge family in Northamptonshire to Northumberland.

Anne Ward's [12-3,133] parents were Thomas Ward [13-6,266] and Frances Taylor [13-6,267]. Thomas Ward [13-6,266] was christened in 1561 in Middleton Cheney, Northamptonshire, England with Richard Ward [14-12,532] and Agnes [14-12,533] as his parents. Thomas Ward [13-6,266] married Frances Taylor [13-6,267] on June 10, 1588 in Middleton Cheney and was her second husband. Thomas Ward [13-6,266] was buried in 1613 in Middleton Cheney, and Frances [13-6,267] was buried on December 5, 1635 in Middleton Cheney.[1344] Richard Ward [14-12,532] was buried in 1585 in Middleton Cheney, and was the son of Thomas Ward [15-25,064] and Emma [15-25,065]. Thomas Ward [15-25,064] died before 1566.[1345]

Frances Taylor [13-6,267] was christened on April 4, 1558 in Middleton Cheney, and was the daughter of John Taylor [14-12,534] and Joyce Murcote [14-12,535]. John Taylor [14-12,534] was born about 1535 and married Joyce [14-12,535] on August 5, 1553 in Bishop's Tachbrook, Warwickshire, England. John died on April 24, 1562 and Joyce was buried on May 21, 1609 in Middleton Cheney. The parents of Joyce have not been traced, but the father of John Taylor [14-12,534] was Hugh Taylor [15-25,068]. Hugh died on February 2, 1551/2.[1346] There is an older Taylor genealogy that is a little different and has two more generations, but it is questionable so I went with the modern Taylor genealogy based on wills and vital records.

[12-3,200] Walter Carleton and [12-3,201] Jane Gibbon

Walter Carleton [12-3,200] was christened on December 29, 1582 in Beeford, East Riding of Yorkshire, England, and was the son of John Carleton [13-6,400] and Ellen Strickland [13-6,401]. Walter [12-3,200] married Jane Gibbon [12-3,201] in 1607 in Hornsea, East Riding of Yorkshire, England[1347]

1342   Ibid.
1343   Ibid., Vol 167: pp. 166-7.
1344   Ibid., Vol 167: pp. 174-6.
1345   Ibid., Vol 111: p. 319.
1346   Ibid., Vol 167: pp. 172-4.
1347   Tracy Elliot Hazen, "The English Ancestry of Edward Carleton of Rowley, Mass.," *The New England Historical and Genealogical Register*, Vol 93: p. 39.

and they had at least four children.[1348] Jane was the daughter of Peter Gibbon [13-6,402] and Margery [13-6,403].   Walter Carleton [12-3,200] died on October 4, 1623 in Hornsea, and Jane [12-3,201] then married William Birkell, Jr on January 23, 1626 in Hornsea.[1349] Jane was still living in 1639.[1350] The Carleton genealogy through the Strickland family continues into the Medieval times and will have to be covered separately from this book. The children of Walter Carleton [12-3,200] and Jane Gibbon[12-3,201] are listed below:

1.   Edward Carleton [11-1,600], christened on October 20, 1610 in Beeford. He married Ellen Newton [11-1,601].
2.   Thomas Carleton, christened on January 10, 1612/3 in Beeford, and still living in 1643.
3.   Anne Carleton, born about 1615 in Hornsea.
4.   William Carleton, born about 1617 in Hornsea, and died in 1639.

[12-3,202] Lancelot Newton and [12-3,203] Mary Lee

Lancelot Newton [12-3,202] was born about 1580 to John Newton [13-6,404] and Marie [13-6,405].   Lancelot [12-3,202] married Mary Lee [12-3,203] on January 3, 1610 in Barmston, East Riding of Yorkshire, England, and they had at least five children together.[1351] Lancelot became a bailiff in Hedon, East Riding of Yorkshire, England in 1613, then became the mayor of Hedon in 1616.[1352] When Lancelot was buried on August 30, 1622 in Hedon,[1353] he was listed as an alderman.[1354] Mary was buried on March 12, 1632 in Hedon.[1355] Newton genealogy continues into Medieval times and will have to be covered separately. The children of Lancelot Newton [12-3,202] and Mary Lee [12-3,203] are listed below:

1.   Thomas Newton, christened on June 18, 1611 in Hedon.
2.   Ellen Newton [11-1,601], christened on September 4, 1614 in Hedon. She married Edward Carleton [11-1,600].
3.   Margery Newton, christened on May 2, 1617 in Hedon.
4.   Elizabeth Newton, christened on January 2, 1619 in Hedon, and still living in 1635.

1348   Ibid., Vol 93: p. 40.
1349   Ibid., Vol 93: p. 39.
1350   Frederick Lewis Weis, *Ancestral Roots of Certain American Colonists Who Came to America before 1700*, 8 ed., (Baltimore: Genealogical Publishing Company, 2008), p. 7, line 2-41.
1351   Tracy Elliot Hazen, "The Ancestry of Ellen Newton, Wife of Edward Carleton of Rowley, Mass.," *The New England Historical and Genealogical Register*, Vol 94: p. 17.
1352   Ibid., Vol 94: p. 18.
1353   Ibid., Vol 94: p. 17.
1354   Ibid., Vol 94: p. 18.
1355   Ibid., Vol 94: p. 17.

5. Frances Newton, christened on January 2, 1621 in Hedon.[1356]

[12-3,204] Edward Jewett and [12-3,205] Mary Taylor

Edward Jewett [12-3,204] was born about 1580 in Bradford, West Yorkshire, England.[1357] I was not able to verify parents for Edward. Edward sold cloth in Bradford,[1358] and married Mary Taylor [12-3,205] on October 1, 1604 in Bradford.[1359] Mary was the daughter of William Taylor [13-6,410]. Edward was buried on February 4, 1614/5 in Bradford,[1360] and was survived by Mary who proved his will on July 12, 1615 in Yorkshire, England.[1361] The children of Edward Jewett [12-3,204] and Mary Taylor [12-3,205] are listed below:

1. William Jewett, christened on September 15, 1605 in Bradford.
2. Maximilian Jewett, christened on October 4, 1607 in Bradford.
3. Joseph Jewett [11-1,602], who was christened on December 31, 1609 in Bradford. He married Mary Mallinson [11-1,603].
4. Sarah Jewett.[1362]

1356   Ibid., Vol 94: p. 18.
1357   William Richard Cutter, ed., *New England Families: Genealogical and Memorial*, (New York: Lewis Historical Publishing Company, 1914), Vol IV: p. 1719; PDF e-book, https://archive.org/details/newenglandfamili041847 accessed 30 July 2018.
1358   William Richard Cutter, ed., *Genealogical and Personal Memoirs: Relating to the Families of Boston and Eastern Massachusetts*, (New York: Lewis Historical Publishing Company, 1908), Vol II: p. 941; PDF e-book, https://archive.org/details/genealogicaland01cuttgoog accessed 10 July 2018.
1359   William Richard Cutter, ed., *New England Families: Genealogical and Memorial*, (New York: Lewis Historical Publishing Company, 1914), Vol IV: p. 1719; PDF e-book, https://archive.org/details/newenglandfamili041847 accessed 30 July 2018.
1360   Tracy Elliot Hazen, "Two Founders of Rowley, Mass., " *The New England Historical and Genealogical Register*, Vol 94: p. 103; database, *American Ancestors*, accessed 26 July 2018.
1361   William Richard Cutter, ed., *New England Families: Genealogical and Memorial*, (New York: Lewis Historical Publishing Company, 1914), Vol IV: p. 1719; PDF e-book, https://archive.org/details/newenglandfamili041847 accessed 30 July 2018.
1362   William Richard Cutter, ed., *Genealogical and Personal Memoirs: Relating to the Families of Boston and Eastern Massachusetts*, (New York: Lewis Historical Publishing Company, 1908), Vol II: p. 941; PDF e-book, https://archive.org/details/genealogicaland01cuttgoog accessed 10 July 2018.

[12-3,206] Richard Mallinson and [12-3,207] Sara Waterhouse

Richard Mallinson [12-3,206] was born about 1580. He married Sara Waterhouse [12-3,207] on October 29, 1601 in Bradford, West Yorkshire, England and they had at least three children. Richard was buried on May 14, 1638 in Bradford, and Sara was buried on November 16, 1643 in Bradford.[1363] Not much else is known about this couple and their parents, except that Richard's father was Thomas Mallinson [13-6,412]. Thomas [13-6,412] was born about 1550 and was buried on August 6, 1624 in Bradford.[1364] The children of Richard Mallinson [12-3,206] and Sara Waterhouse [12-3,207] are listed below:

1. Thomas Mallinson, christened on March 6, 1602/3 in Bradford.
2. Mary Mallinson [11-1,603], christened on May 29, 1606 in Bradford. She married Joseph Jewett [11-1,602].
3. Sara Mallinson, christened on August 13, 1609 in Bradford. She married William Goodall on January 31, 1630 in Bradford.[1365]

[12-3,210] Henry Scott and [12-3,211] Martha Whatlocke

The first mention I could find for Henry Scott [12-3,210] in the parish register of Rattlesden, Suffolk County, England, was when he married Martha Whatlocke [12-3,211] there on July 25, 1594.[1366] There are two different genealogies online for Henry Scott, but I did not find strong enough evidence to continue his genealogy. There were two Scott families (Robert Scoote, or Edmund Scoot and Joane) having children recorded in the parish registers of Rattlesden between 1558 when the register started and 1580. Neither was recorded as having a Henry, so he might have been christened in another location or even in a non-Conformist church. Henry Scott was buried in Rattlesden on December 24, 1624.[1367]

Martha Whatlocke [12-3,211], Henry's wife, was christened on July 18, 1568 in Rattlesden,[1368] and was still living on January 10, 1624 when Henry

---

1363   Tracy Elliot Hazen, "Two Founders of Rowley, Mass., " *The New England Historical and Genealogical Register*, Vol 94: p. 112; database, *American Ancestors*, accessed 26 July 2018.
1364   Ibid., Vol 94: p. 111.
1365   Ibid., Vol 94: p. 112.
1366   J. R. Olorenshaw, *Notes on the History of the Church and Parish of Rattlesden, in the County of Suffolk,* (Peterborough: Geo. C. Caster, Market Place, 1900), p. 240; PDF e-book, https://dcms.lds.org/delivery/DeliveryManagerServlet?from=fhd&dps_pid=IE3997643 accessed 31 July 2018.
1367   Ibid., p. 267.
1368   Ibid., p. 225.

Scott wrote his will.[1369] Martha was the daughter of Thomas Whatlocke [13-6,422] and Joane [13-6,423].[1370] Thomas Whatlocke was buried on 25 January 1608/9 in Rattlesden and was described in the parish register as being very old.[1371] The children of Henry Scott [12-3,210] and Martha Whatlocke [12-3,211] are listed below:

1. Thomas Scott, christened on February 26, 1595 in Rattlesden.[1372]
2. Ursula Scott [11-1,605], christened on February 14, 1598 in Rattlesden.[1373] (She married Richard Kimball [11-1,604].)
3. Roger Scott, christened on November 15, 1604 in Rattlesden.[1374] He married Sarah Grimwood on February 26, 1627/8 in Rattlesden.[1375]

[12-3,212] Robert Haseltine

Robert Haseltine [12-3,212] was christened on February 27, 1582/3 in Howden, East Riding of Yorkshire, England,[1376] and his parents were Edward Haseltine [13-6,424] and Margaret Williamson [13-6,425].[1377] Even though the marriages and christenings were in Howden, this family actually lived in Knedlington, East Riding of Yorkshire, England and traveled to the parish church in Howden for christenings and marriages. Online genealogies often have more information on this family, but I did not have access to evidence to verify the information. The children of Robert Haseltine [12-3,212] are listed below:

1. Edward Haseltine, christened on February 6, 1608 in Howden.[1378]

1369   Henry F. Waters, "Genealogical Gleanings in England," *The New England Historical and Genealogical Register,* Vol 52, p. 248; database, *American Ancestors,* accessed 31 July 2018.
1370   J. R. Olorenshaw, *Notes on the History of the Church and Parish of Rattlesden, in the County of Suffolk,* (Peterborough: Geo. C. Caster, Market Place, 1900), p. 225; PDF e-book, https://dcms.lds.org/delivery/DeliveryManagerServlet?from=fhd&dps_pid=IE3997643 accessed 31 July 2018.
1371   Ibid., p. 252.
1372   "England Births and Christenings, 1538-1975," s.v. "Thomas Scoote" (birth "1595" place "Rattlesden"), database, *FamilySearch,* accessed 16 July 2017.
1373   "England Births and Christenings, 1538-1975," s.v. "Urslaye Scoote" (birth "1598" place "Rattlesden"), database, *FamilySearch,* accessed 16 July 2017.
1374   J. R. Olorenshaw, *Notes on the History of the Church and Parish of Rattlesden, in the County of Suffolk,* (Peterborough: Geo. C. Caster, Market Place, 1900), p. 248; PDF e-book, https://dcms.lds.org/delivery/DeliveryManagerServlet?from=fhd&dps_pid=IE3997643 accessed 31 July 2018.
1375   Ibid., p. 269.
1376   G. E. Weddall, ed., *The Registers of the Parish of Howden, Co. York,* (Leeds: Oriel Press, 1904), Vol I: p. 140; PDF e-book, https://archive.org/details/registersofparis21howd accessed 1 August 2018.
1377   Ibid., Vol I: p. 21.
1378   "England Births and Christenings, 1538-1975," s.v. "Edward Haseltine" (birth "1608" place "Howden"), database, FamilySearch, accessed 1 August 2018.

2. Robert Hazelton/Haseltine [11-1,606], christened on January 2, 1609/10 in Howden.[1379] (He married Ann [11-1,607].)
3. John Hazeltine, christened on August 23, 1612 in Howden.[1380]
4. George Haseltine, christened on March 23, 1614 in Howden.[1381]

[12-3,216] George Dalton

George Dalton [12-3,216] was possibly born about 1535 and was buried on February 24, 1613/4 in Dennington, Suffolk, England.[1382] His children are listed below:

1. Edmund Dalton, born about 1575 and married Susan.
2. Timothy Dalton, born about 1577 and married Ruth Leete.
3. John Dalton, who married Ann Cranmore on October 28, 1622 in Culford, Suffolk, England and was buried there on February 23, 1668.
4. Philemon Dalton [11-1,608], who was born about 1590 and married Anne Cole [11-1,609] on October 11, 1625 in Dennington.
5. Sarah Dalton, who was born about 1595 and married Richard Everard.[1383]

[12-3,244] Thomas Osgood and [12-3,245] Margaret Skeat

Thomas Osgood [12-3,244] married Margaret Skeat [12-3,245] on July 13, 1595 in Newton Tony, Wiltshire, England.[1384] As for his parents, there is a theory that Christopher Osgood and Alice are his parents because they were of the right age at the right time and place. However, there are no surviving birth or christening records in the 1570's when he would have been born, nor am I aware of any wills that would provide a strong link to the next generation. So I will stop with Thomas Osgood.

1379 "England Births and Christenings, 1538-1975," s.v. "Robart Haseltine" (birth "1610" place "Howden"), database, FamilySearch, accessed March 2018.
1380 "England Births and Christenings, 1538-1975," s.v. "John Hesseltine" (birth "1612" place "Howden"), database, FamilySearch, accessed 1 August 2018.
1381 G. E. Weddall, ed., *The Registers of the Parish of Howden, Co. York,* (Leeds: Oriel Press, 1904), Vol I: p. 216; PDF e-book, https://archive.org/details/registersofparis21howd accessed 1 August 2018.
1382 George F Sanborn, Jr. and Melinde Lutz Sanborn, "The Dalton Cluster: Timothy Dalton, Philemon Dalton, Richard Everard, and Deborah (Everard) Blake," *The New England Historical and Genealogical Register*, Vol 154: p. 281; database with digital images, *American Ancestors*, accessed November 2019.
1383 Ibid.
1384 Jane Fletcher Fiske, "New Light on the English background of the Osgoods of Essex County, Massachusetts," *The American Genealogist*, Vol 83: p. 57; database with digital images, *American Ancestors*, accessed 24 October 2019.

Margaret Skeat [12-3,245] was possibly the daughter of Roger Skete and Alice, because a will from Roger mentioned having children named Arthur, William, Margaret, and Margaret the younger. Furthermore, it is known from records that Margaret had a brother named William. However, I am not convinced this is strong enough evidence to further trace this family, because there were other families with variations of the name Skeat in Wiltshire at the time who might have had children named William and Margaret.[1385]

Margaret Skeat was buried on May 1, 1616 at Newton Tony. Thomas Osgood was also buried at Newton Tony, on June 16, 1634. The children of Thomas Osgood [12-3,244] and Margaret Skeat [12-3,245] are listed below:

1. Peter Osgood, christened on September 12, 1596 in Newton Tony.
2. Richard Osgood, christened on January 28, 1598/9 in Newton Tony.
3. William Osgood, christened on April 12, 1602 in Newton Tony.
4. Thomas Osgood, christened on April 10, 1604 in Newton Tony.
5. Christopher Osgood [11-1,622], christened on April 17, 1606 in Newton Tony. (He married Mary Everatt [11-1,623].)
6. Hestor Osgood, christened on March 29, 1608 in Newton Tony.
7. Elizabeth Osgood, christened on December 30, 1610 in Newton Tony.
8. Moses Osgood, christened on March 14, 1612/3 in Newton Tony.
9. Adam Osgood.[1386]

[12-3,286] George Marsh and [12-3,287] Elizabeth

George Marsh [12-3,286] married his wife Elizabeth [12-3,287] by about 1621. By 1635 they were in Hingham, Plymouth County, Massachusetts, and he became a freeman there on March 3, 1635/6. George Marsh made a will on July 2, 1647 and may have died the same day. Then in November 1648, Elizabeth married Richard Bowen.[1387] The children of George Marsh [12-3,286] and Elizabeth [12-3,287] are listed below:

1. Mary Marsh [11-1,643], born about 1621 and married before 1641 John Page [11-1,642].
2. Thomas Marsh, born about 1623 and married Sarah Beal on March 20, 1648/9 in Hingham.
3. Elizabeth Marsh, born about 1627 and married before 1647 John Turner.
4. Onesiphorus Marsh, born about 1630. He married first to Hannah Cutler in 1654/5 in Hingham, second to Elizabeth (Parrot) Worcester in 1686 in Haverhill, Essex County, Massachusetts, and third to Sarah

---

1385   Ibid.
1386   Ibid., Vol 83: p. 58.
1387   Robert Charles Anderson, "The Great Migration: Immigrants to New England, 1634-1635, Vol V, M-P," p. 24; database with digital images, *American Ancestors,* accessed 8 November 2019.

(Travers) Wallingford in 1691 in Haverhill.[1388]

[12-3,290] Henry Palmer and [12-3,291] Elizabeth Masy

Henry Palmer [12-3,290] was born about 1601 based on his age at death.[1389] His family has been traced to Frampton, Dorset, England through online databases matching the names of his wife and children. He married Elizabeth Masy [12-3,291] on June 26, 1632 in Frampton,[1390] then emigrated to Massachusetts sometime between 1637 when his youngest daughter was born in Frampton[1391] and June 22, 1642 when he became a freeman in Massachusetts.[1392]

Elizabeth Masy [12-3,291] died on November 22, 1664 in Haverhill, Essex County, Massachusetts,[1393] and Henry Palmer [12-3,290] then became involved in politics. He was a representative in 1667, 1674, and from 1676 to 1679,[1394] and he died on July 15, 1680 in Haverhill at the age of 79.[1395] The children of Henry Palmer [12-3,290] and Elizabeth Masy [12-3,291] are listed below:

1. Elizabeth Palmer [11-1,645], christened on June 23, 1633 in Frampton.[1396] She married Robert Ayer [11-1,644] on February 27,

---

1388   Ibid., pp. 24-25.
1389   Topsfield Historical Society, *Vital Records of Haverhill Massachusetts: to the End of the Year 1849,* (Topsfield, Massachusetts: Topsfield Historical Society, 1911), Vol II: p. 455; PDF e-book, https://archive.org/details/cu31924099427654/page/n8 accessed 25 June 2019.
1390   "England, Dorset, Parish Registers, 1538-2001," s.v. "Henry Palmer" (spouse "Elizabeth Masy" marriage "1632"), database, FamilySearch, accessed 8 November 2019.
1391   "England, Dorset, Parish Registers, 1538-2001," s.v. "Bathshua Palmer" (birth "1637"), database, FamilySearch, accessed 8 November 2019.
1392   James Savage, *A Genealogical Dictionary of the First Settlers of New England: Showing Three Generations of Those Who Came Before May 1692*, (Boston: Little, Brown and Company, 1860), Vol III: p. 340; PDF e-book, http://archive.org/details/genealogicaldic03savarich accessed 17 July 2018.
1393   Topsfield Historical Society, *Vital Records of Haverhill Massachusetts: to the End of the Year 1849,* (Topsfield, Massachusetts: Topsfield Historical Society, 1911), Vol II: p. 455; PDF e-book, https://archive.org/details/cu31924099427654/page/n8 accessed 25 June 2019.
1394   James Savage, *A Genealogical Dictionary of the First Settlers of New England: Showing Three Generations of Those Who Came Before May 1692*, (Boston: Little, Brown and Company, 1860), Vol III: p. 340; PDF e-book, http://archive.org/details/genealogicaldic03savarich accessed 17 July 2018.
1395   Topsfield Historical Society, *Vital Records of Haverhill Massachusetts: to the End of the Year 1849,* (Topsfield, Massachusetts: Topsfield Historical Society, 1911), Vol II: p. 455; PDF e-book, https://archive.org/details/cu31924099427654/page/n8 accessed 25 June 2019.
1396   "England, Dorset, Parish Registers, 1538-2001," s.v. "Elizabeth Palmer" (birth "1633"), database, FamilySearch, accessed 8 November 2019.

1650/1.[1397]

2. Mehitable Palmer (possibly [10-805]), christened on February 8, 1634/5 in Frampton.[1398] She married Samuel Dalton [10-804][1399] but the year is in dispute which makes a difference in whether she mothered his children in this genealogy.

3. Bathshua Palmer, christened on June 25, 1637 in Frampton.[1400] She died on February 26, 1654/5 in Haverhill.[1401]

[12-3,292] Edmund Johnson and [12-3,293] Mary

Edmund Johnson [12-3,292] was born about 1612 based on his age at emigration on July 13, 1635 from London, England, and he was a carpenter. He traveled alone, so he probably married Mary [12-3,293] between 1635 and 1639 in New England. In 1639 they were in Hampton, Rockingham County, Massachusetts, where Edmund died on March 10, 1650/1. His widow Mary went on to marry Thomas Coleman on July 16, 1651 in Hampton.[1402] The children of Edmund Johnson [12-3,292] and Mary [12-3,293] are listed below:

1. Peter Johnson [11-1,646], christened in 1639 in Hampton. He married Ruth Moulton [11-1,647] on April 3, 1660 in Hampton.

2. John Johnson, christened on May 16, 1641 in Hampton. He was still living in 1689 in Newport, Newport County, Rhode Island.

3. James Johnson, born about 1643 in Hampton. He married first to Sarah Daniel on March 26, 1675 in Hampton, and second to Hannah after 1704. James died on June 10, 1715 in Hampton.

4. Dorcas Johnson, born about 1650 and married Samuel Pearson on April 16, 1672.[1403]

1397   "Ayer Genealogy," *The Essex Antiquarian,* Vol 4: p. 145; database with digital images, *American Ancestors,* accessed 4 July 2019.

1398   "England, Dorset, Parish Registers, 1538-2001," s.v. "Mehetabell Palmer" (birth "1634"), database, FamilySearch, accessed 8 November 2019.

1399   James Savage, *A Genealogical Dictionary of the First Settlers of New England: Showing Three Generations of Those Who Came Before May 1692,* (Boston: Little, Brown and Company, 1860), Vol III: p. 340; PDF e-book, http://archive.org/details/genealogicaldic03savarich accessed 17 July 2018.

1400   "England, Dorset, Parish Registers, 1538-2001," s.v. "Bathshua Palmer" (birth "1637"), database, FamilySearch, accessed 8 November 2019.

1401   "Massachusetts, Town Clerk, Vital and Town Records, 1626-2001," s.v. "Bathshua Palmer" (death "1654" place "Haverhill"), database, *FamilySearch,* accessed 8 November 2019.

1402   Robert Charles Anderson, "Great Migration: Immigrants to New England, 1634-1635, Volume IV, I-L", p. 62; database with digital images, *American Ancestors,* accessed 28 October 2019.

1403   Ibid.

[12-3,294] John Moulton and [12-3,295] Ann Grene

There is some dispute about this genealogy, but I believe this genealogy to be correct since it uses wills and parish registers. John Moulton [12-3,294] was born about 1599 and was the son of Robert Moulton [13-6,588] and Mary Smith [13-6,589]. John Moulton [12-3,294] married Ann Grene [12-3,295] on September 24, 1623 in Ormesby, Norfolk England, Ann Grene [12-3,295] was also born about 1599, based on her age at emigration in 1637. John died before October 1, 1650 , which was the date his will was probated. Ann died on April 12, 1668 in Hampton, Rockingham County, New Hampshire.[1404] The children of John Moulton [12-3,294] and Ann Grene [12-3,295] are listed below:

1. Henry Moulton, christened on November 12, 1623 in Hemsby, Norfolk, England.
2. Mary Moulton, christened on November 24, 1626 in Hemsby.
3. Ann Moulton, christened on September 27, 1629 at Hemsby.
4. Bridget Moulton, christened on April 8, 1632 at Hemsby, and buried February 17, 1633/4.
5. Jane Moulton, christened on April 8, 1634 at Hemsby.
6. Bridget Moulton, christened on April 8, 1634 at Hemsby.
7. John Moulton, christened on March 16, 1638/9 at Newbury, Essex County, Massachusetts.
8. Ruth Moulton [11-1,647], christened on May 7, 1640 at Hampton, and married Peter Johnson [11-1,646] on April 3, 1660 at Hampton.[1405]

More information on this line, like children and some more dates, is available at the source cited in the footnotes. An outline with the ancestors is given here. Robert Moulton [13-6,588] was born about 1565 in Ormesby to Thomas Moulton [14-13,176] and Joan Grene [14-13,177], who was the daughter of Richard Grene [15-26,354]. He married Mary Smith on May 15, 1595 in Hemsby, and died in October 1633 in Scratby, Norfolk, England. Mary was the daughter of Henry Smyth [14-13,178] of Hemsby and Brydgett [14-13,179], and Mary was buried on April 27, 1636 at Ormesby.[1406]

Thomas Moulton [14-13,176] was born about 1513 in Ormesby, and was the son of Robert Moulton [15-26,352] and Margaret [15-26,353]. He married Joan Grene [14-13,177] probably between 1555 and 1560, and died in September 1587 in Ormesby. Robert Moulton [15-26,352] was born around 1480 and died before September 1535. Margaret [15-26,353] died before 1553.[1407]

1404   Joy Wade Moulton, "Some Doubts about the English Background of the Moulton Family," *The New England Historical and Genealogical Register,* Vol 144: pp. 260-1; database with digital images, *American Ancestors,* accessed 9 November 2019.
1405   Ibid., Vol 144: p. 262.
1406   Ibid., Vol 144: p. 259.
1407   Ibid., Vol 144: p. 256.

[12-3,304] Edward Gilman

Edward Gilman [12-3,304] was christened on April 20, 1557 in Caston, Norfolk, England, and was the son of Edward Gilman [13-6,608] and Rose Rysse [13-6,609].[1408] His children are listed below:

1. Edward Gilman [11-1,652], born about 1587 and married Mary Clark [11-1,653] in Hingham, Norfolk, England in 1614.
2. Margaret Gilman, christened on August 1, 1602 in Hingham, England.
3. Sarah Gilman, christened on December 4, 1603 in Hingham, England.
4. Mary Gilman, who married first to Nicholas Jacob about 1629, and second to John Beal, Sr on March 10, 1658/9. She died on June 15, 1681 in Hingham, Plymouth County, Massachusetts.[1409]

[12-3,310] Alexander Shapleigh

It is difficult to sort out fact from fiction because a genealogy of this family was done by a Gustave Anjou, who allegedly faked some of his sources. Alexander Shapleigh died before 1650 in England, and was the father of Catherine Shapleigh [11-1,655], who married James Treworthy [11-1,654].[1410]

[12-3,312] Thomas Appleton and [12-3,313] Mary Isaacke

Thomas Appleton [12-3,312] was born about 1529, based on his age at inheriting the title Esquire in 1534 for Little Waldingfield, Suffolk, England. His parents were William Appleton, Esq, [13-6,624] of Waldingfield Parva and Rose Sexton [13-6,625]. Thomas married Mary Isaacke [12-3,313] probably around 1580 or earlier, based on the birth of their third son being in 1585. Mary Isaacke was the daughter of Edward Isaacke [13-6,626] of Well Court and Margery Wheathill [13-6,627]. He died about 1604 in London, since his will was probated on May 16, 1604. Mary died after 1612.[1411] The genealogy of the Appleton family continues, but will have to be covered separately due to

---

1408   Clarence Almon Torrey, "English Origin of Edward Gilman," *The American Genealogist*, Vol 11: p. 137; database with digital images, *American Ancestors,* accessed 30 October, 2019.
1409   Ibid., Vol 11: pp. 137-8.
1410   James Savage, *A Genealogical Dictionary of the First Settlers of New England: Showing Three Generations of Those Who Came Before May 1692,* (Boston: Little, Brown and Company, 1860), Vol IV: p. 330; PDF e-book, http://archive.org/details/genealogicaldic04savarich accessed 17 July 2018.
1411   Joseph James Muskett, ed., *Suffolk Manorial Families: Being the County Visitations and Other Pedigrees,* Vol I: p. 329; PDF e-book, https://archive.org/details/bub_gb_ZxANnBnHKBQC/page/n335 accessed 15 October 2019.

size limitations. The known children of Thomas Appleton [12-3,312] and Mary Isaacke [12-3,313] are listed below:

1. Thomas Appleton, the third son, christened in 1585 in Little Waldingfield and still living in 1603.
2. Samuel Appleton [11-1,656], the fourth son, christened in 1586 in Little Waldingfield. He married first to Judith Everard [11-1657], and second to Martha.
3. Sara Appleton, christened in 1589 in Little Waldingfield. She married first to Edward Bird of Walden, and second to Henry Smyth.
4. Mary Appleton, who married Robert Ryson of Preston.
5. Judith Appleton, who married first to ___ Allen, and second to Luwos Bayley, Bishop of Bangor.[1412]

[12-3,314] John Everard and [12-3,315] Judith Bourne

John Everard [12-3,314] was a goldsmith in London, England who married Judith Bourne [12-3,315] on May 11, 1579 in St. Mary Aldermanbury parish of London, England. Judith was born on August 19, 1557 in St. Mary Aldermanbury parish to John Bourne [13-6,630].[1413] She had a will in 1598,[1414] so she might have been a widow by that time. The daughter of John Everard [12-3,314] and Judith Bourne [12-3,315] was Judith Everard [11-1,657] who married Samuel Appleton in Preston, which is now called Preston St. Mary in Suffolk, England.[1415]

[12-3,318] ___ Goodale and [12-3,319] Elizabeth

Elizabeth Goodale [12-3,319] emigrated from Yarmouth in Norfolk, England with her daughters, and died on April 8, 1647 in Newbury, Essex County, Massachusetts.[1416] Although I found a marriage between a Robert

---

1412   Ibid.

1413   Society of Genealogists, "Boyd's Inhabitants Of London & Family Units 1200-1946," s.v. "John Everard" (year "1598" place "London"), database with digital images, *FindMyPast*, accessed 11 November 2019.

1414   Leslie Mahler, "Confirmation of the Parentage of Judith Everard, Wife of Samuel Appleton o f Ipswich, Massachusetts," *The New England Historical and Genealogical Register,* Vol 160: p. 109; database with digital images, *American Ancestors*, accessed 31 October 2019.

1415   Joseph James Muskett, ed., *Suffolk Manorial Families: Being the County Visitations and Other Pedigrees,* (Exeter: William Pollard & Co., 1900) Vol I: p. 330; PDF e-book, https://archive.org/details/bub_gb_ZxANnBnHKBQC/page/n335 accessed 15 October 2019.

1416   Charles Henry Pope, *The Pioneers of Massachusetts, A Descriptive List, Drawn from the Records of the Colonies, Towns, and Churches, and other*

Goodalle and Elizabethe Bonan on November 17, 1596 in Yarmouth in the *FamilySearch* databases, I did not find a christening record for their daughters near Yarmouth where they came from. So I believe further information, like Yarmouth christening records for the family or wills, will be needed as evidence to further trace this family. The daughters of ___ Goodale [12-3,318] and Elizabeth [12-3,319] are listed below:

1. Susanna Goodale, who married Abraham Toppan.
2. Elizabeth Goodale, who married John Lowle.
3. Joanna Goodale [11-1,659], who married first to John Oliver [11-1,658] of Newbury, and second to Captain William Gerrish in 1645.[1417]

[12-3,324] Richard Symonds and [12-3,325] Elizabeth Plume

Richard Symonds [12-3,324] was the son of John Symonds of Newport [13-6,648] and Anne Benbow [13-6,649]. (For further information on the Symonds genealogy, see the chart showing the descendants of John Symonds of Croft, which is in the Appendix.[1418]) Richard Symonds [12-3,324] married Elizabeth Plume [12-3,325] on January 9, 1580,[1419] and she was the daughter of Robert Plume [13-6,650] of Yeldham and Elizabeth Purcas [13-6,651].[1420] Robert Plume [13-6,650] was the son of John Plume [14-13,300] of Yeldham.

Elizabeth Plume [12-3,325] was buried on January 24, 1611, and Richard Symonds [12-3,324] died on July 8, 1627.[1421] The children of Richard Symonds [12-3,324] and Elizabeth Plume [12-3,325] are listed below:

1. John Symonds of Yeldham, who married Ann Elliot.

Contemporaneous Documents, (Boston: Charles H. Pope, 1900) p. 191; PDF e-book, https://archive.org/details/pioneersofmassac00pope/page/8 accessed 1 November 2019.

1417   Ibid.

1418   Walter Charles Metcalfe, ed., *The Visitations of Essex by Hawley, 1552; Hervey, 1558; Cooke, 1570; Raven, 1612; and Owen and Lilly, 1634. To which Are Added Miscellaneous Essex Pedigrees from Various Harleian Manuscripts: and an Appendix Containing Berry's Essex Pedigrees.* (London: Mitchell and Hughes, 1878) p. 495; PDF e-book, https://archive.org/details/visitationsofess1314metc/page/n8 accessed 3 November 2019.

1419   William S. Appleton, *Ancestry of Priscilla Baker, Who Lived 1674-1731, and Was the Wife of Isaac Appleton, of Ipswich,* (Cambridge: Press of John Wilson and Son, 1870) p. 20; PDF e-book, https://archive.org/details/ancestrypriscil00applgoog/page/n16 accessed 16 October 2019.

1420   Clifford L. Stott, "John Plumb of Connecticut and his Cousin, Deputy Governor Samuel Symonds of Massachusetts," *The American Genealogist,* Vol 70: p. 65; database with digital images, *American Ancestors,* accessed 14 November 2019.

1421   William S. Appleton, *Ancestry of Priscilla Baker, Who Lived 1674-1731, and Was the Wife of Isaac Appleton, of Ipswich,* (Cambridge: Press of John Wilson and Son, 1870) p. 20; PDF e-book, https://archive.org/details/ancestrypriscil00applgoog/page/n16 accessed 16 October 2019.

2. Edward Symonds of Black-Notley, who married Anne Draper.
3. Samuel Symonds [11-1,662], who married first to Dorothy Harlakendon, (second to Martha Read [11-1,663], and third to Rebecca.)
4. Richard Symonds of Yeldham.[1422]

[12-3,326] Edmund Reade and [12-3,327] Elizabeth Cooke

Edmund Reade [12-3,326] of Wickford was christened on May 23, 1563 in England and was the son of William Reade [13-6,652] of Wickford and Mary [13-6,653]. William Reade [13-6,652] of Wickford was the son of Roger Reade [14-13,304], who died in 1558, and Elizabeth [14-13,305]. Roger Reade [14-13,304] was the son of William Reade [15-26,608] of Wickford, who died in 1584 or 1534 (the print is difficult to read).[1423]

Edmund Reade [12-3,326] married Elizabeth Cooke [12-3,327], who was the daughter of Thomas Cooke [13-6,654] of Pebmarsh, who died in 1621, and his third wife Susan Brand [13-6,655] of Boxford. Thomas Cooke [13-6,654] of Pebmarsh was the son of Robert Cooke [14-13,308] of Pebmarsh and Joane Syday [14-13,309], and Robert Cooke [14-13,308] was the son of John Cooke [15-26,616] of Horkesley and ___ Newton [15-26,617].[1424]

Edmund Reade [12-3,326] of Wickford was buried on December 1, 1624 in Wickford.[1425] The children of Edmund Reade [12-3,326] and Elizabeth Cooke [12-3,327] are listed below:
1. Martha Read [11-1,663], who married first to Daniel Epes, and second to Samuel Symonds [11-1,662].

1422   Walter Charles Metcalfe, ed., *The Visitations of Essex by Hawley, 1552; Hervey, 1558; Cooke, 1570; Raven, 1612; and Owen and Lilly, 1634. To which Are Added Miscellaneous Essex Pedigrees from Various Harleian Manuscripts: and an Appendix Containing Berry's Essex Pedigrees.* (London: Mitchell and Hughes, 1878) p. 495; PDF e-book, https://archive.org/details/visitationsofess1314metc/page/n8 accessed 3 November 2019.

1423   Joseph James Muskett, ed., *Suffolk Manorial Families: Being the County Visitations and Other Pedigrees* (Exeter: William Pollard & Co., 1900) p. 164; PDF e-book, https://archive.org/details/bub_gb_ZxANnBnHKBQC/page/n335 accessed 15 October 2019.

1424   Walter Charles Metcalfe, ed., *The Visitations of Essex by Hawley, 1552; Hervey, 1558; Cooke, 1570; Raven, 1612; and Owen and Lilly, 1634. To which Are Added Miscellaneous Essex Pedigrees from Various Harleian Manuscripts: and an Appendix Containing Berry's Essex Pedigrees.* (London: Mitchell and Hughes, 1878) p. 383; PDF e-book, https://archive.org/details/visitationsofess1314metc/page/n8 accessed 3 November 2019.

1425   Joseph James Muskett, ed., *Suffolk Manorial Families: Being the County Visitations and Other Pedigrees* (Exeter: William Pollard & Co., 1900) p. 164; PDF e-book, https://archive.org/details/bub_gb_ZxANnBnHKBQC/page/n335 accessed 15 October 2019.

2. Margaret Reade, who married John Lake.
3. Elizabeth Reade, born in 1617 in Wickford, Essex, England and married John Winthrop, Jr.[1426]

[12-3,332] Joshua Batcheller

Joshua Batcheller [12-3,332] was born in Kent, England and was the son of Daniel Batcheller [13-6,664].[1427] He had at least three children and four brothers.[1428] His children are listed below:
1. John Batcheller/Batchelder [11-1,666], who died on March 3, 1676 in Reading, Middlesex County, Massachusetts.
2. Elizabeth Batcheller.
3. Hannah Batcheller.[1429]

[12-3,360] Robert Parker and [12-3,361] Judith

Robert Parker [12-3,360] was born about 1603, probably in England. By March 9, 1634 he was in Boston, Suffolk County, Massachusetts when he became a member of the Boston church. On March 4, 1635, Robert was admitted as a freeman of Boston, and around this time he probably got married to Judith [12-3,361] (aka Jude). Judith was the widow of Richard Bugby of Roxbury. Even though Robert's occupation was that of a butcher, he was described as a servant of William Aspenwall when admitted to the Boston church. So he was probably a recent immigrant at the time who became a servant for a number of years to pay for passage to New England. Robert and Judith had at least five children together,[1430] and Judith died in Cambridge, Middlesex County, Massachusetts on March 8, 1682.[1431] Robert Parker died before April 7, 1685, when his will was probated.[1432] The children of Robert

---

1426   Ibid.
1427   Ezra S. Stearns, ed., *Genealogical and Family History of the State of New Hampshire*, (New York: The Lewis Publishing Co, 1908), Vol III: p 1536; PDF e-book, https://archive.org/details/genealogicalfami03stea , accessed 9 July 2018.
1428   Frederick Clifton Pierce, *Batchelder, Batcheller, Genealogy*, (Chicago: W B Conkey Company, 1898), pp. 343, 347; PDF e-book, https://archive.org/details/batchelderbatche1898pier accessed 15 July 2018.
1429   Ibid.
1430   James Savage, *A Genealogical Dictionary of the First Settlers of New England: Showing Three Generations of Those Who Came Before May 1692*, (Boston: Little, Brown and Company, 1860), Vol III: p. 355; PDF e-book, http://archive.org/details/genealogicaldic03savarich accessed 17 July 2018.
1431   "Massachusetts, Town Clerk, Vital and Town Records, 1626-2001," s.v. "Judith Parker "(death 1682), database, *FamilySearch*, accessed 4 May 2018.
1432   James Savage, *A Genealogical Dictionary of the First Settlers of New*

Parker [12-3,360] and Judith [12-3,361] are listed below:
1. Benjamin Parker [11-1,680] (who married Sarah Hartwell [11-1,681]).
2. Sarah Parker, born in April 1640.
3. John Parker, who was christened on March 27, 1642 in Roxbury, which is now in Boston, Suffolk County, Massachusetts.
4. Nathaniel Parker, born on July 28, 1643.
5. Rachel Parker.[1433]

[12-3,362] William Hartwell and [12-3,363] Jazan

William Hartwell was born about 1613[1434] in England and married Jazan who was born about 1608[1435] in England. About 1636 William was in Concord, Middlesex County, Massachusetts, where he was made a freeman on May 18, 1642.[1436] He died on March 12, 1690 and was buried at Old Hill Burying Ground in Concord, Middlesex County, Massachusetts.[1437] Jazan died on August 5, 1695 and shares a headstone with William at Old Hill Burying Ground.[1438] The children of William Hartwell [12-3,362] and Jazan [12-3,363] are listed below:
1. William Hartwell, born in 1638.
2. John Hartwell, born on February 23, 1641.
3. Mary Hartwell, born in 1643.
4. Samuel Hartwell, born on March 26, 1645.
5. Martha Hartwell, born on April 25, 1649.
6. Sarah Hartwell [11-1,681][1439] (who married Benjamin Parker [11-

England: Showing Three Generations of Those Who Came Before May 1692, (Boston: Little, Brown and Company, 1860), Vol III: p. 355; PDF e-book, http://archive.org/details/genealogicaldic03savarich accessed 17 July 2018.
1433   Ibid.
1434   William Hartwell, grave marker, Old Hill Burying Ground, Concord, Middlesex County, Massachusetts, digital image, *FindAGrave,* s.v. "William Hartwell" (death 1690, memorial 24277132), accessed 2 March 2017.
1435   Jazan Hartwell, grave marker, Old Hill Burying Ground, Concord, Middlesex County, Massachusetts, digital image, *FindAGrave,* s.v. "Jazan Hartwell" (death 1695, memorial 24277216), accessed 2 March 2017.
1436   James Savage, *A Genealogical Dictionary of the First Settlers of New England: Showing Three Generations of Those Who Came Before May 1692*, (Boston: Little, Brown and Company, 1860), Vol II: p. 369; PDF e-book, http://archive.org/details/genealogicaldic02savarich accessed 17 July 2018.
1437   William Hartwell, grave marker, Old Hill Burying Ground, Concord, Middlesex County, Massachusetts, digital image, *FindAGrave,* s.v. "William Hartwell" (death 1690, memorial 24277132), accessed 2 March 2017.
1438   Jazan Hartwell, grave marker, Old Hill Burying Ground, Concord, Middlesex County, Massachusetts, digital image, *FindAGrave,* s.v. "Jazan Hartwell" (death 1695, memorial 24277216), accessed 2 March 2017.
1439   James Savage, *A Genealogical Dictionary of the First Settlers of New England: Showing Three Generations of Those Who Came Before May 1692*, (Boston:

1,680]).

[12-3,382] William Towne and [12-3,383] Joan Blessing

William Towne [12-3,382] married Joan Blessing [12-3,383] on April 28, 1620 in Yarmouth, Norfolk England.[1440] Most of their children were born in Yarmouth.[1441] William Towne arrived in Salem, Essex County, Massachusetts by 1640, but moved to Topsfield, Essex County, Massachusetts in 1651. William Towne died about 1672 and Joan died about 1682.[1442]

Joan Blessing [12-3,383] was christened on June 22, 1595 in Caister next Yarmouth, Norfolk, England. Her parents were John Blessing [13-6,766] and Jane [13-6,767].[1443] Some believe that John Blessing and Jane were the John and Joan couple married in Suffolk, England, but since that was in a different county I am hesitant to go with that connection without more evidence.

The children of William Towne [12-3,382] and Joan Blessing [12-3,383] are listed below:

1. Rebecca Towne [11-1,691], christened on February 21, 1621 in Yarmouth, Norfolk, England and married Francis Nurse [11-1,690].
2. John Towne, christened on February 16, 1623 in Yarmouth.
3. Susan Towne, christened on October 20, 1625 in Yarmouth.
4. Edmund Towne, christened on June 28, 1628 in Yarmouth.
5. Jacob Towne, christened on February 11, 1631 in Yarmouth.
6. Mary Towne, christened on August 24, 1634 in Yarmouth and married Isaac Easty.
7. Sarah Towne, who was born in Salem. She married first to Edward Bridges on January 11, 1660 and second to Peter Cloyes.
8. Joseph Towne, who was born about 1639 in Salem.[1444]

Little, Brown and Company, 1860), Vol II: p. 369; PDF e-book, http://archive.org/details/genealogicaldic02savarich accessed 17 July 2018.

1440   "England Marriages, 1538-1973," s.v. "William Towne" (marriage 1620, spouse "Jone Blessing"), database, *FamilySearch*, accessed 3 May 2017.

1441   William B. Towne, "Notes and Memoranda Relating to Persons of the Name of Towne," *The New England Historical and Genealogical Register*, Vol 21: p. 16; database, *American Ancestors*, accessed 13 August 2018.

1442   Ibid., Vol 21: p. 15.

1443   "England Births and Christenings, 1538-1975," s.v. "Jone Blessing" (christened 1595), database, *FamilySearch*, accessed 3 May 2017.

1444   William B. Towne, "Notes and Memoranda Relating to Persons of the Name of Towne," *The New England Historical and Genealogical Register*, Vol 21: p. 16; database, *American Ancestors*, accessed 13 August 2018.

[12-3,440] Robert Mears and [12-3,441] Elizabeth Johnson

Robert Mears was born about 1592 and married Elizabeth Johnson. Elizabeth was born about 1605. They immigrated to Boston, Suffolk County, Massachusetts in 1635 in the ship *Abigail*. Robert was a tailor, and died before September 10, 1667 when his will was proven. Elizabeth was still living at the time of the will.[1445] The children of Robert Mears [12-3,440] and Elizabeth Johnson [12-3,441] are listed below:

1. Samuel Mears, who died before June 1641.
2. John Mears, who died in 1635.
3. Stephen Mears, born in 1637 in Boston.
4. Samuel Mears, who was born on June 7, 1641 in Boston and married Mary. He died in 1676.
5. James Mears [11-1,720], who was born on March 9, 1644 in Boston. (He married Elizabeth Mellowes [11-1,721]).
6. John Mears, who married Mercy and died on September 27, 1663.[1446]

[12-3,442] Edward Mellowes and [12-3,443] Hannah Smith

Edward Mellowes [12-3,442] was christened on September 10, 1609 in Odell, Bedfordshire, England[1447] and his parents were Abraham Mellowes [13-6,884] and Martha Bulkeley [13-6,885]. Edward and his parents immigrated to Charlestown, which is now part of Boston, Suffolk County, Massachusetts, by 1633 when they were admitted to the Charlestown church. Around this time, Edward Mellowes probably married Hannah Smith, whose ancestry is in some dispute. Edward became a freeman on March 4, 1634 in Charlestown, and was constables in 1637. He was literate, as evidenced by him being town clerk of Charlestown, and he was also a selectman. Edward died on May 5, 1650 in Charlestown, and Hannah married Joseph Hills on June 24, 1651.[1448] Hannah died about 1655.[1449] The children of Edward Mellowes [12-3,442] and Hannah

---

1445   James Savage, *A Genealogical Dictionary of the First Settlers of New England: Showing Three Generations of Those Who Came Before May 1692*, (Boston: Little, Brown and Company, 1860), Vol III: p. 192; PDF e-book, http://archive.org/details/genealogicaldic03savarich accessed 17 July 2018.
1446   William Richard Cutter, ed., *Genealogical and Personal Memoirs: Relating to the Families of Boston and Eastern Massachusetts*, (New York: Lewis Historical Publishing Company, 1908), Vol III: p. 1480; PDF e-book, https://archive.org/details/genealogicaland00cuttgoog accessed 15 June 2018.
1447   "England Births and Christenings, 1538-1975," s.v. "Edward Mellowes" (birth 1609), database, *FamilySearch*, accessed 19 August 2018.
1448   James Savage, *A Genealogical Dictionary of the First Settlers of New England: Showing Three Generations of Those Who Came Before May 1692*, (Boston: Little, Brown and Company, 1860), Vol III: p. 195; PDF e-book, http://archive.org/details/genealogicaldic03savarich accessed 17 July 2018.
1449   William Richard Cutter, ed., *Genealogical and Personal Memoirs: Relating to*

Smith [12-3,443] are listed below:
1. Hannah Mellowes, born in 1636.
2. Mary Mellowes, born in 1638.
3. Martha Mellowes, born in 1640 and died in 1642/3.
4. Edward Mellowes.
5. Elizabeth Mellowes [11-1,721] (she married James Mears [11-1,720]).
6. Abraham Mellowes, born in 1645.[1450]

Abraham Mellowes [13-6,884] was born about 1570 in the United Kingdom and married Martha Bulkeley [13-6,665] about 1595.[1451] He died in 1639,[1452] probably in Massachusetts. Martha Bulkeley was born about 1572 in the United Kingdom, and her parents were the Reverend Edward Bulkeley [14-13,330] and Olive Irby [14-13,331].[1453] Martha's genealogy continues and will have to be covered elsewhere.

[12-3,448] Edmund Frost and [12-3,449] Thomasine Clench

Edmund Frost [12-3,448] married Thomasine Clench [12-3,449] on July 3, 1634 in Earls Colne, Essex, England.[1454] It was recorded as the fifth month of the year, which in the Julian calendar was July. They immigrated to Massachusetts in 1635 in the ship *Great Hope* out of Ipswich, England, and Edmund Frost became a freeman of probably Cambridge, Middlesex County, Massachusetts on March 3, 1636.[1455] Thomasine died before December 15,

the Families of Boston and Eastern Massachusetts, (New York: Lewis Historical Publishing Company, 1908), Vol II: p. 906; PDF e-book, https://archive.org/details/genealogicaland01cuttgoog , accessed 10 July 2018.

1450   James Savage, *A Genealogical Dictionary of the First Settlers of New England: Showing Three Generations of Those Who Came Before May 1692*, (Boston: Little, Brown and Company, 1860), Vol III: p. 195; PDF e-book, http://archive.org/details/genealogicaldic03savarich accessed 17 July 2018.

1451   Robert Charles Anderson, *The Great Migration Begins: Immigrants to New England 1620-1633*, (Boston: New England Historic Genealogical Society, 1995), p. 1249; database with digital images, *American Ancestors,* accessed 19 August 2018.

1452   James Savage, *A Genealogical Dictionary of the First Settlers of New England: Showing Three Generations of Those Who Came Before May 1692*, (Boston: Little, Brown and Company, 1860), Vol III: p. 195; PDF e-book, http://archive.org/details/genealogicaldic03savarich accessed 17 July 2018.

1453   Donald Lines Jacobus, *The Bulkeley Genealogy: Rev. Peter Bulkeley,* (New Haven, Connecticut: The Tuttle, Morehouse & Taylor Company, 1933), p. 15; PDF e-book, https://archive.org/details/bulkeleygenealog00jaco_0 accessed 19 August 2018.

1454   "England Marriages, 1538-1973," s.v. "Thomasin Clench" (marriage 1634, spouse "Edmond Frost"), database, *FamilySearch,* accessed 20 August 2018.

1455   James Savage, *A Genealogical Dictionary of the First Settlers of New England: Showing Three Generations of Those Who Came Before May 1692*, (Boston: Little, Brown and Company, 1860), Vol II: p. 211; PDF e-book, http://archive.org/details/genealogicaldic02savarich accessed 17 July 2018.

1665 when Edmund married Reana. Edmund died on July 12, 1672 in Cambridge.[1456]

Some genealogical works, like Savage cited earlier, say that Edmund had another wife named Mary by 1653, but that was probably due to a clerical error since Thomasine was still living and married to Edmund Frost in January 1658/9 according to church records. Also, some respected genealogists trace Thomasine Clench to Cambridgeshire, England. However that connection is circumstantial, and when one considers that there was a Clench family already living in Earls Colne where Thomasine got married, the connection to the Clench family in Cambridgeshire becomes too weak to include in this genealogy.

The children of Edmund Frost [12-3,448] and Thomasine Clench [12-3,449] are listed below:

1. John Frost, born before 1635 in England. He married Rebecca Andrews on June 26, 1666 in Cambridge, Massachusetts.
2. Thomas Frost, born in March 1637 in Cambridge.
3. Samuel Frost, born in February 1639 in Cambridge and married Mary Cole on October 12, 1663 in Cambridge.
4. Joseph Frost, born on January 13, 1639/40 in Cambridge and married Hannah Miller on May 22, 1666 in Charlestown.
5. James Frost [11-1,724], born on April 9, 1643 in Cambridge. He married first to Rebecca Hamlet on December 7, 1664, and second to Elizabeth Foster [11-1,725] on January 22, 1666/7 in Billerica.
6. Mary Frost, born on July 24, 1645 in Cambridge.
7. Ephraim Frost, born about 1651.
8. Sarah Frost, born about 1653 in Cambridge.
9. Thomas Frost, born about 1655. He married first to Mary (Gibbs) Goodridge on November 12, 1678, and second to Hannah Johnson on July 9, 1691 in Sudbury.[1457]

[12-3,450] Thomas Foster

Thomas Foster [12-3,450] was in Weymouth, Norfolk County, Massachusetts before 1640. By March 1648 Thomas was married to Elizabeth, and she had at least two of their children. However, there is no record of Elizabeth before 1648, so it is not proven that she was the mother of any children before 1648. Thomas Foster was a blacksmith, and was repeatedly brought to court after October 4, 1671 for not attending the established

---

1456   Robert Charles Anderson, George F. Sanborn, Jr., and Melinde Lutz Sanborn, *The Great Migration: Immigrants to New England, 1634-1635, Volume II, C-F* (Boston: New England Historic Genealogical Society, 2001), p. 596; database with digital images, *American Ancestors*, accessed 20 August 2018.
1457   Ibid.

Church's services. Thomas was an Anabaptist, and died on April 20, 1682.[1458] [1459] [1460] The children of Thomas Foster [12-3,450] are listed below:

1. Thomas Foster, born on August 18, 1640 in Weymouth, and died in 1679.
2. John Foster, born on October 7, 1642 in Weymouth and died on June 13, 1732.
3. Increase Foster.
4. Elizabeth Foster [11-1,725] (she married James Frost [11-1,724]).
5. Hopestill Foster, born on March 26, 1648 in Braintree, Norfolk County, Massachusetts and died on May 26, 1679.
6. Joseph Foster, born on March 28, 1650 in Braintree, and died on December 12, 1721.[1461]

[12-3,454] John Gorton and [12-3,455] Mary

John Gorton [12-3,454] is first mentioned in Roxbury, which is now in Boston, Massachusetts, in August of 1636 in a record of his daughter's burial.[1462] John's wife's name was Mary [12-3,455], but it is not certain where or when they married. John became a freeman in 1669, presumably in Roxbury, and died in 1676. Mary was still living at the time that John wrote his will.[1463] The children of John Gorton [12-3,454] and Mary [12-3,455] are listed below:

1. Mary Gorton, who died in August 1636.
2. Mary Gorton, born in 1641 and died before 1648.
3. Sarah Gorton, christened on January 21, 1644.
4. Hannah Gorton, born in 1646 and died 1669.
5. Mary Gorton [11-1,727], born in 1648 and died in 1703. (She married Daniel Mascroft [11-1,726]).
6. Alice Gorton, born on March 8, 1652.

1458   Lucius R. Paige, "Family of Thomas Foster," *The New England Historical and Genealogical Register*, Vol 26: pp. 394-5; database, *American Ancestors*, accessed 21 August 2018.
1459   Henry A Hazen, *History of Billerica, Massachusetts: With a Genealogical Register,* (Boston: A Williams and Co, 1883) p. 54 of Genealogical Register; PDF e-book, https://archive.org/details/historyofbilleri00hazenhe , accessed 9 July 2018.
1460   Clarence Almon Torrey, *New England Marriages Prior to 1700*, (Baltimore, Maryland: Genealogical Publishing Co., Inc, 2004), p. 278; database with digital images, *Ancestry.com,* accessed 10 May 2018.
1461   Ibid.
1462   "Massachusetts, Town Clerk, Vital and Town Records, 1626-2001," s.v. "Mary Gorton" (death 1636), database, *FamilySearch*, accessed 24 August 2018.
1463   James Savage, *A Genealogical Dictionary of the First Settlers of New England: Showing Three Generations of Those Who Came Before May 1692*, (Boston: Little, Brown and Company, 1860), Vol II: p. 282; PDF e-book, http://archive.org/details/genealogicaldic02savarich accessed 17 July 2018.

7. Elizabeth Gorton, born and died in 1654.
8. John Gorton, born in 1655 and died before 1676.
9. Abraham Gorton, born in 1659.[1464]

1464   Ibid.

211

Appendix

GENEALOGY CHARTS

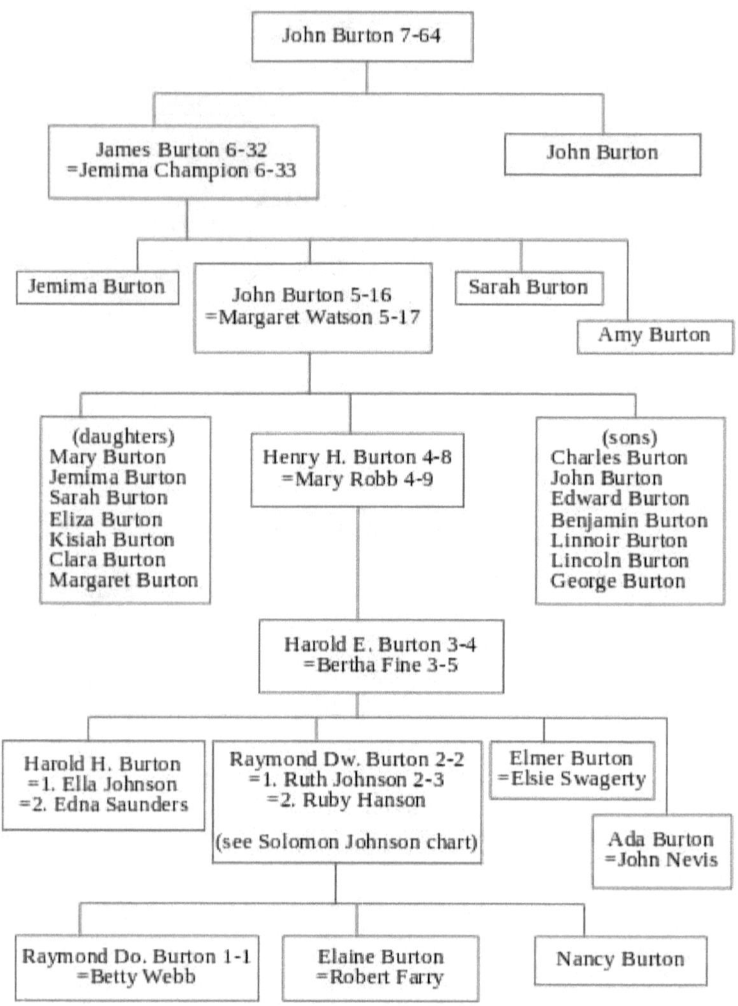

John Burton 7-64
James Burton 6-32
=Jemima Champion 6-33
John Burton
Jemima Burton
John Burton 5-16
=Margaret Watson 5-17
Sarah Burton
Amy Burton
(daughters)
Mary Burton
Jemima Burton
Sarah Burton
Eliza Burton
Kisiah Burton
Clara Burton
Margaret Burton
Henry H. Burton 4-8
=Mary Robb 4-9
(sons)
Charles Burton
John Burton
Edward Burton
Benjamin Burton
Linnoir Burton
Lincoln Burton
George Burton
Harold E. Burton 3-4
=Bertha Fine 3-5
Harold H. Burton
=1. Ella Johnson
=2. Edna Saunders
Raymond Dw. Burton 2-2
=1. Ruth Johnson 2-3
=2. Ruby Hanson
(see Solomon Johnson chart)
Elmer Burton
=Elsie Swagerty
Ada Burton
=John Nevis
Raymond Do. Burton 1-1
=Betty Webb
Elaine Burton
=Robert Farry
Nancy Burton

Ancestors of Raymond Donald Burton

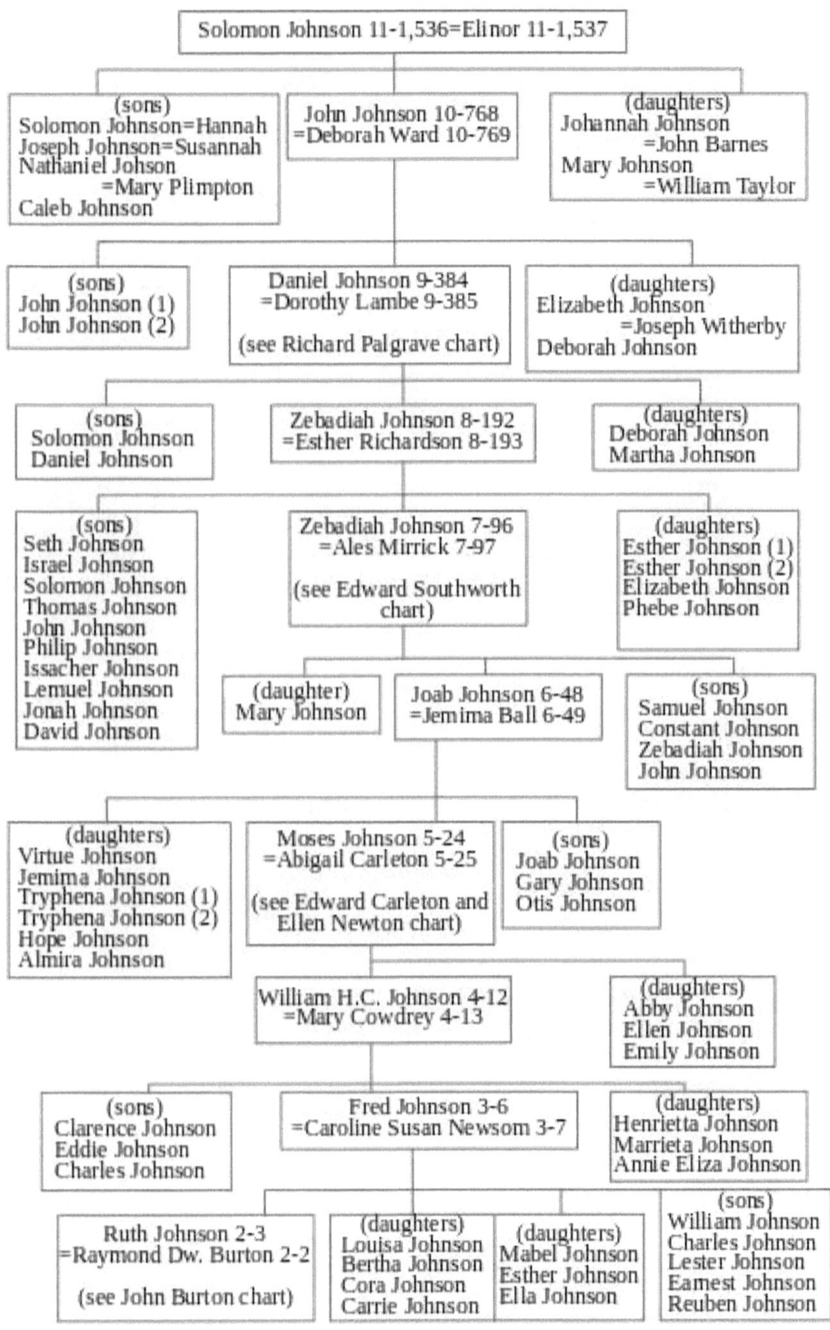

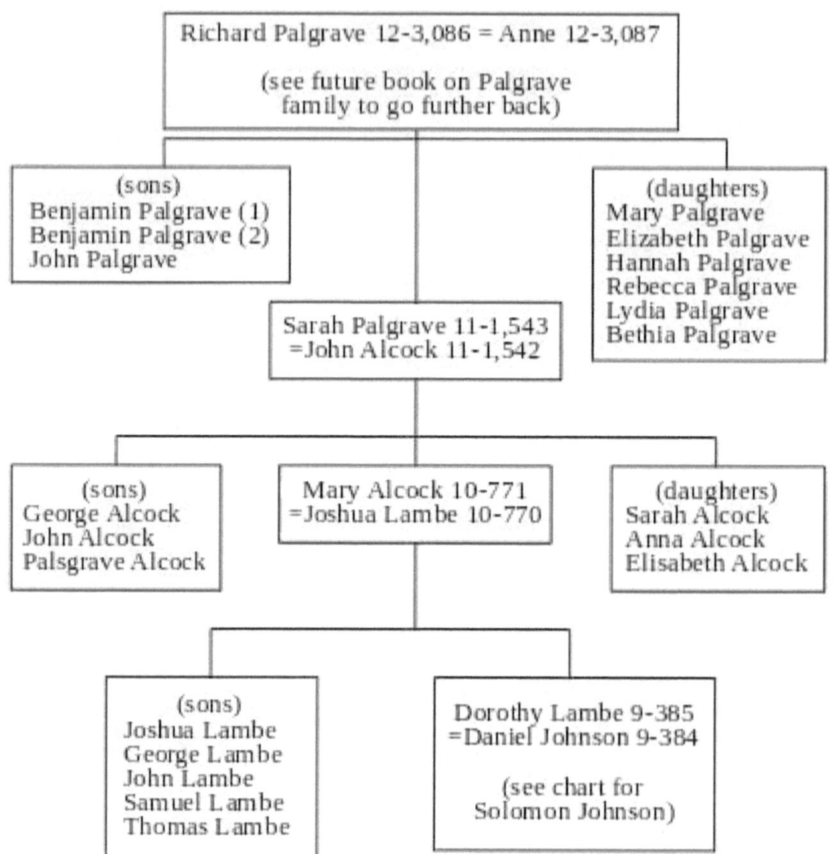

Richard Palgrave 12-3,086 = Anne 12-3,087
(see future book on Palgrave
family to go further back)
(sons)
Benjamin Palgrave (1)
Benjamin Palgrave (2)
John Palgrave
(daughters)
Mary Palgrave
Elizabeth Palgrave
Hannah Palgrave
Rebecca Palgrave
Lydia Palgrave
Bethia Palgrave
Sarah Palgrave 11-1,543
=John Alcock 11-1,542
(sons)
George Alcock
John Alcock
Palsgrave Alcock
Mary Alcock 10-771
=Joshua Lambe 10-770
(daughters)
Sarah Alcock
Anna Alcock
Elisabeth Alcock
(sons)
Joshua Lambe
George Lambe
John Lambe
Samuel Lambe
Thomas Lambe
Dorothy Lambe 9-385
=Daniel Johnson 9-384
(see chart for
Solomon Johnson)

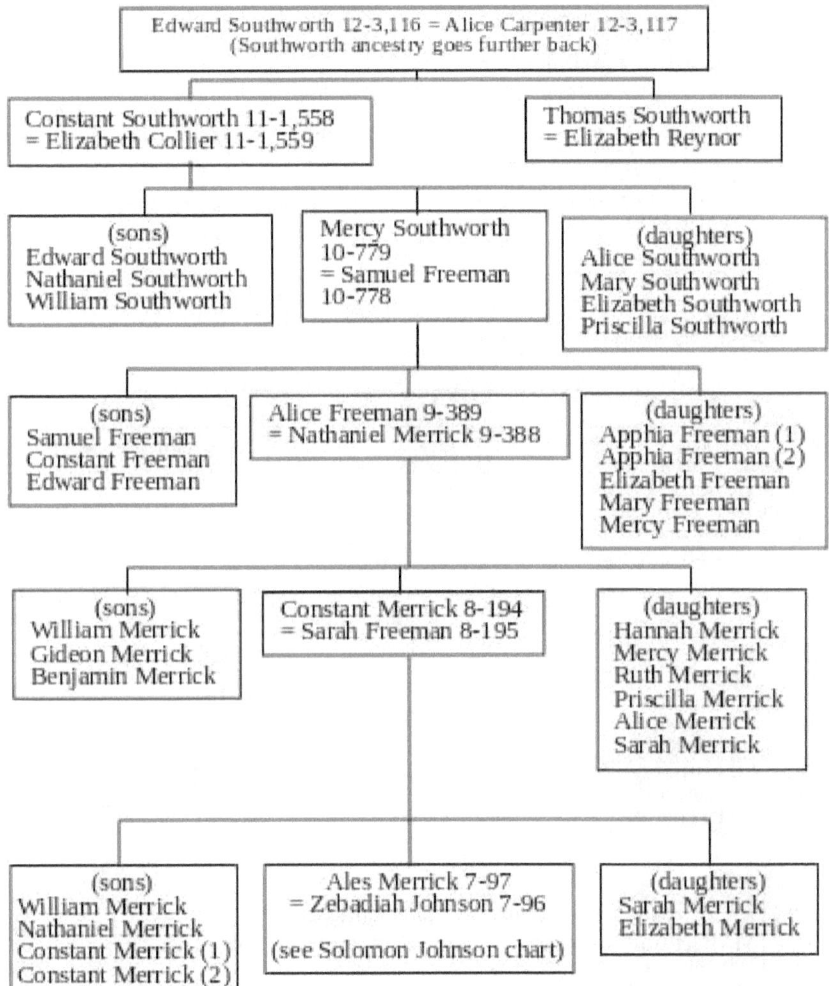

Edward Southworth 12-3,116 = Alice Carpenter 12-3,117
(Southworth ancestry goes further back)

Constant Southworth 11-1,558
= Elizabeth Collier 11-1,559

Thomas Southworth
= Elizabeth Reynor

(sons)
Edward Southworth
Nathaniel Southworth
William Southworth

Mercy Southworth
10-779
= Samuel Freeman
10-778

(daughters)
Alice Southworth
Mary Southworth
Elizabeth Southworth
Priscilla Southworth

(sons)
Samuel Freeman
Constant Freeman
Edward Freeman

Alice Freeman 9-389
= Nathaniel Merrick 9-388

(daughters)
Apphia Freeman (1)
Apphia Freeman (2)
Elizabeth Freeman
Mary Freeman
Mercy Freeman

(sons)
William Merrick
Gideon Merrick
Benjamin Merrick

Constant Merrick 8-194
= Sarah Freeman 8-195

(daughters)
Hannah Merrick
Mercy Merrick
Ruth Merrick
Priscilla Merrick
Alice Merrick
Sarah Merrick

(sons)
William Merrick
Nathaniel Merrick
Constant Merrick (1)
Constant Merrick (2)

Ales Merrick 7-97
= Zebadiah Johnson 7-96

(see Solomon Johnson chart)

(daughters)
Sarah Merrick
Elizabeth Merrick

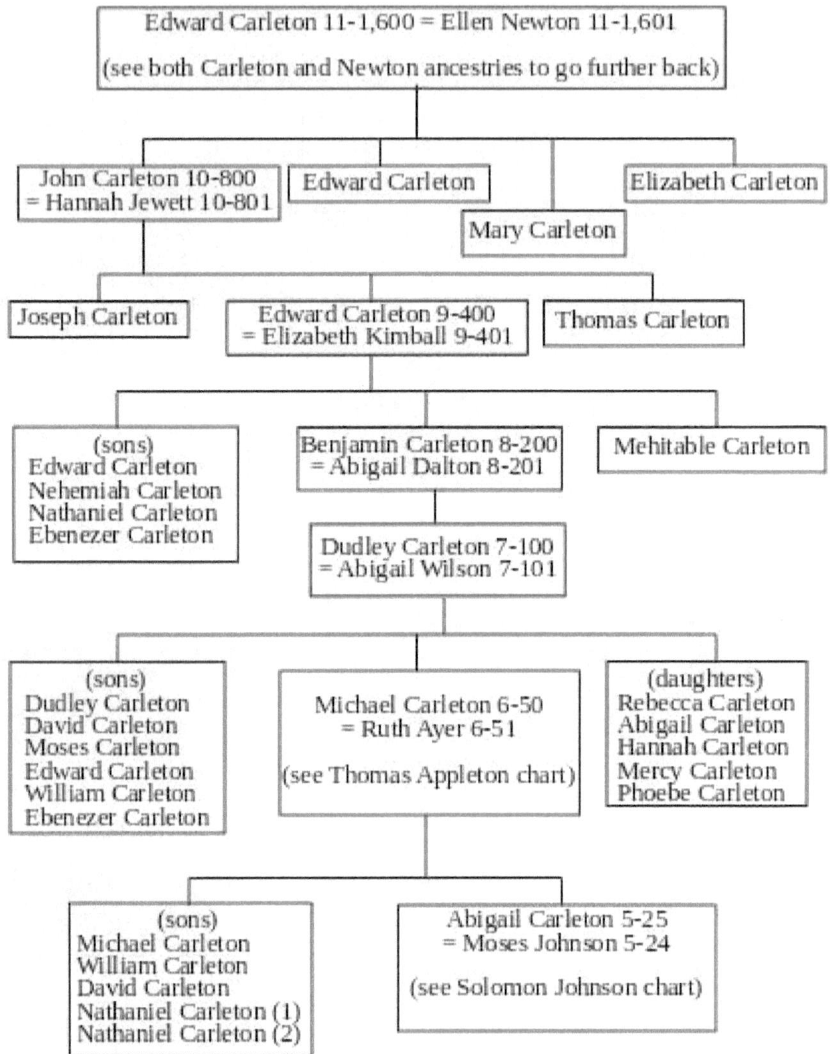

Edward Carleton 11-1,600 = Ellen Newton 11-1,601
(see both Carleton and Newton ancestries to go further back)
John Carleton 10-800 = Hannah Jewett 10-801
Edward Carleton
Elizabeth Carleton
Mary Carleton
Joseph Carleton
Edward Carleton 9-400 = Elizabeth Kimball 9-401
Thomas Carleton
(sons)
Edward Carleton
Nehemiah Carleton
Nathaniel Carleton
Ebenezer Carleton
Benjamin Carleton 8-200 = Abigail Dalton 8-201
Mehitable Carleton
Dudley Carleton 7-100 = Abigail Wilson 7-101
(sons)
Dudley Carleton
David Carleton
Moses Carleton
Edward Carleton
William Carleton
Ebenezer Carleton
Michael Carleton 6-50 = Ruth Ayer 6-51
(see Thomas Appleton chart)
(daughters)
Rebecca Carleton
Abigail Carleton
Hannah Carleton
Mercy Carleton
Phoebe Carleton
(sons)
Michael Carleton
William Carleton
David Carleton
Nathaniel Carleton (1)
Nathaniel Carleton (2)
Abigail Carleton 5-25 = Moses Johnson 5-24
(see Solomon Johnson chart)

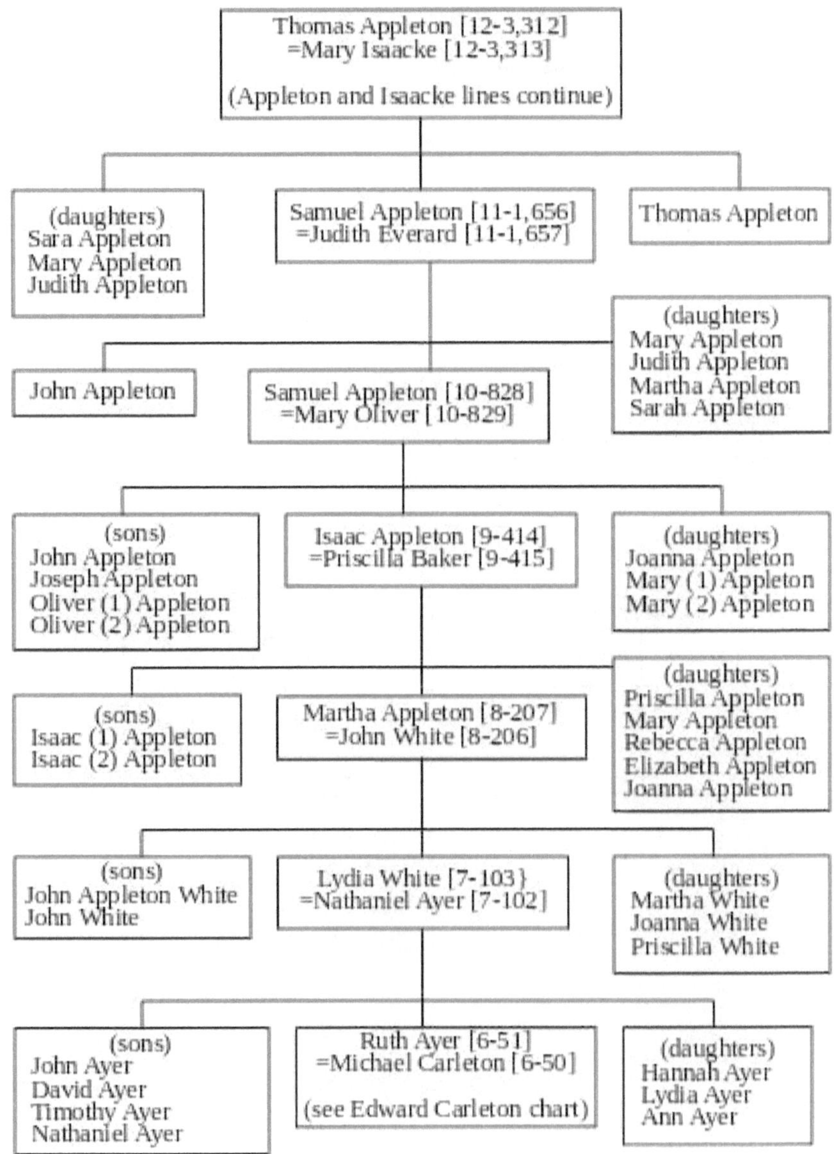

Thomas Appleton [12-3,312]
=Mary Isaacke [12-3,313]

(Appleton and Isaacke lines continue)

(daughters)
Sara Appleton
Mary Appleton
Judith Appleton

Samuel Appleton [11-1,656]
=Judith Everard [11-1,657]

Thomas Appleton

John Appleton

Samuel Appleton [10-828]
=Mary Oliver [10-829]

(daughters)
Mary Appleton
Judith Appleton
Martha Appleton
Sarah Appleton

(sons)
John Appleton
Joseph Appleton
Oliver (1) Appleton
Oliver (2) Appleton

Isaac Appleton [9-414]
=Priscilla Baker [9-415]

(daughters)
Joanna Appleton
Mary (1) Appleton
Mary (2) Appleton

(sons)
Isaac (1) Appleton
Isaac (2) Appleton

Martha Appleton [8-207]
=John White [8-206]

(daughters)
Priscilla Appleton
Mary Appleton
Rebecca Appleton
Elizabeth Appleton
Joanna Appleton

(sons)
John Appleton White
John White

Lydia White [7-103]
=Nathaniel Ayer [7-102]

(daughters)
Martha White
Joanna White
Priscilla White

(sons)
John Ayer
David Ayer
Timothy Ayer
Nathaniel Ayer

Ruth Ayer [6-51]
=Michael Carleton [6-50]

(see Edward Carleton chart)

(daughters)
Hannah Ayer
Lydia Ayer
Ann Ayer

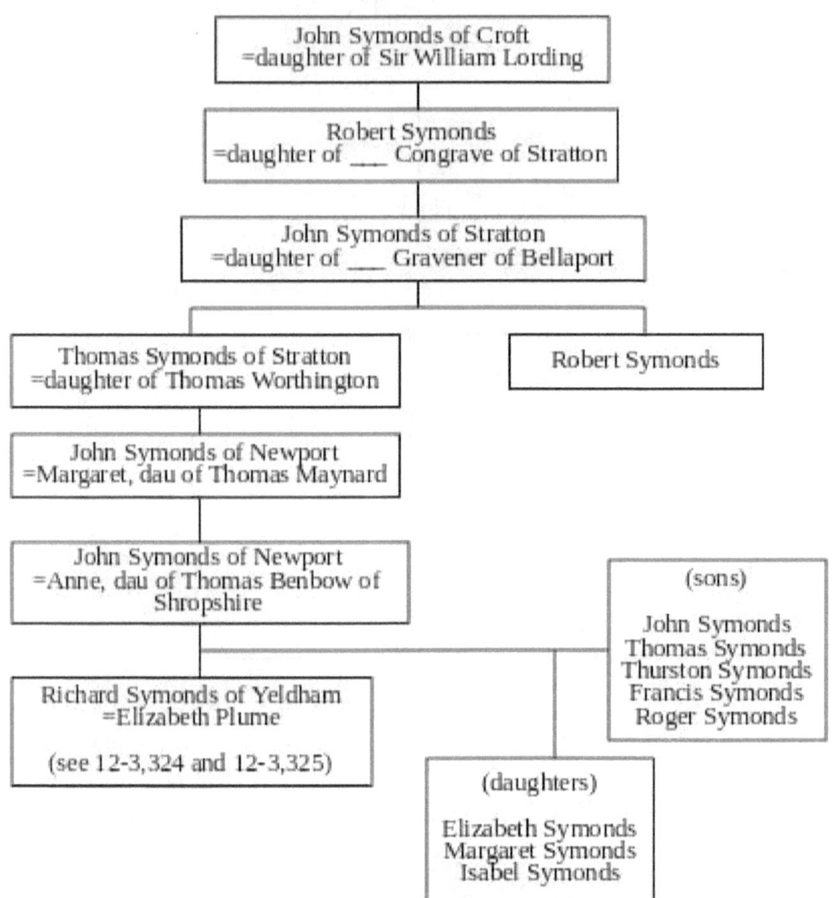

John Symonds of Croft
=daughter of Sir William Lording

Robert Symonds
=daughter of ___ Congrave of Stratton

John Symonds of Stratton
=daughter of ___ Gravener of Bellaport

Thomas Symonds of Stratton
=daughter of Thomas Worthington

Robert Symonds

John Symonds of Newport
=Margaret, dau of Thomas Maynard

John Symonds of Newport
=Anne, dau of Thomas Benbow of Shropshire

(sons)

John Symonds
Thomas Symonds
Thurston Symonds
Francis Symonds
Roger Symonds

Richard Symonds of Yeldham
=Elizabeth Plume

(see 12-3,324 and 12-3,325)

(daughters)

Elizabeth Symonds
Margaret Symonds
Isabel Symonds

Descent from William Brewster, who immigrated on the Mayflower

GENERATION	INDIVIDUAL	AND	SPOUSE
1	William Brewster (came on the Mayflower) abt 1567-1644	and	Mary Abt 1569-1627
2	Patience Brewster ?-1634	and	Thomas Prence Abt 1601-1673
3	Mercy Prence Abt 1631-1711	and	John Freeman 1627-1719
4	John Freeman 1651-1721	and	Sarah Merrick 1654-1696
5	John Freeman 1678-?	and	Mercy Watson 1683-?
6	Sarah Freeman 1704-?	and	Constant Merrick Abt 1701-1792
7	Ales Mirrick ?-1737	and	Zebediah Johnson 1732-?
8	Joab Johnson 1765-1840	and	Jemima Ball 1772-1816
9	Moses Johnson 1794-1880	and	Abigail Carleton 1789-?
10	William Henry Carleton Johnson 1827-1910	and	Mary Eliza Cowdrey 1830-1900
11	Fred Henry Johnson 1860-1932	and	Caroline Susan Newsom 16867-1946
12	Ruth Elma Johnson 1910-1951	and	Raymond Dwight Burton 1907-1970
13	Raymond Donald Burton 1929-1986		

Descent from Stephen Hopkins, who immigrated on the Mayflower

GENERATION	INDIVIDUAL	AND	SPOUSE
1	Stephen Hopkins (immigrated on Mayflower) ?-bef 1644	and	Mary ?-1613
2	Giles Hopkins 1607-1690	and	Catherine Wheldon 1617-aft 1689
3	Abigail Hopkins 1644-?	and	William Merrick 1643-1732
4	Nathaniel Merrick 1675-1743	and	Alice Freeman
5	Constant Merrick Abt 1701-1792	and	Sarah Freeman 1704-?
6	Alice Mirrick 1731-?	and	Zebadiah Johnson 1732-?
7	Joab Johnson 1765-1840	and	Jemima Ball 1772-1816
8	Moses Johnson 1794-1880	and	Abigail Carleton 1789-?
9	William Henry Carleton Johnson 1827-1910	and	Mary Eliza Cowdrey 1830-1900
10	Fred Henry Johnson 1860-1932	and	Caroline Susan Newsom 1867-1946
11	Ruth Elma Johnson 1910-1951	and	Raymond Dwight Burton 1907-1970
12	Raymond Donald Burton 1929-1986		

Descent from Rebecca (Towne) Nurse, who was accused of witchcraft at Salem

GENERATION	INDIVIDUAL	AND	SPOUSE
1	Rebecca (Towne) Nurse (alleged Salem witch) 1621-1692	and	Francis Nurse 1618-1695
2	Mary Nurse Abt 1659-1749	and	John Tarbell Abt 1654-1715
3	John Tarbell 1680-1757	and	Hannah Flint 1685-1779
4	Anna Tarbell 1716-?	and	Samuel Parker 1722-1752
5	Rebecca Parker 1752-?	and	Nathaniel Cowdry 1745-?
6	Joseph Cowdry 1781-1859	and	Lucy Brown 1778-1856
7	Joseph Cowdry 1807-?	and	Ann Eliza Foster ?-1847
8	Mary Eliza Cowdrey 1830-1900	and	William Henry Carleton Johnson 1827-1910
9	Fred Henry Johnson 1860-1932	and	Caroline Susan Newsom 1867-1946
10	Ruth Elma Johnson 1910-1951	and	Raymond Dwight Burton 1907-1970
11	Raymond Donald Burton 1929-1986		

Bibliography

The American Genealogist. New Haven, CT: D.L. Jacobus, 1937- . Database. *American Ancestors.* https://www.americanancestors.org (Accessed 2018).

Anderson, Robert Charles. *The Great Migration Begins: Immigrants to New England 1620-1633.* Boston: New England Historic Genealogical Society, 1995. Database with digital images. *Ancestry.com.* (Accessed 2018).

Anderson, Robert Charles. *The Great Migration Begins: Immigrants to New England 1620-1633,* 3 Volumes. Boston: New England Historic Genealogical Society, 1995. Database with digital images. *American Ancestors.* https://www.americanancestors.org (Accessed 2018).

Anderson, Robert Charles, George F. Sanborn, Jr., and Melinde Lutz Sanborn. *The Great Migration: Immigrants to New England, 1634-1635, Volume II, C-F.* Boston: New England Historic Genealogical Society, 2001. Database with digital images, *American Ancestors,* https://www.americanancestors.org (Accessed 2018).

Anderson, Robert Charles. *Great Migration: Immigrants to New England, 1634-1635, Volume IV, I-L.* Boston: New England Historic Genealogical Society, 1995. Database with digital images. *American Ancestors.* https://www.americanancestors.org (Accessed 2019).

Anderson, Robert Charles. *The Great Migration: Immigrants to New England, T-Y.* Boston: New England Historic Genealogical Society, 2012. Database with digital images. *American Ancestors.* https://www.americanancestors.org (Accessed 2019).

Appleton, William S. *Ancestry of Priscilla Baker, Who Lived 1674-1731, and Was the Wife of Isaac Appleton, of Ipswich.* Cambridge: Press of John Wilson and Son, 1870. PDF e-book. *Internet Archive.* https://archive.org (Accessed 16 October 2019).

Buffa, Elizabeth Berry. "Cox Family Outline." Report, 1977. PDF e-book. *Internet Archive.* https://archive.org (Accessed 8 July 2018).

"California, County Marriages, 1850-1952." Database with digital images. *FamilySearch.* https://www.familysearch.org . (Accessed 2017).

"California Death Index, 1905-1939." Database with digital images. *FamilySearch,* https://www.familysearch.org . (Accessed 2017).

"California Death Index, 1940-1997." Database with digital images. *FamilySearch,* https://www.familysearch.org . (Accessed 2017).

California. Los Angeles County. 1900 U.S. Census, population schedule. Database with digital images. *FamilySearch.* https://www.familysearch.org . (Accessed 2017).

"California Marriages, 1850-1877." Database. *Ancestry.com.* https://www.ancestry.com . (Accessed 2012).

California, Santa Clara County. 1860 U.S. Census, population schedule. Database with digital images. *Ancestry.com.* https://www.ancestry.com . (Accessed   2015).

California, Santa Clara County. 1880 U.S. Census, population schedule. Database with digital images. *FamilySearch.* https://www.familysearch.org . (Accessed 2017).

California. Santa Clara County. 1910 U.S. Census, population schedule. Database with digital images. *FamilySearch.* https://www.familysearch.org . (Accessed 2016).

California. Santa Clara County. 1920 U.S. Census, population schedule. Database with digital images. *FamilySearch.* https://www.familysearch.org . (Accessed 2016).

California. Santa Clara County. 1930 U.S. Census, population schedule. Database with digital images. *FamilySearch.* https://www.familysearch.org . (Accessed 2016).

California. Santa Clara County. 1940 U.S. Census, population schedule. Database with digital images. *FamilySearch.* https://www.familysearch.org . (Accessed 2016).

California. Tuolumne County. 1930 U.S. Census, population schedule. Database with digital images. *FamilySearch.* https://www.familysearch.org . (Accessed 2016).

Celebration of the Two Hundredth Anniversary of the Incorporation of Billerica, Massachusetts, May   29th, 1855. Lowell, Mass.: S. J.

Varney, 1855. PDF e-book. *Internet Archive.* https://archive.org .
(Accessed 13 July 2018).

Chapman Bros. *Portrait and Biographical Album of Johnson and Pawnee
Counties, Nebraska.*   Chicago: Chapman Bros., 1889. PDF e- book.
Google Books. https://books.google.com . (Accessed 27 March 2017).

Cleveland, Horace Gillette. *A Genealogy of Benjamin Cleveland.* Chicago:
n.p., 1879. PDF e-book. *Internet Archive.* https://archive.org
(Accessed 15   July 2018).

Colorado. Otero County. 1920 U.S. Census, population schedule. Database
with digital images. *FamilySearch.* https://www.familysearch.org
(Accessed 2016).

"Convict Records."   Database.   *Convict Records of Australia.*
https://convictrecords.com.au (Accessed 2017).

Cutter, William Richard, ed. *Genealogical and Family History of Western
New York.* New York: Lewis Historical Publishing Company, 1912.
PDF e-book. *Internet Archive.* https://archive.org (Accessed 9 July
2018).

Cutter, William Richard, ed. *Genealogical and Personal Memoirs: Relating to
the Families of Boston and Eastern Massachusetts.* New York: Lewis
Historical Publishing Company, 1908. PDF e-book. *Internet Archive.*
https://archive.org (Accessed 10 July 2018).

Cutter, William Richard, ed. *Genealogical and Personal Memoirs: Relating to
the Families of the State of Massachusetts.* New York: Lewis
Historical Publishing Company, 1910. PDF e-book. *Internet Archive.*
https://archive.org (Accessed 9 July 2018).

Cutter, William Richard, ed. *New England Families: Genealogical and
Memorial.* New York: Lewis Historical Publishing Co, 1913. PDF e-
book. *Internet Archive.* https://archive.org (Accessed 2018).

Cutter, William Richard, ed. *New England Families: Genealogical and
Memorial.* New York: Lewis Historical Publishing Company, 1914.
PDF e-book. *Internet Archive.* https://archive.org (Accessed 2018).

"Devon Baptisms Transcriptions." Database with digital images. *FindMyPast.*
https://www.findmypast.com . (Accessed 2015-2017).

"Devon Burials."   Database with digital images.   *FindMyPast.*
https://www.findmypast.com (Accessed 2015).

"Devon Marriages and Banns." Database with digital images. *FindMyPast.* https://www.findmypast.com (Accessed 2015).

"England Births and Christenings, 1538-1975." Database. *American Ancestors.* https://www.americanancestors.org (Accessed 2018).

"England Births and Christenings, 1538-1975." Database. *FamilySearch.* https://www.familysearch.org   (Accessed 2017-2018).

"England Births and Christenings 1538-1975." Database. *FindMyPast.* https://www.findmypast.com (Accessed 2019).

"England, Dorset, Parish Registers, 1538-2001." Database. *FamilySearch.* https://www.familysearch.org   (Accessed 2019).

"England, Lancashire, Parish Registers 1538-1910." Database. *FamilySearch,* https://www.familysearch.org (Accessed 2017).

"England Marriages, 1538-1973." Database. *FamilySearch.* https://www.familysearch.org (Accessed 2018).

"England, Sussex Parish Registers, 1538-1910." Database. *FamilySearch.* https://www.familysearch.org (Accessed 2018).

The Essex Antiquarian. Salem, MA: The Essex Antiquarian, 1897-1909. Database with digital images. *American   Ancestors.* https://www.americanancestors.org (Accessed 2019).

Flint, John and Stone, John H, compilers. *A Genealogical Register of the Descendants of Thomas Flint of Salem.* Andover: Warren F. Draper, 1860. PDF e-book. *Internet Archive.* https://archive.org (Accessed 2018).

"Find A Grave Memorial." Database with digital images. *Find A Grave.* https://www.findagrave.com   (Accessed 2016-2018).

Fine, Dorothy Wilson. *A Fine Branch of the Family Tree.* San Jose, CA: El Camino Real Chapter, DAR, 1991.

Gage, Arthur E. *Some Descendants of John Gage of Ipswich, Mass.* Boston: New England Historic Genealogical Company, 1908. PDF e-book. *Internet Archive.* https://archive.org (Accessed 2018).

Gilman, Arthur. *The Gilman Family: Traced in the Line of Hon. John Gilman, of Exeter, N.H., with an Account of Many Other Gilmans, in England*

and America. Albany, NY: Joel Munsell, 1869. PDF e-book. *Internet Archive.* https://archive.org (Accessed 2019).

The Goodspeed Publishing Co. *History of Hickory, Polk, Cedar, Dade, and Barton Counties, Missouri.* Chicago: The Goodspeed Publishing Co, 1889. PDF e-book. *Google Books.* https://books.google.com (Accessed 2017).

Greene, Samuel S. *A Genealogical Sketch of the Descendants of Thomas Green of Malden, Mass.* Boston: Henry W. Dutton & Son, 1858. PDF e-book. *Internet Archive.* https://archive.org (Accessed 2018).

Gove, William Henry. *The Gove Book: History and Genealogy of the American Family of Gove and Notes of European Goves.* Salem, MA: Sydney Perley, 1922. PDF e-book. *Internet Archive.* https://archive.org (Accessed 2019).

Hazen, Henry A. *History of Billerica, Massachusetts: With a Genealogical Register.* Boston: A Williams and Co, 1883. PDF e-book. *Internet Archive.* https://archive.org (Accessed 2018).

Hills, William Sandford. *Genealogical Data Relating to the Ancestry and Descendants of William Hills and of Joseph Hills.* Boston: Hills Family Genealogical and Historical Association, 1902. PDF e-book. *Internet Archive.* https://archive.org (Accessed 2018).

Hoyt, David W. *The Old Families of Salisbury and Amesbury Massachusetts: With Some Related Families of Newbury, Haverhill, Ipswich, and Hampton.* Providence, RI: Snow& Farnham, 1897. PDF e-book. *Internet Archive.* https://archive.org (Accessed 2018).

Illinois. Adams County. 1860 US Census, population schedule. Database with digital images. *FamilySearch.* https://www.familysearch.org (Accessed 2016).

Jacobus, Donald Lines. *The Bulkeley Genealogy: Rev. Peter Bulkeley.* New Haven, Connecticut: The Tuttle, Morehouse & Taylor Company, 1933. PDF e-book. *Internet Archive.* https://archive.org (Accessed 2018).

Jas. A Tartt & Co. *History of Gibson County, Indiana.* Edwardsville, Ill: Jas. A Tartt & Co, 1884. PDF e-book. *Google Books.* https://books.google.com (Accessed 3 July 2017).

Johnson, William W. *Johnson Genealogy: Records of the Descendants of John Johnson of Ipswich and Andover.* North Greenfield, Wisconsin:

William W Johnson, 1892. PDF e-book. *Internet Archive.* https://archive.org (Accessed 14 July 2018),

Kansas. Meade County. 1910 U.S. Census, population schedule. Database with digital images. *FamilySearch.* https://www.familysearch.org (Accessed 2016).

Kansas. Pratt County. 1900 U.S. Census, population schedule. Database with digital images. *FamilySearch.* https://www.familysearch.org (Accessed 2016).

Kansas. Russell County. 1880 U.S. Census, population schedule. Database with digital images. *FamilySearch.* https://www.familysearch.org (Accessed 2017).

"Kentucky, County Marriages, 1797-1954." Database with digital images. *FamilySearch.* https://www.familysearch.org (Accessed 2017).

Lake City Publishing. *Portrait and Biographical Album of Jefferson and Van Buren Counties, Iowa.* Chicago: Lake City Publishing, 1890. PDF e-book. *Internet Archive.* https://archive.org (Accessed 5 May 2019).

Lamb, Charles Francis. *Nathan Lamb of Leicester, Massachusetts: His Ancestors and Descendants.* Madison, Wisconsin: n.p., 1930. e-book. *Internet Archive Lending Library.* https://archive.org (Accessed 2018).

The Lewis Publishing Company. *The Bay of San Francisco: The Metropolis of the Pacific Coast and its Suburban Cities.* Chicago: The Lewis Publishing Company, 1892. PDF e-book. *Internet Archive.* https://archive.org (Accessed November 2017).

"Lincolnshire Baptisms." Database with digital images. *FindMyPast.* https://www.findmypast.com (Accessed 2019).

"Lincolnshire Marriages." Database with digital images. *FindMyPast.* https://www.findmypast.com (Accessed 2019).

"London, England, Church of England Baptisms, Marriages and Burials, 1538-1812." Database with digital images. *Ancestry.com.* https://www.ancestry.com (Accessed 2017-9).

Mackay, Scott. Personal Papers. Ca. 2000-2018. Privately held by Scott Mackay. Irondale, MO.

"Maryland Marriages, 1666-1970." Database. *FamilySearch.*

https://www.familysearch.org (Accessed 2017).

"Massachusetts Births, 1841-1915." Database. *FamilySearch.* https://www.familysearch.org . (Accessed 2017).

"Massachusetts Births and Christenings, 1639-1915." Database. *FamilySearch.* https://www.familysearch.org . (Accessed 2016-2017).

"Massachusetts, Compiled Marriages, 1633-1850." Database. *Ancestry.com.* https://www.ancestry.com (Accessed 2017).

"Massachusetts Deaths, 1841-1915." Database. *FamilySearch.* https://www.familysearch.org (Accessed 2017-2019).

"Massachusetts Deaths and Burials, 1795-1910." Database. *FamilySearch.* https://www.familysearch.org   (Accessed 2018).

Massachusetts. Essex County. 1850 U.S. Census, population schedule. Database with digital images. *FamilySearch.* https://www.familysearch.org . (Accessed 2016-2017).

"Massachusetts Marriages, 1695-1910." Database. *FamilySearch,* https://www.familysearch.org (Accessed 2016-2018).

"Massachusetts Marriages, 1841-1915." Database with digital images. *FamilySearch.* https://www.familysearch.org . (Accessed 2017).

"Massachusetts, Plymouth County, Probate Records, 1633-1967." Database with digital images. *FamilySearch.* (Accessed 2018).

"Massachusetts, Town and Vital Records, 1620-1988." Database. *Ancestry.com.* https://www.ancestry.com (Accessed 2016).

"Massachusetts, Town Clerk, Vital and Town Records, 1626-2001." Database with digital images. *Ancestry.com.* https://www.ancestry.com . (Accessed 2017).

"Massachusetts, Town Clerk, Vital and Town Records, 1626-2001." Database with digital images. *FamilySearch.* https://www.familysearch.org (Accessed 2016-2019).

"Massachusetts, Town Death Records, 1620-1850." Database. *Ancestry.com.* https://www.ancestry.com (Accessed 2017).

Metcalf, Henry Harrison, ed. *Probate Records of the Province of New Hampshire,* Vol 32. Bristol, NH: R W Musgrove, Printer, 1914. PDF e-book. *Internet Archive.* https://archive.org (Accessed 2019).

Metcalfe, Walter Charles, ed. *The Visitations of Essex by Hawley, 1552; Hervey, 1558; Cooke, 1570; Raven, 1612; and Owen and Lilly, 1634. To which Are Added Miscellaneous Essex Pedigrees from Various Harleian Manuscripts: and an Appendix Containing Berry's Essex Pedigrees.* London: Mitchell and Hughes, 1878. PDF e-book. *Internet Archive.* https://archive.org (Accessed 2019).

Merrick, George Byron. *Genealogy of the Merrick-Mirick-Myrick Family of Massachusetts: 1636-1902.* Madison, WI: Tracy, Gibbs & Co, 1902. PDF e-book. *Internet Archive.* https://archive.org (Accessed 2018).

Missouri. Carroll County. 1880 U.S. Census, population schedule. Database with digital images. *FamilySearch.* https://www.familysearch.org . (Accessed 2016).

"Missouri Birth & Death Records Database." Database. *Missouri Digital Heritage,* https://www.sos.mo.gov//mdh . (Accessed 2017).

"Missouri, County Marriage, Naturalization, and Court Records, 1800-1991." Digital images not indexed. *FamilySearch.* https://www.familysearch.org   (Accessed 2019).

"Missouri, Marriage Records, 1805-2002." Database with digital images. *Ancestry.com.* https://www.ancestry.com (Accessed 2017).

"Missouri Marriages, 1750-1920." Database. *FamilySearch.* https://www.familysearch.org . (Accessed 2016-2017).

Missouri. Marion County. 1870 US Census, population schedule. Database with digital images. *FamilySearch.* https://www.familysearch.org (Accessed 2016).

Missouri. Polk County. 1870 U.S. Census, population schedule. Database with digital images. *FamilySearch.* https://www.familysearch.org . (Accessed 2017).

Missouri. Texas County. 1860 U.S. Census, population schedule. Database with digital images. *FamilySearch.* https://www.familysearch.org . (Accessed 2017).

Morrison, Leonard Allison and Stephen Paschall Sharples. *History of the Kimball Family in America: From 1634 to 1897, and of its Ancestors the Kemballs or Kemboldes of England.* Boston: Damrell & Upham, 1897. PDF e-book. *Internet Archive.* https://archive.org (Accessed

2018).

Munro-Fraser, J. P. *History of Santa Clara County, California: including its Geography, Geology, Topography, Climatography and Description.* San Francisco: Alley, Bowen & Co, 1881. PDF e-book. *Internet Archive.* https://archive.org . (Accessed 16 March 2017).

Muskett, Joseph James, ed. *Suffolk Manorial Families: Being the County Visitations and Other Pedigrees.* Exeter: William Pollard & Co., 1900. PDF e-book. *Internet Archive.* https://archive.org (Accessed 2019).

National Historical Society. *History of Caldwell and Livingston Counties, Missouri.* St Louis: National Historical Society, 1886. PDF e-book. *Google Books.* https://books.google.com (Accessed 2017).

New England Family History. New York City: Henry Cole Quinby, 1907- . PDF e-book. *Internet Archive.* https://archive.org (Accessed 2018).

The New England Historical and Genealogical Register. Boston: New England Historic Genealogical Society, 1847- . Database with digital images. *American Ancestors.* https://www.americanancestors.org (Accessed 2018).

The New England Historical and Genealogical Register. Boston: New England Historic Genealogical Society, 1847- . PDF e-book. *Internet Archive.* https://archive.org (Accessed 2019).

"New Hampshire Birth Records, Early to 1900." Database with digital images. *FamilySearch.* https://www.familysearch.org (Accessed 2017).

"New Hampshire Deaths and Burials, 1784-1949." Database. *FamilySearch.* https://www.familysearch.org (Accessed 2019).

"New Hampshire Marriage Records, 1637-1947." Database with digital images. *FamilySearch.* https://www.familysearch.org (Accessed 2016).

"New Hampshire, Town Clerk, Vital and Town Records, 1636-1947." Digital images. *FamilySearch.* https://www.familysearch.org (Accessed 2019).

Society of Genealogists. "Boyd's Inhabitants Of London & Family Units 1200-1946." Database with digital images. *FindMyPast.* https://www.findmypast.com (Accessed 2019).

Topsfield Historical Society. *Vital Records of Haverhill Massachusetts: to the*

End of the Year 1849. Topsfield, Massachusetts: Topsfield Historical Society, 1911. PDF e-book. *Internet Archive.* https://archive.org/details/cu31924099427654 (Accessed 2018).

"Record of Commissions of Officers in the Tennessee Militia." Database with digital images. *Ancestry.com.* https://www.ancestry.com (Accessed 2017).

Roberts, Gary Boyd. *English Origins of New England Families.* Baltimore, MD: Genealogical Publishing Co, Inc, 1984. Database. *Ancestry.com.* https://www.ancestry.com (Accessed 2018).

Olorenshaw, J. R. *Notes on the History of the Church and Parish of Rattlesden, in the County of Suffolk.* Peterborough: Geo. C. Caster, Market Place, 1900. PDF e-book. ExLibris Rosetta. https://books.familysearch.org (Accessed 31 July 2018).

Oregon. Multnomah County. 1900 U.S. Census, population schedule. Database with digital images. *FamilySearch.* https://www.familysearch.org . (Accessed 2017).

Oregon. Yamhill County. 1860 U.S. Census, population schedule. Database with digital images, *FamilySearch,* https://www.familysearch.org . (Accessed 2015).

Oregon Territory. Yamhill County. 1850 U.S. Census, population schedule. Database with digital images. *FamilySearch.* https://www.familysearch.org . (Accessed 2015).

Paige, Lucius R. *History of Hardwick, Massachusetts. with a Genealogical Register.* Boston: Houghton, Mifflin and Company, 1883. PDF e-book. *Google Books.* https://books.google.com (Accessed 2018).

Pierce, Frederick Clifton. *Batchelder, Batcheller, Genealogy.* Chicago: W B Conkey Company, 1898. PDF e-book. *Internet Archive.* https://archive.org (Accessed 2018).

Pope, Charles Henry. *The Pioneers of Massachusetts, A Descriptive List, Drawn from the Records of the Colonies, Towns, and Churches, and other Contemporaneous Documents .* Boston: Charles H Pope, 1900. PDF e-book. *Internet Archive.* https://archive.org (Accessed 2019)

"Probate records 1648-1924 (Middlesex County, Massachusetts)." Database with digital images. *FamilySearch.* https://www.familysearch.org (Accessed 2018).

Savage, James. *A Genealogical Dictionary of the First Settlers of New England: Showing Three Generations of Those Who Came Before May 1692.* Boston: Little, Brown and Company, 1860. PDF e-book. *Internet Archive.* https://archive.org (Accessed 2018).

Sawyer, Eugene T. *History of Santa Clara County California: with Biographical Sketches.* Los Angeles: Historic Record Company, 1922. PDF e-book. *Internet Archive.* https://archive.org (Accessed 2016).

"Scotland: Births and Baptisms, 1564-1950." Database. *American Ancestors.* https://www.americanancestors.org (Accessed 2018).

"Scotland: Marriages, 1561-1910." Database. *American Ancestors.* https://www.americanancestors.org (Accessed 2018).

Sibley, John Langdon. *Biographical Sketches of Graduates of Harvard University: in Cambridge, Massachusetts.* Cambridge, Massachusetts: University Bookstore, 1873. PDF e-book. *Internet Archive.* https://archive.org (Accessed 17 July 2018).

Slaughter, John. *Massachusetts Vital Records Project.* Website. https://ma-vitalrecords.org (Accessed 2018).

Stearns, Ezra S., ed. *Genealogical and Family History of the State of New Hampshire.* New York: The Lewis Publishing Co, 1908. PDF e-book. *Internet Archive.* https://archive.org (Accessed 9 July 2018).

"Tasmania Marriages 1803-1899." Database with digital images. *FindMyPast.* https://www.findmypast.com . (Accessed 2015).

"Tennessee Births and Christenings, 1828-1939." Database. *FamilySearch.* https://www.familysearch.org (Accessed 2017).

"Tennessee, Marriage Records, 1780-2002." Database. *Ancestry.com.* https://www.ancestry.com (Accessed 2018).

Texas. Fannin County. 1880 US Census, population schedule. Database with digital images. *FamilySearch.* https://www.familysearch.org . (Accessed 2016).

Topsfield Historical Society. *Vital Records of Haverhill Massachusetts: to the End of the Year 1849.* Topsfield, MA: Topsfield Historical Society, 1911. PDF e-book. *Internet Archive.* https://archive.org (Accessed 2019).

Torrey, Clarence Almon. *New England Marriages Prior to 1700.* Baltimore, Maryland: Genealogical Publishing Co., Inc, 2004. Database with digital images. *Ancestry.com.* https://www.ancestry.com (Accessed 2016-2019).

Upham, Charles W. *Salem Witchcraft: With an Account of Salem Village, and a History of Opinions on Witchcraft and Kindred Subjects.* Boston: Wiggin and Lunt, 1867. PDF e-book. *Internet Archive.* https://archive.org (Accessed 20 July 2018).

Upham, F K. *Upham Genealogy: the Descendants of John Upham, of Massachusetts.* Albany, NY: Joel Munsell's Sons, 1892. PDF e-book. https://archive.org/details/uphamgenealogyde00upha (Accessed 22 July 2018).

"US and Canada, Passenger and Immigrant Archive Lists Index, 1500s-1900s." Database. *Ancestry.com.* https://www.ancestry.com (Accessed 2016-2018).

"US and International Marriage Records, 1560-1900." Database. *Ancestry.com.* https://www.ancestry.com (Accessed 2016).

"U.S., Civil War Draft Registrations Records, 1863-1865." Database with digital images. *Ancestry.com.* https://www.ancestry.com . (Accessed 2018).

"U.S., Union Soldiers Compiled Service Records, 1861-1865." Database. *Ancestry.com.* https://www.ancestry.com . (Accessed 2018).

"United States Revolutionary War Rolls, 1775-1783." Database with digital images. *FamilySearch.* https://www.familysearch.org (Accessed 2017).

"United States War of 1812 Index to Service Records, 1812-1815." Database with digital images. *FamilySearch.* https://www.familysearch.org (Accessed 2017).

"United States World War I Draft Registration Cards, 1917-1918." Database with digital images. *FamilySearch.* https://www.familysearch.org . (Accessed 2016).

Vermont. Caledonia County. 1800 U.S. Census, population schedule. Database with digital images. *FamilySearch.* https://www.familysearch.org (Accessed 2017).

Vermont. Orange County. 1790 U.S. Census, population schedule. Database with digital images. *FamilySearch.* https://www.familysearch.org (Accessed 2017).

"Vermont, Town Clerk, Vital and Town Records, 1732-2005." Digital image not indexed. *FamilySearch.* https://www.familysearch.org (Accessed 2016).

"Vermont Vital Records, 1760-1954." Database with digital images. *FamilySearch.* https://www.familysearch.org (Accessed 2016).

"Virginia, Wills and Probate Records, 1652-1983." Database with digital images. *Ancestry.com.* https://www.ancestry.com . (Accessed 2018).

Vinton, John Adams. *The Richardson Memorial: Comprising a Full History and Genealogy of the Posterity of the Three Brothers.* Portland, Maine: Brown Thurston and Co, 1876. p. 521. PDF e-book. *Internet Archive.* https://archive.org (Accessed 10 July 2018).

Ward, Andrew Henshaw. *Ward Family: Descendants of William Ward, who settled in Sudbury, Mass, in 1639.* Boston, MA: Samuel Drake, 1851. PDF e-book. *Internet Archive.* https://archive.org (Accessed 17 July 2018).

Weddall, G. E., ed. *The Registers of the Parish of Howden, Co. York.* Leeds: Oriel Press, 1904. PDF e-book. *Internet Archive.* https://archive.org (Accessed 1 Aug 2018).

Weis, Frederick Lewis. *Ancestral Roots of Certain American Colonists Who Came to America before 1700*, 8 ed. Baltimore: Genealogical Publishing Company, 2008.

Weis, Frederick Lewis. *The Ancestry of Ensign Constant and Captain Thomas Southworth of Plymouth and Duxbury, Massachusetts.* Dublin, New Hampshire: n.p., 1958. PDF e-book. *ExLibris Rosetta.* https://dcms.lds.org/delivery/DeliveryManagerServlet?dps_pid=IE6282139 (Accessed 22 July 2018).

White, Daniel Appleton and Annie Frances Richards. *The Descendants of William White, of Haverhill, Mass.* Boston: American Printing and Engraving Company, 1889. PDF e-book. *Internet Archive.* https://archive.org (Accessed 2019).

Wisconsin. Bad Ax County. 1860 US Census, population schedule. Database with digital images. *FamilySearch.* https://www.familysearch.org . (Accessed 2016).

"Wisconsin, County Marriages, 1836-1911." Database. *FamilySearch.* https://www.familysearch.org . (Accessed 2017).

Wisconsin. Vernon County. 1870 US Census, population schedule. Database with digital images. *FamilySearch.* https://www.familysearch.org . (Accessed 2017).

Alphabetical Index

ABOUT THE AUTHOR

Scott R. Mackay is a grandson of Raymond Donald Burton, and has a BA in history from San Jose State University in California. Scott has been working on genealogy for about twenty years, and after military service moved to rural Missouri.